FU SSU-NIEN: A LIFE IN CHINESE HISTORY AND POLITICS

Fu Ssu-nien, Chinese scholar, educator, and political and social critic, was one of the most colorful and influential intellectual figures in twentieth-century China. Wang Fan-sen's biography of Fu's extraordinary life and contributions offers the first in-depth examination and serious recognition of his role in the intellectual and educational development in modern China.

Fu's life, spanning five decades of tumultuous political change in China, in many ways embodies the dilemma faced by modern Chinese intellectuals; dissatisfied with the model of the traditional literati, they lacked a professional, academic model to take its place. Fu's early years as a student leader of the May Fourth Movement and subsequent life as an activist were born of intellectual dissatisfaction; as an educator and as founder of the Institute of Philology and History at Peking University and the Academia Sinica, he worked to fill the void by professionalizing Chinese research and education.

Wang traces Fu's leading role in cultivating modern Chinese academe and, in particular, his efforts to establish a "modern" historical discipline with an emphasis on objective analysis of primary sources. He also tells the less well known story of Fu's struggles with political foes and his involvement in wartime politics. Fu's efforts to improve history as a professional discipline in China made him the target of attacks by left-wing intellectuals on the one hand and of conservative Chinese historians on the other. A liberal intellectual in wartime China, he was caught between his opposition to communism and his opposition to corrupt elements within the ranks of the Kuomintang. His attempts to separate historical studies from politics, along with his hostility to the Communist Party, brought particularly harsh criticism after he left the mainland for Taiwan in 1948. All of the above have served to obfuscate Fu's role. Wang's analysis offers a new, scholarly account of Fu's intellectual life and that of the academic community he helped to shape in the 1930s and 1940s. Incorporating an impressive array of archival material, including original papers and correspondence from Fu's private collection, this book fills a major gap in the cultural and intellectual history of modern China.

Wang Fan-sen is a Research Fellow at the Institute of History and Philology, Academia Sinica, in Taipei. He also teaches at National Taiwan University and Ch'inghua University.

Cambridge Studies in Chinese History, Literature and Institutions

    Victor H. Mair   Tunhuang Popular Narratives
    Ira E. Kasoff   The Thought of Chang Tsai
Chih-P'ing Chou   Yüan Hung-tao and the Kung-an School
Arthur Waldron   The Great Wall of China: From History to Myth
Hugh R. Clark   Community, Trade, and Networks: Southern Fujian Province from the Third to the Thirteenth Centuries
Denis Twitchett   The Writing of Official History under the T'ang
J. D. Schmidt   Stone Lake: The Poetry of Fang Chengda
Brian E. McKnight   Law and Order in Sung China
Jo-Shui Chen   Liu Tsung-yüan and Intellectual Change in T'ang China, 773–819
David Pong   Shen Pao-chen and China's Modernization in the Nineteenth Century
J. D. Schmidt   Within the Human Realm: The Poetry of Huang Zunxian, 1848–1905
Arthur Waldron   From War to Nationalism: China's Turning Point, 1924–1925
Chin-Shing Huang   Philosophy, Philology, and Politics in Eighteenth-Century China: Li Fu and the Lu-Wang School under the Ch'ing
Glen Dudbridge   Religious Experience and Lay Society in T'ang China: A Reading of Tai Fu's "Kuang-i chi"
Eva Shan Chou   Reconsidering Tu Fu: Literary Greatness and Cultural Context
Frederic Wakeman Jr.   The Shanghai Badlands: Wartime Terrorism and Urban Crime, 1937–1941
Sarah A. Queen   From Chronicle to Canon: The Hermeneutics of the Spring and Autumn Annals according to Tung Chung-shu
J. Y. Wong   Deadly Dreams: Opium, Imperialism, and the *Arrow* War (1856–1860) in China
Norman Kutcher   Mourning in Late Imperial China
Thomas M. Buoye   Manslaughter, Markets, and Moral Economy: Violent Disputes over Property Rights in Eighteenth-Century China

Fu Ssu-nien
A Life in Chinese History and Politics

Wang Fan-sen
Academia Sinica

PUBLISHED BY THE PRESS SYNDICATE OF THE UNIVERSITY OF CAMBRIDGE
The Pitt Building, Trumpington Street, Cambridge, United Kingdom

CAMBRIDGE UNIVERSITY PRESS
The Edinburgh Building, Cambridge CB2 2RU, UK http://www.cup.cam.ac.uk
40 West 20th Street, New York, NY 10011-4211, USA http://www.cup.org
10 Stamford Road, Oakleigh, Melbourne 3166, Australia
Ruiz de Alarcón 13, 28014 Madrid, Spain

© Cambridge University Press 2000

This book is in copyright. Subject to statutory exception
and to the provisions of relevant collective licensing agreements,
no reproduction of any part may take place without
the written permission of Cambridge University Press.

First published 2000

Printed in the United States of America

Typeface Baskerville 10/12 pt.   *System* QuarkXPress [BTS]

A catalog record for this book is available from the British Library.

Library of Congress Cataloging in Publication data

Wang, Fan-sen.
Fu Ssu-nien: a life in Chinese history and politics / Wang Fan-sen.
p. cm. – (Cambridge studies in Chinese history, literature and institutions)
Includes bibliographical references and index.
ISBN 0-521-48051-5 (hb)
1. Fu, Ssu-nien, 1896–1950.   2. Historians – China – Biography.
3. China – Intellectual life – 1912–1949.   I. Title.   II. Series.
DS734.9.F8 W36 2000
951.04′092 – dc21
[B]   99-053801

ISBN 0 521 48051 5 hardback

To Professor Yü Ying-shih

Contents

Acknowledgments xi

List of Abbreviations xii

Chronology xiii

Introduction: Fu Ssu-nien and Post-1895 Intellectual Trends   1

1   Fu Ssu-nien's Early Years   11

2   The Shaping of a New Historical School   55

3   Toward a Theory of Plural Origins of Chinese Civilization: Hypotheses on Ancient Chinese History   98

4   Contra-Introspective Moral Philosophy   126

5   The Burden of the May Fourth Mentality   140

6   Statism and the Later Days of a May Fourth Youth   164

Conclusion: The Defeat of a May Fourth Youth   197

Appendix I   A Fragment from a Short Story Attacking Ku Chieh-kang   205

Contents

Appendix II   A Transcript of a Conversation between Fu Ssu-nien and Ch'en Pu-lei   207

Glossary   209

Bibliography   229

Index   255

Acknowledgments

This book would not have been completed without the generous assistance of many individuals. I wish to thank first and foremost my advisor, Professor Yü Ying-shih, for his unfailing guidance, inspiration, and kindness while I was studying at Princeton University from 1987 to 1992. I am also deeply grateful to Professor Chang Hao for his valuable comments on my work and to Professors Denis C. Twitchett, Marius Jansen, Frederick W. Mote, Willard J. Peterson, Chou Chih-p'ing, Thomas Metzger, and the late James T. C. Liu for their valuable input.

During the writing of this book, my friends David C. Wright, Markus Keller, Xiao-bin Ji, John Kieschnick, and my tutor, Professor Jeremiah Finch, helped me polish my English. My friends Peter Zarrow, David Wright, Axel Schneider, and Wang Qingjia provided useful suggestions during the preparation of the manuscript. Brian MacDonald, Cambridge University Press production editor, was especially helpful during the final revisions of the manuscript.

The project would not have been possible without the support of my colleagues in the Institute of History and Philology, Academia Sinica, Taipei. My gratitude goes especially to Professor Kuan Tung-kuei.

Last but not least, thanks are also due to my wife, Wen-fang, to whom I am indebted beyond words.

Abbreviations

CCP	Chinese Communist Party
FSNC	*Fu Ssu-nien ch'üan-chi*, Taipei, 1980
FSNP	Fu Ssu-nien Papers, Institute of History and Philology, Taiwan
IHP	Institute of History and Philology, Academia Sinica
KMT	Kuomintang (Nationalist Party)
PRC	People's Republic of China

Chronology

1896 On February 13 Fu is born in Liao-ch'eng, Shantung.
1898 The Hundred Days Reform.
1901 Fu enters the village school.
1904 Outbreak of the Russo-Japanese War.
1905 China abolishes the civil service examination system. Fu enters a new elementary school but continues to be tutored by his grandfather in the Confucian Classics.
1909 Fu continues in elementary school with tutoring by his grandfather and enters the middle school of Tientsin prefecture, where he develops a close association with Manchu nobility (the family of Ying Hua, who was the founder of the *Ta-kung pao*).
1911 Outbreak of the Wuchang Revolution.
1913 Fu enters the preparatory school of Peking University.
1914 Fu reads and admires K'ang Yu-wei's *Pu-jen tsa-chih*.
1916 In autumn Fu enters the Chinese department of Peking University.
1917 Late in this year Fu has his first contact with Hu Shih, which changes Fu from a conservative to a zealot.
1918 In August Fu organizes about twenty classmates to establish the New Tide Society.
1919 In January Fu heads the editorial board of the journal *New Tide* and writes the opening remarks of the journal. The *New Tide* immediately becomes very popular, its influence nearly equal to that of the *New Youth*, published by a group of professors.
      On May 4 Fu leads the student demonstration.
      In winter Fu goes to England to study experimental psychology at University College of London University.
1923 Fu moves to Berlin to study at Berlin University and completes

	an in-depth study of Mach's *Analysis of the Sensations* and *Mechanics*.
1925	Fu's interests gradually turn to history and comparative linguistics.
1926	Northern Expedition launched in June.
	In winter Fu leaves Berlin University and returns to Shantung, later assuming the post as dean of the School of Letters at Chungshan University, Kwangchow.
1927	In March KMT armies reach Nanking and Shanghai.
	In autumn Fu sets up the Institute of Philology and History in Chungshan University.
	In winter during the Kwangchow Riot instigated by Chang T'ai-lei, a radical activist of the Chinese Communist Party (CCP), Fu is almost executed by the CCP.
1928	Fu founds the Institute of History and Philology (IHP) of Academia Sinica and begins the archaeological excavation of Yin-hsü of Anyang, Honan.
1929	In spring Fu moves the Institute of History and Philology to Peking.
	In autumn Fu teaches at Peking University.
1931	In September the Mukden Incident and the Japanese seizure of Manchuria occur. Fu challenges his colleagues with the question, How should intellectuals serve their country?
1932	In May Fu sets up *Tu-li p'ing-lun* with Hu Shih, Ting Wen-chiang, and others.
	In October Fu publishes the first volume of *Tung-pei shih-kang*, an abstract of which is sent to the Lytton Commission in an attempt to prove that from ancient times the Chinese government had controlled Manchuria. *Tung-pei shih-kang* is severely criticized. Fu debates with Chu Hsi-tsu on Ming history.
1933	In February the Japanese conquer Jehol.
	In spring the IHP is moved to Shanghai, but Fu remains in Peking and teaches at Peita.
	Fu is jointly appointed director of the Institute of Social Science, Academia Sinica, and director of preparations for the National Central Museum.
1934	After divorcing his wife, Fu marries Yü Ta-ts'ai.
	Fu takes part in debates on the issue of national medicine.
	In winter the Institute of History and Philology moves to Nanking.

1935	Fu publishes *I Hsia tung hsi shuo*. Fu confronts the particularization of northern China, which stirs up the December Ninth student movement.
1936	In spring Fu moves to Nanking. In winter the Sian Incident occurs. Fu strongly supports Chiang Kai-shek and severely denounces Chang Hsüeh-liang.
1937	Fu serves as acting secretary-general of the Academia Sinica. After the outbreak of the Marco Polo Bridge Incident, Fu participates in the *Kuo-fang ts'an-i hui*. In autumn Fu moves the Institute of History and Philology to Changsha.
1938	In spring Fu moves the Institute of History and Philology to Kunming. In July Fu serves as representative of the *Kuo-min ts'an-cheng hui*.
1940	Fu publishes *Hsing ming ku-hsün pien-cheng*, largely drafted before 1937. In autumn Fu again serves as acting secretary-general of the Academia Sinica. He becomes seriously ill and almost dies.
1945	In April Fu serves as fifth-term representative in the *Kuo-min ts'an-cheng hui*. In July Fu represents the *Kuo-min ts'an-cheng hui* in a visit to Yenan. In the *Kuo-min ts'an-cheng hui* Fu attacks the premier H. H. Kung and his clique. This contributes to Kung's resignation. On August 14 Japan surrenders. In autumn Fu serves as acting president of Peita. In winter Fu settles unrest in the wake of student demonstrations.
1946	In January Fu attends the *Cheng-chih hsieh-shang hui-i*. In May Fu announces his decision to exclude all "turncoat professors" from Peita.
1947	In February, after witnessing the drastic deterioration of the economy, Fu attacks the premier T. V. Soong and his clique. Fu's three famous articles calling for Soong's resignation are published, contributing to Soong's resignation. In June Fu goes to the United States for surgery and lives in New Haven, Connecticut.
1948	In August Fu returns to Nanking from the United States.

	In winter Fu attempts suicide and later moves the Institute of History and Philology to Taiwan.
1949	In January Fu is appointed president of Taiwan University.
1950	In December Fu dies of hypertension suddenly in the Provincial Assembly of Taiwan.

Introduction: Fu Ssu-nien and Post-1895 Intellectual Trends

Fu Ssu-nien was born in 1896, in the immediate aftermath of the First Sino-Japanese War of 1894–1895, a major event in modern Chinese history and a shocking defeat at the hands of the Japanese. The war exerted enormous influence on the lives of Fu Ssu-nien and the men of his generation.

The outcome of the war was described by Liang Ch'i-ch'ao (1873–1929), who was old enough to feel the shock firsthand, as "the smashing of the dream of the past two thousand years."[1] Although China had repeatedly been defeated after the Opium War, its defeat at the hands of the Japanese was devastating and traumatic. Japan, after all, was an East Asian nation, one long viewed by the Chinese as having strong civilizational ties to China. What is more, Japan had begun transforming itself on the Western model after China had.

Some major transformations involving various Chinese intellectuals took place immediately after 1894–1895. In 1895 the leader of a revolutionary group, Sun Yat-sen (1866–1925), called the Japanese victory an unforeseeable event in Chinese history. He decided to organize his first anti-Manchu group, the Revive China Society (Hsing-chung-hui), in the winter of 1894, right after China had suffered a number of military defeats. K'ang Yu-wei (1858–1927), who later led the reform party, decided to convene about thirteen hundred *chü-jen* (provincial graduates) in Peking to encourage the emperor on reform. Yen Fu (1854–1921), the intellectual leader who played the most important role in introducing European utilitarian political and economic philosophy into China, published four groundbreaking articles: "On the Speed of World Change," "On Strength," "On Our Salvation," and "In Refutation of Han Yü." In 1895 he began working on a Chinese translation of Huxley's *Evolution and Ethics*, which appeared with the title of

---

1 Ting Wen-chiang, *Liang Jen-kung nien-p'u ch'ang-pien ch'u-kao* (Taipei, 1958), 24.

T'ien-yen-lun and became the most influential publication in modern China.[2] And T'an Ssu-t'ung (1865–1898), the young martyr of the 1898 Reformation, decided to give up the traditional literati life-style in 1894–1895.[3]

Several new developments in the Chinese intellectual world shaped and molded Fu Ssu-nien's intellectual development, the first being the radicalization of ideas. Several individuals contributed to this phenomenon. Yen Fu made a sharp black-and-white distinction between Chinese and Western traditions and argued forcefully that China was vastly inferior to the West, especially in the realm of culture. This charge came as a surprise because heretofore the Chinese had been extremely proud of their culture.[4] T'an Ssu-t'ung criticized the tradition of "three bonds" (*san-kang*) by which the ruler guides his subject, the father guides his son, and the husband guides his wife. K'ang Yu-wei came close to denouncing almost the whole scholastic tradition of the past two millennia as "false learning." Chang Ping-lin (1869–1936) unrelentingly criticized Confucius's personality. Liang Ch'i-ch'ao's New Citizen theory held that Chinese traditional moral values were outdated because none was related to public spirit, something that every modern citizen needed.[5]

Traditional value systems, however, were buttressed by a number of social and political systems. Among these, monarchy, Confucian ritual, classical education, civil service examinations, and the legal system were the most important. Although radical ideas burgeoned in the late Ch'ing, it was only after the collapse of the five pillars just mentioned that the intellectual revolution took off. The civil service examinations were abolished in 1905, and the monarchy collapsed in 1911. In 1912 Ts'ai Yüan-p'ei, then minister of education, announced that students did not need to worship Confucius and that classical education would no longer be required in the curriculum. The Ch'ing legal code was also abolished in the same year.

The traditional values system so denigrated after 1895 had been a rather coherent one in the past. After the breakdown of the value system, the elements that originally correlated with one another became diametrically opposed to or competed with each other.

---

2 See Benjamin Schwartz, *In Search of Wealth and Power: Yen Fu and the West* (New York, 1969), 43, 91.
3 T'an Hsün-ts'ung, *Ch'ing T'an Fu-sheng hsien-sheng Ssu-t'ung nien-p'u* (Taipei, 1980), 14–19.
4 See Li Tse-hou, *Chung-kuo chin-tai ssu-hsiang shih-lun* (Peking, 1979), 249–285.
5 See ibid., especially chapters on Tan Ssu-t'ung, K'ang Yu-wei, Chang T'ai-yen, and Liang Ch'i-ch'ao. See also Wang Fan-sen, *Chang T'ai-yen (Ping-lin) te ssu-hsiang* (Taipei, 1985), 185–89, and *Ku-shih-pien yü-tung te hsing-ch'i* (Taipei, 1987), chs. 2–3.

Introduction

The second major intellectual development was the formation of a new intellectual community, one whose loyalty gradually shifted from the Manchu court to the country as a whole. After China's defeat by Japan in 1894–1895, many young intellectuals gradually gave up studying for the traditional imperial civil service examinations for entry into officialdom. They became what Max Weber described as "free-floating resources" and were later enormously influential in the transformation of the country. They were described as cutting themselves off from the examination system, imperial China's ladder to success. Without official positions[6] and no longer constrained by official ideology, they made themselves the agents of political and intellectual transformation. But when the examinations were abolished by the government in 1905, however, it was as though the government itself was cutting the ties between the literati and the official ideology, which basically comprised of Confucian teaching. This decision opened up the possibility for plural developments and was a major impetus for intellectual liberation. The abolition of the examination system was a drastic event that also shook a great many intellectuals out of their lethargy. With no future and no income, some of them managed to become new intellectuals, while others sank into depravity.[7] They could no longer lead the life of traditional intellectuals whose duty was to govern the nation and "pacify all under heaven." The position of the intellectual and the scholar in this new China became problematic. Should they adapt, become professionals, and then form a stratum of professionals to constitute the core of the new society?

After 1895 two axes coexisted in China: one political and the other cultural. The former was motivated by a will to power, the latter by a will to truth. They were seen by intellectuals as the means for saving the country from its disastrous fortune. Politics was not always antagonistic to culture, but the two were frequently in tension. The subject of the political axis was to save the nation from crisis, to pursue wealth and power. As for the cultural sphere, a group of intellectuals emerged whose goal was to establish an autonomous academic world and prevent learning from being determined by any utilitarian mentality or political agenda. Its aim was also, finally, to cope with Western countries in a more fundamental way. They viewed the lack of an academic society as the real weakness of the old tradition.

To those who called for the establishment of an academic society, learning should be divorced from immediate concerns. The autonomy of

---

6 Li Tse-hou, *Chung-kuo chin-tai ssu-hsiang shih-lun*, 289.
7 On the shock brought about by the abolition of the civil service examinations, see Liu Ta-p'eng, *Tui-hsiang-chai jih-chi* (Shanghai, 1990), 146–147.

learning – that is, learning for learning's sake – was an article of faith that kept getting stronger and stronger. Yen Fu was the harbinger of this concept. He proclaimed that the strength of Western countries was to be found in the realm of ideas and values. To pursue this "real" strength, China should discard false learning that was tainted by practical purposes and hold to true learning (*ch'ü wei ts'ung chen*).[8] He contended that the fundamental reason for China's backwardness was its lack of real learning. Although true learning might seem to be useless, he argued, in the long run it would have the greatest use. Accordingly, he championed the separation of scholarship and statecraft.[9] "Cure stupidity" was the name of Yen Fu's studio, and this expressed his conviction about the importance of overcoming ignorance. "In overcoming ignorance we must exert our utmost efforts to seek out knowledge."[10] The overcoming of ignorance leads to the cure of poverty and weakness.

Chang Ping-lin also contributed considerably in this regard. Many youths believed that what Chang championed, the divorce of classical study from practical use, led to the consideration of classics and ancient learning as objects of scholastic research.[11] Wang Kuo-wei (1877–1927), another keen-minded intellectual, had also believed even during the late Ch'ing that learning should be divorced from practicality and elevated to higher purposes.[12]

Wu Chih-hui (1865–1953) insisted that if China had several accomplished scholars to form a center of gravity, these scholars could gradually transform the country into a modern nation.[13] There was a circle of mostly Western-educated students who believed that the importance of culture was preeminent over that of politics. Ts'ai Yüan-p'ei (1868–1940), Wu Chih-hui, Li Shih-tseng (1881–1973), Wang Ching-wei (1883–1944), and a number of veterans of the 1911 revolution also thought this way. But as China was repeatedly plagued by political crises, they did not have the time or opportunity to build up gradually an academic community.

The wish to establish a purely academic community was crystalized when Ts'ai Yüan-pei was appointed president of Peking University (here-

---

8 Yen Fu, "Lun shih-pien chih chi," in Chiang Chen-chin, ed., *Yen Chi-tao wen-ch'ao* (Taipei, 1971), 19.
9 Yen Fu, "Lun chih-hsüeh chih-shih yi feng erh t'u," in ibid., 163–168.
10 Schwartz, *In Search of Wealth and Power*, 49.
11 See, for example, Ku Chieh-kang in his long preface for the first volume of *Ku-shih pien* (Peking and Shanghai, 1926–1941), 7 vols., 1:25–26.
12 Wang Kuo-wei, "Lun chin-nien chih hsüeh-shu chieh," in *Wang Ching-an wen-chi* (Taipei, 1978), 173–174.
13 Wu Ching-heng, "Ssu-shih-sui jih-chi hsüan-lu," in *Wu Ching-heng hsüan-chi* (Taipei, 1967), *hsü-pa, yu-chi, tsa-wen* volume, 221.

Introduction

after Peita) in 1917. Ts'ai opened his inauguration speech as president with a simple sentence: "The university is the place for high and profound learning."[14] This announcement drastically transformed the nature of the university from an institution for training government officials into a modern academic community. No longer was it the responsibility of the literati to govern the country. From now on, intellectuals could pursue rigorous academic work with their colleagues as their audience. Their ultimate aim still consisted of serving society, but as scholars and not as officials. Their achievements were to be judged by members of the academic community rather than by society. Nine days after Ts'ai's appointment, he appointed Ch'en Tu-hsiu (1879–1942) as dean of the School of Letters. A group of scholars was then appointed, and they radically changed the rather conservative environment of Peita. Ts'ai Yüan-p'ei, Wu Chih-hui, and Li Shih-tseng later became staunch supporters of the Academia Sinica, believing that if several dozen intellectuals devoted to serious academic work were assembled, an intellectual center could be established. Gradually, such a group could influence and transform the society in a more profound way than the revolutionaries of 1911 had been able to do.[15]

Radicalization, free-floating literati, and a vision of advancing an academic society in China were, then, three trends that influenced the life of Fu Ssu-nien.

Fu Ssu-nien's Role in the Modern Chinese Intellectual World

Although students of modern Chinese intellectual history have written numerous studies on the "teachers" of the May Fourth generation, such as Hu Shih (1891–1962), Ch'en Tu-hsiu, and Li Ta-chao (1888–1927), little attention has been paid to the "student" generation.[16] Among this group, Fu Ssu-nien (Meng-chen, 1896–1950), an important leader of the movement, remains almost completely neglected. As a student leader of the May Fourth Movement, a scholar, a political and social critic, and an academic leader, Fu Ssu-nien was one of the most colorful and influential figures in twentieth-century China. Except for Alan

---

14 Ts'ai Yüan-pei, "Chiu-jen Pei-ching-ta-hsüeh hsiao-chang chih yen-shuo," in Shen Shan-hung, *Ts'ai Yüan-pei hsüan-chi* (Hangchow, 1993), 2 vols., 1:490.
15 Wu Ching-heng, "Ssu-shih-sui jih-chi hsüan-lu," in *Wu Ching-heng hsüan-chi, hsü-pa, yu chi, tsa-wen* volume, 221.
16 See Vera Schwarcz, *The Chinese Enlightenment: Intellectuals and Legacy of the May Fourth Movement of 1919* (Berkeley, 1986), an excellent study on the student generation of May Fourth youth.

Moller's work, however, there has been no serious biographical study of Fu in any Western language.[17] In the Chinese academic world, the study of Fu Ssu-nien's life is just beginning.[18]

Fu is almost forgotten in mainland China. Because of his close relationship with the Nationalist government led by Chiang Kai-shek (1887–1975), Mao Tse-tung's (1894–1976) condemnation of Fu as a war criminal in 1949, and the severe criticism of him during the "Criticize Hu Shih Campaign," the mere mention of Fu's name is often avoided by mainland writers, even when events centrally involving him

---

17 Alan Gordon Moller, "Bellicose Nationalist of Republican China: An Intellectual Biography of Fu Ssu-nien" (Ph.D. diss., University of Melbourne, 1979).

18 The "Fu Ssu-nien Institute" in Shangtung and two centennial memorial conferences convened in his memory, one in Taipei and one in Shangtung, have signaled this trend. "Fu Ssu-nien Institute" was established by the Liao-ch'eng Normal College. See Liao-ch'eng shih-fan ta-hsüeh li-shih-hsi, Liao-ch'eng ti-ch'ü cheng-hsieh kung-wei, and Shan-tung-sheng cheng-hsieh wen-shih-wei, eds., *Fu Ssu-nien* (Shantung, 1991), 359. The two centennial memorial conferences were held in 1995 in Taipei and in May 1996 in Liao-ch'eng.

The major materials I have used to reconstruct Fu's life and thought are collected in *The Complete Collection of Fu Ssu-nien's Work* (*Fu Ssu-nien ch'üan-chi*, hereafter *FSNC*). Soon after Fu Ssu-nien's death in December 1950, Taiwan University compiled *Fu Meng-chen hsien-sheng chi* (Taipei, 1952), a five-volume set of Fu's works. In 1967 Wen-hsing Publishing Company published a ten-volume set of Fu's works entitled *Fu Ssu-nien hsüan-chi*, a collection of selected articles. The edition added forty-three essays that were not included in the 1952 edition. In 1980 Fu's widow, Yü Ta-ts'ai, initiated the compilation of a new set of Fu's works entitled *Fu Ssu-nien ch'üan-chi* in seven volumes. The compilers added nine articles not included in the 1967 edition. Although this work is called a "complete collection," I have found more than ten articles and a number of unpublished manuscripts that could still be added.

I have also made use of the Fu Ssu-nien Papers (which includes five large chests of Fu's personal documents shipped to Taiwan when Fu moved the Institute of History and Philology [IHP] to Taiwan in late 1948), the Archives of the History of the Institute of History and Philology (Shih-yü-so tang-an), and essays not included in Fu's collected works. A considerable number of personal interviews were also conducted. These sources were complemented by several memorial pieces composed by Fu's contemporaries. I also made one trip to the archives of the University of London and another trip to Liao-ch'eng, Fu's hometown, but to my disappointment I uncovered no significant new material on Fu.

Fu Ssu-nien has long been labeled a "reactionary scholar" in mainland China, so I am pessimistic about any substantial amount of private papers relating to Fu surviving the political turmoil there. Given Fu's wide association with the Chinese academic world, if any of his papers did in fact survive the Cultural Revolution and other political upheavals, this would be very helpful in studying Fu's life.

Although the Fu Ssu-nien Papers consists of about four thousand pieces of documentation, it still has some limitations, which need to be noted here. Fu's papers on the whole have been kept in good condition. In these materials, however, items after 1937 far outnumber those prior to that year. Material pertaining to academic administration is far more abundant than material on other topics, and material about the IHP and Peita is more abundant than other material. Despite this shortcoming, the papers still provide a new key to understanding the life and thought of Fu Ssu-nien.

are narrated.[19] Historians have also largely failed to acknowledge Fu's contributions to their field.[20] In Taiwan, Fu is legendary as an academic administrator and is well known for his academic accomplishments. The research methodologies and styles he and Hu Shih espoused have been targets of continuous criticism from those of various persuasions. For instance, Fu's reluctance to theorize has been criticized by the younger generation of historians, while Fu and the school he established were severely criticized by New Confucianists such as Hsü Fu-kuan (1903–1982) for being intentionally negligent of the moral (especially introspective) values in Chinese traditional learning. As a result, an important part of the intellectual and political history between 1919 and 1949 remains obscure.

I am compelled to focus on only a few of his many accomplishments for discussion in this book. Of these I include, first, his intellectual life as well as the academic community Fu helped to organize and guide for two decades. By this community I refer not only to his Institute of History and Philology (IHP) but also to Peita and Taiwan University (hereafter T'aita). As one of the major architects of Chinese modern learning, Fu founded the IHP, which was considered representative of the modern historiography of its time. Fu assembled and trained a large group of scholars working under his leadership. The business of this enterprise is in itself a very intricate story, indicative of the mushrooming of scientific learning in the 1920s and 1930s.[21] Fu Ssu-nien and the institute under his leadership produced a number of notable achievements. New projects were undertaken, many of them opening new pages of Chinese historical study. For instance, although it is widely known that archaeological excavations in post-1949 China have been carried out with spectacular results, few realize how much these recent archaeological developments owe to Fu's farsighted leadership. Practically all the People's Republic of China (PRC) leaders in archaeology, most notably

---

19 Sheng-huo Tu-shu Hsing-chih San-lien shu-tien, ed., *Hu Shih ssu-hsiang p'i-p'an* (Peking, 1955), 7 vols. In this movement Fu Ssu-nien's name always appeared with that of Hu Shih as a member of "Hu's clique."

20 For example, when Hsia Nai, a former junior colleague of Fu, was commemorating the Anyang excavations as a landmark of the New Chinese archaeology, Fu's name was never mentioned. See Hsia Nai, "Wu-ssu yün-tung ho Chung-kuo chin-tai k'ao-ku-hsüeh te hsing-ch'i," *K'ao-ku*, no. 3 (1979), 193–196. In a more recent book by P'ang Chen-hao, *Tung-I ku-kuo shih-lun* (Chengtu, 1989), Fu Ssu-nien's point about Tung-I is repeated without acknowledgment. See especially the preface of this book.

21 Chou P'ei-yüan, "Liu-shih-nien lai te Chung-kuo k'o-hsüeh," in Chung-kuo she-hui K'o-hsüeh-yüan Chin-tai-shih yen-chiu-so, ed., *Chi-nien Wu-ssu-yün-tung liu-shih chou-nien hsüeh-shu t'ao lun hui lun wen-chi* (Peking, 1980), 3 vols., 1:44–63. Cf. Tai Nien-tsu, "Wu-ssu-yün-tung ho hsien-tai k'o-hsüeh tsai Chung-kuo te ch'uan-po," in ibid., 3:375–386.

Hsia Nai (1910–1985), were originally trained in Fu's institute. The same can also be said of related fields, such as oracle bone and bronze studies and archival collections and research.

Another enduring contribution is the professionalization of history in China as an academic discipline. Many historians of modern China achieved noteworthy results in their research, but almost none of them established an institutional base as Fu did to exert a shaping influence on Chinese historiography. With his emphasis on methodological rigor and specialization, Fu consciously criticized traditional dilettantism. If we are justified in speaking of a "historical revolution" in modern China, we may well say that it was begun by Ku Chieh-kang (1893–1980) and finished by Fu Ssu-nien. But, whereas Ku has been well known in the West since the late 1920s,[22] Fu, by contrast, remains virtually unknown to the outside world. It is high time to give Fu the scholarly and critical attention he truly deserves.

As a historian, Fu concentrated mostly on the field of ancient Chinese history. Although Fu's working hypotheses on the history of Chinese antiquity have since been challenged and modified, they still provide important insights on the period. The most important hypothesis was the "East-West Theory of Ancient China" (I Hsia tung hsi shou), which divides the Three Dynasties into two antagonistic groups. The process whereby Fu broke up the old unitary system and shaped a new hypothesis is reconstructed in this book, and the interaction between Fu Ssu-nien's historical studies and modern ideas, such as pluralism, is also discussed.

Fu's other major contribution to the study of ancient Chinese history was his reconstruction effort. In the mid-1920s, Fu Ssu-nien was known for his support of the Movement of Doubting Chinese Antiquity, but later, in the 1930s, he contributed much to the repudiation of this movement. Far from being credulous, he and his colleagues in the IHP set as their central task the reconstruction of the history of ancient China. Both Fu's reversal and his effect on the radical movement are considered here.

This study also tries to bring Fu Ssu-nien's case to two broader themes of modern Chinese intellectual history: first, the rise and later development of the cultural iconoclasm of the May Fourth youth; and, second, the success and frustration involved in establishing an academic society in China.

---

22 See, for example, Arthur Hummel's "What Chinese Historians Are Doing in Their Own History," *American Historical Review* 34:4 (July 1929), 715–724, and his *The Autobiography of a Chinese Historian* (Leyden, 1931), and Laurence Schneider, *Ku Chieh-kang and Chinese New History* (Berkeley, 1971).

Introduction

While members of the May Fourth generation tried to reproach Chinese tradition, infuse many new ideas into Chinese society, and establish an academic society, in turn society also challenged them from the late 1920s on. Three factors were most evident: (1) the political turmoil, which challenged the professed apolitical stance with regard to cultural activities;[23] (2) the revival of cultural nativism and the urgent need for national identity, which challenged the May Fourth iconoclasm; and (3) the political collectivism, which challenged May Fourth liberalism.

Such challenges intensified after the Mukden Incident in 1931,[24] which marked the approach of a life-and-death struggle for the nation's destiny. After this incident, many May Fourth youths modified or gave up their early ideas. It is important to observe how Fu Ssu-nien reacted to this challenge and to what extent it was representative of his generation.

Fu Ssu-nien spent his later years in administration and politics. When he was a student, back at Peita, he pleaded with his colleagues of the New Tide Society to refuse to work in society until they reached their thirties and to swear off all political causes, even worthy ones. The demands of political involvement later overcame his youthful resolve, but Fu's involvement in politics was gradual. When a group of May Fourth youths became ministers in the Nationalist government, Fu kept himself out of office and served only in the People's Political Council. As an amateur politician, Fu attacked the two most powerful premiers of the Nationalist government (both family associates of Chiang Kai-shek) and contributed to their resignations. Fu also consistently and persistently criticized the Chinese Communists, a position that accounted for his support of the Nationalist government. He later assumed the

---

23 With the corrupt politics of the early Republican period, antipolitical attitudes were very much in vogue during the May Fourth era. John Dewey (1859–1952) keenly sensed the discontinuity between the scholar-official tradition and the present antipolitical inclination and said "it was in its deeper aspect a protest against all politicians and against all further reliance upon politics as a direct means of social reform" (Chow Tse-tsung, *The May Fourth Movement: Intellectual Revolution in China* [Cambridge, Mass., 1960], 224). "Even the scholars specializing in political science were inclined to avoid practicing political entanglement" (ibid., 223). "The liberals' abhorrence of practical politics was based, on the one hand, upon their pessimistic views of the warlord and bureaucratic government, and on the other hand upon their assumption that political reform could be achieved only after a social and cultural transformation" (ibid., 223).

24 Hu Shih, who once swore to stay away from politics for twenty years, became involved in it again soon after this incident. Early in 1926, when Hu was in England and heard of the success of the Northern Expedition, he admitted that "We may be wrong in trying to avoid politics." See Hu Shih, address given at the Royal Institute of International Affairs, in *Journal of the Royal Institute of International Affairs* 6:6 (1926), 279.

acting presidency of Peita and the presidency of T'aita, which kept him from publishing any serious studies during the last fifteen years of his life. Fu's later career reveals how politics, in fact, ended up dominating his life and eventually consuming him.

1
Fu Ssu-nien's Early Years

Hometown: An Old Society on the Verge of Collapse

Fu Ssu-nien was born on March 26, 1896, in Liao-ch'eng, Shantung, where his ancestors had lived since the fifteenth century. From 1467 to 1487, Fu Ssu-nien's ancestor Fu Hui-tsu, a native of Kiangsi, served as magistrate of the Kuan-hsien district in western Shantung. An epitaph records that when Hui-tsu's tenure was up, the local people begged him to stay, whereupon "he had (three of) his sons remain to comfort the people."[1] Two of Hui-tsu's sons later moved from Kuan-hsien to the neighboring district of Liao-ch'eng. Henceforth Liao-ch'eng became the "hometown" of that branch of Fu's family, which by Fu Ssu-nien's time had lived there for fourteen generations.

The geographical setting and decline of Liao-ch'eng during the late Ch'ing exerted considerable influence on Fu's upbringing. The fate of Fu's hometown followed that of the Grand Canal and the "eight-legged essay" (*pa-ku-wen*). The economic importance of the Grand Canal in this area was pivotal. "Its river network stimulated trade and tied the region together, its commercial traffic was a great source of private and public wealth, and its rhythms shaped the life of millions in the counties along its banks."[2] Liao-ch'eng was an important harbor along the Grand Canal, and its fate hinged very much on the success of the canal. For the residents of Liao-ch'eng, this was both fortunate and unfortunate. For centuries the canal brought easy wealth to the city, making Liao-ch'eng one of four major inland harbors north of the Yangtze River. When the canal was drained, however, the city seemed to have lost its reason for being. During Fu's childhood the area around Liao-ch'eng had already lost its wealth and become extremely backward in the young Fu's eyes. This area

---

1 Fu Le-ch'eng, "Fu Meng-chen hsien-sheng te hsien-shih," in *Shih-tai te chui-i lun-wen-chi* (Taipei, 1984), 111–112.
2 Susan Naquin, *Shantung Rebellion* (New Haven, 1981), 3.

stood in contrast with eastern Shantung, which, though infertile, mountainous, and economically depressed because of a poor traffic network, had struggled to develop factories, commerce, and irrigation and had finally became part of an important commercial area in China. Comparing his native region with eastern Shantung and the coastal areas of China, Fu described western Shantung as a tired place with "good-for-nothing" and "lukewarm" people, an old society powerless to transform itself, awaiting a slow but inevitable death.[3]

As a result the area became a hotbed for uprisings. From the mid-Ch'ing on, western Shantung was one of China's most turbulent areas and became even more so in the late Ch'ing. It witnessed one of the earlier uprisings of the Ch'ing, the Wang Lun Rebellion of 1774.[4] It also witnessed the rebellion of Sung Ching-shih (1824–?) in 1861,[5] and, of course, the Boxer Rebellion. To Ch'ing officials, "Lu-hsi," or western Shantung, and especially the area around Fu Ssu-nien's hometown, was a world with unpleasant associations. But on the other hand, the better-educated inhabitants of Liao-ch'eng were famous for their command of the eight-legged essay, the key to success in the civil service examination, and this created a considerable number of teaching jobs and opportunities for careers in officialdom. Consequently, prior to the death of the eight-legged essay and the abolition of the civil service examination in 1905, Liao-ch'eng fared slightly better than other districts in Lu-hsi. This prevented Liao-ch'eng from being drawn into the cycle of rebellion endemic to the Lu-hsi region as a whole. However, the conservative culture to which the eight-legged essay was tied also limited the ability of Liao-ch'eng's elite to accept new things and the development of the new businesses necessary to transform the local economy.[6]

In Fu's childhood most people of Lu-hsi worked on farms and picked cattle manure from the streets. Women wove clothing, and children helped their parents with minor chores. Although they labored day and night, year in and year out, even the rich among them could lead only minimally prosperous lives. Only on two or three special occasions a year were people able to eat meat.[7] Bandits, soldiers, and local rascals disrupted the lives of the people at will. Most people here were loyal, mild-mannered, and moral but too weak to resist pressure from officials and

---

3 *FSNC*, 2515.
4 Naquin's *Shantung Rebellion* offers a thorough account of this event.
5 Cf. *Sung Ching-shih tang-an shih-liao* (Peking, 1959). In this collection, several informants for the oral records of this event were from Fu's hometown, Liao-ch'eng.
6 Cf. Joseph Esherick, *The Origins of the Boxer Uprising* (Berkeley, 1987), especially ch. 1.
7 *FSNC*, 2520. Fu made this observation when he visited his mother's hometown, a village right beside Liao-ch'eng.

Early Years

intruders. They were also too complacent to change a familiar life-style and adapt to changing circumstances. In short, Fu's bleak depiction of a weak society on its way to an inevitable deterioration was more than the ravings of a young rebel.

But the deterioration of this old society and the abolition of the civil service examination did not diminish the people's adherence to traditional cultural values. Fu lamented in 1919 that what he had witnessed in his hometown was a fruitless old culture too weak to prevent the transformation of local society but still powerful enough to resist new culture, thus preventing its inhabitants from studying abroad. Shantung found it difficult to fulfill the quota assigned by the Ch'ing government for students to be sent to study abroad; the local government even sought students from other provinces. All of Shantung, and especially Liao-ch'eng, lagged far behind other areas in setting up new schools and suffered from a shortage of both students and teachers.[8]

Reflecting back on the place of his birth, Fu Ssu-nien once wrote with a sigh that his hometown was a nest of bandits and soldiers. Nevertheless, it is also undeniable that this area was the hometown of many sages. The Liao-ch'eng of Fu's childhood has been variously characterized as militant, nationalistic, conservative, mystic, and anti-Christian. This mixture of chivalries and sages was somewhat embodied in the character of Fu's grandfather, Fu Li-ch'üan (1844–1922), who was most influential in shaping Fu Ssu-nien's character.

According to Fu's family records, Fu Li-ch'üan was a prominent master of the martial arts and of literature.[9] It was rare in traditional China for a literatus to be so versed in the martial arts, but local Liao-ch'eng tradition was at home with both the brush and the sword. The Boxer Rebellion was initiated and patronized, at least at its inception, by several similarly prestigious literati from this area.[10] There is no evidence to indicate that Fu's family had anything to do with this uprising, but the climate of opinion in the area was shared by Fu's family members. Fu Li-ch'üan, for example, was well known in his hometown

---

8 FSNP, I-1282, a manuscript written by Teng Kuang-ming (1897–1998), entitled "Chi i-wei Shantung te lao chiao-yü-chia – Wang Chu-ch'en hsien-sheng."

9 An extant piece of calligraphy also indicated that he was elegant with the brush. See FSNP, II-60, a photo of Fu Li-ch'üan's calligraphy scroll. His family members believed that the most famous righteous knight-errant of the late Ch'ing, Big Blade Wang the Fifth (Ta-tao Wang Wu, a close friend of T'an Ssu-t'ung), became a disciple of Fu Li-ch'üan after a dramatic competition in which Wang Wu was defeated by Fu in combat with bamboo poles. See Fu Le-ch'eng, "Fu Meng-chen hsien-sheng te hsien-shih," in *Shih-tai te chui i lun-wen-chi*, 121–122.

10 T'ao Fei-ya, "Shantung shih shen yü fan Chiao-hui tou-cheng," in *I-ho-t'uan yün-tung yü chin-tai Chung-kuo she-hui* (Szechwan, 1987), 278–286.

for his rejection of Christianity. After the Boxer Rebellion, when German priests were replaced by American evangelists, Fu Li-ch'üan, then in his fifties, was extremely active in creating disturbances and disrupting the efforts of these American missionaries to proselytize the locals. During the 1910s, when an American priest was relating to the Liao-ch'eng public the story of the Virgin Mary, Fu promptly jumped onto the stage and announced: "It is absolutely not true that Jesus was born without a father; what really happened was that Jesus did not know who his father was!" Stunned and aroused, the audience shouted the preacher down. On another occasion, when it was explained that "Jesus had himself crucified to save the world," Fu Li-ch'üan jumped onto the stage and said, "[As all of you know], in traditional China, loyalists and righteous people died willingly for their causes. When they died, they had a smile on their faces. Behold, in the portrait here Jesus lowers his head and closes his eyes as if he had no way out; was he not a bit cowardly?" The crowd then shouted at the minister, and the preaching was once again disrupted.[11]

Fu Ssu-nien's wayward grandfather was largely responsible for the decline of his family. Although he had obtained the title of graduate for preeminence (*pa-kung*) in the late Ch'ing, such a title was not very promising for government service.[12] Although he had good family connections, Fu Li-ch'üan never formally held office. He sometimes taught at private schools but spent most of his time wandering the streets. His family led a life of extreme poverty.

During the 1930s Fu Ssu-nien drew up an autobiographical sketch in which he mentioned that his father was a director of the Lungshan Academy (Lung-shan-shu-yüan), his grandfather a graduate for preeminence, and his great-grandfather a governor of Anhwei.[13] Fu did not trace his family origins further because one of his ancestors, Fu I-chien (1609–1665), was an embarrassment to him. Fu I-chien had served in

---

11 Only after his beloved grandson Fu Ssu-nien had returned from Peita for the summer intercession was Fu Li-ch'üan persuaded to stay away from the Christian preachers. Nonetheless, later, when Fu Li-ch'üan was invited to Liao-ch'eng Normal School to deliver a speech, he vehemently denounced Christianity again. Fu Le-ch'eng, "Fu Meng-chen hsien-sheng te hsien-shih," in *Shih-tai te chui-i lun-wen-chi*, 122–123.
12 Graduates for preeminence (*Pa-kung*) were senior licentiates chosen at examinations held once every twelve years. Holders of this degree were qualified to present themselves at the triennial examination for the third degree (*chin-shih*). If a graduate for preeminence successfully passed the triennial examination, he might be able to have a brilliant official career. However, because every graduate for preeminence was allowed to stand for the triennial examination only once in his life, the chances for success at this were rather slim. See Shang Yen-liu, *Ch'ing-tai k'o-chü k'ao-shih shu-lun* (Peking, 1958), 28–30.
13 FSNP, III-432, a short autobiography of Fu.

Early Years

the early Manchu regime and was legendary for passing the first civil service examination held by the newly founded Ch'ing government (1645) with the rank of *chuang-yüan* or *optimus*. He was finally promoted to the position of grand secretary in 1654 and also took charge of several imperially sponsored compilation projects.[14] Fu I-chien was famous not only for his success in the civil examination but also for his unrestrained knight-errant (*hsia*)[15] character and his obesity, both hereditary characteristics passed down to many of his descendants, including Fu Ssu-nien. But Fu Ssu-nien considered Fu I-chien a traitor to the Han Chinese and is reported to have blushed at the very mention of his name.[16]

Fu Ssu-nien's Upbringing

In a diary entry approximately datable to 1926, Fu Ssu-nien wrote that the most decisive period of a man's education is his childhood, especially the days he spends with his family.[17] The effect of one's family upbringing lasts even after one's full maturity, he added. Fu's family upbringing was on his mind even when he announced that "the family is the source of all manner of evil" (*chia wei wan o chih yüan*) in 1919.[18] In his middle age Fu confided to his brother: "all that constituted my

---

14 *Han-ming-ch'en chuan* (rpt., Taipei, 1970), 10, 50a–52b. Arthur Hummel, ed., *Eminent Chinese of the Ch'ing Period* (rpt., Taipei, 1972), 253. Because of Fu I-chien's great success in the first civil examination held by the Ch'ing government, his examination essays were collected and published under the title *Fu-ku-chai shih-i*, which was prefaced by Fu I-chien in 1679. See Fu Tseng-hsiang, *Ts'ang-yüan ch'ün shu ching-yen lu* (Peking, 1982), 5 vols., 5:1430.
15 Before taking the civil examinations, Fu I-chien was alleged to have been extremely attracted to a beautiful girl, Wang Su-yün, and to have traveled thousands of miles to visit her. He despaired that she had already been taken as a concubine by a local wealthy man, I Mi-chih. Fu nonetheless asked for a glance at her and left immediately. He was overtaken by a servant of the wealthy man and finally persuaded to accept the beautiful girl as his concubine. A subsequent story relates that years later the wealthy family was implicated in a political inquisition and was in real danger of destruction, but Fu I-chien, then grand secretary, saved it. Fu I-chien was later accused of improperly making a concubine his major wife. This story is recorded in Li Huan, ed., *Kuo-ch'ao ch'i-hsien lei-cheng ch'u-pien* (1884–1890; rpt., Taipei, 1966), *chüan* 463, 46. Fu I-chien was ordered by the emperor to compile the *I-ching t'ung-chu* in 9 *chüan*. He also wrote a preface for Ku Ying-t'ai's *Ming-shih chi-shih-pen-mo*. See Li Huan, ed., *Kuo-ch'ao ch'i-hsien lei-cheng ch'u-pien*, *chüan* 3, 1–2. As for the preface Fu wrote for Ku Ying-t'ai's book, see *Ming-shih chi-shih pen-mo* (Taipei, 1968), preface, 1.
16 Wang Shih-chieh's (1891–1981) speech at the conference about Fu Ssu-nien, "Fu hsien-shen tsai cheng-chih shang te erh-san shih," *Chuan-chi wen-hsüeh*, 28:1 (1976), 14.
17 *FSNP*, I-433, a notebook of 1926.
18 *FSNC*, 1553–1558. Fu's article "Wan o chih yüan" was published in January 1919 and was echoed by his teacher Li Ta-chao in a very short essay also entitled "Wan o chih yüan," *Mei-chou p'ing-lun* (July 1919). See *Li Ta-chao hsüan-chi* (Peking, 1959), 227. However, this was not an entirely new idea. Liu Shih-p'ei (1884–1919) had a similar idea back in 1907.

world of thought was from the teachings of our grandfather. What he taught me was loyalty [*chung*], filial piety [*hsiao*], integrity [*chieh*], and uprightness [*i*] without any trace of uncleanliness or impropriety."[19] Fu's father, Fu Hsiao-lu, died at age thirty and was survived by his wife and two sons, Fu Ssu-nien, then nine, and Fu Ssu-yen, then four. Even while Fu Hsiao-lu was alive, Fu Ssu-nien's mother and particularly his grandfather were in charge of his education in the absence of his father, who taught in the Lung-shan Academy, which resided at the neighboring district of Liao-ch'eng. A member of Fu's family sensed the similarity both in learning and character between grandfather and grandson. Fu's mother, née Li, was the daughter of a local landlord. She was semiliterate and reportedly very courageous. In 1928, when bandits pointed rifles at her, her shouting persuaded them to leave. Fu's nephew may have been correct in suggesting that Fu's courage in denouncing premiers H. H. Kung (K'ung Hsiang-hsi, 1880–1967) and T. V. Soong (Sung Tzu-wen, 1894–1971) in the 1940s was to some extent the result of his mother's influence.[20]

Fu's childhood fell into the culturally transitional Kuang-hsü (1875–1908) and Hsüan-t'ung (1909–1911) reign periods. Educational reform was the major component of this transformation.[21] In 1901 the Ch'ing court ordered that new-style hierarchical schools be established in every district and prefecture. Elementary schools (*hsiao-hsüeh-t'ang*) were not erected in Liao-ch'eng until Fu was ten years old (1905), when he followed most children of his generation and entered the new elementary school in which classical study was the least important item on the curriculum. For example, Liang Shu-ming (1893–1988), Ch'ien Mu (1895–1990), and most members of the generation born after 1890 were given only superficial instruction in the classics in the new elementary schools.[22] But Fu Ssu-nien's conservative grandfather paid special attention to him, insisting that he study the Confucian Classics.

---

19 Fu Le-ch'eng, "Fu Meng-chen hsien-sheng te hsien-shih," in *Shih-tai te chui-i lun-wen-chi*, 124. It is also recorded that even when Fu was a very prominent academic leader in China, he knelt all day in the presence of his mother whenever she turned angry. This again was extremely uncommon during Fu's generation, and it is all the more remarkable because it was done by a severe critic of the traditional Chinese family.
20 Fu Le-ch'eng, "Fu Meng-chen hsien-sheng te hsien-shih," in *Shih-tai te chui-i lung-wen-chi*, 126.
21 Cf. Shu Hsin-ch'eng, *Chin-tai Chung-kuo chiao-yü-shih tzu-liao* (Peking, 1961), 3 vols., 2:398–645.
22 See Ch'ien Mu, *Pa-shih i shuang-ch'in, Shih-yu tsa-i* (Taipei, 1983), 4, 65, 120. Ch'ien Mu writes that during his childhood he found that hardly any of his relatives had read the Five Classics. As for himself, he admitted that throughout his life he never finished reading the Thirteen Classics. See also Liang Shu-ming, *Chao-hua* (Shanghai, 1941), 140.

Early Years

In the *Ch'eng-shih chia-shu fen-nien jih-ch'eng* (*A Chronologically Arranged Syllabus for Classical Studies Used in the Ch'eng Family School*), one of the most popular curriculum guides in traditional China, parents were advised to begin their children's education at eight and ensure that their children finished reading the Five Classics at age eleven.[23]

Thanks to his grandfather, Fu was one of the very few members of his generation to have received a classical education, which in Fu's case began at the age of six. Fu reflected on his early years with bitterness, writing that his arduous classical training had seriously impaired his health.[24] Fu finished memorizing most of the Thirteen Classics by age thirteen.[25] The pace of this course, which was called "building work" (*kung-ch'eng*) in the *Ch'eng shih chia-shu fen-nien jih-ch'eng*, would have been considered too fast in traditional China. As a young boy, Fu also studied classics under another *pa-kung*, Sun Ta-ch'en. Later, at age ten, when the civil service examination was about to be abolished, Fu entered a local new school but continued his traditional classical training at home under the supervision of his grandfather. It is not too much to say that the abolition of the civil service examination system drew Fu to the first stage of new learning. But he also maintained his classical training in the event that the civil examination system were to be revived.[26] In fact, many literati of Fu's generation still lingered in their attachment to the eight-legged essay and expected that the civil examination system might be revived one day as it had been shortly after its abolition in 1898.

The new school system consisted of an elementary school in every district, a middle school (*chung-hsüeh-t'ang*) in every prefecture, and a high school (*kao-teng hsüeh-t'ang*) in every provincial capital. These schools would, it was expected, confer upon their students the degrees of licentiate (*sheng-yüan*), candidate in the provincial civil service examination (*chü-jen*), and candidate of the national civil service examination (*chin-shih*) respectively. When Fu was thirteen, his family, perhaps fearing that the old civil examination would not be revived, sent him to study in the middle school of Tientsin prefecture. Even though there were several

---

23 See Ch'eng Tuan-li, *Ch'eng-shih-chia-shu tu-shu fen-nien jih ch'eng*, in Yang Chia-lo, ed., *Tu-shu fen-nien jih-ch'eng, Hsüeh-kuei lei-pien* (Taipei, 1962), 8–9.
24 FSNP, I-708, a set of lecture notes entitled "Chung-kuo chin san-pai-nien lai tui wai-lai wen-hua chih fan-ying."
25 There are general reports that Fu committed many of the classics to memory. See, for example, Chung Kung-hsün, "Meng-chen hsien-sheng tsai Chung-shan ta-hsüeh shih-ch'i te i-tien pu-ch'ung," *Chuan-chi wen-hsüeh*, 28:3 (1976), 51; Yang Lien-sheng, review of *Fu Meng-chen hsien-sheng chi*, *Harvard Journal of Asiatic Studies*, 16:3–4 (1953), 489.
26 Ku Chieh-kang was also such a case. See Howard Boorman, ed., *Biographical Dictionary of Republican China* (New York, 1968), 4 vols., 2:245.

other middle schools in western Shantung, people still thought of Tientsin, then a rather westernized city, as a more advanced place in which access to new things was more readily available. After the abolition of the civil examinations, familiarity with things Western became a major qualification for getting into officialdom. It is worth noting that the old pursuit of prestige drove many youths to turn to things Western to obtain access to the so-called new degrees (*hsin-kung-ming*). No longer able to pass the examinations simply by studying in village schools, students were drawn from their hamlets into towns and cities to attend the new schools.[27]

The patron of Fu's study in Tientsin was Hou Yen-shuang, a *chin-shih* who had been a beggar in his teens and was reared and educated by Fu's father.[28] When Hou finally passed the *chin-shih* examination, he buoyantly returned to Liao-ch'eng to visit his beloved teacher. Upon his arrival he found that his teacher had already died and that his family was in a desperate situation. Ho swore in front of his mentor's tomb to help in bringing up Fu Ssu-nien and Fu's brother. The former students of Fu Hsiao-lu had donated a certain amount of money as a fund to sustain the Fus. On the eve of every lunar new year, an oxcart carrying a large quantity of food donated by these students would arrive at Liao-ch'eng for the Fu family. When Hou Yen-shuang decided to take Fu Ssu-nien to Tientsin, his intention was probably only to help Fu pursue things Western and thereby have a new channel into an official career. In his hometown Fu was always surrounded by people who asked him, "When are you going to start your official career [*ch'u-kuan*]?"[29] Even after the abolition of the civil service examinations, people still thought that any earned degree should lead to official rank; if not, it seemed to serve no purpose.

In Tientsin Fu's early hostility toward Christianity gradually diminished, owing mainly to his frequent contact with Ying Hua (1866–1926), a devout Catholic and publisher of the *Ta-kung pao*. Although Ying Hua firmly supported the Ch'ing government's effort to implement a parliamentary system, he opposed revolutionaries, whom he referred to as "packs of troublemakers" (*luan-tang*). Fu's enthusiastic discussion of contemporary politics with the Yings, who were reformist Manchu noble-

---

27 Kuo Mo-jo, *Shao-nien shih-tai* (Shanghai, 1948), 141, 179; Ch'ien Mu, *Pa-shih i shuang-ch'in, Shih-yu tsa-i*, 686.
28 Hou later became a congressman in early Republican China. Some biographical material about him can be found in Ling Yün, "P'eng Chao-hsien cheng-hai fu-ch'en hua tang-nien (–)," *I-wen-chih*, 80 (1972), 20–26.
29 *FSNC*, 2002.

men, was highly commended by that family during the last years of the moribund Ch'ing house.[30]

The purpose of the middle school curriculum was obviously to educate people for strengthening the nation. The curriculum covered thirty-seven hours a week, about half of which was devoted to English and mathematics and the remaining time to moral cultivation, classical reading, composition, Chinese and world history, Chinese and world geography, painting, biology, physics, chemistry, and physical exercise.[31] In 1913 Fu graduated from the Tientsin Middle School and was faced with at least two choices: entering high school (*kao-teng hsüeh-t'ang*) or entering the preparatory school (*yü-k'o*) of Ching-shih-ta-hsüeh-t'ang (later Peita). Fu chose the latter.

At Peita

Fu did extremely well in middle school, excelling in mathematics, English, and Chinese.[32] With credentials and achievements such as these, one was then expected to enter the Department of Science or the Law School, both of which were prestigious pathways to successful careers.[33] Fu, however, decided to enter the preparatory school's College of Letters, surprising many by entering the Department of Chinese upon graduation. Fu's enthusiasm for traditional Chinese learning is also evidenced by his persuading several other preparatory school students at Peita to enter the Department of Chinese.[34]

When Fu entered the Peita Preparatory School, the university was gradually being transformed from an old-style career-training school for government officials into a modern university.[35] Fu's performance in preparatory school was impressive. Upon graduation he was first in his

---

30 Cf. Ying Ch'ien-li, "Hui-i yu-nien shih-tai te Fu-hsiao-chang," in *Fu ku hsiao-chang ai-wan-lu* (Taipei, 1951), 8. Ying Hua's animosity toward revolutionaries has been discussed by Fang Hao, "Ying Lien-chih hsien-sheng nien-p'u chi ch'i ssu-hsiang," *Kuo-li T'ai-wan ta-hsüeh li-shih-hsüeh-hsi hsüeh-pao*, 1 (1974), 91. Fu Ssu-nien came to know the Yings through Hou Yen-shuan's introduction. Hou was then an editorial writer for Ying's newspaper. See *Ying Lien-chih hsien-sheng jih-chi i-kao* (Taipei, n.d.), 1174–1204.
31 Shu Hsin-ch'eng, *Chin-tai Chung-kuo chiao-yü-shih tzu-liao*, 2:499.
32 The people of the time tended to think of mathematics and English as the two key paths to new learning.
33 Cf. Mao Tun (Shen Yen-ping), *Yu-chih che* (Shanghai, 1938), 110–111. Mao Tun was Fu's classmate in Peita.
34 Li Ch'üan and Hsü Ming-wen, "T'ai Kang chih-ming jen-shih i Fu Ssu-nien", in *Fu Ssu-nien* (Shantung, 1991), 281.
35 Both Ho I-shih (1878–1961) and Hu Jen-yüan (1883–1942), two presidents of the university who served before Ts'ai Yüan-p'ei, had modern visions of college education but did not contribute significantly to the remolding of the university.

class among students of the humanities. Although Fu was by no means the only talented student, he was known in a very exaggerated way as "number one in Shantung after Confucius" or "the most talented youth in the Yellow River area." Such fame later helped him to become a student leader on several occasions.[36]

When Fu was in Peita, political and cultural conservatism was on the upswing, as evidenced by the attempts of Yüan Shih-k'ai (1859–1916) and Chang Hsün (1854–1923) to revive traditional imperial governance and ideology. This convinced many youths that traditional literature, rotten old politics, and traditional ethics were members of the same family.[37] Conscientious intellectuals concluded that old politics, old ethics, and old literature were parts of an organic whole that had to be eliminated in toto. Warlordism could be defeated and Peking politics cleansed only if traditional literature and ethics were also destroyed.

In 1916 Yüan Shih-k'ai managed to ascend to the throne of the emperor. Yüan's cultural policies contrasted sharply with those of Ts'ai Yüan-p'ei, the first minister of education of the Nationalist government in Nanking. Ts'ai ruled that Confucius could no longer be worshiped and that Confucian classics would no longer be read in schools. However, Yüan Shih-k'ai represented a great number of conservatives and reversed Ts'ai's decisions after his rise to power in 1913. In June 1913 Yüan decreed that Confucius was to be worshiped in every school. Four months later, in the Temple of Heaven Draft Constitution (T'ien-t'an hsien-fa ts'ao-an), Yüan proclaimed Confucianism the basis of civil education. In February 1915 Yüan's government declared that all schools should venerate the ancient sages as their models. They should base themselves on Confucianism and read the classics as part of the required curriculum. Some literati even sent in memorials urging that the constitution declare Confucianism the state religion.[38] Yüan Shih-k'ai rejected this suggestion, however, despite his closeness to the conservatives. The movement to turn Confucianism into the state religion was also supported by K'ang Yu-wei.[39] It is noteworthy that it

---

36 When Fu was at Peita, he had already become a legendary figure even in the neighboring district of Liao-ch'eng. Teng Kuang-ming recalled that when he was a child, he heard that Fu was "the number one genius along the Yellow River." See Teng Kuang-ming, "Hui-i wo te lao-shih Fu Ssu-nien hsien-sheng," in *Fu Ssu-nien*, 2. Wu T'i, Fu's classmate at Peita, also attested that when he was at Peita he heard students saying that Fu was "the most talented person of Shantung after Confucius." See Wu T'i, "I Meng-chen," in *Fu ku hsiao-chang ai-wan-lu* (Taipei, 1951), 62.
37 Cf. Ch'en Tu-hsiu, "Wu-jen tsui-hou chih chüeh-wu," in *Ch'en Tu-hsiu chu-tso hsüan* (Shanghai, 1993), 179. "Yüan Shih-k'ai fu-huo," in ibid., 239–240.
38 Ernest Young, *The Presidency of Yüan Shih-k'ai* (Ann Arbor, 1977), 202–204.
39 Ibid., 202–203.

was in the same year (1915) Ch'en Tu-hsiu decided to establish his journal *Youth* (*Ch'ing-nien*), which called for culture reformation and was deemed to be the beginning of the New Culture Movement by Hu Shih.[40]

In the summer and autumn of 1917 Chang Hsün led his Queue Army to Peking to restore the Manchu regime. This further convinced the new intellectuals that it was time to purge China of old ethics and old literature, the two pillars of the traditional regime.

Ch'en Tu-hsiu insisted that Yüan Shih-k'ai and numerous men like him were phenomena of the traditional Chinese political culture. The Confucian political culture was the ultimate cause of the recurrent vicious cycle of political chaos, which only an ethical and moral revolution could end. Only after the old bottle had been emptied could new Western ideas be poured into it. Ch'en Tu-hsiu asserted that if China did not transform itself in this manner, many more men like Yüan Shih-k'ai would arise and launch attempts to abolish the republic and revive the imperial system. A unique aspect of Ch'en Tu-hsiu's cultural agenda was his focus on a cultural approach to solving various imminent problems China faced, especially politics. This agenda was the major difference between Ch'en and his contemporaries. Yüan Shih-k'ai's cultural and educational policies and Chang Hsün's attempted restoration of the Manchu regime contributed significantly to the radicalization of these years. This growing conservatism bothered young students who were imbued with the liberal tendencies of 1911–1912. They were becoming fed up with all of the restoration movements.

At the height of these conservative reactions, Fu Ssu-nien attended the preparatory school of Peita. When Yüan Shih-k'ai died immediately after having become emperor, Fu was in the third class of the preparatory school.[41] When Chang Hsün tried to restore the Ch'ing in 1917, Fu was a freshman at Peita. During Fu's freshman year, Ts'ai Yüan-p'ei joined Peita. Ts'ai formed a new academic community in Peking that was independent of Peking politics and was to play a significant role in China's modern intellectual development.

A senior member of the revolutionary group, Ts'ai is generally regarded as the grand architect of the New Culture Movement. His appointment to Peita was later described as a "bomb in the stomach of the Monkey [*Sun-wu-k'ung*]." (The "bomb" was Ts'ai, and "monkey" the northern warlords.) Ts'ai's threat to the conservative North was not, however, recognized at the beginning. His appointment was by no

---

40 Hu Shih, "Wu-ssu yün-tung shih ch'ing-nien ai-kuo te yün-tung," in *Hu Shih chiang yen chi* (Taipei, 1978), 3 vols., 3:568.
41 Mao Tun, *Wo tsou-kuo te tao-lu* (Hong Kong, 1981), 86–87.

means made from any intention of the Peking government to improve the university but was simply the unexpected outcome of political maneuvers.[42]

An enthusiastic revolutionary in the late Ch'ing, Ts'ai was famous for being a *Han-lin*, the highest honor a literatus could attain after passing the civil service examinations. Ts'ai's literary achievements attracted many young people in the Yangtze area, and his reputation sometimes exceeded even that of Sun Yat-sen.[43] Ts'ai once became a true believer in anarchism and advocated replacing religion with aesthetic education. His moral qualities and his amicable, serene personality were assets to him in working with people of different orientations and backgrounds. He was, however, strong-minded when threatened. His unique bipolar personality was crucial in shaping two premier academic institutions: Peita and the Academia Sinica. Ts'ai confessed years later to Fu Ssu-nien that all he did at Peita was to allow various elements to grow freely and compete with each other. "What I did was simply let some teachers and students (of Peita) freely express their ideas according to their own personal inclinations. I merely did not block their developments."[44] During his tenure Ts'ai diverted funds from the university's limited financial resources to support both radical and conservative journals, although in his innermost self he supported the new culture. Another advancement of Ts'ai's was the transformation of Peita from a college providing training for official careers into a research university. The influence of Ts'ai's new policy was crucial. Before Ts'ai Yüan-p'ei was sworn in as president of Peita, professional research merited no respect and was even ridiculed. After Ts'ai, however, academic research gained in popularity.[45]

The limited number of universities in existence at that time also helped Peita to become an educational focal point. Of the other two universities in China at the time, Shansi University in T'ai-yüan was obscure, and the Peiyang University in Tientsin was very small and thus negligible as an institution of higher learning.[46] The Peita president's

---

42 T'ao Ying-hui, "Ts'ai Yüan-p'ei yü Pei-ching ta-hsüeh (1917–1923)," *Chung-yang yen-chiu yüan Chin-tai-shih yen-chiu-so chi-k'an*, 5 (1976), 272–273.
43 Wu Ching-heng, "Ssu-shih-nien ch'ien te hsiao ku-shih," in *Ts'ai Yüan-p'ei hsien-sheng chi-nien-chi* (Peking, 1984), 89.
44 FSNP, III-735, a letter from Ts'ai Yüan-p'ei to Fu, written when Ts'ai was in Europe.
45 Lü Ssu-mien, "Ts'ai Chieh-min (Yüan-p'ei)," in *Hao-lu wen-hsüeh chi* (Peking, 1996), 440–445.
46 Cf. *Kuo-li Pei-yang ta-hsüeh chi-wang* (Taipei, 1979). During the late Ch'ing, the Peking government ordered that many provincial *ta-hsüeh-t'ang* be set up. Most of them, however, did not function and were very obscure. Cf. Chu Yu-hsien, ed., *Chung-kuo chin-tai hsüeh-chih shih-liao* (Shanghai, 1986), Part I, 2 vols., 2:811–827.

attitude toward the new culture was, therefore, crucial in allowing new ideas to surface on the national scene.

But some traditions of the old Peita – that is, the Peita before Ts'ai Yüan-p'ei – remained. For example, in the old Peita the official status of students was sometimes higher than that of the teachers,[47] thus making the standing between students and teachers more equal and sometimes leading to debates between students and teachers, a situation unheard of in traditional teacher-pupil relationships. Freedom of expression quickly and unexpectedly led to much vigorous discussion. Free expression included posting "big-character posters" (*ta-tzu-pao*) slandering classmates,[48] a practice that later became an important medium in student movements.

But the major catalyst of the new Peita was the arrival of several new faculty members, especially Hu Shih, who arrived in 1917, apparently the first Ph.D. among the Peita faculty (though, in fact, his degree was not conferred until 1927). But even before Hu Shih's arrival, a new climate had already been forming. Only nine days after Ts'ai's appointment to Peita, he appointed as dean of the College of Letters Ch'en Tu-hsiu, who had been very interested in literary and moral reforms. Outside the College of Letters, professors like Chang Shih-chao (1881–1973), then a professor of logic and the university librarian, inspired students like Fu Ssu-nien to study logic and psychology. Owing to this influence, Fu later went to England to study Freudian psychology.

Fu apparently had access to Western books prior to the arrival of Hu Shih and Ch'en Tu-hsiu at Peita.[49] Although thoroughly imbued with Western knowledge by this time, Fu was not yet necessarily an iconoclast. On the contrary, he was once an enthusiastic reader of K'ang Yu-wei's *Pu-jen tsa-chih*, a periodical that advocated cultural and political conservatism and strongly condemned the unselective adoption of Western

---

47 Many students of old Peita were government officials. Moreover, once the students graduated, many of them tended to have more promising official careers than the faculty members. For these reasons Ch'en Han-chang (1863–1938) refused appointment as a teacher at Peita and instead became a student.
48 Fu Ssu-nien was very enthusiastic in writing posters mocking the private lives of his fellow students. He once ridiculed a classmate on a poster to such an extent that Ts'ai Yüan-p'ei publicly denounced it. Fu later admitted that Ts'ai did this to help him quit his bad habit of humiliating his classmates. See *FSNC*, 2375, and T'ao Ying-hui, "Ts'ai Yüan-p'ei yü Pei-ching ta-hsüeh," 280.
49 In Fu's personal library there are still some English books dated 1918 and before, such as Windelband's *History of Philosophy*. According to a written note in the front of the book, it was bought in 1916. I have also found that there is a copy of Bertrand Russell's *Scientific Method in Philosophy*, purchased in 1918. A copy of John Dewey et al., *Creative Intelligence: Essays in the Pragmatic Attitude*, was also purchased in 1918.

institutions and culture. The theme of *Pu-jen* (unbearableness) was that concern for the survival of the nation should supersede concerns about parliament and democracy. The *Book of Great Harmony* (*Ta-t'ung-shu*), the treatise outlining K'ang's utopian ideas, was also published in the same journal. Fu disliked K'ang's utopian ideas but enthusiastically endorsed the rest of his thought.[50]

In late 1917 Chang Shih-chao resigned his post as university librarian, and Li Ta-chao took his place. Hu Shih was appointed professor in September and began offering courses in the "history of Chinese philosophy." His criticism of ancient texts shocked as well as inspired a group of keen-minded students. In addition, Fu was attracted in early 1918 by two seminars offered by Liu Fu (1891–1934) and Chou Tso-jen (1884–1966): the history of European literature and the history of the Chinese novel, which were offered for the first time by the Department of Chinese at Peita, a department in which classical study was dominant. Fu Ssu-nien was receptive to the new learning they introduced. In the seminar for these courses, Fu was attracted to the study of the mentality of the common people and the language of the Chinese novel. Chou's course attracted a group of students who later became organized and founded the journal *New Tide* (*Hsin-ch'ao*).

Li Ta-chao's influence on Fu Ssu-nien and Lo Chia-lun (1897–1969) has been seriously neglected, sometimes deliberately so. In several versions of Fu's collected works, one important article bearing the marks of the influence of the Russian Revolution on Li have been left out.[51] Li encouraged the formation of the New Tide Society (Hsin-ch'ao she) and set aside a room in the university library for its activities. As one of Li's favorite students, Lo Chia-lun, an editor of the society's journal, was then echoing Li's image of the Russian Revolution as the great tide about to sweep over all mankind.[52] Fu Ssu-nien made a similar claim that the French Revolution had been superseded by the Russian Revolution and that the Russian model of revolution was the hope of the whole world and the only solution to China's problems.[53]

The activities of these new professors severely threatened the conservative group. The conservatives were mostly evidential research scholars and were disciples or friends of Chang Ping-lin. In 1915 the quarrel

---

50 K'ang yu-wei, ed., *Pu-jen tsa-chih hui-pien* (Shanghai, 1914; rpt., Taipei, 1968), 2 vols. Mao I-heng, "Kuan-yü Fu Ssu-nien te i-feng-hsin," *T'ien-wen-t'ai* (January 2, 1951).
51 For example, the most popular edition of Fu's works, *Fu Ssu-nien ch'üan-chi* (*FSNC*).
52 Maurice Meisner, *Li Ta-chao and the Origins of Chinese Marxism* (Cambridge, Mass., 1967), 71.
53 "She-hui-ko-ming: E-kuo (Russia)-shih te ko-ming," *Hsin-ch'ao*, 1:1 (1919), 128–129. This article was left out by the compilers of *FSNC*.

Early Years

between this group and the T'ung-ch'eng school, an even more conservative literary school established during the Ch'ing dynasty, resulted in the exclusion of the most conservative members of the Peita faculty. At Peita, Chang Ping-lin's circle could be divided into three groups: the conservatives, with such members as Huang K'an (1886–1935); the radicals, with members such as Ch'ien Hsuan-t'ung (1887–1939) and Shen Chien-shih (1886–1947); and the moderates, with members such as Ma Yü-tsao (1878–1945). Hu Shih allied with the radical group.[54] Fu was, however, extremely fond of the courses offered by Huang K'an and Ch'ien Hsüan-t'ung.[55]

Huang K'an and Liu Shih-p'ei (1884–1919) were extremely radical during 1900–1909, but around 1917, for reasons still unknown and deserving of further research, they turned to rather conservative causes.[56] They were not, however, as conservative as was imagined. Neither were they devoted to old cultural practices, least of all "Confucianism." They were committed to their scholarship as the exclusive investigator of truth. They studied classics and philology rigorously without adhering too closely to traditional values. They did, however, resist replacement of the literary language with the vernacular. Except for the young warriors of this group, such as Chang Hsüan, they did not preach the old morality and were relatively accommodating to the moral values of Chinese culture.[57] They did exactly what the title of their journal implied – they studied the "national past" (*Kuo-ku*).

Fu Ssu-nien was originally considered by Liu Shih-p'ei and Huang K'an as the most promising student and the one to whom the leading role of traditional learning should be extended. Nevertheless, Fu was quickly won over by the New Culture group in 1918. Due to the paucity of historical materials, it is rather difficult to explain Fu's change.[58] In

---

54 Shen Yin-mo, "Wo ho Pei-ta," in *Wu-ssu yün-tung hui-i-lu* (Peking, 1979), 3:157–170.
55 It has been argued that Ch'ien Hsüan-t'ung's linguistic theories somewhat coincided with the propositions of the Vernacular Language Movement. See Mao I-heng, "Kuan-yü Fu Ssu-nien te i-feng hsin," *T'ien-wen-t'ai* (January 4, 1951).
56 Liu Shih-p'ei's radical thought is best analyzed by Chang Hao in his *Chinese Intellectuals in Crisis: Search for Order and Meaning, 1890–1911* (Berkeley, 1987), 146–179.
57 Chang Hsüan was a very obscure figure. According to Ch'ien Mu, Chang's middle school classmate, Chang was an extremely enthusiastic nationalist who died not long after the end of the New Culture Movement. See *Pa-shih i shuang-ch'in, Shih-yu tsa-i*, 57–59. Liu Shih-p'ei also died soon after the end of the movement.
58 There is an anecdote that might also account for why Fu finally decided to join the new group. One day Fu was asked by his mentor Huang K'an to clean a spittoon. Fu did not do this job neatly, so Huang slapped Fu's face. Fu was fed up with this and decided to walk away. This anecdote was given to me by Ch'en Hsin-hsiung, a professor at Taiwan Normal University whose mentor, the late Lin Yin, was a student of Huang K'an.

fact, his conversion took place so quickly that when he joined the activity of the New Culture group, the group suspected Fu of being an agent sent by the conservatives.[59] Because Fu was the only one from the Department of Chinese who became a member of the new group, he was threatened constantly by his classmates.[60]

In sum, Fu's change was caused by two factors. On the one hand, ideologically the conservative group had become an "empty shell." The destructive power of the Ch'ing evidential research scholarship, especially as represented by K'ang Yu-wei and Chang Ping-lin, had overturned many traditional values. Fu was well versed in K'ang and Chang's works. Fu observed immediately after his turn to the New Culture group that K'ang and Chang contributed enormously to the fall of Confucianism. He claimed that by his time the Ch'ing learning was trivial and useless and that Confucianism was an empty shell. Fu said that Chang Ping-lin treated Confucius and the various pre-Ch'in schools of thought equally. In his various writings, Chang criticized Confucians severely.[61] Hsü Chih-heng, then a faculty member at Peita, wrote that "after the publication of Chang Ping-lin's 'Brief Discussions of Noncanonical Philosophies' [*Chu-tzu-hsüeh lüeh-shuo*], denouncing Confucianism came into vogue."[62] As for K'ang Yu-wei, Fu felt that although K'ang was known for revering Confucius, some of his works were in fact most detrimental to Confucian authority. K'ang pointed out that the Six Classics were mostly forgeries made by Confucius to reform and to establish Confucianism as a state religion. This implied that Confucius was a bold forger and that the Six Classics, which were the main content of the Confucian tradition, were forged texts. Strongly influenced by the works of K'ang and Chang, Fu's confidence in traditional values was definitively shaken. Thus, on the eve of the May Fourth Movement, Fu announced that Confucianism was in a hopeless situation and about to collapse.[63]

On the other hand, the old conservative group did not offer answers to immediate issues, such as how best to save China, or the meaning of life, marriage, clan, and so on. Fu's early experiences in his hometown, a stubbornly conservative society on the verge of collapse, might have contributed to his change. Fu's conviction that the old society was incapable of rejuvenating itself must have led him to be suspicious of the traditional value system and to look for any available alternative. Like a

---

59 T'ang Pao-lin and Lin Mao-sheng, eds., *Ch'en Tu-hsiu nien-p'u* (Shanghai, 1988), 87–88.
60 Ku Ch'ao, "Ku Chieh-kang yü Fu Ssu-nien tsai ch'ing-chuang shih-tai te chiao-wang," *Wen-shih-che*, 2 (1993), 12, 17.
61 *FSNC*, 1458–1459.
62 Hsü Chih-heng, "Tu Kuo-tsui-hsüeh-pao kan-yen," *Kuo-tsui hsüeh-pao*, 6 (1905), 1.
63 *FSNC*, 1458–1459.

long-ill patient losing confidence in his old doctor, Fu shopped around for any medicine that might cure the nation's ills. On the other hand, new things and ideas were pouring into the Peita community. A group of new professors persuasive in general issues introduced a cluster of new values. The old value system had been washed away, and the inflow of new things enticed Fu to join the new group.

Fu Ssu-nien and the New Tide

During the New Culture period, there were three Peita student groups representing three different inclinations: New Tide, Citizens, and National Past (Kuo-ku). On November 18, 1918, about twenty young student leaders of the New Culture Movement decided to organize the New Tide Society. The students had been inspired by Hu Shih, Li Ta-chao, and Chou Tso-jen, their professors at Peita, and many had enrolled in the latter's class on "The History of European Literature." They established a new monthly journal entitled the *New Tide*. This journal was modeled after the *New Youth*, which itself was published by their teachers as a revival of the defunct *Youth*. Financed by the university, the students successfully published the first issue in January 1919, with Fu Ssu-nien as its chief editor. The journal specialized in introducing Western thought to China and aimed to emancipate the minds of China's youth from the rigid conventions of the past. While society members were mostly in their twenties, they closely affiliated themselves with the publishers of the teachers' journal, the *New Youth*.

It is interesting to note that few if any articles in the *New Tide* overtly encouraged nationalism. Instead, their authors tended to expound on lofty idealistic theories, often without regard for practical realities. It was also ironic that, in a way, the *New Tide* writers were even more radical than those of the *New Youth* journal in criticizing Chinese traditions. Some of them also advocated revolution after the Russian model, although their understanding of it was vague and entailed only a trifling acquaintance with socialism and democracy.

The New Tide Society's ardent iconoclasm toward Chinese tradition eventually reached the point where it contradicted the agenda of the standard definition of "nationalism" – the glorification of a nation's heritage. The New Tide Society launched negative attacks against Chinese traditions and values. In their place, the society deemed acceptable the importation of whatever Western ideas and teachings might be needed to bolster national strength. This posture has amazed many scholars, and in the 1950s a major critic concluded that "in all the world there was nothing more strange than the May Fourth youths who championed nationalism by means of washing away the history and culture of their nation."⁶⁴ Almost simultaneous with the founding of the *New Tide*, the conservative student group set out to organize the National Past Society and published its journal.⁶⁵

The confrontation between the *New Tide* and the *National Past* was a most dramatic one. Both were run by students, both were funded by Ts'ai Yüan-p'ei, and both were assigned to neighboring rooms. The confrontation between the two groups was so intense that some members of the groups carried knives in their pockets for unexpected quarrels.⁶⁶ But the *New Tide* soon won over the greater audience, and after publishing only four issues, the *National Past* folded.⁶⁷ In this confrontation, with minor exceptions most members of the "conservative" group were actually more compromising than conservative; they were not determined to refute their enemies. Liu Shih-p'ei even proclaimed publicly that they did not oppose all propositions of the *New Tide* and that the students, and not he himself, were the leaders of this organization.⁶⁸ In contrast, members of the *New Tide* were militant and ready to exclude any ideas incompatible with their propositions. Fu Ssu-nien complained that the landslide victory of the New Culture group occurred because there was no qualified conservative equal to the fight. This, according to Fu, also showed what a cowardly nation China was.⁶⁹

The purpose of the *New Tide* was to influence high school students,⁷⁰ but its readers ranged from professors to middle school students. More radical than the *New Youth*, to a large extent the *New Tide* superseded the teachers' journal.⁷¹ The *New Tide* attracted significant attention when

---

64 Hsü Fu-kuan, "San-shih-nien lai chung-kuo te wen-hua ssu-hsiang wen-t'i," *Hsüeh-shu yü cheng-chih chih-chien* (Taichung, 1963), 2 vols., 2:145.
65 Before then, Liang Shu-ming, a lecturer in Indian philosophy, also founded a society for studying Eastern philosophy and Confucian philosophy. He also held public lectures. *Pei-ching-ta-hsüeh jih-k'an* (Peking), October 4, 1918.
66 Hsiao Ch'ao-jan, *Pei-ching ta-hsüeh hsiao-shih (1898–1949)* (Peking, 1988), 79.
67 In the *Kuo-ku* journal, we find that except for a short preface written by Huang K'an, conservative faculty members never published any article explicitly attacking the New Culture group. But two students, Chang Hsüan and Hsüeh Hsiang-sui, were active in rebuking the New Culture group on issues such as vernacular language.
68 See *Pei-ching-ta-hsüeh jih-k'an*, March 24, 1919. The passive disposition of the conservative professors was attested to by Liang Shu-ming. Liang said that they were too devoted to their own teaching and leisurely life-styles to be bothered with refuting the New Culture group. Liang confessed that it was strange that he, having only a scant knowledge of the Confucian classics, rose up to fight. See Liang Shu-ming, *Chao-hua*, 140.
69 *FSNC*, 1203.   70 *FSNC*, 2402.
71 This is Hu Shih's testament; see T'ang Te-kang, *Hu Shih k'ou-shu tzu-chuan* (Taipei, 1981), 176.

the minister of education, complaining about the rampant new culture, mentioned the journal.[72]

The success of the *New Tide* can also be explained by the emergence of new audiences. In this regard the students of Peita were crucial. Only after Peita was transformed by Ts'ai Yüan-p'ei from a career-training school into a modern university (in other words, when the students lost their channels to official careers) were the students able to divorce themselves from the official ideology. New audiences formed in Peita, and, relying on their prestige, they propagated their views throughout the nation. Outside Peita the potential audience also expanded greatly after the abolition of the civil examinations in 1905. After this, the number of new students increased tenfold within two years. During the New Culture Movement, the number of students was forty times what it had been in 1905 (i.e., 4 million to 4.5 million). These students could have been an audience for the conservatives[73] or for the proponents of New Culture, but ultimately they opted for the latter group.

The *New Tide* won the war with *National Past* easily, but its victory over another journal, the *Citizen* (*Kuo-min*), was less easy. In fact, among non-conservative students there were two discernible groups: the political reformists and the radicals. The group led by Fu Ssu-nien was politically reformist and culturally radical. The *Citizen* group was composed of political radicals, yet culturally it was rather reform-minded. The journals of these two groups also targeted different strata of their audiences. The *New Tide* targeted middle and high school students, whereas the *Citizen* targeted common people. The members of the *Citizen* even conducted a series of public lectures for the people of the lower classes, yet ironically their journal was still written in the classical language. The *New Tide* strove for plain expression and promoted radical ideas, a combination that struck a responsive chord with the younger generation.[74]

The enormous success of the *New Tide* attracted the attention of an assistant librarian at Peita, one Mao Tse-tung, who sought opportunities to discuss national affairs with Fu Ssu-nien and Lo Chia-lun in the periodicals room.[75] But, as attested by Mao, both Fu and Lo were too busy

72 See *Wu-ssu shih-ch'i te she-t'uan* (Peking, 1979), 4 vols., 2:65–66.
73 Perry Link, "Traditional-Style Popular Urban Fiction in the Tens and Twenties," in Merle Goldman, ed., *Modern Chinese Literature in the May Fourth Era* (Cambridge, Mass., 1977), 331.
74 Cf. *Wu-ssu shih-ch'i te she-t'uan*, 124–126.
75 On Mao's activity at Peita, see Ch'en P'o, "Ch'ing-nien Mao Tse-tung yü Pei-ching ta-hsueh," *Pei-ching ta-hsüeh hsüeh-pao*, no. 6 (1984), 90–94. A graduate of a provincial normal school, Mao enthusiastically participated in various student associations at

to talk to him. The two of them had unbelievably high rates of absenteeism from classes. By May 1919 Fu's reputation was already high in Peking student circles.

Fu Ssu-nien as Marshal of the May Fourth Demonstrations

In May 1919 Ts'ai Yüan-p'ei informed the students that the Chinese delegation had failed to win back Shantung due to the secret agreement reached by Chinese diplomats with Japan. In response, the students decided to stage a demonstration.[76] Demonstrating was not new to Peita students. At the beginning of 1919 the members of the *Citizen* had already launched an interschool demonstration against the Peking government and had therefore acquired experience in organizing students from different schools into a unified front. Student demonstrations did not come hand in hand with the New Culture Movement; it was the *Citizen* group that launched that protest. Fu Ssu-nien was believed to be opposed to the interschool demonstration launched by the *Citizen* group in early 1919.[77] But upon hearing the disheartening news from Ts'ai Yüan-p'ei and knowing that this time not only the Chinese warlord government but also imperialist countries would be the targets of protest, Fu actively participated in the protests and soon became marshal of the demonstrations. The reasons why Fu became the leader were many. During his undergraduate years, Fu had already become a potential student leader at Peita by virtue of his outstanding academic performance and his wide participation in newly founded societies, such as the Peita Co-op. His leadership qualities were further indicated by his teaching continuing education courses for clerks of Peita, his leading the debate team, and his election with the highest number of votes as appraisal member of the Moral Exhortation Society (Chin-te hui), an

---

Peita; see Hsiao Ch'ao-jan, *Pei-ching ta-hsüeh hsiao-shih (1898–1949)*, 85. He later confessed that "my office was so low that people avoided me. One of my tasks was to register the names of people who came to read newspapers, but to most of them I did not exist as a human being. Among those who came to read, I recognized the names of famous leaders of the Renaissance movement, men like Fu Ssu-nien, Lo Chia-lun, and others, in whom I was intensely interested. I tried to begin conversations with them on political and cultural subjects, but they were very busy men. They had no time to listen to an assistant librarian speaking southern dialect." See Edgar Snow, *Red Star over China* (New York, 1978), 139–140. Mao was apparently deeply hurt and repeated stories of this kind many years later.

76 Hsü Te-heng, "Wu-ssu yün-tung liu-shih chou-nien," *Wen-shih-tzu-liao hsüan-chi*, 61 (1979), 19.
77 Ibid., 12.

organization founded by Ts'ai Yüan-p'ei and the largest single organization at Peita.[78]

Outside Peita, the wide circulation of the *New Tide* among other students in Peking was facilitated by a loose network of student distribution agents. As the chief editor of this journal, Fu was very visible in Peking student circles.[79] Fu's identity as a student from Shantung, part of which had just been lost to Japan,[80] might also have been considered as some sort of qualification for leading a protest against the Peking government.

On the morning of May 4, 1919, Fu led a group of about three thousand students[81] and proceeded toward the diplomatic compounds of Peking to present a protest letter to the American ambassador. The conflict between the *New Tide* group and the *Citizen* group was discernible in the two manifestos drafted by these two groups. The former manifesto was rather temperate in wording, while the latter was radical. The former was in the vernacular language, the latter in the literary language. The discrepancy also surfaced after the protest letter to American diplomats was presented. Fu believed that his mission had already been accomplished, but the *Citizen* group insisted on proceeding to Ts'ao Ju-lin's (1877–1966) home to insult this chief negotiator who had made the secret agreement with Japan. A quarrel between Fu Ssu-nien

---

78 On the organization of Peita Co-op, see *Pei-ching ta-hsüeh jih-k'an*, December 27, 1917. For the other examples of Fu's leadership, see *Pei-ching ta-hsüeh jih-k'an*, May 21, 1918: Fu got 54 votes as appraisal member, and Hu Shih got 66 votes as the inspector; *Pei-ching ta-hsüeh jih-k'an*, October 8, 1918: Fu published a long letter to Ts'ai Yüan-p'ei discussing the failure to make the Department of Philosophy part of the Humanities School, the first time Ts'ai Yüan-p'ei was impressed by Fu; and *Pei-ching ta-hsüeh jih-k'an*, October 17, 1918: Fu headed the Debate Society. It is noteworthy that I Tsung-k'uei observed in 1918 that there were four leaders of the New Culture Movement: Ch'en Tu-hsiu, Hu Shih, Ch'ien Hsüan-t'ung, and Fu Ssu-nien, and that, in people's perception, Fu was a major leader of the movement; See I's *Hsin shih-shuo* (1918; rpt., 1982), preface, 39b–40a.
79 The most important reason might have been Fu's prominent reputation in student circles through the circulation of the *New Tide*. According to Li Hsiao-feng (1897–1971), due to the limitations of the circulation network, the *New Tide* was more popular in Peking than in other places. Most of its circulation was in schools rather than bookstores. The major portion of its publications probably fell into the hands of young students in Peking. See Li, "Hsin-ch'ao she te shih-mo," *Wen-shih tzu-liao hsüan-chi*, 61 (1979), 82–128.
80 The number of Shantung students at Peita was small, although the exact number is unknown. We do know, however, that there were forty students who received Shantung provincial government aid. See *Pei-ching ta-hsüeh jih-k'an*, April 30, 1918.
81 Chow Tse-tsung, *The May Fourth Movement*, 105. The number of students participating in this demonstration is disputed. There were, according to Chow, fifteen thousand students in all of Peking. See ibid., 99.

and Hsü Te-heng (1890-1990), the leader of the *Citizen* group, occurred on May 5. After receiving a slap in the face, Fu refused to participate in any further activity. It is worth noting that many of the members of the *Citizen* group later became Chinese Communists, while those of the *New Tide* group split afterward.[82] Fu Ssu-nien and Lo Chia-lun favored the Nationalist Party (KMT), while T'an P'ing-shan (1886-1956), Chang Shen-fu (1895-1986), and others sympathized with the Communist Party (CCP). The two groups also represented two approaches of the young students: to take political action to save the country or to devote themselves to academic and cultural activities. Many of the members of the citizen group later became involved in politics, while many *New Tide* members went on to enjoy success as writers, including Yeh Shao-chün (1894-1988), Chu Chih-ch'ing (1898-1948), Yü P'ing-po (1900-1990), and K'ang Pai-ch'ing (1896-1959). Others became leading academicians, such as Fu Ssu-nien and Ku Chieh-kang in history, Wang Ching-hsi (1897-1968) in psychology, and Feng Yu-lan in the history of Chinese philosophy.

The May Fourth Movement was politically influential. During its course, several groups began to sense that ideas could be transformed into political weapons. Students demonstrated on the street with nothing in their hands, yet they greatly changed Peking politics. Party leaders found that it was very much in their interest to include students in their organizations. Party organs also began to publish literary supplements in the vernacular language.[83] The KMT restructured itself. The CCP was born. Numerous new political parties appeared. According to Hu Shih, the New Culture Movement that began in 1915 was interrupted by the May Fourth Movement four and a half years later.[84]

Fu's role in the editing of the *New Tide* remained unchanged until October 1919, when he left Peking for England to study. Lo Chia-lun succeeded him in the editorial work, and the *New Tide* gradually declined. The *New Tide* ceased publication in March 1922 after only twelve issues. Afterward, Sun Fu-yüan (1894-1966) and Li Hsiao-feng (1897-1971) transformed the society into a study and publishing organization. The name of the Pei-hsin publishing company is in fact an abbreviation of Peita and the *New Tide*. Its prestigious reputation as a publisher of intellectual thought carries on its inheritance from the *New Tide* movement.

---

82 P'eng Ming, *Wu-ssu yün-tung shih* (Peking, 1984), 227.
83 T'ang Te-kang, *Hu Shih k'ou-shu tzu-chuan*, 190.
84 Hu Shih, "Wu-ssu yün-tung shih ch'ing-nien ai-kuo te yün-tung," in *Hu Shih chiang-yen-chi*, 3:568.

In retrospect, it is curious that, in a nation where seniority was of such importance, the leading role in the enlightenment movement was played by a group of undergraduates.⁸⁵ Fu, one of these undergraduate leaders, even provoked two debates with teachers at Peita, Ma Hsü-lun (1884–1970) and Liang Shu-ming, and announced that one of his tasks was to provoke his elder enemies, or "to ride on the tigers' backs."⁸⁶

Why were the youth so confident and proud? In their minds, only Western learning showed the final measure of the value of learning; tradition had little value. Therefore, those who were less tainted by traditional culture, such as children and the insane, were more free of errors.⁸⁷ Ch'ien Hsüan-t'ung, a professor who supported the new cause, even announced that "all Chinese over forty years old should be executed."⁸⁸ The more access people had to Western learning, the closer they were to "the truth." Proficient in English, Fu obtained Western books from the Maruzen bookstore in late 1916.⁸⁹ Armed with these new weapons, Fu and his group may have felt that they were on an equal if not higher footing with their professors who could not read English.

The Young Proselyte

Being less tainted with outdated ideas and better able to get access to what he regarded as true learning, Fu wrote about fifty articles within ten months to enlighten his young compatriots, a number almost equal to the number of nonacademic articles he published after 1920. Because most of these articles became extremely popular and influential, it is worthwhile to discuss their contents. It is not, however, easy to explore Fu's complex mind during the *New Tide* period. The enthusiasm and agony behind these writings are still discernible. It is puzzling that several sparkling pieces on traditional learning were mixed with immature outbursts, but this frame of mind was perhaps typical of such transitional periods.

The formation of Fu Ssu-nien's opinions during the New Culture Movement and its aftermath was rather unsystematic. Many of his ideas were not original but were further developments of ideas inherited from Hu Shih, Lu Hsün (1881–1936), Chou Tso-jen, and Ch'en Tu-hsiu.

---

85 *FSNC*, 2406.   86 *FSNC*, 2407.   87 For example, *FSNC*, 1193.
88 This is a widely known saying of Ch'ien in his early ages. See Lu Hsün, "Chiao-shou tsa-yung," in *Lu Hsün ch'üan-chi* (Peking, 1981), 16 vols., 7:435–436.
89 Mao I-heng, "Kuan-yü Fu Ssu-nien te i-feng-hsin," *T'ien-wen-t'ai* (January 2, 1951).

However, it is discernible that Fu Ssu-nien called for a fundamental change, one that involved discarding the culture of the "men of letters" (*wen-jen*). Anything related to traditional "men of letters" incurred flamboyant attacks from him. This was tantamount to attacking the core of traditional Chinese history.

Fu claimed that "once a man becomes a man of letters, he is no longer a human being."[90] "Once someone becomes a man of letters, he escapes from the real world and enters a dream world."[91] He detested everything pertaining to "men of letters," including their mental attitudes and their life-style.[92] His opinion was that if China were to save itself, it would have to discard the men of letters. He was, in essence, questioning who represented the real "China." This is a theme inherent in many of Fu's writings of the *New Tide* period.

In Fu's writings of this period, there were two tendencies that were shared to a certain extent by many of the youth in his generation. The first of these tendencies was popularism, which manifested itself in Fu as a deep animosity toward traditional literati culture. New China should "go to the people" and take the common people's feelings as the yardstick for measuring the value of traditional cultural forms.

For Fu, as for many of his contemporaries, the common people were a positive aspect of Chinese society. Fu reevaluated everything against the standard of the common people and their real feelings. This was part of his desire to transform the traditional literati-dominated society.

The second tendency, one common to many during the May Fourth era, was a desire to enlighten the people, both literati and the common man. Fu and his generation knew that the prerequisite for enlightening the masses of common people was adopting their language and cultural forms. According to Fu Ssu-nien, this transformation was not conforming to common society, but adopting the ways of the commoners to transform them.[93]

Fu Ssu-nien as Cultural Critic

Fu Ssu-nien viewed the entire enterprise of the New Culture Movement as an attempt to become closer to "human nature" (*jen-hsing*). Unlike previous thinkers, Fu believed that humanity (*jen*) was a goal to be achieved, not an established state of being. Chinese philosophers, Fu

---

90 *FSNC*, 1192.
91 A letter from Fu Ssu-nien to Hu Shih, in *Hu Shih lai-wang shu-hsin hsüan* (Hong Kong, 1983), 3 vols., 1:105.
92 For example, *FSNC*, 1184, 1191.   93 *FSNC*, 1092.

Early Years

argued, had always endeavored to drive people away from human nature, whereas in the West people were urged to move closer to it. According to Fu, Chinese culture had been distracted from the essential question of what being human entailed because Confucianism, especially Neo-Confucianism, had been so wrong in leading people to separate themselves from social realities and the actualities of human life. The view of sagehood (*sheng-jen-kuan*) had diverted people from real life. The basic assumption of Chinese traditional ethics was that human beings were born for the realization of morality and the pursuit of the moral code set by sages; people were not allowed to have "selves."[94] What appeared in Chinese operas, novels, and literature were all man-made feelings and artificial sentiments, only a very few of which were in tune with the ordinary people (*ch'ang-jen*). Fu contended that it was not the pronouncements of the "sage" but the most basic sentiments and feelings that constituted true human nature.[95]

Fu suggested that the healthy, common desires long suppressed into the unconsciousness should be, as Ch'en Tu-hsiu had said, the unchanging value, and that it was time to redeem them. *A Nun Regretting Monasticism* (*Ni-ku ssu-fan*), a Kunshan opera (*K'un-ch'ü*), was highly regarded by Fu because in it normal human desires find expression.[96] He praised

---

94 *FSNC*, 1245.
95 In Fu's essays we often encounter the term "human nature," a term and concept from which, according to Fu, Chinese philosophers had been distracted. The mundane nature of human beings had been fully attested to later when Fu began his study at London University of two Western intellectual trends: Darwinism and Freudianism. Darwin's theory of evolution alerted us to our animal origins. With this new assumption, Fu asked, how could the idea of achieving sagehood still be sustainable? (*FSNC*, 1261). With the aid of psychoanalysis, Fu had acquired another forceful weapon for dismissing sagehood. In psychoanalysis, human consciousness is divided into several levels. People had come to realize that even Neo-Confucianism did not fully penetrate into the unconscious level to probe the sometimes animal-like, irrational, and dark nature of human beings (*FSNC*, 1260–1261). Fu advocated that the "libido" (*pen-neng*) is far more powerful than the "id" and asserted that "id" is to "libido" as slave is to master (*FSNC*, 1263). He implied that the suppressed "libido" was the essence of the human mind, and that many mundane desires (desires to which the New Culture Movement sought to draw attention) were in fact the constituents of human nature. This view also led Fu to become one of the earliest people in China who were attracted by behaviorism in 1926 (*FSNC*, 1237). Reason is only "to decorate and cover up" the impulses (*FSNC*, 1263). Therefore, law, religion, morality, and politics are, as reason, always changeable (*FSNC*, 1264, 1266, 1289). The old Confucian proverb "Heaven does not change, neither does the Tao change" was thus called into question. Human beings were now viewed as very ordinary, if not inferior, creatures (*FSNC*, 1261). This represented a radical conceptual departure from the old Confucian proverb that "man is the most dignified creature under Heaven" (*T'ien-ti-chih-hsing jen-wei-kuei*). The sentence first appeared in *Po-hu-t'ung*, and it later became a common proverb of Confucianism. Cf. Yü Ying-shih, *Chung-kuo ssu-hsiang ch'uan-t'ung te hsien-tai ch'üan-shih* (Taipei, 1987), 19.
96 *FSNC*, 1087.

the nun in this opera for being conscious of herself (*yu-i-shih*) in expressing her sexual desire.[97]

The adoption of the vernacular language was instrumental in Fu's agenda to move closer to the common people. The change of genre is very important. During the New Culture Movement, vernacular language replaced the classical language. Before then, in most schools parallel prose was most popular.[98] The use of vernacular language even on very formal occasions marked a great change from the previous period. During the Ch'ing, much vernacular material was written by literati to educate the common people, but they still used the classical language to express themselves. Now the new intellectuals argued that everyone should use the vernacular language for all occasions. Previously some literati appreciated Sung and Yüan vernacular novels, but only now did they use this language to convey serious thoughts. Most new intellectuals could not write in the vernacular language easily. They had to learn to write it.[99]

However, Fu Ssu-nien wrote in his article "Vernacular Literature and the Psychological Transformation" that it was not enough for new intellectuals merely to use the vernacular language. They should do so as a tool for psychological transformation. Fu complained that the political chaos in the early Republican period was due to the odd phenomenon of all sorts of old thoughts being present in the new regime. The political revolution bore no fruit. What China needed was a cultural and spiritual revolution. Fu wrote, "The Republic of China was not republican at all." He argued that in the long run a truly republican China could be constructed only by means of a literary revolution.[100] Hu Shih pointed out that this was the most important article Fu had written in the New Culture Movement.[101]

It is also believed that Fu's articles in 1918 and 1919 advanced the popularity of the literary reform among students.[102] Fu showed students how to write in the vernacular language, and in this he was rather unusual, because many people promoted the vernacular-language movement without giving actual instruction in how to write in it. In his essay "How to Write in the Vernacular Language" (Tsen-yang hsieh

---

97 Fu certainly knew the dark side of the unconsciousness. He even believed that "lechery and violence" (*yin sha*) were the two most common elements of the Chinese unconsciousness. See *FSNC,* 1080.
98 Mao Tun, *Wo tsou-kuo te tao-lu,* 107.
99 Ku Ch'ao, *Ku Chieh-kang hsien-sheng nien-p'u* (Peking, 1993), 43.
100 *FSNC,* 1183–1184.
101 Hu Shih, "Fu Meng-chen hsien-sheng te ssu-hsiang," in *Hu Shih chiang-yen-chi,* 340.
102 Chow Tse-tsung, *The May Fourth Movement,* 276.

pai-hua-wen), he advised his readers to pay attention to their spoken language and to borrow as much as possible from Western composition skills.[103]

Fu was very much influenced by Chou Tso-jen's famous article "Humane Literature" (Jen te wen-hsüeh), which called for a Chinese literature that describes real human emotions. Fu even went a step farther, asserting that the so-called humane literature was in fact "Europeanized literature" (*Ou-hua*) and that the best way to produce this new form of "humane literature" was to model Chinese writing as closely as possible on Western writing.[104] To avoid being divorced from social reality, the new Chinese literature should pay full attention to "human feelings" (*jen-lei ch'ing-kan*). Fu asserted that, although "feeling" was far more powerful than reason, Chinese authors had always insisted on imitating sages to the neglect of human feelings. Fu believed that "human feeling" was the source of the success of Russian literature and the Russian Revolution and implied that the main task of the current Chinese culture movement was not only to revolutionize literary thought (a subject on which he expounded in several articles) but also to develop "human feeling."[105] With these beliefs, Fu's aesthetic views changed immensely. He appreciated art that reflected "real feeling" (*ch'ing-chen*), "naturalness" (*tzu-jan*),[106] and "the feelings of the common people and even prostitutes" (*shu-min ch'ang-you*). The artistic taste of the elite should give way to the taste of the common people, and man-made beauty should give way to natural beauty. Beauty, for Fu, was what was closest to the reality of things.[107]

Fu appreciated the pathbreaking work of Wang Kuo-wei in writing the history of Sung and Yüan opera (*Sung Yüan hsi-ch'ü shih*), because these operas, Fu believed, truly reflected the feelings of the common people. Measured by this new aesthetic standard, Fu claimed that throughout the history of Chinese literature only a few works of poetry and dramatic literature of the lower people were valuable, because they reflected the sentiments of ordinary people.[108] In sum, Fu's broad-ranging aesthetic agenda encompassed the redemption of cultural forms, politics, ethics, and morality, and the yardstick of the quality of literature was no longer represented by literati but by the common people.

Fu's opinion of Chinese opera is illustrative in this regard. Fu was very familiar with Chinese opera and often singled out operas as targets of special criticism. He was so disappointed with Chinese opera that he

---

103 *FSNC*, 1127–1134.   104 *FSNC*, 1133.   105 *FSNC*, 1182–1183.
106 *FSNC*, 1430.   107 *FSNC*, 1068.   108 *FSNC*, 1428.

attached his favorite term to it: "a bundle of contradictions" (*i-t'uan mao-tun*).[109] Chinese opera, he believed, adopted too many symbolic expressions and only very rarely reflected genuine human sentiment,[110] developing to such an extreme that it valued performance above human reality.[111] The excessive emphasis placed on performance was reflected in gestures,[112] stage arrangements,[113] and the inevitable happy ending,[114] all at the expense of true human feeling. It all amounted to nothing more than simpleminded juggling acts.[115] Fu asserted that performance and juggling pursued two different goals; the former emphasized imitating the human situation, whereas the latter emphasized pointless invention. The former had as its ideal the resemblance of reality, whereas the latter resembled nothing; the former paid attention to plot, whereas the latter played tricks. According to Fu's assessment, although these characteristics of performance and juggling were in diametrical opposition, they coexisted in Chinese opera in a contradictory stasis heretofore unperceived.[116]

In contrast, Fu treasured Sung and Yüan opera because it was natural and real, was not written by learned scholars, and was not intended to be preserved forever.[117] Sung and Yüan opera was, then, free in its style of language and unconcerned about the refinement of its content or audience. Fu believed that actors in plays should portray common people and their common lives. He argued further that there should be no sharp division between good and evil characters in plays.[118]

The fundamental way to transform literature, however, was to transform the Chinese language. Fu asserted that Chinese ideographs were created in a most primitive time and that the standard style currently in use was more difficult to learn than even the ancient seal script.[119] Like some of his contemporaries, Fu called for abolishing all Chinese ideographs within ten years.[120] He believed that a new phonetic language should be created to replace the ideograph system and that the phonetic language would totally destroy traditional Chinese literature before the establishing of a new literature.[121] Fu even dreamed, as had many of his contemporaries, that one day a universal language would naturally be formed.[122] But Fu, Hu Shih, and others did have their doubts about the adaptability of Esperanto in China, because they

109 *FSNC*, 1080.   110 *FSNC*, 1077.   111 Ibid.   112 *FSNC*, 1102.
113 *FSNC*, 1101.   114 *FSNC*, 1109.   115 *FSNC*, 1077–1078.   116 *FSNC*, 1078.
117 *FSNC*, 1430. Few modern scholars would accept Fu's entire interpretation of Sung and Yüan opera.
118 *FSNC*, 1110.
119 *FSNC*, 1140. For example, the character *yeh*, the original meaning of which is believed to be "snake," was widely used to mean "also." *FSNC*, 1142.
120 *FSNC*, 1138.   121 *FSNC*, 1164.   122 *FSNC*, 1151.

thought it almost impossible to learn a new, man-made language.[123] Fu did, however, suggest that romanizing the Chinese spoken language would be a worthwhile experiment.[124]

Critics of the Chinese Mental Attitude

Fu Ssu-nien was pessimistic about the destiny of the New Culture Movement. Like Lu Hsün, whose works are filled with sharp and sarcastic insights into the Chinese mentality, Fu also assumed a pessimistic attitude toward everything Chinese, including the destiny of the vernacular-language movement. As usual, Fu was pessimistic about the Chinese mental attitudes and the "flu" syndrome of adopting and then discarding new things.[125] He believed that even if all new cultural forms such as vernacular language and new opera were to succeed in the future, these new things would soon become shelters for the old if there was not a tremendous and fundamental change in the Chinese "mental structure."

Fu Ssu-nien devoted much attention to discussing the question of how to train agents of the enlightenment movement. Fu perceived a weakness in the Chinese character and asserted that only after a thoroughgoing change of Chinese mental attitudes could the New Culture Movement truly succeed. He believed that several factors had produced the deficiencies in the Chinese mental attitudes, but that the prime influence on the way Chinese thought and acted was the Chinese family system. Fu was fond of his family and had benefited greatly from his early family life.[126] Yet, like many of his contemporaries, he felt that Chinese families restrained the individual development of their members. This, he thought, was a debilitating liability because individuality is essential to the development of responsible modern citizens.

For Fu, the Chinese family was "the source of all manner of evils" (*wan-o chih yüan*);[127] good originated with the individual,[128] and the family hindered the development of individuality.[129] In families, "people progress day by day to become non–human-beings";[130] in other words, children were taught to conform to a hierarchical family order irrespective of their individualities. Fu regarded the "Eight Steps" of the

---

123 *FSNC*, 1150–1151.   124 *FSNC*, 1155.
125 Fu singled out Shanghai as a city representative of this kind of mentality.
126 Fu Le-ch'eng, *Fu Meng-chen hsien-sheng nien-p'u*, in *FSNC*, 7:2633.
127 It is worth noting that during the late Ch'ing, there was an anarchist movement that called for the destruction of the Chinese family system. It was especially championed by Liu Shih-pei. See Wang Fan-sen, "Liu Shih-p'ei yü Ch'ing-mo te wu-cheng-fu chu-i yün-tung," *Ta-lu-tsa-chih*, 90·6 (1995), 6.
128 *FSNC*, 1553.   129 *FSNC*, 1555–1558.   130 *FSNC*, 1557.

Great Learning (*Ta-hsüeh*) as a bundle of contradictions; for example, "self-cultivation" (*hsiu-shen*) required individuality, whereas "ordering one's family" (*ch'i-chia*) requires one to suppress one's individuality. Fu encouraged people to set aside considerations of parents, brothers, and wives and act solely by the dictates of their own consciences. He even encouraged people to be single.[131] Ku Chieh-kang recollected a scroll hung on the wall of Fu's dormitory that read: "Within the four seas, I have no family. I do not recognize the six relationships (parents, brothers, wife and children)."[132]

Like many others, Fu believed that despotism also retarded the development of individuality. Under despotic politics, there was no healthy growth in the people's sense of responsibility, which prevented the Chinese people from expressing their own will and fighting for causes they believed in. Because the Chinese are too "weak" (*hsin-ch'i po-jo*) to stand up for any cause, Fu noted with a sigh, the conservatives of his time were so fragile, so numb, so unresponsive, and so morally inconsistent that few of them were capable of standing up to oppose the New Culture Movement. He accordingly worried that the New Cultural Movement would succeed too fast because people simply fell into step with the trends of the time, and that the movement itself would be frustrated not long after its success.

Transevaluation of Traditional Learning

In Fu Ssu-nien's opinion, Confucian tradition had already lost its persuasive power in the late Ch'ing and early Republican periods. Fu asserted that Confucianism failed to cope with the change of society and offered no help to the numerous difficulties Chinese society faced. Evidential research scholars paid no attention to practical problems, whereas the revived Sung learning, which aimed for moral cultivation and statecraft, turned the clock back. Confucian classics did not have any real influence on people's lives anymore. Fu agreed with Ch'ien Hsüan-t'ung that the Six Classics and the Three Histories (*Records of the Grand Historian* [*Shih-chi*], *History of the Former Han Dynasty* [*Han-shu*], and *History of the Later Han Dynasty* [*Hou-Han-shu*]) should be burned and that the *Erh-ya* (*Progress toward Correctness*) and *Shuo-wen* (*Analysis of Characters as an Explanator of Writing*) should be used to cover windows[133] because these texts were only read by literati and had nothing to do with

---

131 Ibid.
132 Ch'en Yü-hsien, "Hung Yeh i ku-yu," *Ming-pao yüeh-k'an*, no. 12 (1987), 106.
133 *FSNC*, 1143.

the common people and everyday life.¹³⁴ Writings other than the Six Classics, Fu felt, were far more influential in people's real lives. With regard to governing, the *Important Deliberations on Government of the Chen-kuan Period* (627–649) (*Chen-kuan cheng-yao*) was more instructive to emperors than the *Book of Documents*. As for the education of the local elite, the *Tract of T'ai-shang on Action and Response* (*T'ai-shang kan-ying-p'ien*) was more useful than the *Book of Rites*. The *Reflections on Things at Hand* (*Chin-ssu-lu*) was easier to grasp than the *Analects* in terms of moral cultivation. As for teaching people loyalty, the *Spring and Autumn Annals* was much less efficient than the "Song of Righteousness" (Cheng-ch'i ko) of Wen T'ien-hsiang (1236–1282). As for exhorting people to order their families, the *Great Learning* was much less efficient than Chu Po-lu's (Yung-ch'un, 1627–1699) *Proverbs for Regulating Family* (*Chih-chia ko-yen*). Ninety percent of the content of the classics was only for window dressing and a source for writing compositions.¹³⁵

Fu argued that the textual resources of traditional Chinese spirituality, be they Confucian Classics, Taoist tracts, or Buddhist Sutras, did little to help people cultivate their minds. Even Neo-Confucianism failed in this respect. Fu noticed that the common people were very much in need of moral guidance. For Fu, this lack of moral guidance explained why various religious sects attracted so many followers in late imperial China and why some religious movements evolved into full-scale uprisings.

When all of the traditional moral resources had been abandoned as dysfunctional, what moral code could the citizens resort to? Likely inspired by John Stuart Mill, Fu proclaimed a view of life shared by Hu Shih and Ting Wen-chiang (1887–1936): "Freely develop the individual for the sake of public welfare."¹³⁶

But Fu still treasured one branch of traditional learning. During the May Fourth period, he published an article entitled "The Fundamental Error in the Chinese Intellectual World" (Chung-kuo hsüeh-shu-ssu-hsiang-chieh chih chi-pen miou-wu), which severely criticized the methodological shortcomings of traditional Chinese scholarship. Such shortcomings included excessive use of analogy, excessive generalizations, and vagueness.¹³⁷ But Fu still clung to Ch'ing philological learning. He believed that Ch'ing evidential research was the only branch of Chinese learning imbued with a scientific spirit and a logic of sequence.¹³⁸ He compared Ch'ing research methods favorably with the Western scientific method but was saddened that whereas Western

---

134 *FSNC*, 1136–1137. 135 *FSNC*, 2050. 136 *FSNC*, 2411.
137 *FSNC*, 1218–1219. 138 *FSNC*, 1456, 1459.

scholars searched for "truth," Ch'ing scholars took the word of Confucius and Mencius as "truth" and therefore devoted all their energies to investigating useless textual matters.[139] Thus he was among the first to envision the enterprise of employing the methods of Ch'ing scholars in "rearranging the nation's past" (*cheng-li kuo-ku*).[140] Fu cautioned his readers that he was not holding up Ch'ing learning as a science in itself but was, instead, suggesting that Ch'ing philological methods be applied to such fields as Chinese linguistics.[141] Fu Ssu-nien was by no means convinced, as was Hu Shih, that the evidential research of Ch'ing scholars fully embodied the scientific spirit. The methodology employed by Ch'ing scholars had its drawbacks, and Western learning was indispensable.

Creating a "Society"

Fu never discussed "democracy" as enthusiastically as his colleagues did. In this he stood in contrast to most of his contemporaries, who advocated or envisioned a democracy brought about by means of political revolution.[142]

Fu may have felt that the problem in Chinese politics was not so much a lack of democracy as an overabundance of freedom, which resulted in nongovernance. The focus of Fu's message during this period was always social construction. Fu singled out the Russian socialist revolution as an acceptable pathway for China. But Fu had only very vague ideas about the so-called Russian Revolution. The major characteristic of this event, as seen by Fu, was its great social revolution, which promised to reform an outdated, hollow, and guilt-laden society. Fu therefore saw the Russian Revolution as a revolution that transformed the "masses" into a "society." As such, it was for Fu a model case of mobilizing and organizing people to fight for an unified cause. Yet he never mentioned class struggle or other key elements of Communist theory.[143]

In reading Fu's writings from this period, we can sense a gradual shift of concern away from literary reform and toward societal construction. Fu Ssu-nien's discussion of societal construction began with the discus-

---

139 *FSNC*, 1457.
140 *FSNC*, 1463. It is worth noting that the idea of "scientifically rearranging the nation's past" (*k'o-hsüeh te cheng-li kuo-ku*) was first mentioned by Mao Tzu-shui (1893–1988) and Fu Ssu-nien. See *FSNC*, 1258–1259.
141 *FSNC*, 1463.
142 He only used the term *min-chu* (democracy) twice when discussing whether the late Ch'ing revolutionaries knew what democracy was. See *FSNC*, 1184.
143 Fu Ssu-nien, "She-hui-ko-ming: E-kuo (Russia) – shih te ko-ming," 128–129.

sion of the destructive power of despotism. He argued that traditional despotism had at least four bad effects: (1) It dispersed the Chinese into an unorganized mass that never formed into any "society" (*she-hui*) or organized community. Moreover, whenever collective actions did occur, they tended, because of a lack of genuine cohesion, to be excessive.[144] (2) Because no "society" really existed, people tended to rely on politics to solve all social problems. (3) Because of despotic politics, China's so-called government was in fact "nongoverning" (*wu-chih*). The government, on the one hand, was unable to extend its governance to society and, on the other hand, it inhibited society from taking charge of itself. (4) Under despotic politics, there was no healthy growth in the people's sense of responsibility.

Fu also saw the civil service examination system as a reason for China's lack of society:

> But how is it that China ultimately has no society today? Can it be that the Chinese people lack all organizational ability? There is a historical reason for this as well. In the past, the autocratic dynasty was the center of Chinese political organization, and the civil service examination system was the center of the organization of culture. All of society was controlled by these two systems. Under these two systems, organizational strength could only develop to a certain degree. Because autocracy could not coexist with social power, for it to exist even a day autocracy had to destroy social power forcefully. On the level of thought, the examination system made it so that the people would not demand organizational power. This created today's state of fragmentation [a loose sheet of sand].[145]

Autocracy could not tolerate social power, and success in the civil examination system required no organizational effort.

Fu denounced Chinese "politics" as nonpolitics. Chinese governments, he argued, were full of oligarchy, eunuchs, courtiers, usurpers, able scoundrels, strategists, and deceitful men. The history of Chinese politics was filled with usurpations, struggles for sovereignty, the exercise of sovereign powers in regions under the control of contending warlords, annexations, plots, and idle comforts. China's so-called society, moreover, consisted of nothing more than roaming robbers, adulation of riches, power, official titles, and belief in evil spirits, goblins, devils, demons, monsters, Taoist charlatans, and omens.[146] Living in this kind of "society," Fu argued, the Chinese people had in fact no real "lives" at all.[147]

---

144 *FSNC*, 1207.
145 Fu Ssu-nien, "Ch'ing-nien te liang-chien shih-yeh," *Ch'en-pao* (July 3, 1920).
146 *FSNC*, 1105.   147 *FSNC*, 1084–1085.

Fu's utmost concern for establishing a "society" led him to study the formation of Western "society." He believed that in Western feudal society the middle class existed with an organization. Once this organization was in place, he argued, there were then "lives" and a "sense of responsibility" – in other words, a real "society."[148] It was the May Fourth Movement, Fu hoped, that would heighten his compatriots' sense of responsibility and society.[149] Fu Ssu-nien argued that psychological transformation and "creating a society" should be the major task of his generation.

As for the definition of creating a society, Fu was influenced by Auguste Comte's social organism theory, which was introduced into China by Yen Fu and further expanded by Liang Ch'i-ch'ao's *New Citizen* (*Hsin-min shuo.*)[150] The theory of social organism held that elements of a society should cooperate with each other efficiently like healthy organs in which molecules were bound together as crystals to diamonds. A good society should be composed of healthy voluntary organizations. Fu argued that society in China more closely resembled a mob organization than a society in the Western sense. All organizations in China – whether official associations, industrial organizations, or guilds – were loose and weak. It was society in name but a mob in reality. As China's peasants had no self-governing ability, they resembled the mob. He even compared the student organizations of his time with this same mob.[151] For Fu, the mob was like a sack of potatoes, whereas society was an organism. Fu was convinced that the Chinese liked mob life and disliked society.[152]

Fu wanted people to distinguish clearly between the social order (*she-hui shang chih-hsü*) and order within society (*she-hui nei chih-hsü*). The former could be achieved by any autocratic political system, whereas the latter could only be established if society itself formed its rules and regulations. The former referred to the government's maintaining stability, whereas the latter referred to the internal social order. China lacked vitality because of its lack of a true society, and the individual could not develop his ability. It was, then, the task of the Chinese to establish order within society.[153]

Fu reflected on his own times and concluded that, because there was no "society" in China, there was consequently no means to supervise

---

148 *FSNC*, 1597.   149 Ibid.
150 Fu did not mention this linkage. See Yen Fu's, "I-yü chui-yü," in *Ch'ün-hsüeh i-yen* (Shanghai, n.d.), 2, and Liang Ch'i-ch'ao's *Hsin-min shuo* (Taipei, 1978), 61, 131, 152.
151 *FSNC*, 1578–1579.   152 *FSNC*, 1579.   153 *FSNC*, 1579–1580.

the government; the people simply accepted the bullying of those in power.[154] Before China could solve its political problems, therefore, it had first to create a society.[155]

Fu argued that society could be created by cultivating social responsibility and "adhesiveness between individuals." New unities had to be made out of disparate elements. Within these unities one could experiment with social ethics, and then these ethics could be used to unite the dispersed Chinese Republic.[156]

Fu argued in an unpublished draft that, after China had entered the modern world, its history could be divided into four periods. In the first period China was awakened to search for wealth and power; in the second it was awakened to undertake political reforms; the third period consisted of a cultural awakening; and the fourth period involved learning how to create a society. Fu believed that over the past few decades the special feature of the political history of Western countries was social reformation, a trend that would occur in China in the near future. Fu insisted that the first step in creating a society consisted of reforming oneself, at which point one could proceed to creating society from scratch. In this process China should not jump from one stage to another. He furthermore confessed in the May Fourth period that he himself naively believed such a leap was possible.[157]

Fu believed that only after the May Fourth Movement had the Chinese become aware of the methods of dealing with social problems. The May Fourth Movement was a new invention by Chinese youth to perform their social responsibility. During these gloomy months there was a very vivid social movement originating from people's social responsibilities scarcely seen under the autocratic regime.

For creating a society, Fu repeatedly talked about bringing "causes" (*chu-i*) to China. He believed that having any kind of cause was better than having none at all, for only by championing a cause would the Chinese develop into disciplined citizens. Without a true belief in any cause, he believed his compatriots would continue to conduct their business in accordance with the "flu" model: when the flu comes, there is

---

154 Fu Ssu-nien, "Ch'ing-nien te liang-chien shih-yeh," *Ch'en-pao* (July 3, 1920).
155 Ibid.
156 Fu Ssu-nien, "Ch'ing-nien te liang-chien shih-yeh," *Ch'en-pao* (July 5, 1920).
157 I found this draft, entitled "Shih-tai te shu-kuang yü wei-chi," mixed up with the administrative archives of the IHP without any serial number on it. However, I published part of it in Wang Fan-sen and Tu Cheng-sheng, eds., *Fu Ssu-nien wen-wu tzu-liao hsüan-chi* (Taipei, 1995), 34.

no way to avoid contracting it, and when it goes away, there is no way to keep it.[158] Without a true belief in a cause, new trends would easily achieve a certain measure of popularity but never really take root. Similarly, Fu described and criticized a syndrome he termed *su-ch'eng* (a training class for quick mastery of a subject within a short time to become qualified to serve as a government official). This approach to learning had, he maintained, wasted Chinese energy in numerous useless enterprises.

Fu emphasized that the Chinese should undertake certain kinds of "citizenship training" (*kuo-min hsün-lien*) under the rubric of certain "causes." He thought that if there were no transformation in the quality of citizens, no solid results would be apparent no matter how extensively new culture was introduced. He even equated the Chinese people with Chinese dogs in a provocative essay entitled "Chinese Dogs and Chinese People" (Chung-kuo-kou ho Chung-kuo-jen), in which he proclaimed that both Chinese dogs and people are poorly disciplined and easily diverted from real learning.[159] Fu asked variations of the same question repeatedly. Is there a "cause" in Chinese politics? Are Chinese revolutionaries pursuing a cause? Do Chinese parties have a cause? How many Chinese really have a cause? Among new organizations, how many of them have a cause?[160]

But Fu was pessimistic toward the business of creating a society. Fu lamented that after China had passed through its feudal age, it would still be incapable of developing a politics at once sophisticated and good (*hsiao-er-hao*). This was not contrary to the perspective of Chang Ping-lin, who viewed the feudal period as the only period during which China could have developed a representative system, an opportunity China missed. Although Fu encouraged his compatriots to overtake the Western world within several decades,[161] he nevertheless pessimistically announced that if there were no profound changes beneath the superficial politics, China's political future would be hopeless,[162] because social construction would require careful work and long-term endeavors in mental transformation and social organization.

After 1920, however, arguments for "creating a new society" do not appear in Fu's writings. For Fu, there was a dilemma. It is obvious that members of the *New Tide* were followers of both Hu Shih and Li Ta-chao. Under the influence of Li and the news of the triumph of the Russian Revolution, students naturally had roseate views of the revolution and concluded that wholesale social revolution was possible. The Russian

158 *FSNC*, 2438. 159 *FSNC*, 1595–1598.
160 *FSNC*, 1574. 161 *FSNC*, 1166. 162 *FSNC*, 1207.

Revolution should, then, displace the French Revolution, which (in their estimation) emphasized individualism and liberalism.[163]

Hu Shih's influence, however, was also strong. Hu represented the ideal of piecemeal reformation, which emphasized that societal progress should be a process of gradual improvement, with individual effort as most instrumental in the process. These two ideals or approaches coexisted in a youth like Fu Ssu-nien and became a major source of tension. He sensed that the problem of his time was so serious that it had to be solved in toto, which, of course, required wholesale change. However, he was also realistic and pessimistic. He abhorred any superficial change without substantial transformation, which smacked of the "flu" syndrome. He therefore believed in piecemeal change.

Thus, we see Fu constantly emphasizing on the one hand that China should create a society from scratch and on the other hand that society is created by individuals – that every person's innermost being is a small society, and so the first step in reforming society is reforming oneself.[164] We also see him insisting that in the process of creating society, China should not jump from one stage to another.

It is discernible that after Fu studied in Europe the latter approach gradually won out over the former. He wrote nothing about creating a society after his studies in Europe. He became a follower of Hu Shih, not Li Ta-chao or Ch'en Tu-hsiu. In July 1919, when Fu was still in China, the tension between Li Ta-chao's wholesale approach and Hu Shih's piecemeal approach finally came to a boiling point. The Debate of Problem and Cause (Wun-t'i yü chu-i lun-chan) erupted, but Fu did not participate.

When Fu Ssu-nien was in Europe, socialism was very much in vogue in China. Right before his return to China, the number of writings on these topics mushroomed. The intellectual atmosphere in China at the time has been described in the following terms: "There is now a change in the atmosphere. The social aspect of our life has come to the forefront and now dominates the whole outlook of students. It is not such social problems as family and sex relations, illiteracy, narcotics, and the reform of certain time-worn customs, matters in which students were once intensely interested, but the problem of the fundamental reconstruction of society."[165] But Fu Ssu-nien never went into this topic again.

---

163 Fu Ssu-nien, "She-hui-ko-ming: E-kuo (Russia)-shih te ko-ming," 128–129.
164 A draft entitled "O yu t'u-chung shui-kan-lu" was also mixed up with the administrative archives of the IHP without any serial number. I published part of it in Wang Fan-sen and Tu Cheng-sheng, *Fu Ssu-nien wen-wu tzu-liao hsüan-chi*, 35.
165 W. T. Wu, "Movements among Chinese Students," 259, quoted in Arif Dirlik, *Revolution and History: Origin of Marxist Historiography in China, 1919–1937* (Berkeley, 1978), 42.

The business of his later life he devoted to the piecemeal, incremental transformation of China.

"A Bundle of Contradictions"

Although Fu Ssu-nien vehemently denounced Chinese tradition, his inner world was never so clear-cut. On the one hand, new intellectuals argued that the only solution to the problem of old China was to imitate Western civilization as accurately as possible. Therefore, a plethora of Western knowledge was introduced. But the old selves still clung to traditional feelings. The biblical metaphor "new wine in old bottles" could be obverted: "old wine in new bottles." For sharp-minded literati, their whole selves were new bottles with old wine in them. This divided mind was of course reflected in Fu Ssu-nien. The divided mind was succinctly described by Wu Mi (1894–1978) as "a dead body torn by two horses."[166]

The business of enlightenment was a very complicated story. It happened not only in the public sphere but also in the individual's private mental world. There could be contradictions within one's own mind, contradictions between what one preached and how one acted, and contradictions between the private and public spheres, some of which can be discerned in Fu's activities during this period.

In the editor's opening statement in the *New Tide*, Fu wrote in the literary language, the style he and his friends had sworn to demolish. This choice surprised many of Fu's colleagues, but Fu announced that he had strategic considerations in mind. It is worth noting that in the eyes of its critics, the purpose of the New Culture Movement was nothing more than an excuse to avoid difficulties and take an easier way out. For example, the purpose of the ethical revolution was to avoid observing moral codes; and the literary revolution, which called for adopting the vernacular as the written language, was criticized as promoting the unlearned writing of rickshaw boys and peddlers. This anxiety is reflected even in Ts'ai Yüan-p'ei's reply to an attack by Lin Shu (1852–1924):

It is true that one has to read thousands of books in order to master either the literary or the vernacular language, but how can you say that professors such as Hu Shih, Ch'ien Hsüan-t'ung, and Chou Ch'i-ming [Chou Tso-jen] do not read thousands of books and are not able to write in good literary language? As a

---

166 Wu Hsüeh-chao, *Wu Mi yü Ch'en Yin-k'o* (Peking, 1992), 47.

matter of fact, all of these professors had written excellent classical literature before they started the new movement.[167]

Proving that Hu Shih could also write excellent classical literature silenced some critics, but another daunting task was proving that people like Hu Shih advocated the new culture in order to improve the wellbeing of society and not to mask their own lack of familiarity with the Chinese tradition. This kind of tension was always on the minds of the movement's promoters. Sometimes they would show that they were well versed in the old culture to prove that launching the enlightenment movement was not a cover for their incompetence. In *New Youth*, Ch'en Tu-hsiu told Ch'ien Hsüan-t'ung: "You are a master of phonetics and philology and yet promote the vernacular literature. Why worry that the whole country will not immediately follow [your innovations]?"[168] The logic Ch'en Tu-hsiu employed was that people would tend to think that if a specialist in classical philology like Ch'ien Hsüan-t'ung advocated vernacular language, there must be some reason for it. This logic also explained why Fu Ssu-nien decided to write the editor's opening statement of the *New Tide* in the classical style.

The inner struggles between the old self and the new, between how one was brought up and how one hoped things would turn out, between the familiar and the ideal were always evident.

The first contradiction was that people did not practice what they preached. In the earlier generation, Lu Hsün, who had had considerable influence on Fu Ssu-nien, advised people not to read books bound in the traditional Chinese style, yet he himself read such books frequently, if not every day. Wu Chih-hui, who was very close to Fu, claimed to throw all old books into the toilet, yet he wrote in the seal style and wore the long robe of the Chinese literatus. They led contradictory lives. The same was also true of the 1890s generation. Lo Chia-lun had called for women's liberation and free marriage and yet allowed Ts'ai Yüan-p'ei to arrange a marriage for him without even meeting his bride.[169] In his essay "I Will Not Keep It" (wo pu-yao le), Mao Tse-tung wrote, "I will not read *Selections of Refined Literature* [*Chao-ming-wen-hsüan*] any more." He also denounced certain other works as well.[170] But throughout his

167 Ts'ai Yüan-p'ei, "Wei shuo-ming pan-hsüeh fang-chen ta Lin Ch'in-nan chün han," in Sun Te-chung, ed., *Ts'ai Yüan-p'ei hsien-sheng i-wen lei-ch'ao* (Taipei, 1961), 35. I adopt Chow Tse-tsung's translation; see *The May Fourth Movement*, 71.
168 Ch'en Tu-hsiu, "Ta Ch'ien Hsüan-t'ung," in *Ch'en Tu-hsiu chu-tso hsüan*, 3:376.
169 Shu Wu, "Ts'ai Yüan-p'ei te liang-tz'u shuo-mei," *Chung-kuo shih-pao* (February 5, 1992).
170 Li Jui, "Hsiang-chiang p'ing-lun yü Wen-hua shu-she," in Chang Ching-lu, ed., *Chung-kuo hsien-tai ch'u-pan shih-liao* (Peking, 1954–1959), 5 vols., 1:33–34.

life, the *Chao-ming-wen-hsüan* was Mao's favorite literary text.[171] Mao Tzu-shui (1893–1988), a classmate of Fu at Peita and later professor of Chinese classics, also had such a split mentality. He told his students that he taught the *Analects* for several decades only in order to totally discredit it.[172] A similar feeling was also manifested by Shen Yen-ping (1896–1981), Fu's classmate, whose alias "Mao Tun" meant "contradiction." The same sense of inner conflict is manifested in Fu's epithet, "a bundle of contradictions" (I-t'uan mao-tun).[173] Such mentalities were the results of conflicts between what they were, what they were most familiar with, and what they felt in their innermost selves on the one hand, and what they felt the future of themselves and the country should be on the other. They worried that their traditional value system was detrimental to the strength of their nation and felt that the old self with which they were the most familiar should be completely eliminated. But the leap from custom to ideal was more difficult than most of these men imagined.

Fu Ssu-nien suffered from the same trouble. In his innermost self Fu cherished traditional family relationships,[174] but he honestly believed that the traditional family system was detrimental to society's future. He had thus obligated himself to suppress his most natural inclinations for the sake of the common good of his nation. He even hung a scroll in his study that read he should "make home nowhere." His split mentality was especially true in his being torn between things Western and things Chinese. In "Nature" (Tzu-jan), a poem Fu wrote while waiting for a ship to Europe, his ambivalence toward enlightenment was strongly expressed. In that poem, things Western were expressed in a sentimental way as being of "bad will," "powerful" yet "ugly," and Chinese tradition was of "good will" but "weak" and "useless." The ambivalence was between what Erik Erikson terms "aim-conscious self denial" and "authentic being."[175] For the future of the self and the nation, intellectuals of Fu's generation were determined to give up what they were most familiar with in order to pursue Western learning.

But given the difficulties of becoming successfully westernized, many readily found that they, as educators to their compatriots, needed to be

---

171 Chao K'o, "Mao Tse-tung tu-shu i-wen," *Li pao*, 14 (1981), 71, 73. Cf. also Kung Yü-chih, P'ang Hsien-chih, and Shih Chung-ch'üan, *Mao Tse-tung te tu-shu sheng-huo* (Peking, 1986), 218.
172 This was reported by Hsü Fu-kuan in his "K'ao-chü yü i-li chih cheng chih ch'a-ch'ü," *Hsüeh-shu yü cheng-chih chih chien* (Taichung, 1963), 2:263.
173 *FSNC*, 2365.   174 See, for example, *FSNC*, 2550–2552, a poem written in 1919.
175 Erik Erikson, *Young Man Luther* (New York, 1962), 52–53.

educated themselves. They also found it extraordinarily difficult to eliminate the old self. Their mental state can perhaps be epitomized by Wang Kuo-wei's lament: "I opened my eyes to glance at the world of red dust, only to find that I too am in the midst of [the red dust] I see."[176] As agents of enlightenment committed to changing their compatriots, they found that they themselves were among the "compatriots." Fu Ssu-nien seems to have sensed this with some measure of distress: "Carrying two or three thousand years of history about on our backs, we can only be viewed as people who know the value of the new thinking yet are unable to replace the old thinking with new."[177] Fu acutely felt the struggle between the old and new selves in October 1919. After ten tumultuous months of editing the *New Tide* and participating in the May Fourth Movement, Fu Ssu-nien, who had proclaimed repeatedly that China should be thoroughly westernized, found himself wavering in ambivalence while he was in Shanghai. This sudden moment had afforded Fu an opportunity to reflect on the drastic changes in his mental world that had occurred over the past few years. On this occasion he found his old self reemerging to remind him of what he had experienced before being converted to the New Culture Movement. The remnants of his first eight thousand days could not be obliterated by the experiences of the last six hundred days. Later, Fu admitted that the "subconsciousness" is more powerful than the "consciousness" and that "feeling" is more powerful than "reason." Fu began analyzing himself and putting down the elements of his innermost struggles.

He wrote of his feeling not in prose but in "modern poetry" (*hsin-shih*). "Modern poetry" and "jottings of feeling" (*sui-kan-lu*) were two of the several new literary genres that enabled Chinese writers to express their feelings more freely.[178] Thanks to these new genres, Fu expressed some of his deepest personal feelings in several poems.[179] The poem Fu wrote in a small hotel in Shanghai was the last piece of modern poetry he ever wrote. A letter to Yü P'ing-po and Ku Chieh-kang was attached to the poem as a "preface." In the poem, Fu discusses the conflict between what he had been, what he was, and what he hoped to become. He wrote:

176 Wang Kuo-wei, "Wan-hsi-sha," in *Wang Kuan-t'ang hsien-sheng ch'üan-chi* (Taipei, 1968), 16 vols., 4:1517.
177 *FSNC*, 1598.
178 Several new genres enabled writers to freely express their feelings. For example, Hu Shih sensed that the "short critique" (*tuan-p'ing*) was a powerful new genre. See *Hu Shih te jih-chi* (Taipei, 1989), 18 vols., September 4, 1921, n.p.
179 After the May Fourth period, Fu never wrote any more new-style poems. Only several old-style poems were published, to commemorate a hero who died resisting the Japanese during the Sino-Japanese War. See *FSNC*, 2573–2574.

When you see this clumsy, inelegant poem, [you] may be surprised at [its] differing from my usual arguments. Therefore I have to explain [this] clearly.

In my breast I have always harbored many questions and few answers. This is as you know. In the past two or three years many more questions have been accumulated and stirred up. In the past four or five months, the questions have increased even more, and at the same time [I have] overturned all of [my] earlier undigested answers altogether. All of this has made me hungry for learning – deadly hungry. I resent that I cannot fly out of China this very second. Right now I am like a little child who is just learning to talk. . . . Also, originally I had many instinctive feelings which [I] had no time to think over. And these have been time and again suppressed by my theories. Now I also set them free, let them enjoy the same right as my theories do, and place them on [my] list of questions.

Now I am naturally in a situation of danger and confusion, like a straw afloat on the ocean, like an animal in a maze of thousands of layers.

The poem read:

In this present world, I peep at this world with my eyes open.
While peeping without analyzing anything, [I] only see lines of interest (*ch'ü-wei*) intertwined together.
"Interest!" "Interest!" Are you really the most intimate to me?
Why can't you explain yourself?
Aren't you truly the most intimate to me?
Why do you have the power to make me betray my knowledge to be on good terms with you?
A color sad and wretched – weeping tears all day long.
[You] really have the carriage of Athena.
From my distant ancestors stretching back for thousands of years straight down to me, you have stolen innumerable souls.
Clearly, clearly knowing that intimacy with you will [lead to] tragedy,
Yet artists of many ages have spat out their heart blood for you,
[And] billions of "ones with interest" have suffered billions of catastrophes.
The result is still a great failure.[180]

In this freely written poem, Fu showed his ambivalence toward "theory" and "instinct" and toward "life" and "nature." The "theory" and "life" represented the goals for which he and his country should strive, while "instinct" and "nature" represented what he and his compatriots held the dearest.[181] This sort of tension never appeared in his essays written during the *New Tide* period. During that time, as an enlightened edu-

---

180 *FSNC*, 2569–2572.
181 In this poem "life" was the goal the Chinese should pursue and was synonymous with things Western. Fu believed that the Chinese never knew what "life" really was. Moreover, the Chinese could only feel at ease with what they were; therefore, "nature" was what they should struggle to cast off. Cf. *FSNC*, 1084, 1136, 1180.

Early Years

cator he had proclaimed that what he advocated was unassailable.[182] But in this poem he expressed the feeling that what he loved he found untenable, and what he found tenable he did not love.

A similar struggle surfaced again several months after Fu's arrival in London. His concern was once again almost the same as before: how to reconcile the old self with the new. He confessed that,

> Last month I came to the realization that the reason why I have not been studying as diligently as when I was in the Preparatory School of Peita, the period devoted to the study of the National Past [*kuo-ku shih-tai*], is simply because that was a period during which I studied what I felt fond of.... But when I finally left the confines of *kuo-ku*, my old confidence was totally shattered. What I have recently studied is far more relevant to real needs than what I studied before.... But I still find it difficult to form a close friendship with this "learning" [*hsüeh-wen*].[183]

This inner tension continued to trouble Fu for some time. In 1929 Fu told Hu Shih: "Our thinking is new. Our beliefs are new. In thought we are entirely westernized. However, in [the way] we settle down our lives and enjoy what we do, we are still traditional Chinese." Hu Shih noted in his diary that on this point he wholeheartedly agreed with Fu.[184]

In sum, Fu Ssu-nien had strong ideas about what China had been and what it should *not* become, but had only very vague ideas of what it *should* become. He felt that he did not have a full understanding of what Western society, literature, and learning really were like. He therefore had high hopes for pursuing "real learning" (*chen-hsüeh-wen*) abroad and solving "the big problems" (*ta-wen-t'i*) – the psychological and sociological origins (*ken-yüan*) of the nation's troubles.[185] Because Fu was disappointed with Neo-Confucianism, Taoism, and Buddhism, he never resorted to traditional moral philosophy for an understanding of the Chinese mental world. Under the influence of Chang Shih-chao, Fu turned instead to psychology. The study of psychology was not unique to Fu Ssu-nien but was a major interest of the New Tide Society.[186] In 1919 and 1920, when members of the New Tide Society were going abroad for new learning, many of them, including Fu Ssu-nien, Yang Chen-sheng (1890–1956), and Wang Ching-hsi, devoted themselves to the study of psychology. They were motivated by the task of "revolu-

---

182 *FSNC*, 1189.
183 Fu Ssu-nien, "Liu Ying chi-hsing," *Ch'en-pao* (August 7, 1920).
184 *Hu Shih te jih-chi*, April 27, 1929, n.p.
185 Fu Ssu-nien, "Liu Ying chi-hsing," *Ch'en-pao* (August 7, 1920).
186 Schwarcz, *The Chinese Enlightenment: Intellectuals and Legacy of the May Fourth Movement of 1919*, 104. See also Lin Chi-ch'eng, "Fu-lo-i-te (Freud) hsüeh-shuo tsai Chung-kuo te ch'uan-po, 1914–1925," *Erh-shih-i shih-chi*, no. 4 (1991), 20–31.

tionizing the mind (*ko-hsin*)."[187] People like Wu K'ang (1895–1976) were committed to constructing a scientific explanation of the Chinese spiritual world. Wu went so far as to write an essay calling for the establishment of "a mathematical formula to explain why filial piety was an outworn, irrational variable in the equation of life and morality."[188] Fu was also optimistic that psychology could yield the solution to this "big problem." It was with these hopes in mind that he went to England to study psychology.

187 Schwarcz, *The Chinese Enlightenment: Intellectuals and Legacy of the May Fourth Movement of 1919*, 118.
188 Ibid., 116.

2
The Shaping of a New Historical School

No matter how ambivalent Fu himself felt, at a time when young people believed that the *tao* had already shifted from Confucian texts to Western books (*hsi-shu*), he was very much envied by his contemporaries. In a letter from Ku Chieh-kang to Fu Ssu-nien, Ku confessed his frustration at his inability to grasp just "what is learning" (*she-mo shih hsüeh-wen*); his inability to read foreign books was equivalent to being unable to gain access to the new *tao*. Ku contemptuously announced that there was not a single chapter in Chinese books worth reading.[1] It was also true for Fu Ssu-nien that nothing other than Western learning could be called true learning (*hsüeh-wen*), and he described himself as extremely hungry for "learning."[2] Given this scenario, when Fu and five other members of the New Tide Society went abroad to study, they were nicknamed "Five Ministers Sent Abroad" (*Wu-ta-ch'en ch'u-yang*), reminiscent of the five ministers of the late Ch'ing who went abroad to study the Western constitutional system.[3]

Studying in London and Berlin

Fu characterized his time in London as *yu-hsüeh*, or general study, not study in pursuit of a degree. But when he left China in the winter of

---

1 *FSNC*, 2417.   2 *FSNC*, 2568.
3 The nickname was also given for another reason. In late 1919 a successful industrialist named Mu Ou-ch'u (1876–1943) offered a certain amount of money to send five student leaders of the May Fourth Movement (most of whom were members of the New Tide Society) to study abroad. These students received higher stipends from Mu than those who were subsidized by the Republican government. See Feng Yu-lan, *San-sung-t'ang tzu-hsü*, in *San-sung-táng ch'üan-chi*, vol. 1 (Honan, 1985), 53. It has been argued that after the leading members of the New Tide Society went abroad to study, the leadership vacuum they left behind caused the rise of the leftist students in the Peita community. See Fu Le-ch'eng, "Fu Meng-chen hsien-sheng yü Wu-ssu yün-tung," in *Shih-tai te chui-i lun-wen-chi*, 137.

1919, his plan was probably to get a degree from a Western country if possible. Fu first registered in the Department of Psychology at the University College of London University. He originally planned to register as an M.A. student, but on the advice of Charles E. Spearman, the department chair and a pioneer in experimental psychology, Fu decided to take courses at the undergraduate level. He also spent a considerable amount of time taking courses from the medical school. And he was remorseful that he spent too many years studying Chinese learning. While he was at London, his study was unfortunately disrupted by the sudden disappearance of Yü P'ing-po, a close friend of his who had accompanied him all the way to England. Because of hardships experienced in London, Yü stealthily fled away. Fu took a trip to France to try to fetch Yü back but was ultimately unsuccessful in doing so. In this way Fu wasted part of a semester, and he had to resume his learning at the start of the new school year, in October 1920. This marked the beginning of a series of academic setbacks and failures.[4]

Because Fu had embraced a great plan to study "Western learning" as a whole when he arrived at London, he decided to start his study with the basic sciences to find a "real" solution to "fundamental [ken-yüan] problems."[5] We have almost no materials for this period except a notebook with several jottings in it.

Fu lived on Sisters Lane in South London. On the wall of his room hung portraits of three scholars and writers he admired the most: Bernard Shaw, Charles Darwin, and John Stuart Mill.[6] During Fu's three undergraduate years at Peita, he had taken almost no courses in natural science, making it somewhat difficult for him to pick up subjects such as chemistry, and mathematics at London University. During his years at the university, his major goals must have been, on the one hand, to discard the ambiguity, overgeneralizations, and metaphysical ways of thinking that characterized Chinese thought and, on the other hand, to explore the depths of the human mind with some experimental, observable, and numerical measurements. His attraction to experimental psychology was mainly owing to this kind of impetus.

Applying experimental psychology, Fu hoped to probe collective psychology, a topic related to his concern for the Chinese character. This explains why he produced an incomplete translation project while he studied in Europe. Fu translated William Mcdougall's *The Group Mind*.

---

4 See *Hu Shih lai-wang shu-hsin hsüan*, 1:103–108.
5 Fu Ssu-nien, "Liu Ying chi-hsing," *Ch'en pao* (August 7, 1920).
6 FSNP, II-3, Fu's family album.

The subtitle of this book, which Mcdougall labeled "A Sketch of the Principles of Collective Psychology with Some Attempt to Apply Them to the Interpretation of National Life and Character," well represents Fu's concern.[7] He also paid particular attention to psychoanalysis, with which he hoped to probe into traditionally forbidden areas with an eye to liberating the Chinese from the shackles of their tradition and to redirect the Chinese attitude toward these hidden pockets of potential.[8]

Fu spent three years at London University with the intention of obtaining an M.A. degree in psychology,[9] but he was unable to do so.[10] Nevertheless, these three years were an important period in Fu's intellectual development.

According to the record of Mao I-heng (1895–1968), one of Fu's classmates at Peita and then in France, after becoming disillusioned with experimental psychology and especially collective psychology, Fu abandoned his dream of becoming a scholar of psychology.[11] Fu's chief objection to the discipline was the notion that human behavior can be extrapolated from studies on animal behavior.[12]

In London Fu became acquainted with the novelist and social critic H. G. Wells and helped him with Chinese medieval history for his book

7 *The Group Mind* was published by Cambridge University Press in 1920. Fu's translation manuscript was mixed in with the administrative documents of the IHP and has thus never been found. The manuscript did not indicate its original title. However, I finally found its original source and located the book in Fu's own book collection.
8 Mao I-heng, "Kuan-yü Fu Ssu-nien te i-feng-hsin," *T'ien-wen-t'ai* (January 4, 1951). A considerable number of books about sexual psychology were in Fu's collection. See FSNP, no serial number, a book collection list.
9 Fu never mentioned what kind of degree he held. In 1946 Fu received an honorary Ph.D. degree from Oslo University of Norway. See FSNP, III-1322, a letter from the Ministry of Foreign Affairs.
10 In the M.A. degree record of the Senate House of London University, I did not find Fu's name. At London University I found three records concerning Fu. The first (no. 2755 98) recommended "that Szenien Fu be registered as an Internal Student as from Oct. 1920 and admitted as a candidate for the degree of MA in Psychology upon his complying with the Regulations under statute 113 resolved." The source listed was "University of London, minutes of the Senate for the sessions Oct. 1921 to Sept. 1922, U. C. (University College) archives 387 7050 college archivist:" The second (no. 4334 92) read " Considered: – an application (28 April 1922) from S. Fu, who is registered under statute 113 as a candidate for the MA degree in Psychology, for exemption from part of the BA Honours qualifying examination." The higher-degree subcommittee recommended that Mr. Fu be excused from writing the paper in philosophy but not the two papers in general psychology). The third document (no. 4335 93) recommended "that Szenien Fu be excused the paper in the History of Modern Philosophy (Descartes to Kant) at the BA Honours examination in psychology as a qualifying examination for candidature at the MA examination / resolved under headline: LXIII: exemption from part of Honours qualifying examination for MA degree in psychology."
11 Mao I-heng, "Kuan-yü Fu Ssu-nien te i-feng-hsin," *T'ien-wen-t'ai* (January 4, 1951).
12 Ibid.

The Outline of History.[13] Fu also actively attended various cultural activities, including public speeches (e.g., Bertrand Russell's speeches) and operas, and was particularly fond of Bernard Shaw. Fu's interest in opera might have been a continuation of his student days at Peita, where he was an active promoter in the new theater movement.[14] Western opera had been his model for reforming Chinese opera back in his Peita years. He also seems to have read quite a few novels; on New Years Day of 1923 he promised himself in his pocket notebook that he would not "indulge in opera" and not "be poisoned any more by Hardy."[15] Unfortunately, owing to the extreme paucity of data, it is impossible to reconstruct fully Fu's social intercourse in London.[16]

Fu's studies in London proved difficult. One may surmise that the horizontal Western alphabetical or "crab-walk language" (*hsieh-hsing-wen*), which troubled Hu Shih more than ten years earlier, might also have bothered Fu.[17] This difficulty perhaps led Fu to realize that becoming westernized, as he advocated during the *New Tide* period, was not as easy as he had thought.

In June 1923 Fu left London for Berlin.[18] The high inflation in 1923 and 1924 in Germany[19] helped the Chinese students staying in Germany because Chinese currency was exchanged at a favorable rate. This probably explained why there were about a thousand Chinese students living in Berlin at the time. Better economic conditions in Germany probably constitute one of the major reasons for Fu to give up his study in England and leave for Germany. At that time Berlin was the capital of Germany, home to about three million inhabitants and a very rich cultural center. The social-democratic movement was rather strong there. Some of Fu's old friends, such as Mao Tzu-shui, Yao Shih-ao (Ts'ung-wu) (1894–1970), and Ho Ssu-yüan (1896–1982), were all in Berlin when Fu arrived.

Fu registered in Berlin University as a student in the School of Humanities, again as an undergraduate. According to regulations, he

---

13 See H. G. Wells, *The Outline of History* (New York, 1971), 6, 487–489. This book was first published in 1920 and sold one and a half million copies within twelve years.
14 FSNP, III-431, a draft of a self-sketch. In Peita, Fu was active in promoting the New Theater Movement. See *FSNC*, 1075–1111.
15 FSNP, V-28, a pocketbook of 1923. These sentences were written in English.
16 There were almost no English names or addresses listed in Fu's pocketbook. See FSNP, V-28.
17 Hu Shih, *Hu Shih chia-shu shou-chi* (Anhwei, 1989), 36. Hu confessed that he was seriously troubled by the difficulty of learning English.
18 While arranging Fu's papers, I discovered that when Fu moved to Berlin, he threw most of his belongings away. This has made the reconstruction of his life in London very difficult.
19 Cf. Jerome Grieder, *Intellectuals and the State in Modern China* (New York, 1981), 211.

would have needed about four years with a senior thesis to fulfill graduation requirements, but it seems that Fu never intended to obtain a B.A. degree. He advised his friends that instead of devoting most of their time to dissertations, they should utilize this rare chance to pursue as much learning as possible.[20] He enjoyed auditing several courses in physics, especially those on Einstein's relativity theory, and in comparative philology, two areas that were dominant trends at Berlin University at that time.[21] Fu also spent time in mathematics and several other branches of learning. Among these, statistics and, more specifically, probability were major interests.[22] One of his notebooks dating to 1925 shows that he believed probability theory could help him acquire the solution to some social problems.[23]

During this time it was fashionable for Chinese students in Berlin to neglect the divisions of what they perceived to be "Western learning." Fu Ssu-nien, Yü Ta-wei, Ch'en Yin-k'o (1890–1969), and Mao Tzu-shui tended to study a very wide array of disciplines.[24] Certain characteristics of what they chose to learn are, however, discernible. They tended to study subjects that gave scientific explanations for diverse phenomena. Fu's ideal was to extend scientific explanations to social phenomena. Four recognizable influences to which Fu exposed himself in Europe are the employment of statistics in humanistic study, positivism, the positivized Rankean school, and comparative linguistics.

In Europe Fu was first attracted by the applicability of statistics to humanistic studies. Following on the rapid progress in natural science of the late nineteenth century, historical works such as Walter Bagehot's *Physics and Politics* and *Thoughts on the Application of the Principles of Natural Selection and Inheritance to Political Society* were very much in vogue.[25] Although Fu Ssu-nien did not read Bagehot's book, he was impressed by this trend. In his notebook for the 1925–1926 winter semester in Berlin, we find such titles as Karl Pearson's *Contribution to the Mathematical Theory of Evolution*.[26] The ideas of Karl Pearson (1857–1936), a scholar whose work helped lay the foundation for modern statistical

---

20 Mao I-heng, "Kuan-yü Fu Ssu-nien te i-feng-hsin," *T'ien-wen-t'ai* (January 4, 1951).
21 It was once reported that Fu was a student of Albert Einstein ("Fu Ssu-nien hsien-sheng erh-san shih," *Fu ku hsiao-chang ai-wan-lu* [Taipei, 1951], 7), but David Yule (Yü Ta-wei), in an interview on November 10, 1990, in Taipei dismissed this story. Fu did, however, audit some of Einstein's seminars.
22 FSNP, V-49, a notebook of 1925–1926 on college-level probability.
23 *FSNC*, 2365–2366.
24 *Fu ku hsiao-chang ai-wan-lu*, 7.
25 James Thompson and Bernard Hohn, *A History of Historical Writing* (New York, 1942), 2 vols., 1:439–460, especially 457–458.
26 FSNP, IV-49, a notebook of mathematics from the 1925–1926 winter semester.

theory, attracted Fu for some time. He once planned to translate T. Buckle's *History of Civilization in England* into Chinese and argued that the statistical methods demonstrated in that book would be very fruitful for understanding Chinese history.[27]

When Fu left China, he wrote in an unpublished essay that he hoped to go to Europe to purge all tangles from his mind and train himself in "reliable" thinking.[28] Fu had already suggested how he would obtain this "reliable" thinking in the *New Tide*. In March 1919 he noted that positivism is the best, most advanced product of the Western intellectual world and should be introduced to China to correct the farfetched, confused, and imprecise mental attitudes of many Chinese.[29] Positivism is outdated and discredited today, however. It was the belief of Ting Wen-chiang, Wang Hsing-kung (1889–1951), and a group of Chinese scholars that positivism could remedy the mystic Chinese mental attitudes.[30] Thus, in Europe Fu was naturally attracted by a group of European positivists. The characteristics of this school were not only akin to Fu's early training – that is, Ch'ing evidential research – but also fulfilled his hope to pursue an objective, scientific understanding of the world.

Fu acknowledged that the positivists who exerted the most influence on him were scholars like Ernest Mach (1838–1916) and Karl Pearson. When Fu was first attracted by their works, he was by no means preparing himself to become a historian. But he believed that the methodology of natural science could benefit any branch of learning.[31]

The major characteristic of the late-nineteenth- and early-twentieth-century positivists was the assignment of relatively narrow limits to the

---

27 See FSNP, 610, a letter from Fu to Ting Wen-chiang. In addition to works by Pearson and Buckle, several other scholars' works with which Fu was very familiar were those on statistics or probability. C. Spearman (1863–1945), whose fame attracted Fu to London University to study experimental psychology, was considered to have made one significant contribution to the development of psychology – namely, the establishment of the statistical method for psychology in the early decades of the twentieth century. (Cf. Paul Edwards, ed., *The Encyclopedia of Philosophy* [New York, 1967], 8 vols., 7:23.) *A Treatise on Probability*, by the economist John Maynard Keynes (1883–1946), one of Fu's favorite authors, was published in London right after Fu's arrival there (*The Encyclopedia of Philosophy*, 4:333–334). The most impressive part of Buckle's work, at least to East Asian scholars, was its scientific spirit. This spirit is well summarized by the following statement: "the actions of men are subject to regularities as strict and mathematically exact as those that operate in other spheres of scientific inquiry.... As a conclusive demonstration of his thesis, Buckle cited the evidence afforded by large-scale statistical surveys concerning the numbers of marriages contracted, and of murders and suicides committed" (*The Encyclopedia of Philosophy*, 1:414).
28 Wang Fan-sen and Tu Cheng-sheng, *Fu Ssu-nien wen-wu tzu-liao hsüan-chi*, 35.
29 *FSNC*, 1447.
30 Ch'en Yüan-hui, "Chung-kuo te Ma-ho (E. Mach) chu-i che," in *Ch'en Yüan-hui wen-chi* (Foochow, 1993), 3 vols., 2:79–96.
31 *FSNC*, 2365–2366.

human mind. Laszek Kolakowski summed up the characteristics of this intellectual trend as the philosophical destruction of the subject; the biological and practical conception of cognitive functions, reduction of intellectual behavior to purely organic needs, and renunciation of "truth" in the transcendental sense; and a desire to get back to the most concrete datum, to a "natural" view of the world not mediated by metaphysical functions. Mach, the one from whom Fu benefited the most, believed that the basis and origin of all scientific knowledge is sense experience. He was thus hostile toward "any a priori condition of synthetic";[32] "so-called principles, laws, theories" he argued, "all are subject to the control of experience."[33] "Science is not a collection of individual facts, gathered and added to in view of making generalizations."[34] When Fu later launched a new historical school in China, he was opposed to any philosophy of history, "systematic philosophy" (*hsi-t'ung-che-hsüeh*), or generalizations.[35]

The affinity between Mach's magnum opus, *Analysis of the Sensations* (1886), and Fu's historical methodology is readily discernible. Fu's most renowned maxims, "presenting evidence but never elaborating" and "points A and B should never be bridged without sufficient evidence,"[36] were probably borrowed from Mach. On the opening page of the *Analysis of the Sensation*, Mach elaborated on the chief point of his work, "the principle of sufficient determinateness," by saying that:

When once the inquiring intellect has gained, through adaption, the habit of connecting two things, A and B, in thought, it always thereafter seeks to retain this habit, even where the circumstances are slightly altered. Wherever A makes its appearance, B is added in thought. The principle here formulated, which has its root in an effort for economy, and is particularly noticeable in the work of great investigators, may be termed the principle of continuity.[37]

He argued further:

We have become accustomed to seeing light deflected in passing from air to glass, and *vice versa*. But the deflexion differs noticeably in different cases, and

---

32 Laszek Kolakowski, *The Alienation of Reason: A History of Positivist Thought*, trans. Norbert Guterman (New York, 1968), 119.
33 Ibid., 121.   34 Ibid., 123.   35 *FSNC*, 1310–1311, 1303.
36 *FSNC*, 1310. It is widely believed that Fu's historical view was from Ranke. See, for example, Chang Chih-yüan, "Lan-k'o (Ranke) te sheng-p'ing yü chu-tso," *Tzu-yu Chung-kuo*, 7:12 (1952), 382–387, an article dedicated by Chang to commemorate Fu Ssu-nien. Chang noted at the beginning of this article that he wrote it because Fu was the Chinese Ranke. See also Li Wen-p'ing, "Fu Ssu-nien te shih-hsüeh kuan-tien yü chih-shih fang fa," in *Fu Ssu-nien*, 121.
37 Ernst Mach, *Analysis of the Sensations*, trans. C. M. Williams (Chicago, 1897), 27.

the habit gained in some cases cannot be carried over undisturbed to new cases.[38]

The methodology championed by Mach may have been compatible with Fu's interest in Ch'ing evidential research. The rigorous, solid, meticulous style of Ch'ing scholarship, as Chang Ping-lin observed, emphasized evidence and forbade flowery prose and farfetched deduction.[39] In sum, Fu was susceptible to an intellectual trend that championed objectivity by doing away with subjectivity. The "subject" or "self" was viewed as "something added to the content of experience either illegitimately or purely for convenience."[40] As he became increasingly committed to positivism, the broad intellectual adventurousness of his early years gave way to a more rigid, conservative agenda.

In Berlin, Fu never registered in any historical course. He attended a very wide variety of courses, including logic, medical psychology, anthropology, Sanskrit, and phonetics.[41] From late 1924 on, Fu's interest shifted to the German historiographical tradition, especially the Rankean school. But when Fu was in Berlin, topics such as historical relativism were in hot dispute and the Rankean school was no longer dominant in Germany. That Fu chose Ranke and not another historian as his primary model mirrored his inclination to pursue a historiography of objective and scientific rigor. This new interest, it turned out, could also easily be bridged with Ch'ing evidential scholarship.

Although Fu Ssu-nien and the IHP have long been viewed as the embodiment of China's Rankean school, none of Ranke's works have been found in any of Fu's collections.[42] The low ebb of the Rankean school while Fu was in Berlin might account for this. Nevertheless, since Rankean historical ideas had already been disseminated into professional historical study in Germany and had become a shared element among most German historians, Fu likely came into contact with Ranke's work. As with many American Rankean historians who never widely read Ranke's works,[43] Fu might also have picked up Rankean ideas without

38 Ibid., 27–28.
39 Chang Ping-lin, "Shuo-lin," in *T'ai-yen wen-lu ch'u-pien, chüan* 1. Quoted in Wang Fan-sen, *Chang T'ai-yen te ssu-hsiang*, 25.
40 Kolakowski, *The Alienation of Reason*, 104.
41 Cf. Wang Fan-sen and Tu Cheng-sheng, eds., *Fu Ssu-nien wen-wu tzu-liao hsüan-chi*, 53.
42 It is surprising that there are none of Ranke's works in Fu Ssu-nien's collections. During his life Fu did mention Ranke's name once (*FSNC*, 1404). When Fu stayed in America in 1947–1948, he proposed to purchase a collection of Ranke's works, but never did. Cf. FSNP, I-817, a piece of paper with information about an edition of Ranke's work. But the absence of books from an author's library is not necessarily significant, since they may have been, for example, loaned and not returned.
43 Peter Novick, *That Noble Dream* (Cambridge, 1988), 29.

The Shaping of a New Historical School

delving deeply into any particular book. The major discrepancies between Ranke's and Fu's ideas are also very evident.[44] However, Fu Ssu-nien did read Ernst Bernhheim's works, which were the gist of the hybrid of positivism and Rankean ideas. This reading can explain some of the origin of Fu's historical ideas.[45] As far as we can recognize, Fu's persistent interest in gathering primary sources, opening up and publishing archives, and earnestly pursuing historical objectivity probably stemmed from the influence of Ranke. The establishment of the IHP and the publication of the institute's journal, *Bulletin of the Institute of History and Philology (Chung-yang yen-chiu yüan Li-shih yü-yen yen-chiu-so chi-k'an*, hereafter *Bulletin*), were modeled on Rankean ideas and the school's major journal, *Historische Zeitschrift* (1859).[46]

Under the influence of Ch'en Yin-k'o, the elder brother of one of Fu's classmates back at Peita, Fu was gradually attracted to a group of Orientalists at Berlin University. There he and Ch'en Yin-k'o attended

---

44 Several differences between these two scholars can be discerned. First of all, Fu attempted to build a historiography as scientific as biology or geology, an intention never voiced in Rankean theory. Later, many Western historians planned to develop scientific history, but not Ranke. What characterized Ranke's historiography most was his use of archives in historical study, especially diplomatic history. However, Fu never studied diplomatic history. Although Ranke emphasized primary sources, he never held such a radical view as to argue that "the study of data is historiography" (*shih-hsüeh chi shih-liao-hsüeh*). Ranke did say that history should be written "the way it really happened" (*wie es eigentlich gewesen*), but this meant that the historian should be true to the facts; interpretation was not forbidden in the sense proposed by Fu Ssu-nien. Nor did Ranke rule out all metaphysical thinking. He esteemed Christianity to the extent that he claimed religion as the major motivation for the historian. Fu, on the other hand, despised metaphysics. Ranke was originally trained as a philologist and later widely employed a philological approach in his research, but he never coined the phrase "history and philology." The combination of history and philology was an important feature of the Rankean school and German historiography, but the slogan was Fu Ssu-nien's. Cf. Theodore H. von Laue, *Leopold Ranke: The Formative Years* (Princeton, 1950), especially 42–54, 137.

45 I examined a copy of Ernst Bernheim's *Lehrbuch der historischen Methode und Geschichts-philosophie*, which was included in Fu's collection, and found that it had apparently been thoroughly read; the binding was broken, and Fu noted that it was rebound in 1937. But if we are too obsessed with the question of what Western historical school the IHP fell in with, we will be guilty of "elementalism," and this will not lead to a better understanding of the school.

46 The *Historische Zeitschrift* was entirely the work of Ranke's pupils, though Ranke himself kept aloof from it. In its first issue, Ranke called for establishing a national organization for German historians and noted the need for a journal; Fu carried out similar projects in China. But as the editor Heinirich von Sybel claimed, the *Zeitschrift* was to publish only materials that had some "connection with the life of the present." (Heinirich von Sybel, foreword to the first issue of the *Historische Zeitschrift* [Munich, 1859], and Leopold Ranke's "Congratulatory Remarks," ibid., 28–35. See also Thompson and Hohn, *A History of Historical Writing*, 1:213.) Fu Ssu-nien viewed the IHP and its bulletin as diametrically opposed to this approach. Fu established the principle that the IHP and its bulletin should be absolutely divorced from politics.

several courses in Tibetan taught by Herman Franke (1870–1930).[47] Fu even developed interest in Sanskrit and Burmese.[48] He gradually turned toward an orientological and philological approach to learning in 1925 and 1926.[49] Thus, after seven years of wandering, Fu gradually reverted to the field with which he was most familiar.[50]

Fu's failure to earn a degree after seven long years of study disappointed many people. When Hu Shih and Fu Ssu-nien met in 1926 in France, Hu wrote in his diary that "Fu has led an undisciplined life (in the past years in Europe). He has not been as diligent as Ku Chieh-kang."[51] He must have been disappointed that his most promising student in Peita, a student who had once made him feel threatened when attending his class, had failed to become a specialist in any field of Western learning.[52] Disorderly and undisciplined though they were, those seven years exerted considerable influence on Fu's intellectual

47 Herman Franke was *ausserordentlicher Professor* of Tibetan. See Johannes Asen, ed., *Gesamtverzeichnis des Lehrkörpers der Universität Berlin, Bd. I, 1810–1945* (Leipzig, 1955), 50. FSNP, V-96 was Fu's notebook of Tibetan. Ch'en Yin-k'o's notebook of this class is still extant. Cf. Chi Hsien-lin, "Ts'ung pi-chi-pen k'an Ch'en Yin-k'o hsien-sheng te chih-hsüeh fan-wei ho t'u-ching," in *Chi-nien Ch'en Yin-k'o chiao-shou kuo-chi hsüeh-shu t'ao-lun-hui lun-wen-chi* (Kwangtung, 1989), 76.
48 Wang Fan-sen and Tu Cheng-sheng, *Fu Ssu-nien wen-wu tzu-liao hsuan-chi*, 52.
49 In his conversation with Hu Shih in Paris in 1926, however, Fu said that he regretted that in the past seven years he had failed to purge from his mind all the Chinese texts he memorized in his early years. See FSNP, I-1678, a letter from Hu Shih to Fu Ssu-nien.
50 Fu's switch from science to philology and finally to history coincided somewhat with the writing of a long letter he mailed to Ku Chieh-kang in late 1926. According to Ku's postscript to this letter, Fu started writing it in January 1924. However, the letter remained incomplete even when finally mailed out in October 1926. It is quite unusual for anyone to take three years to write a letter. This letter was written to honor Ku Chieh-kang's request to review several articles Ku had published. These articles were responsible for instigating the Movement of Doubting Chinese Antiquity. While reviewing these articles, Fu had a chance to engage in the study of ancient Chinese history, a field he had avoided for the preceding four years (from early 1920 to early 1924). But until his return to China, Fu does not seem to have decided that his future profession would be history. This explains why in the letter to Ku Chieh-kang, Fu said that he was not a historian. But after three years of pondering ancient Chinese history while writing that letter, Fu might have regained his interest in history. Moreover, he might have also found that he could achieve prominence only in this field, a field involved heavily with Confucian Classics, a subject with which he was most familiar. See *FSNC*, 1499–1542.
51 See *Hu Shih te jih-chi*, September 5, 1925. Nine consequent lines in the diary were crossed out by Hu Shih. It is not farfetched to believe that Hu's criticism of Fu was far more severe. We also learn from one of Lu Hsün's letters that Hu Shih was disappointed that Fu spent seven years in Europe studying without any focus. According to Lu Hsün, Fu was also very saddened by Hu's comments. See Lu Hsün *Liang-ti-shu*, in *Lu Hsün ch'üan-chi*, (Peking, 1981), 16 vols., 11:550.
52 Hu Shih once admitted that when he first taught at Peita, students like Fu Ssu-nien, well versed in traditional learning, were very threatening. See Fu Le-ch'eng, *Fu Meng-chen hsien-sheng nien-p'u*, in *FSNC*, 2607.

The Shaping of a New Historical School

development. And his undisciplined style of learning also enabled him to become an architect of the Chinese modern academic world. As director of the IHP and later the president of T'aita, his wide exposure to various kinds of learning brought him good vision. Nowadays, anyone walking into Fu's private library[53] may surmise that Fu wanted to devote his energies to studying in many fields of Western learning. Fu's collection of Western books was so wide-ranging that almost no meaningful sequence of them can be formed. It is also impossible for us to tell how many of these books Fu actually read, but his selections and purchases themselves afford us some reflection of his interests and concerns at the time.

Fu's Western books are chiefly on history, psychology, linguistics, mathematics, chemistry, physics, biology, Darwinism, and history. Also included are anthologies of ancient Greek and Roman works, along with the literary works of England, France, and Germany.[54] There are very few books on politics, economics, sociology (not even any by scholars, who were popular in the 1920s), theology, or religion. It is interesting to find that there are also very few works by Marx or Lenin or studies of the Russian Revolution. This is remarkable, considering that the revolution had once held such attraction for this enthusiastic young man. On previous occasions he had predicted that the Russian Revolution would be the model of development for the whole world.[55] One reason for the relative paucity of such books might be that after seven years of exposure to the English and German political systems, Fu's former enthusiasm for the Russian Revolution had waned.

When Fu was in Berlin, he became a staunch supporter of the Nationalist government in Kwangchow.[56] Upon learning of the success of the Northern Expedition, he returned to China with an appointment as dean of the School of Letters of Chungshan University in Kwangchow. He was thirty-one years old at the time. He had remained faithful to the oath taken seven years ago with his colleagues of the New Tide Society – he did not begin working in society until the age of thirty.[57] Before Fu arrived in Kwangchow, a good number of other intellectuals, including Kuo Mo-jo (1892–1978), Yü Ta-fu (1896–1945), and Lu Hsün made

---

53 Now in the Fu Ssu-nien Library at the Academia Sinica.
54 This observation is based on the list of Fu's non-Chinese book collection, prepared in 1938. However, from 1927 to 1936, Fu had almost no chance to buy any books in Western languages. I therefore believe that almost all the foreign books were purchased in Europe and that they reflect Fu's interest during those years. The list is in FSNP, no serial number.
55 Fu Ssu-nien, "She-hui-ko-ming: E-kuo (Russia)-shih te ko-ming," *Hsin ch'ao*, 1:1 (1919), 128–129.
56 *FSNC*, 2371.   57 *FSNC*, 1209.

allegiance to the government in Kwangchow. Ku Chieh-kang also felt that the KMT regime was the most suitable for saving China and convinced Hu Shih that, if he were to do political work, he should join the KMT.[58]

In Paris, Fu and Hu Shih had several days of intense conversation. Hu later recalled that Fu's historical enterprise launched later in his life had already been formed by this time. Hu was correct; Fu's notebook for 1926 contains several simple sentences sketching his future plans.[59] Most of his provocative articles on ancient Chinese history written over the next ten years were sketched out here for the first time. Some of the entries are:

1 "Geographical relevance between the Six Classics and Confucianism" (*Liu-ching yü ju-chia ti-li shang chih kuan-hsi*).
2 The "five ranks of nobility" (*wu-teng chüeh*).
3 "The evolution of the texts of '*tzu*'" (*chu-tzu wen-chi chih yen-pien*).
4 The "period of transition between *Yin* and *Chou*" (*Yin Chou chih chi*).
5 "The Pohai" (A gulf of the Yellow Sea).[60]
6 "There was territory beyond the seas" (*hai wai yu chieh*).
7 "Reversing the (traditional) ideas concerning the period between *Yin* and *Chou*."

As for historical methodology, Fu jotted: "We now have to apply European history to [the study of] our history, the European heritage to our heritage, European intellectual skills (in interpreting history, *hsin-shu*) to our intellectual skills."[61] Although these titles were concerned with history rather than philology, when Fu established the *Philology and History Weekly* (*Yü-yen li-shih chou-k'an*) at Chungshan University, he placed philology first in the title, suggesting that Fu still esteemed philology over history. Fu announced in the editorial's opening remarks of this weekly that philology and historiography were two fruitful traditional fields of Chinese learning, implying that the Institute of Philology and History of Chungshan University was to carry on this tradition.[62] One year later, Fu was to establish the Institute of History and Philology

---

58 Ibid.
59 Ku Chieh-kang's two articles questioning the reliability of Chinese ancient history, which were mailed by Ku to Berlin to Fu, should have persuaded Fu to reconsider Chinese ancient history.
60 Fu believed the Pohai area to be the cradle of Chinese civilization. He later explicated this idea in some of his historical writings.
61 FSNP, I-433, a notebook of 1926.
62 Fu Ssu-nien, "Fa-k'an-ts'u," *Chung-shan ta-hsüeh yü-yen li-shih hsüeh yen-chiu-so chou-k'an*, 1:1 (1927), 3.

in the newly founded Academia Sinica.⁶³ This was the first institute for professional historical research in modern Chinese history. By putting history before philology, Fu seemed to imply that he deemed history as prior to philology. It is worth noting that Ch'en Yin-k'o also shifted from philology to history. The careers of Fu and Ch'en were similar to that of Ranke, who also developed from a philologist into a historian.⁶⁴

During the seven years of Fu's absence from China, the Chinese intellectual world was turned upside down. Fu was not well informed of all the changes. First was the gradual rise of Marxism, which had attracted the attention of many intellectuals during the May Fourth period. After the May Fourth Incident, its popularity soared. Many Chinese intellectuals were encouraged by the Russian Revolution and felt that their social concerns should be articulated into organized actions. There was also a major social change in the intellectual world, one that Fu Ssu-nien had foretold. A growing dissatisfaction with the individualistic approach toward social and political reformation gradually led to widespread enthusiasm for the communitarian, holistic approach. Concepts such as individualism, democracy, and liberation, which had been in vogue during the New Culture Movement, now gave way to holistic approaches that emphasized social, economic, or class interpretations. People hoped to create a community according to their intellectual powers, and various kinds of utopian organizations emerged. Most of them lasted no more than a year, and their failures always led the participants to radicalization, especially with regard to the construction of an ideal community.⁶⁵ In addition to this, many activities with "social" names or concerns also appeared, and they tended to work more closely with the common people. In other words, a better society was now the fashion. The differences were over how to achieve this goal.

Given the post–May Fourth developments described here, splits in the New Culture groups seemed inevitable. Most of the groups split into two parts, liberal and leftist. Some of them even predicted that they would meet each other again on the battlefield.⁶⁶ The first split occurred within

---

63 Ts'ai Yüan-p'ei did not include the IHP in the original plan of the Academia Sinica. However, Fu Ssu-nien successfully persuaded Ts'ai to add this institution. Fu was originally appointed by Ts'ai to set up the Institution of Psychology. See Su T'ung-ping, "Shih-yü-so fa-chan-shih" (an unfinished and unpublished manuscript prepared for the IHP), ch. 2, 19. The page numbering of this manuscript is inconsistent.
64 Cf. George P. Gooch, *History and Historians in the Nineteenth Century* (Boston, 1965), ch. 6.
65 P'eng Ming, *Wu-ssu yün-tung shih*, 500–565.
66 Chow Tse-tsung, *The May Fourth Movement*, 253.

the *New Youth* group. Ch'en Tu-hsiu turned to Marxism in 1920, while Hu Shih and his group remained loyal to liberalism. As for the New Tide Society, most of its members remained liberal scholars, writers, and educators. Some later joined the KMT. In Hunan, the New People Society (Hsin-min hsüeh-hui) led by Mao Tse-tung was also divided into right and left wings. The Young China Association (Shao-nien Chung-kuo hsüeh-hui) also witnessed the same kind of split. Some of its members turned to the CCP, but a good many others set up the Chinese Youth Party later, calling for democracy and nationalism. The others joined the KMT and the Progressive Party (Chin-pu tang).[67] Fu Ssu-nien drifted away from his earlier inclination toward socialism and separated himself from his leftist colleagues of the May Fourth generation.

Fu Ssu-nien and the Institute of History and Philology

When Fu returned to China, his ambition was to establish a new academic world. In the "Opening Remarks" of the *New Tide* (1919), Fu did not even mention politics. He did, however, talk about how to save Chinese academia from its desperate situation. He firmly believed that the Chinese academic community could not be separated from the international academic world. Those who dared argue that Chinese scholarship could be separated from international academic society did so, he held, because they did not realize the extent of Western scholastic achievement and the backwardness of Chinese academic society. He complained that the Chinese had no true love of study. In his "Remarks" he revealed his ultimate goal: that Peita would one day achieve academic excellence on a par with Western universities.[68] During the 1920s Hu Shih and Ku Chieh-kang also argued that the prominent task of their time was excellence in academic work. As Ku Chieh-kang put it, "to establish an academic society" (*chien-li hsüeh-shu she-hui*).[69]

After his seven-year sojourn in Europe, Fu was dismayed to find that the world's foremost centers of Orientology were Paris and Berlin.[70] His longing to bring the world's orientological center back to Peking reflected a complicated mentality Nietzsche called "resentment,"[71] or a hate-and-envy complex. His desire was, as mentioned earlier, "to apply European history to the study of our history, the European heritage to our heritage, European intellectual skills to our intellectual skills," and one day to supersede the Western scholars. An observation from Ku Chieh-kang attested to this. Ku noted in his diary that

67 Ibid., 248–253. 68 *FSNC*, 1397–1401.
69 Ku Ch'ao, *Ku Chieh-kang hsien-sheng nien-p'u*, 169.   70 *FSNC*, 1314.
71 See Max Scheler, *Ressentiment*, trans. William Holdheim (New York, 1961), 68.

Fu [Ssu-nien] studied in Europe for a long time. He wanted to follow French sinologists and ultimately compete with them. Thus, his policy was to heighten [research quality]. My opinion is different. . . . We must pay attention to popularization first. Popularization is not to lower the academic quality, but serves as the basis for heightening it [in the future].[72]

Fu believed that the establishment and professionalization of an academic culture was the way to advance Chinese scholarship so that it could finally compete with Western scholars. This sentiment was echoed by many eminent Chinese scholars and led to the founding of the Institute of History and Philology (IHP). One of Fu's major contributions was his bringing together the new, first-rate scholars of his time to form the IHP. Among the most prominent of these were Ch'en Yin-k'o, an outstanding historian of medieval Chinese history; Chao Yüan-jen (1892–1982), the father of modern Chinese linguistics; and Li Chi (1896–1976), the father of modern Chinese archaeology.

The Academia Sinica, the first research institute in China, was established in the wake of the success of the Northern Expedition. Ts'ai Yüan-p'ei acquired the financial resources to set up this academy because of his support for Chiang Kai-shek. From 1926 to 1928, Ts'ai supported Chiang Kai-shek in his bid to become the leader of the KMT, and together with Wu Chih-hui he endorsed Chiang's moves to rid the party of Communists. Ts'ai Yüan-p'ei, Wu Chih-hui, Li Shih-tseng, and Chang Ching-chiang (1877–1950) hoped to establish an educational system on the French model, one independent of political intervention, but ironically it was only through political means that they could realize this ideal. The establishment of the Academia Sinica was approved by the Nationalist government three months after the party purge or "purification" (*ch'ing-tang*).

After the Northern Expedition, the KMT implemented "ideological indoctrination according to the party line" (*tang-hua chiao-yü*), a policy that severely clashed with Ts'ai's ideals. From 1928 on, Ts'ai's pro–human rights activities and his criticism of the fascist tendencies of the KMT caused his relationship with Chiang Kai-shek to worsen steadily.[73] When the financial resources of the Nationalist government were limited, the budget of Academia Sinica was almost the lowest priority, sometimes receiving as low as 20 percent of the amount originally apportioned for it. The Peiping Academy (Pei-p'ing yen-chiu-yüan) (1929), headed by another elder statesman of the KMT party, Li Shih-

---

72 Ku Ch'ao, *Ku Chieh-kang hsien-sheng nien-p'u*, 152.
73 Allen Linden, "Ts'ai Yüan-p'ei yü Chung-kuo-kuo-min-tang (1926–1940)," in Ts'ai Yüan-p'ei yen-chiu hui, ed., *Lun Ts'ai Yüan-p'ei* (Peking, 1989), 281–303.

tseng, competed strenuously with the Academia Sinica for government funding despite the close friendship between Li and Ts'ai. In addition, Academia Sinica's prospects worsened whenever Ts'ai criticized Chiang. According to Yang Hsing-fo (1893–1933), the first secretary-general of Academia Sinica, "In this tumultuous world, any academic study is absurd and runs against the current."[74] Apparently, the economic and political difficulties came as no surprise. Whenever pressure came from party staff, Ts'ai or Yang Hsing-fo would ask Fu Ssu-nien to rush for help to Wu Chih-hui, the only one close to Chiang Kai-shek who still supported the Academia Sinica.[75]

During these tumultuous days, private resources for academic work were almost nonexistent. Appeals to political figures proved the only way to sustain a research institute. With Ts'ai's ties to Chiang Kai-shek strained to the breaking point, any of the party staff members, such as Kuei Ch'ung-chi (1901–?) or Yeh Ch'u-ts'ang (1887–1946), who were hostile to Academia Sinica, could cause enormous trouble.[76] Despite these difficulties, under Ts'ai Yüan-p'ei's leadership Fu Ssu-nien and a group of May Fourth students successfully established thirteen institutes in the Academia Sinica.[77] From 1928 to 1937, the IHP gradually became unanimously recognized as the most successful of the thirteen.[78]

The years from 1927 to 1937 also constituted a dramatic period in Fu's personal life. When Fu arrived at Kwangchow in early 1927, Kuo Mo-jo had left that school not long before Fu's arrival. Lu Hsün was still at Chungshan University. Back in the New Culture Movement, Fu and Lu Hsün showed appreciation for each others' works. Lu Hsün highly praised the *New Tide*, which Fu edited. When Chang Tung-sun (1887–1973) attacked the *New Youth*, both Fu and Lu struck back. They formed quite an amicable friendship. When they met each other again at Chungshan University, their relationship was congenial at first. After the party purge, however, their different attitudes toward the KMT (Fu agreed with it, whereas Lu opposed it) caused them to gradually drift apart. Their relationship worsened when Fu decided to appoint

---

74 FSNP, I-278. This file number includes all letters from Yang Hsing-fo to Fu Ssu-nien.
75 FSNP, I-278.
76 Hu Shih once noted that in Western history a "charter" is necessary to protect the independence of an institution. Because the budget of the Academia Sinica was controlled by the Ministry of Finance, Ts'ai Yüan-p'ei's dream of an independent research institution was always in peril. See *Hu Shih te jih-chi*, February 1, 1930, n.p.
77 See E-tu Zen Sun, "The Growth of the Academic Community 1912–1946)," in John K. Fairbank and Albert Feuerwerker, eds., *The Cambridge History of China* (Cambridge, 1986), 13.2:402–403.
78 Ibid., 398, 403.

Ku Chieh-kang to the faculty of Chungshan University. Lu Hsün, who abhorred Ku[79] (mainly because Ku had accused him of plagiarizing from the work of a Japanese scholar in his history of the Chinese novel), finally left Kwangchow for Shanghai, and this marked the end of the friendship between Fu and Lu Hsün. Fu stayed in Kwangchow, the base of the KMT government, for only three years. There, with the help of Ku Chieh-kang and others, he established the School of Humanities at Chungshan University. At approximately the same time, Fu joined the KMT.[80] As a close associate of Chu Chia-hua (1893–1963), then vice-president of the university and an active member of the KMT, Fu barely escaped execution during the coup of December 1927 led by the Communist Chang T'ai-lei (1898–1927). During this bloody coup, Fu was singled out for arrest by the Communists. Thanks to a secret informant, Fu fled to the house of Ch'en Shou-i (1899–1977) and hid there. Later, when recollecting this event, Fu wrote that thereafter he never treasured his own life as before. This event also produced his lifelong abhorrence of the CCP.[81] In 1929 Fu decided to move the IHP to Peking, the cultural center of the nation. In addition to serving as director of the IHP during these years, Fu also occasionally taught historical methodology and the history of Chinese antiquity at Peita.

In Peking, Fu's life was divided between history and politics. These were the only peaceful years in his life, and some of his most valuable articles on Chinese ancient history were drafted and published during this period. On the other hand, when Japanese militarism was on the rise, he was an ardent patriot or, as Moller has called him, a "bellicose nationalist."[82]

Motivated by strong feelings of patriotism, Fu was instrumental in establishing the *Tu-li p'ing-lun* (*Independent Critic*) in 1932. This was the most important journal in the Chinese intellectual world after the Mukden Incident. It lasted until July 1937, right after the Marco Polo Bridge Incident. Hu Shih, Ting Wen-chiang, and Fu Ssu-nien were its core editors.

In Peking, Fu provoked two major debates. The first was about education (1932), and the second concerned Chinese medicine (1934). Fu believed that the core stratum of a modern society should be a professional class, not the traditional literati,[83] and that students of modern society should be trained to use their hands and feet. These ideas were

---

79 Fu Le-ch'eng, "Meng li te tien-hsing," in *Shih-tai te chui-i lun-wen-chi*, 203–204.
80 *Kuo-li Chung-shan ta-hsüeh jih-pao* (Kwangchow) (June 21, 1927).   81 Ibid.
82 Alan Moller, "Bellicose Nationalist of Republican China: An Intellectual Biography of Fu Ssu-nien" (Ph.D. diss., University of Melbourne, 1979), 151–191.
83 *FSNC*, 2002.

consistent with his ideas of building the new historiography – to be a professional historian and to use your hands and feet. Fu insisted that, if China hoped to be a modern state, it should "burn the books and bury the scholars alive" (said of Shih Huang of Ch'in Dynasty).

Fu complained that the modern Chinese educational system could not transform itself from raising up traditional literati, a group of useless people, because most students were not educated to be professional men. In modern times they could only become government officials, party officials, and so on. Thus, the more people they educated, the more parasites were produced, and they became the source of numerous student movements and social turmoil. In this regard, Fu even claimed that the modern Chinese educational system was on the verge of collapse.[84]

He attributed various shortcomings to the influence of Teacher's College, Columbia University, the alumni of which were dominant in the Chinese educational system after 1917–1918. The first point was that it was not right to view pedagogy as the major element in cultivating a teacher. Pedagogy should only be supplemental. Educational testing, teaching methods, educational psychology, and so on should not be the main topics of investigation. Rather, a good teacher should be deeply versed in his major field, which would then be supplemented by some pedagogical training.[85] He complained that too many "shallow courses," such as philosophy of life, were offered in schools. But the most fundamental courses, such as history, physical exercise, chemistry, physics, and mathematics, were not fully covered.[86] Not surprisingly, Fu incurred much criticism.

In modern China, Fu was the first to base himself in modern medical training to rebuke and dispute traditional Chinese medicine.[87] His medical training in London played an important role in this debate.

The most important event during Fu's stay in Peking, however, was when he met his new wife, Yu Ta-ts'ai (1907–1990), in 1934. Through an old-style arrangement by his mother, Fu had been married to his wife, née Ting, the daughter of a prestigious member of the gentry of Fu's hometown, while he was at Peita. This was a common arrangement for Fu's generation. During Fu's seven years abroad, his young wife lived with his mother to take care of her. There is, however, no available information about her. We do not even know her full name. This tragic marriage lasted until 1934, when Fu arranged a loan through the good offices of Hu Shih and Ting Wen-chiang to settle the divorce

---

84 *FSNC,* 1999. 85 *FSNC,* 2015, 2026.
86 *FSNC,* 2008. 87 *FSNC,* 2633.

case.[88] Divorcing old-style wives and remarrying women versed in the "new education" was common among May Fourth youth; it reflects the drastic transition that occurred not only in their ideas but also in their private lives.

The Mukden Incident disrupted the quiet lives of most Chinese intellectuals. It is widely remembered that in a meeting summoned by Hsiao Chen-ying (1886–1947), a high official under Sung Che-yüan (1885–1940), the nominal leader of North China who was afraid of provoking the Japanese, Hsiao threatened that if any anti-Japanese actions were carried out, the perpetrators would be risking their lives. While most professors kept their silence, Fu, followed by Hu Shih, heroically stood up, denounced Hsiao, and persuaded people to stand firm. The meeting soon turned chaotic and was disbanded. This event was later recollected as an important move in stabilizing the popular mood in Peking for several years. It is also believed that it finally contributed to the rise of the so-called December Ninth Student Movement, a large-scale movement to protest the Nationalist government's weak policies toward Japanese aggression that later led to mass arrests of students.[89]

The Goals and Scope of the IHP

In October 1928 Fu published an editorial manifesto (*chih-ch'ü*) in the first issue of the *Bulletin of the Institute of History and Philology* explaining the necessity for such an institute and why historical study should be the equal of natural science. The message carried by this manifesto later proved extremely influential.

After Liang Ch'i-ch'ao's *New History* (*Hsin-shih-hsüeh*, 1902), *The Method of Historical Study* (*Li-shih yen-chiu-fa*, 1922) and its *Supplement* (*Pu-pien*, 1926), and Hu Shih's "Opening Remarks" in the *Kuo-hsüeh chi-k'an* (1923), Fu Ssu-nien's manifesto was the most systematic blueprint for historical studies that had yet appeared. It did, however, meet with the opposition of some scholars. The focus of this blueprint was the pursuit of objective historical study and the training of professional historians. Fu highlighted the significance of primary sources to an unprecedented extent and also emphasized the need to widen the scope of historical data.

In the 1920s some scholars, including Hu Shih, Fu Ssu-nien, Ku

---

88 The loan, however, haunted Fu almost all of his adult life. See FSNP, 610, a letter from Fu to Ting Wen-chiang.
89 T'ao Hsi-sheng, "Fu Meng-chen hsien-sheng," in *Fu ku hsiao-chang ai-wan-lu*, 51. For Fu's reaction to student demonstrations, see John Isreal, *Student Nationalism in China, 1927–1937* (Stanford, 1966), 104–105.

Chieh-kang, and Li Chi, were dissatisfied with the obsession with written data as the sole major source of historical study. Hu Shih complained that although Ch'ing scholars applied the scientific method, their materials were always written data, thus resembling a closed recycling system. Thus, the scholarship of the past three hundred years was scholarship on books, scholarship on paper, and efforts on paper. All in all, the only achievements of the past three hundred years were innumerable classical exegeses.[90]

They all agreed that not only written data were valuable but that all materials, no matter how scattered, were of equal historical value.[91] In 1927 Ku Chieh-kang was collecting historical data for the library of Chungshan University. He found that even bookdealers were influenced by scholars and that they were obsessed with the Six Classics and the Three Histories (i.e., *Shih-chi, Han-shu, Hou Han-shu*). What bookdealers sent to him for selection were always books related to this category. Data other than these were considered as worthless by booksellers, and booksellers hesitated to collect them for Ku.[92]

The extent to which Fu highlighted the importance of primary sources and his methods for obtaining them impressed many of his contemporaries.[93] The importance of primary sources was frequently discussed by traditional historians, but singling them out as the most important element of historical study and organizing teams to locate them were new developments. Fu contended that scholars should change their attitudes from book to book, from viewing and reading, synonyms for researching.[94] He expressed his concern for primary sources in this way:

Modern historiography is nothing more than the study of historical data, using all the tools provided by natural science to put into order all the available historical data.... What we pay the most attention to is the acquisition of new data.... In short, we are not book readers. We go all the way to Heaven above and Yellow Spring below, using our hands and feet, to search out the stuff of history.[95]

---

90 Hu Shih, "Chih-hsüeh te fang-fa yü ts'ai-liao," in *Hu Shih wen-ts'un* (Taipei, 1968), 4 vols., 3:111, 115.
91 Ku Ch'ao, *Ku Chieh-kang hsien-sheng nien-p'u*, 119. Li Chi, "Chung-kuo tsui-chin fa-hsien chih hsin shih-liao," *Chung-shan ta-hsüeh yü-yen li-shih hsüeh yen-chiu-so chou-k'an*, 5:57, 58 (1928), 3.
92 Ku Ch'ao, *Ku Chieh-kang hsien-sheng nien-p'u*, 165.
93 Ch'ien Mu, *Pa-shih i shuang-ch'in, Shih-yu tsa-i*, 146.   94 *FSNC*, 1311.
95 *FSNC*, 1301, 1312. I adopt Chang Kwang-chih's translation. See *Shang Civilization* (New Haven, 1980), 60–61.

The Shaping of a New Historical School

Fu asserted that historiography could progress only with new primary sources. Historical study between the Han and T'ang was, he believed, preoccupied with issues such as rhetoric, style, and compilation skills and was less devoted to widening the scope and availability of historical data. According to Fu, the major part of Liu Chih-chi's (661–721) *Generalities on History* (*Shih-t'ung*) devoted to systematic criticism of historical methodology was unfortunately marred by its failure to emphasize the importance of the study of primary sources. During the Sung, Ou-yang Hsiu (1007–1072) in his *Record of Collecting Relics* (*Chi-ku-lu*) employed newly found data to study ancient history, thus dispelling the stereotypes of previous periods and turning attention toward the collection of data. According to Fu, this attention to new data allowed for the flourishing of Sung historical writing. The historical studies of the Yüan and Ming were, according to Fu, "almost dead"; "during the Ch'ing not even a single good historian was produced."

Fu believed that the modern Western historiography owed its success to the abundance of new data. Only by drawing from these new sources, he argued, were historians able to develop new historical criticism.[96]

Fu was not so narrow-minded as to assert that "Historiography is equal to historical data." It was, however, Fu's strategy to exaggerate his proposition slightly in order to call attention to it. When Fu discussed "objectivity," an old issue of contention among historians, he emphasized the pursuit of objectivity based on new primary sources and not on secondary descriptions.

The emphasis on primary sources was also illustrated by Fu's disappointment with traditional official history. Several years after the writing of the manifesto, a debate arose between Fu Ssu-nien and his former teacher Chu Hsi-tsu (1879–1944) because of their different attitudes toward the authority of the standard history of the Ming Dynasty. In that debate, Fu was supported by a group of young historians who had gathered data from nonofficial records to rebut Chu Hsi-tsu, who defended the authority of the *History of Ming* (*Ming-shih*).[97]

---

96 FSNP, II-945, a draft entitled "Chung Hsi shih-hsüeh kuan-tien chih pien-ch'ien."
97 The debate concerned the authority of standard histories or other official records. It started in 1934 and ended in 1936 but never reached a conclusion. In this debate Fu did not assert that private data were more reliable, but only that the standard history is not always the final authority and should be compared with other records (*FSNC*, 818). But in a letter to T'sai Yüan-p'ei, Fu went so far as to say that the official histories of the Ming and Ch'ing are completely unreliable (*ch'üan-k'ao-pu-chu*) (*FSNC*, 2441). Fu's proposition was consistently that comparisons between various kinds of data should always be made. He listed sixteen kinds of historical data and suggested that discreet comparison be undertaken regardless of orthodoxy or authoritativeness. Examples include the comparison of direct materials with indirect materials, official records with private records, native records with foreign records, contemporary

The emphasis on the importance of primary sources was also prominent in Fu's discussion of philological study. Fu severely criticized Chang Ping-lin's *New Vernacular* (*Hsin fang-yen*) because Chang relied entirely on textual materials. Fu asserted that, no matter how competent Chang's command of textual material was, he could not achieve much without field investigations. Fu believed that the way to transcend Ch'ing scholarship was to launch large-scale field investigations and experimental phonology. When the Linguistics Section of the IHP was established, instead of appointing traditional philologists, Fu appointed scholars with Western linguistic training such as Chao Yüan-jen. Nevertheless, traditional textual materials such as rhyme charts were not totally discarded; they were utilized as complements to field study.[98]

Fu recognized that modern academic studies in China required new scholars with new mental attitudes. Thus he greatly resented traditional "book readers" (*tu-shu-jen*). As mentioned before, in his essays of the *New Tide* period Fu severely criticized the life-style of the Chinese man of letters. He even said that once a man becomes a man of letters, he is no longer a human being.[99] In the manifesto he leveled various charges against traditional book readers. For traditional book readers, he argued, the source of knowledge is confined to written texts; to study is to read. For traditional book readers, Fu continued, research always meant that one read in solitude in one's own study. Fu argued that much knowledge was available from sources other than books. Scholars, he argued, should use their feet and hands in addition to their eyes.

Fu challenged the traditional book-reading style of research by arguing that field work should be given equal attention. "We are not

records with remote records, unintentionally kept data with intentionally kept data, and oral with written records. The debate arose when Li Chin-hua published an article based on some miscellaneous notes suggesting that the *Ming History* and the *Veritable Record of Ming* (*Ming Shih-lu*) covered up the fact that Emperor Ch'eng of Ming was not born by the empress of the founding emperor of Ming but by his concubine named Kung (Kung-fei), who had also been a concubine of the last Yüan emperor (*FSNC*, 807–821). The article incurred criticism from Chu Hsi-tsu. Chu argued in favor of the traditional authority of the *Ming History* and the *Veritable Record of Ming*, insisting that Emperor Ch'eng was the empress's son. Fu contended that these two official documents should not be deemed final resorts and that private records should not be so easily dismissed (*FSNC*, 1008). On Fu's side were Ch'en Yin-k'o, Li Chin-hua, and Wu Han (1909–1969), who provided a considerable amount of nonofficial evidence. Fu did not lose or win the battle, but the debate did mark his dissatisfaction with official history and his challenge to it.

98 Chao Yüan-jen, "T'ai-shan yü-liao hsü-lun," in *Fu so-chang chi-nien t'e-k'an* (Taipei, 1951), 62.
99 *FSNC*, 1192.

book readers," Fu announced; "(we must) go all the way to Heaven above and Yellow Spring below, using our hands and feet, to search out the stuff of history." This was almost certainly adopted from G. M. Trevelyan's famous saying, "Collect the facts of the French Revolution! You must go down to Hell and up to Heaven to fetch them."[100] It is not too much to say that Fu was making a great leap away from the traditional bookworm type of intellectual (*shu-sheng*). He held that the number of books was limited, whereas unexplored data such as epitaphs, icons, and folk songs existed in virtually unlimited supply. The importance of nontextual historical data was still a relatively new concept to many of Fu's contemporaries. To obtain data, the IHP dispatched a great number of investigation teams all around the nation. These efforts showed the IHP's compatriots that there was learning beyond written records. Other than reading in their studies, scholars should hold instruments, do spadework, and scout around. The institute extended its reach to remote mountains and villages to search for all sorts of materials, many of them heretofore untouched. Conducting research in this way was also unimaginable by most of the IHP's colleagues before.

According to Fu, merely commanding the written record could only make an outdated historian; rigorous scientific study of history involved investigating and exploiting every kind of data and applying all manner of scholarly tools, including those of the natural sciences. For example, as far as the study of ancient history was concerned, those who confined themselves to written records were old-style "book readers," but if one recognized that soil samples or a discarded artifact of an ancient civilization was as significant as one paragraph of the classics, then one was a scientific historian.

Fu believed that research should be a collective enterprise. He was once criticized by a colleague as an "entrepreneur," a label he rejected.[101] But in fact "entrepreneur" is an appropriate term for Fu at this time because he was leading an enterprise or "collective work," as he called it. Fu was aware that in China there had been few enduring private academic organizations comparable with those in Western nations. During the early fourth century A.D., when the Chin court was forced to move from North China to the south, many kinds of learning had ceased to exist, primarily because there had been no continuous academic organizations to perpetuate them. But in the West, Fu argued, the nobility

---

100 Hsü Kuan-san found the origin of this proverb. See Hsü Kuan-san, *Hsin-shih-hsüeh chiu-shih-nien* (Hong Kong, 1986, 1988), 2 vols., 1:221.
101 This is quoted in "Shih-yü-so fa-chan-shih," ch. 7, 453.

and the church had endured political turmoil and perpetuated learning.[102]

In his ideas on collective work, Fu was influenced by Francis Bacon (1561–1626).[103] Bacon believed that a single man could not contribute a great deal to science because science is necessarily a collective enterprise. Owing partly to Bacon's influence, the Royal Society (a society for research) was established in England some years after his death.[104] Thus, Fu advocated that research should be undertaken in a cooperative manner as in the modern West. Fu argued that the time of individual research had long since passed and that scholars now needed libraries or associations to offer them materials and should work within an academic community, discussing work with each other to compensate for individual weaknesses.[105]

Indeed, Fu abhorred traditional Chinese historical compilations, which he believed contained too many moral judgments and political biases.[106] He thus called for the separation of history from morality and politics. His disappointment with the traditional standard histories led him to assert that ideal historical writing is monographical, but not comprehensive or general. Again, he exaggerated his position:

What we hope to do is only to put data in order for the facts to become naturally revealed. . . . If there is a wide gap between two facts, then connecting them with some imagination is sometimes, in certain cases, permissible. But induction is a very dangerous task; to take a possibility as a certainty is a dishonest thing. Therefore, we only lay down evidence without bridging gaps [*ts'un erh pu pu*]. Our attitude toward [arranging] data is that we prove but never overinterpret. We fully explore the meaning within the data. We absolutely do not step out of the data to say anything.[107]

The assertion was startling to his contemporaries and later became the target of considerable criticism.[108] Such an extremely cautious attitude

---

102 FSNP, II-945. Years later, Joseph Needham pointed out to Fu that if China had had academic organizations, A. Stein and Paul Pelliot could not have taken precious materials from China without the notice of the Chinese. See FSNP, I-952, a set of typed manuscripts presented by Joseph Needham to Chiang Kai-shek, one copy of which was sent to Fu by Needham.

103 Hu Shih, "Fu Meng-chen hsien-sheng te ssu-hsiang," *Hu Shih chiang-yen-chi*, 2:346.

104 Cf. Edwards, *The Encyclopedia of Philosophy*, 1:239. Fu did not consider traditional organizational projects for the standard dynastic history or local gazetteers as of the same quality.

105 *FSNC*, 1313.   106 *FSNC*, 1302–1303.

107 *FSNC*, 1310. The translation "to put data in order for the facts to become naturally revealed" was adopted from Dirlik, *Revolution and History*, 12.

108 For example, Tseng Fan-k'ang, "Chung-kuo hsien-tai shih-hsüeh-chieh te chien-t'ao," *Tse-shan pan-yüeh-k'an*, 1:5 (1940), 13–15.

toward induction, interpretation, and generalization was very similar to Mach's suspicion of induction and generalization.[109] It is this guiding rule that shaped the writing style of most members of the IHP and contributed to its strengths and weaknesses. It also affected numerous scholars in their research style whether they liked it or not.

Students of Fu's generation believed that humanistic studies could utilize the methodology of the natural sciences and that there should be no national boundary for any learning. Although the data they dealt with were uniquely Chinese, a universally applicable methodology for exploiting these data should be employed. Fu maintained, for example, that astronomy, geology, and economics were very helpful in tackling historical problems, Thus, modern historical study is a convergence of various kinds of scientific disciplines.[110] Fu believed that it was only through the adoption of such a methodology that the IHP could become a legitimate branch of the Academia Sinica, which championed scientific study. Fu envisioned, for example, that statistics could be a tool for the study of intellectual history. Fu's famous treatise entitled *Studies on the Ancient Meanings of "Nature" and "Destiny"* (*Hsing ming ku-hsü pien-cheng*) was a model to show how statistical methods could be employed to analyze intellectual trends.

To ensure objectivity, Fu was eager to introduce an experimental apparatus into linguistic studies. Although Fu never established "a sort of working historical laboratory for students that shall correspond to chemical laboratories,"[111] he did set up a modern phonetic laboratory in the IHP to solve many problems that had puzzled even prominent phonological experts such as Ch'ien Ta-hsin (1728–1804).[112] For years the IHP operated the best phonetic laboratory in all of Asia.[113] Given the fiscal difficulties Fu faced, the establishment of this laboratory reflected the extent to which he hoped to borrow scientific tools to supersede the Ch'ing scholars.

As has been explained earlier, Fu Ssu-nien called for the professionalization of historiography, which marked a discontinuity with traditional historical writing. In traditional China, historical writing was the job of men of letters. Even during the Republican period, a first-rate historian like Wang Kuo-wei, whose research had always been deemed to

---

109 For a discussion of Mach's point, see John Losee, *A Historical Introduction to the Philosophy of Science* (Oxford, 1980), 168–170.
110 *FSNC*, 1307.
111 Novick, *That Noble Dream*, 33. In the United States it was Henry Adams who hoped to establish this kind of laboratory.
112 *FSNC*, 1307.   113 *FSNC*, 337.

represent new history, never considered himself just a professional historian. Fu wanted to change this. In modern China, the professionalization of historiography consisted of several aspects. Its institutionalization provided a stable income to feed its members, historical research became a full-time occupation, and academic discipline was strictly observed. A redefinition of the audience also ensued. The new historians targeted only their colleagues as their readers, and not the common people. They also tried to detach themselves from moral and political issues.

Professional historians rejected any notion of a grand generalization. Edifices and bricks are useful metaphors to describe their difference. The professional historians tended to make bricks rather than edifices.[114] Fu Ssu-nien repeatedly emphasized that the members of the IHP were expected to do research into the way bricks are made. Bricks lasted a long time, and this job would be accomplished even by men who had only mediocre talent.

Fu's call for problem-oriented study (*chuan-t'i yen-chiu*) and his teaching at Peita on how to conduct it greatly influenced his students.[115] They held that historical study was absolutely not the compilation of general histories; historians should devote themselves, at the most, to the history of one single dynasty.[116] They insisted that strict procedures should be followed. Every conclusion must be backed up by hard evidence. No vague general rhetoric was allowed. They were advised not to be tempted by "a priori construction." Therefore, no "subjective theories" were allowed. Ch'ien Mu's brilliant works were, according to one report, evaluated by Fu as only a good teacher's work.[117]

The IHP and its style were against the current. Prior to the IHP, various historical schools, especially the New Historiography (Hsin shih-hsüeh) upheld by Liang Ch'i-ch'ao, tried to make their concerns related to the practical world in one way or another. Leftist historians who propagated the materialistic conception of history and enthusiastically debated with others on the nature of Chinese society were, in fact, debating about whether China should adopt Marxism. They were applying historical study to political needs, too. In contrast to these, in the meantime, the members of the IHP were earnestly purchasing Ming and Ching archives and excavating the royal tombs of the Shang Dynasty. Fu Ssu-nien claimed that it was not the purpose of the IHP to intentionally

---

114 Novick, *That Noble Dream*, 56.
115 Li Shang-ying, "Yang Hsiang-kuei hsien-sheng hsüeh-shu yen-chiu chi chu-tso pien-nien," *Ch'ing-shih lun-ts'ung* (1994), 1–13.
116 Ch'ien Mu, *Pa-shih i shuang-ch'in, Shih-yu tsa-i*, 146–147.
117 Mao I-heng, "Kuan-yü Fu Ssu-nien te i-feng-hsin," *T'ien-wen-t'ai* (January 4, 1951).

make historical research useful.[118] It turned out that no member of IHP ever participated in political affairs. The general mood of this institute was quite sober.

The IHP at Work

In this section I elaborate on how Fu realized his ideals: first, how he recruited a group of young historians to work under his guidance and, second, how his new perspective on historical data and his idea of "collective work" influenced many undertakings by the IHP. Three projects in particular shed light on these two aspects of Fu's work at this time.

In his manifesto of 1928, Fu announced that he would assemble a group of young scholars who could use new tools and new thinking to write new history. This goal was achieved not only through recruiting members of the IHP but also through Fu's role as an "academic hegemon" (*hsüeh-pa*) who had the power to recommend faculty members to universities, grant study projects, and so forth. For example, Wu T'ing-hsieh (1865–1947), a solid historian recommended by Wang Ching-wei and Lo Wen-kan (1888–1941), was rejected by Fu because Fu recognized that, although Wu's scholarship was commendable and he was at home with traditional historical records (*chang-ku*), he was not equipped with "new tools" or "new thinking."[119]

During his lifelong tenure as director of the IHP, Fu ran the institute with an iron fist, determined to impose his ideas on younger scholars with lenient treatment only for Li Chi, Ch'en Yin-k'o, Chao Yüan-jen, and other early cofounders. His nickname at the time was "fat cat," for whenever the "fat cat" was in the institute, the "mice" worked diligently.[120] Fu also closely scrutinized their research style.[121] In fact, it was only about twenty years after Fu's death, under the impact of Western social science, that the force of Fu's doctrines slowly began to recede.[122]

---

118 A. B. Linden, "Ts'ai Yüan-p'ei yü Chung-kuo-kuo-min-tang (1926–1940)," in Ts'ai Yüan-p'ei yen-chiu hui, *Lun Ts'ai Yüan-p'ei* (Peking, 1989), 281–303.
119 See FSNP, III-74, a letter from Wang Ching-wei to Ts'ai Yüan-p'ei; FSNP, III-77, a letter from Lo Wen-kan to Ts'ai to recommend Wu to the IHP. FSNP, III-82 is a letter from Ts'ai to Fu to recommend Wu. In the early stage of the IHP, Fu recruited a good number of Wang Kuo-wei's students, which showed a certain continuity between Fu's school and that of Wang.
120 Tung Tso-pin, "Li-shih yü-yen yen-chiu-so tsai hsüeh-shu shang te kung-hsien," in *Fu ku hsiao-chang ai-wan-lu*, 67.
121 Ch'ien Mu, *Pa-shih i shuang-ch'in, Shih-yu tsa-i*, 147.
122 During the 1970s the study of socioeconomic history was taboo in Taiwan because of the seeming associations it had with Communist doctrine.

Although Fu taught at the Chungshan University and Peita for only five years, he recruited the top graduates directly from among his students or from other universities. He did not hold seminars as Ranke did in Berlin. Nevertheless, under his guidance the IHP produced a great number of professional historians, philologists, anthropologists, and archaeologists, many of whom achieved prominence.[123] By the late 1930s the "young scholars" recruited by Fu and trained with new tools and new thinking had reached their academic maturity and could counterbalance the power of the cofounders of the IHP.[124]

The war between China and Japan did not diminish the IHP's activities. Being the best environment in southwestern China for humanistic studies, especially during a time when doctoral programs were not yet established, the IHP was the only place to house students for post–master's degree studies.[125] Therefore, in those war years the IHP attracted a group of promising students who were attached to or finally served in the institute and later became its most eminent scholars.

In the manifesto, Fu set forth several investigation projects. The first among them was the Anyang excavation at the sites of the ancient feudal states in eastern Honan. The second was to send archaeological teams to proceed gradually from Loyang to Inner Asia and trace the origins of Western influence in China. The third was to establish a base in Kwangchow and collect anthropological and linguistic materials from the southwestern provinces and, later, to extend the project into Indo-China.[126] Because the IHP was based in Kwangchow, Fu first sent teams to its adjacent provinces. Unfortunately, none of these teams yielded substantial results in the early stages of their work. Fu further secured funding to finance three additional projects: the Szechwan and Sikang ethnological investigations led by Liang Kuang-ming, the Yünnan anthropological trip by Sergei Mikhailovich Shirokogorff and Jung Chao-tsu (1897–1995), and the Chüanchow investigation of Islamic inscriptions and epitaphs. But ultimately, none of these projects came to fruition. It was only with the success of the Anyang excavation that

---

123 According to four lists of IHP personnel, more than one hundred scholars, many of whom had significant achievements, worked in the IHP. See "Shih-yü-so fa-chan-shih," 76, 364, 504, 507–509. However, these lists were far from comprehensive. Some of the persons on the list did not stay in academic work. For example, David Yule, a Harvard Ph.D., later became a successful politician and minister of defense in Taiwan.
124 See "Shih-yü-so fa-chan-shih," 288, where a statistical survey of the rise and importance of these young scholars is given.
125 Yen Keng-wang, "Wo tui Fu Meng-chen hsien-sheng te kan-nien," *Hsien-jen-chang*, 1 (1977), 25–29.
126 *FSNC*, 1311–1312.

Fu and his patrons gained confidence in the soundness of the decision to plan and fund such projects.[127]

When Fu Ssu-nien sent Tung Tso-pin (1895–1963) to investigate the remnants of oracle bones at the Anyang site in 1928, the Movement of Doubting Antiquity was still in its heyday. Perhaps Fu had the words of Li Tsung-t'ung (1895–1974) in mind: "when skeptical historians wrestle with conservative historians, only archaeological findings can settle the dispute."[128] Fu might have thought that it was time to erect a "supreme court" to settle the endless debate of whether the Shang still belonged to the Stone Age, as Anderson, Hu Shih, and Ku Chieh-kang held, by digging into the soil.[129] Immediately after Tung Tso-pin was sent to Anyang to inspect the site of the Shang oracle bones, Fu was informed by Tung that there were still some remnants available. But before long, Tung was dismayed by the fact that after digging at thirty-six places for thirteen days, only a small number of oracle bones was found. At this time when the IHP was facing tremendous fiscal difficulties, Tung was more than ready to persuade Fu to give up the project. But Fu insisted that inscriptions on the oracle bones were not as valuable as the knowledge gained from other sources. Fu once lamented: "I am disappointed that when Lo Chen-yü (1866–1940) excavated [oracle bones] several years ago, the items and soil strata underneath were not recorded and are therefore unknown. He did not have the good sense to pay special attention to this. This is a great loss."[130] Lo was one of the most farsighted historians of his time, with the most advanced perspective on the nature of historical data, and he undertook several visionary activities in preserving and publishing valuable data.[131] But Lo was not advanced enough to recognize the value of materials without characters on them. Even the young Tung Tso-pin did not recognize the importance of such information and attempted to persuade Fu to give up digging when few oracle bones were found.[132] Tung was still accustomed to equating "underground data" (*ti-hsia shih-liao*) with inscriptions, a concept underlying Wang Kuo-wei's work as well. In Wang Kuo-wei's case, the scope of

---

127 On the failure of these investigation teams, see "Shih-yü-so fa-chan-shih," 49–82.
128 Li Tsung-t'ung, "Ku-shih wen-t'i te wei-i chieh chüeh fang-fa," in Ku Chieh-kang, ed., *Ku-shih pien* (Peking and Shanghai, 1926–1941), 7 vols., 1:268–270.
129 *FSNC*, 1317. New excavations did not always settle disputes; they sometimes baffled people further.
130 Fu Ssu-nien, "Li-shih yü-yen yen-chiu-so pao-kao-shu ti-i-ch'i," quoted in "Shih-yü-so fa-chan-shih," 85.
131 Chin Yü-fu, *Chung-kuo shih-hsüeh-shih* (Shanghai, 1944; rpt., Taipei, 1960), 281–288.
132 A letter from Li Chi to Fu Ssu-nien, now kept in Shih-yü so tang-an (which is stored in the Institute of History and Philology, Taipei), *yüan* 25 file.

"underground data" was largely confined to oracle bones and inscribed vessels. He never discussed the problem of stratification.

Nevertheless, in comparison with thirty years previous, when oracle bones were regarded as "dragon bones" for medicine, much progress had been made. In a letter from Li Chi to Fu Ssu-nien, Li complained that "Although the quality of this excavation conducted by Yen-t'ang [Tung Tso-pin] was one level higher than that of Lo Chen-yü, he [Tung] did not record the stratified deposits and viewed everything except oracle bones as of inferior value.... In fact, [the materials neglected by him] were so exciting that I could not believe my eyes."[133] By this time there were several excavations being undertaken by Western scholars with the assistance of Chinese, but to most people archaeology was still conventionally viewed as "digging for treasure" (*chüeh-pao*); to scholars it was more or less epigraphy (*chin-shih-hsüeh*) or even "digging for antiques" (*chüeh ku-tung*). It was no surprise that when Tung was digging, several friends of his suggested, "Why don't you hire someone to dig the things out and then buy them? Why make so much trouble for yourself?"[134]

It may be observed that the perspective of Ch'ing scholars on archaeology was inferior to that of Sung scholars. A comparison of Lü Ta-lin's (1042–1092) *Hsüan-ho k'ao-ku t'u* (1092) and Tuan Fang's (1861–1911) *T'ao-chai chi-chin lu* (1908), two landmark studies of bronze inscriptions, indicates that, as far as making a record of the place where the bronze was unearthed, the latter is far less detailed than the former. The literati of the past eight hundred years seemed never to have come to understand that the precise location of a given find is essential for the study of bronze vessels.[135] What Lü Ta-lin in the Sung prescribed as the basic rules for bronze study were later abandoned, and only the most bookish enterprises, such as collating the inscriptions with textual records, were pursued.[136] "Close investigation was replaced by the colophon; understanding was replaced by appreciation."[137] But Fu Ssu-nien and Li Chi, who had closely observed the development of Western archaeology, were well aware that sophisticated archaeological study demands detailed excavation records. Not only oracle bones and bronze vessels were valuable, but also soil, stone, shells, and pottery – items valuable to the

---

133 This letter was quoted in "Shih-yü-so fa-chan-shih," 98.
134 Tung Tso-pin, "Min-kuo shih-ch'i-nien shih-yüeh shih-chüeh An-yang Hsiao-t'un pao-kao shu." Quoted and translated by Chang Kwang-chih, *Shang Civilization*, 43–45.
135 Li Chi, "Chung-kuo ku ch'i-wu-hsüeh te hsin chi-ch'u," in *Li Chi k'ao-ku-hsüeh lun-wen-hsüan-chi* (Taipei, 1977), 2 vols., 2:867–872.
136 Ibid.   137 Ibid., 869.

modern investigator but worthless to antiquarians. A photograph of the phenomena underground might be more valuable than ten thousand words on a bronze inscription. Li Chi was soon sent by Fu to take Tung Tso-pin's place.[138] This subtle change marked a transition between two different views of archaeological excavation. From 1928 on, archaeologists from the IHP spent seven years on the site, even though they only achieved notable results in 1934.

The success of the Anyang excavation also involved politics. While the Anyang excavation was being undertaken, the Nationalist government had nominal control of Honan province. But the power of the central government was in fact confined to the regions south of the Yangtze River, and the governor of Honan, Han Fu-ch'ü (1890–1938), was still a general under the warlord Feng Yü-hsiang (1882–1948). There was certain kind of correlation between the Academia Sinica and the Northern Expedition. The hidden meaning of Fu Ssu-nien's words was always that, after the Northern Expedition, the institute should be able to carry out a range of projects.[139] But although the Academia Sinica was supposed to have benefited from the success of the Northern Expedition, this did not turn out to be the case. When the excavation team of the IHP was working in Anyang, Honan, it was confronted by a local scholar-official, Ho Jih-chang (1895–?), a student of Lo Chen-yü, who insisted that the Anyang site should be explored by Honanese. Different views of archaeology were also involved in the confrontation. Ho Jih-chang and the local scholars cared mostly about antiques (*ku-wu*), while the national institution was more concerned with the relevance of the site for scholarship. Ho's opposition was tacitly endorsed by the provincial government. Thus, the confrontation between Ho Jih-chang and the IHP was a microcosm of the confrontation between the local authority and the newly formed central government. The idea that archaeological findings should be the property of the whole nation had not yet taken shape in the newly unified country. Although this was a time when the Nationalist government hoped to put education under its direct surveillance, the deteriorating relationship between Chiang Kai-shek and Ts'ai Yüan-p'ei caused Fu to obtain only a trifling amount of help from the Nationalist government, especially when the struggle was not for territory but for "scholarship." At the peak of this struggle, Fu asked Wu Chih-hui, a close friend of Chiang Kai-shek, to have Chiang issue an order to Han Fu-ch'ü. But since Nationalist authority did not fully

---

138 Li was assigned by Fu to replace Tung as the leader of the excavation. See Shih Chang-ju, *K'ao-ku nien-piao* (Taipei, 1952), 11.
139 *FSNC*, 1911.

extend to this area, the Honan government hesitated to attempt to force Ho Jih-chang out of this business. Only after the Central Plains Civil War (1930) and Chiang's defeat of Feng Yü-hsiang was the confrontation between the IHP and local scholars settled.[140]

The field work, laboratory analysis, and scientific study of the results of the Anyang excavation have been recounted in Li Chi's *Anyang*.[141] The meaning and significance of this excavation to the study of ancient Chinese history can be divided into at least three categories. First, the excavations confirmed the authenticity of the oracle bones, previously doubted by Chang Ping-lin. Only after scientific excavation was Chang reported to have secretly read the inscriptions on the oracle bones. The change of Chang's attitude marked the successful persuasion of the foremost philologist of the classical school to accept the authenticity of this new historical data.[142]

Second, during the heyday of the Doubters of Antiquity, traditional belief in ancient Chinese history was dismissed in toto, and the Shang Dynasty was still widely considered as part of the Stone Age. Hundreds of bronze articles were found in Hsiao-t'un alone, ranging from ceremonial vessels to weapons and articles for daily use. All of these show abundantly that the Shang Dynasty was well into a fully developed bronze age.[143] The Doubters of Antiquity gave up some of their more radical assumptions as soon as the discoveries at Anyang were made known.

As leading mainland Chinese archaeologist Su Ping-ch'i later pointed out, only after the Anyang excavation did historians dare to put the Shang Dynasty at the beginning of their books as a truly verified dynasty.[144] Hu Shih and Ku Chieh-kang once insisted that the Shang Dynasty was of the Stone Age, but upon witnessing the findings of the bronze vessels, Hu changed his stance and told Ku in 1929, "Now my thinking has changed. I do not doubt antiquity any longer. I believe in the authenticity of ancient Chinese history." Ku was stunned upon hearing this.[145] Hu even confided to members of the IHP in a public

---

140 *FSNC*, 1317–1318. In the midst of the Central Plains Civil War (1931), Yen Hsi-shan (1883–1960) announced himself commander of the army, navy, and air force of the whole nation and put the IHP under his authority. Only after several old officials of the northern warlords mediated between Yen and the IHP was the latter finally free from the interference of Yen's authority. See "Shih-yü-so fa-chan-shih," 200–202.
141 Li Chi, *Anyang: A Chronicle of the Discovery, Excavation, and Reconstruction of the Ancient Capital of the Shang Dynasty* (Seattle, 1977).
142 Li Chi, "Importance of the Anyang Discoveries in Prefacing Known Chinese History with a New Chapter," in *Li Chi k'ao-ku-hsüeh lun-wen-chi*, 2:964.
143 Ibid.
144 Su Ping-ch'i, "Chien-kuo i-lai Chung-kuo k'ao-ku-hsüeh te fa-chan," in *Su Ping-ch'i k'ao-ku-hsüeh lun-shu hsüan-chi* (Peking, 1984), 300.
145 See Liu Ch'i-yü, *Ku Chieh-kang hsien-sheng hsüeh-shu* (Peking, 1986), 262.

meeting that his erroneous ideas about the Shang Dynasty had been corrected by the Anyang excavations.[146] Fu Ssu-nien himself was also persuaded. A radical May Fourth youth who had once praised Ku Chieh-kang's destruction of Chinese ancient history and nicknamed him "the King of Historiography," Fu now changed his attitudes[147] and set out to piece together concepts that Ku had previously shattered.

Third, the Anyang excavation also refuted the theory of the Western origins of Chinese civilization. During the late Ch'ing even the most learned Chinese scholars accepted this theory in light of the abrupt emergence of the Chou civilization, seemingly from nowhere. The Anyang excavation supplied an abundance of evidence showing that Chinese civilization during the Shang Dynasty had "already attained some of the most fundamental Oriental characteristics, and that early historical Chinese Culture is essentially a northern China creation."[148] Archaeologists also found that there was a continuity of forms between bronze articles discovered in Anyang and their Neolithic prototypes made of pottery, wood, and stone. The continuity of forms indicates the close relationship of the Shang culture with the culture or cultures developed during the Neolithic age.[149]

The excavation achieved its most important contribution by bridging a historical gap. In 1937 Paul Pelliot described this excavation as "the most spectacular discovery made in the field of Asiatic studies in recent years."[150] Through the Anyang excavation, scholars gained evidence about Chinese life more than a millennium before the Christian era; knowledge of this period would have remained very sketchy were it not for the discovery of the royal tombs at Anyang. "At one leap Chinese archaeology had gained a whole millennium."[151] It is also the first time that, according to Ku Chieh-kang, scholars became aware that historical data could be acquired through digging.[152] What is more, the Anyang excavation site left an institutional legacy to its profession by training a generation of Chinese archaeologists. Indeed, the blossoming of archae-

---

146 *Hu Shih te jih-chi*, December 6, 1930, n.p.
147 In 1924–1926 Fu told Ku Chieh-kang that he had become "king of historiography." *FSNC*, 1505.
148 Li Chi, "Importance of the Anyang Discoveries in Prefacing Known Chinese History with a New Chapter," in *Li Chi k'ao-ku-hsüeh lun-wen-chi*, 2:962.
149 Ibid., 2:969. They also asserted that, as the practice of using oracle bones or scapula was unknown to the ancient Mesopotamians, Hebrews, Egyptians, Greeks, Etruscans, and Romans, the Shang people could not have migrated from these areas.
150 Paul Pelliot, "The Royal Tombs of An-yang," in *Independence, Convergence, and Borrowing in Institutions, Thought, and Art* (Cambridge, Mass., 1937), 272.
151 Ibid., 266.
152 Ku Chieh-kang, "Chan-kuo Ch'in Han chien jen te chao-wei yü pien-wei," *Ku-shih pien* (Peking and Shanghai, 1926–1941), 7 vols., 7:64.

ology in the PRC over the past forty years is in large part due to the labor and leadership of the Anyang excavators.[153] The principles Fu laid out in his manifesto still hold true for the field work of archaeological teams in the PRC today.[154]

The second example I shall offer to show the realization of Fu Ssu-nien's ideal is the opening of the Ming and Ch'ing Cabinet Archives. Just as Ranke and his students wandered around Europe seeking new documents, so was Fu Ssu-nien very active in opening up archives and propagating the study of archival materials. Fu and his institute were the first to conduct large-scale archival collecting, cataloging, and research. A new perspective was required for this project. The handling of these archives illustrates how the perspective of the old generation differed from that of the new.

Using archives as a basis for historical work was not totally new to China. But from the Sung on, the significance and value of archives were largely neglected.[155] During the Ch'ing, at least three bureaus permanently operated to compile books based on archival materials.[156] But, overall, scholars still paid more attention to books than to archives.

From the Ming to the early Ch'ing, the Inner Cabinet was a power center of the central government. After the Yung-cheng period (r. 1723–1735) when real policy-making duties were for the most part transferred to the Privy Council of the emperor (Chün-chi-ch'u), the Inner Cabinet became an organ concerned mainly with transmitting documents. An immense number of documents of the Inner Cabinet from Ming and Ch'ing was stored in the Grand Warehouse for hundreds of years.[157] In 1909 this part of the archives was moved out from the Grand Warehouse to its corridors. Finally, Grand Secretary Chang Chih-tung (1833–1909) decided to move them from the Grand Warehouse to the Board of Education (Hsüeh-pu), simultaneously recommending that the books be removed for preservation and that the remaining

---

153 Hsü Kuan-san, *Hsin-shih-hsüeh chiu-shih-nien*, 2:231.
154 This explained why Hsia Nai, a former researcher of the IHP and a prominent leader of archaeology in the PRC, insisted in the debates over the existence of the Hsia Dynasty that unless a good body of direct evidence is acquired, the existence of the Hsia should not be accepted as fact. Hsü Kuan-san, *Hsin-shih-hsüeh chiu-shih-nien*, 2:231–232.
155 Shen Chien-shih, "Ku-kung-po-wu-yüan wen-hsien-kuan cheng-li tang-an pao-kao," in *Shen Chien-shih hsüeh-shu lun-wen-chi* (Peking, 1986), 345.
156 Hsü Chung-shu, "Tsai-shu Nei-ko-ta-k'u tang-an chih yu-lai chi ch'i cheng-li," *Chung-yang yen-chiu yüan Li-shih yü-yen yen-chiu-so chi-k'an*, 3:4 (1933), 563.
157 Ibid., 543, 546. Of these, the documents acquired by the IHP were less well preserved than the documents other institutions acquired.

The Shaping of a New Historical School

archival materials be burned. This order was rescinded after Lo Chen-yü, who was also one of Chang's staff members, argued that there were some valuable historical data in the archives. Chang then recommended that the materials be removed to a safer place.

When the revolution of 1911 necessitated a change of the storage places of these archives, they were moved to the Historical Museum (Li-shih po-wu kuan) in 1912. In 1918 Lu Hsün, then a middle-echelon official of the Ministry of Education, was sent by Fu Tseng-hsiang (1872–1949), the minister of education, to inspect this "small mountain" of papers. Although Lu commented on the sad condition of the documents, no policy was suggested. From then on, the "small mountain" was frequented by officials, many of them well known. But most of these officials were obsessed with finding rare Sung books. Fu Tseng-hsiang, a prestigious book collector, inspected this small "mountain" and decided that the materials were worthless except for some copies printed in the Sung mixed in with the rest. Not until someone with a new perspective on historical data appeared could the documents be rescued.

In 1921 the Historical Museum in Peking, which was then in charge of these archives, decided to sell the materials owing to a budget problem. The 150 tons of paper were sold to a paper mill to be recycled! Lo Chen-yü learned of this and bought the paper at three times the asking price. He then selected and printed part of these archives. But because of Lo's own fiscal difficulties, the archives were later sold to Li Sheng-to (1858–1937), who in turn found the cost of maintaining a storehouse burdensome and planned to sell them to the Japanese or to the Harvard-Yenching Institute.[158] This aroused nationalistic indignation among many Chinese and spurred them to action. Finally, Fu Ssu-nien obtained funds to buy the archives. During the negotiations for the purchase of these archives, Li Sheng-to particularly wished to retain the Sung texts interspersed in the archives. Fu Ssu-nien, however, was more concerned with archival materials. Clearly, Li was an antiquarian; Fu Ssu-nien, a historian with modern perspective.[159] Accordingly, Fu told the middleman that Sung printed texts were valueless to the IHP.[160] Ch'en Yin-k'o said that "The IHP thinks highly of the archives. Li Mu-chai (Sheng-to) thinks highly of Sung printing. What are treasures to us

---

158 Ch'en Yin-k'o said that it would be a "national disgrace" (*kuo-ch'ih*) to do so. See a letter from Ch'en to Fu Ssu-nien, quoted in "Shih-yü-so fa-chan-shih," 186.
159 On Fu Tseng-hsiang's and Li Sheng-to's attitudes, see "Shih-yü-so fa-chan-shih," 117–118, 182. In the IHP, Ch'en Yin-k'o had the same concept of primary sources and played a crucial role in this purchase. See ibid.
160 Ibid., 187–188.

are in fact trash to Li."[161] Fu's thinking was analogous to what he had in mind in 1928 when he persuaded Tung Tso-pin that there were some things more valuable than oracle bones. The differences among Chang Chih-tung, Fu Tseng-hsiang, Li Shang-to, Fu Ssu-nien, and Ch'en Yin-k'o were differences of perspective on historical data.

When Fu decided to save this trash paper from recycling,[162] he definitely had German historiography in mind. The German historical school advocated opening archives, utilizing firsthand documents, and publishing them. When Fu was in Berlin, many massive archives were published in colossal volumes.[163] Although Fu did not follow Ranke in procuring specifically diplomatic documents, he did learn from Ranke the importance of archives. Under Fu's direction, massive manpower was mobilized to organize the archives. Fu rang the bell, and a collective work project was formed. Among the compilers, Li Kuang-t'ao (1902–1984) selected, compiled, and published one hundred volumes of the archives. The compilation and publication continues to this day, and more than three hundred volumes have been published.

Many variations from official records were also found in these archives, especially those concerning the transitional period between the Ming and Ch'ing.[164] While arranging these archives, more than one thousand pages of the original copy of the *Veritable Record of the Hsi-tsung (1621–1627) Reign* (*Hsi-tsung shih-lu*) were found, which for hundreds of years was believed to have been lost, and this enticed Fu to set out on another great project to collate and rearrange the *Ming Shih-lu*. This project lasted forty years, resulting in the publication of 154 volumes.[165] In these efforts, which were organizational projects utilizing collective manpower, the sorts of projects Fu had emphasized in his Manifesto were carried out.

Under the leadership of Fu Ssu-nien, the IHP advanced its efforts by means of systematically collecting and carefully examining all materials concerned. For collecting and studying new data, numerous field work teams were sent out, and projects concerning primary data were launched. Before the institute left mainland China, in addition to large-

---

161 Ibid. Ch'en Yin-k'o's letter was mailed to Fu on March 10, 1929, and is stored in Shih-yü-so tang-an, *yüan* 4 file.
162 It is noteworthy that Lo Chen-yü had already chosen a small part of this archive for publication in *Shih-liao ts'ung-k'an ch'u-pien* (Peking, 1924).
163 On the large-scale source collections in Germany, such as *Monumenta Germarial Historica* and others, cf. Thompson and Hohn, *A History of Historical Writing*, 2:166–168.
164 See "Shih-yü-so fa-chan-shih," 215.
165 Twenty-nine volumes of collated notes entitled *Ming-shih-lu chiao-k'an-chi* (Taipei, 1968) were written by Huang Chang-chien.

scale textual criticism the History Section of the IHP initiated many massive projects concerning primary sources, including the study of the ancient classics and manuscripts of later dynasties. These projects included the editing and transcribing of the comments on wooden slips from the Han Dynasty, found by the Sino-Swedish Expedition led by Sven Hedin; collecting and studying bronze and stone inscriptions; collecting and studying folk literature; and collating, rearranging, and studying the Tun-huang manuscripts.

In addition to traditional phonetic study for clarifying the historical basis of the modern language and drawing up the isogloss atlas of the country, the Linguistic Section sent teams to investigate modern Chinese dialects. The results were that hundreds of dialects in fourteen provinces were surveyed and recorded in phonetic notation (some were even further recorded on aluminum disks). The comparative study of non-Chinese languages of the Sino-Tibetan family was also undertaken.

Fifty-five sites spread over eight provinces were excavated by the Archaeology Section. The sites surveyed and unearthed numbered more than four hundred. Among these enterprises, the Anyang excavations lasted nine years (1928–1937) until it was interrupted by the Sino-Japanese War. In 1932 eighty-eight Chou tombs were excavated, yielding rich collections of Chou bronzes with reliable dating. Prehistoric sites of the Yangshao culture were excavated in Honan in 1934 and 1937. In Ch'eng-tzu-yai, Shantung, one of the prehistoric sites of the Lungshan Black Pottery culture was excavated in 1930 and 1931. In 1936, excavation at the sites of the Black Pottery culture at Liang-ch'eng-chen (Shantung) also led to a number of findings.

The Ethnological Section conducted field studies in northeastern and southwestern China. Hindered by the war, ethnological expeditions focused on the vast southwestern provinces because they were not occupied by the invading Japanese armies. Anthropological study was done on the people of Szechwan and on human bones from cemeteries in Nanking. For twenty years, this section frequently sent out anthropological and ethnological expeditions and investigated many tribes in the southwestern provinces of China.[166] These are only a few examples of the most important projects the IHP carried out at this time.

166 This is a summary of seven memorial articles on Fu's contributions to the development of the IHP. See *Fu so-chang chi-nien t'e-k'an* (Taipei, 1951), 11–60. Up until Fu's death, in addition to seven projects of collecting and publishing historical data, more than 70 volumes of monographs were published. The *Bulletin* carried more than 80 volumes and 448 articles. Starting from zero, the library of the IHP acquired more than 130,000 copies of books that focus on history and philology, 200 complete journals, and a great amount of primary data.

Without Fu Ssu-nien's personal network (*kuan-hsi*), there would have been no such enterprises. In his short life, Fu was nicknamed by his contemporaries an "academic hegemon." Many of his colleagues were amazed at his ability to secure funding and other assistance for implementing many of the IHP's projects. As an organizer in a tumultuous nation in which resources were virtually unavailable to the academic world, Fu Ssu-nien had to develop various kinds of old-fashioned personal networks to secure funding for his new enterprises. This was especially true when IHP projects extended into various areas around the nation and required special support from local governments.

In late 1920 Ts'ai Yüan-p'ei and Wu Chih-hui were two major channels between the Academia Sinica and the central government. The tension during this time between Ts'ai Yüan-p'ei and Chiang Kai-shek made the business of the Academia Sinica more difficult. Fu often recollected sadly how Yang Hsing-fo and Ting Wen-chiang had struggled to gain funding by socializing with high officials of the KMT.[167] Later, when Fu Ssu-nien's close friend Chu Chia-hua was promoted to head of the Organizational Department (Tsu-chih pu) of the KMT, Fu and the IHP gained better access to the core of the government. Due to the increasing power of the KMT party cadres, documents from the Central Committee of the Organizational Department were often necessary for Fu to conduct his business smoothly. Whenever needed, the high tier of the KMT party organ would send telegrams, especially to local governments, to smooth the way for the work of the IHP. After 1937 Fu himself gradually gained access to the highest tier of power.[168] With these extensive personal networks, Fu became a moving force behind many projects and a patron of many scholars.[169] Fu Ssu-nien's close ties with two foundations, the China Foundation (Chung-hua wen-hua chiao-yü chi-chin-

---

167 FSNP, I-92, Fu Ssu-nien to Jen Hung-chün (1886–1961).
168 The 1941 invitation list to the funeral for Fu's mother can serve as a useful index of the extent of his personal networks. The list of names shows that, in addition to the Academia Sinica, Fu had personal relations with the highest echelon of government officials and also with a good number of prestigious universities like Peita, Ch'inghua, Chungshan, and Wuhan, in addition to journalists, foundation administrators, and other important people.
169 For example, Fu tried to gain financial support from Chiang Kai-shek for Liang Ssu-yung (1904–1954) and Liang Ssu-ch'eng (1901–1972), two distinguished scholars. See FSNP, III-1233, Fu to Chu Chia-hua, Hang Li-wu, and FSNP, III-1236, Lin Hui-yin to Fu. FSNP, I-1250, is a letter from Jao Yü-t'ai (1891–1968), a leading scientist, to Fu asking him to urge the government to select young scientists to study abroad. FSNP, II-392, is a letter from Yang Chung-chien (1897–1979), a leading paleontologist, asking Fu to help him to secure a budget to establish a Cenozoic Era laboratory.

The Shaping of a New Historical School

hui) and the Sino-English Boxer Indemnity Foundation (Chung Ying wen-hua chi-chin-hui), funded many IHP projects and other endeavors undertaken by Fu.

However, there were two kinds of demands that kept challenging historians – the first from society and the second from academic colleagues. If a historian closely responded to the demands of society, he should treat history holistically and with regard to contemporary problems. The common people should be his main audience. If a historian entered into dialogue with his colleagues, he should avoid being present-minded. He should strictly obey the rules of the academic community.

In the chaotic 1920s to 1940s, however, society demanded that historians pay more attention to the people than to their colleagues. Audience was crucial. Tradition-minded historians and leftist historians alike demanded that historical writing should be read by the people. Their works were meant to appeal to the common people, and they were meant to influence the course of historical development. The institute, on the other hand, was only interested in reconstructing what had actually happened. The audience that members of the institute appealed to were Chinese and Western academics.[170] What Fu Ssu-nien and his colleagues repeatedly emphasized was enhancing Chinese scholarship and feeling proud and elated in the international world.[171] Thus, it turned out that in terms of historical study the institute was now at the center of the academic world. Yet, in terms of being valued by worldly eyes, it was relegated to the periphery as a failure. Professionalization was a leap into the modern academic world, but it did not make a great contribution to social and political problems.

As for the challenge from the historical community, first of all there were several tensions between old and new historians. For example, in Chungyang University, Liu I-cheng (1880–1956) and Miao Feng-lin (1898–1959) defended traditional historiography. Scholars such as Ch'ien Mu called for writing general history and emphasized that moral principles should not be divorced from historical work. To tradition-minded historians, the nature of knowledge was not as narrow as knowledge only. They could not accept the idea that learning is only satisfying its own ends regardless of this-worldly concerns. Historical study should be related to practical use, either for national identity,

---

170 For example, a letter written by Fu Ssu-nien on December 26, 1932, to Ts'ai Yüan-p'ei reported that the achievements of the IHP could be proved superior to those of Westerners. See Wang Fan-sen and Tu Cheng-sheng, *Fu Ssu-nien wen-wu tzu-liao hsüan-chi*, 79.
171 Cf. ibid., 79.

93

as a mirror, or as a guide for society. They scorned the IHP for lacking an overall comprehensive view of national history. They presupposed that research should be holistic, general, and move from macro to micro – not vice versa. Thus, although they might do research in the same way the new scholars conducted it (i.e., conducting comprehensive investigation into small questions), they emphasized that their research would not stop at details. Historians should not start their work from any new data accidently found but should start with a major concern. Sometimes they were even antagonistic toward new data.[172]

The old and new also could be divided in terms of their attitudes toward what kind of role the mind should play in everything. Intellectuals like Fu Ssu-nien, although never having stated that historical study should take the mind out of everything, were in fact doing research this way. They decided that introspective tradition was a major hindrance for China's progress in every respect. This was a major trend of their generation. Hsiung Shih-li (1885–1968), a leading philosopher of the New Confucian school, later reflected that the idea of "blocking human ability in spiritual cultivation and self-reflection" was widespread. He complained that this was, on the one hand, the legacy of the Ch'ing evidential research and, on the other hand, the influence of positivism; both had converged on the new intellectuals of this generation.[173]

Historians such as Liu I-cheng firmly believed that mind, especially the introspective moral source, should be embodied in historical writings so that the readers could derive moral teaching from them. In other words, learning should not divorce itself from moral teachings. They were not satisfied with being professional men. They still wanted to play a role similar to traditional literati who had wide concerns and general knowledge (*t'ung-shih*).[174]

A third division between old and new was that the new historians, led by Hu Shih and Fu Ssu-nien, believed that without new data, and especially without new archaeological findings, ancient history could not be reconstructed. This idea was opposed by historians such as Ch'ien Mu. At Peita, Ch'ien openly announced that he would trace ancient Chinese history without referring to any new archaeological findings.[175] He repeatedly emphasized that scattered archaeological findings were

---

172 For example, Liu I-cheng, "Lun wen-hua shih-yeh chih cheng-chih," *Shih-hsüeh tsa-chih* 2:1 (1930), 7.
173 Hsiung Shih-li, *Tu-ching shih-yao* (Taipei, 1973), 142, 282.
174 See Liu I-cheng, *Kuo-shih yao-i* (Taipei, 1957), 137.
175 Ch'ien Mu, *Pa-shih i shuang-ch'in, Shih-yu tsa-i*, 142.

simply irrelevant to the reconstruction of ancient history.[176] Liu I-cheng held that the advances in studying new archaeological findings had direct proportional bearings on the retrogression of people's knowledge of China's past.[177] They believed that if ancient history were grasped holistically, traditional records would be sufficient. If historians relied too much on archaeological findings, they could only come up with some small points of ancient history. No useful teaching could be drawn from them.[178]

Leftist historians, of course, constituted the major challenge to the IHP. They called for historians to pay special attention to two factors in history – socioeconomics and class – and, whether they were interpreting the history of thought, literature, or political ideology, the same intellectual apparatus was applied.

In Shanghai and Yenan, leftist historians disdained Fu's group as "slaves to erudition" (*pao-hsüeh te nu-ts'ai*) who cared nothing for the problems of present society and were concerned only with minor, boring, and useless research.[179] Leftist historians also upheld the holistic view for interpreting history. "Long-term socioeconomic processes should receive the primary attention of the historian."[180]

Class was the factor that leftist historians emphasized most strongly. To ignore or to transcend analysis of class was anathema to them. Wu Han (1909–1969), originally a follower of Hu Shih's and Fu Ssu-nien's research style, latter testified that he felt remorse for being above class (*ch'ao chieh-chi*) and that he had tried very hard to overcome this.[181] To employ the category of class in the study of Chinese history was, of course, to take sides with the proletarian. A number of historians changed to this new creed. The change of research style also brought certain changes in their own outlook on life – that is, from an apathetic, disheartened, and hopeless life to a confident and fervently hopeful life. Though exaggerated, the title of an article, "Two Kinds of

---

176 In his late years, even after tremendous archaeological findings proved to be extremely fruitful, Ch'ien Mu still sternly rebuked the archaeological enterprises promoted by the IHP with a most unfriendly tongue. Even the linguistic surveys conducted by the IHP in the sixteen provinces of China were ridiculed by him. See Ch'ien Mu, *Hsien-tai Chung-kuo hsüeh-shu lun-heng* (Taipei, 1984), 147–148, 154.
177 Liu I-cheng, *Chung-kuo wen-hua shih* (Taipei, 1954), 3:287.
178 See Ch'ien Mu, "Yin-lun," *Kuo-shih ta-kang* (Taipei, 1975), 1:3–4.
179 I shall discuss this further in Chapter 5. Even in the 1950s, Fu Ssu-nien's dictum "cheng – erh – pu – shu" was still under fire. Cf. Chou I-liang, "Hsi-yang Han-hsüeh yü Hu Shih," in *Hu Shih ssu-hsiang p'i-p'an* (Peking, 1955), 7 vols., 7:210.
180 Dirlik, *Revolution and History*, 9.
181 Wu Han, "Wo k'o-fu le ch'ao-chieh-chi kuan-tien," *Wu Han wen-chi* (Peking, 1988), 4 vols., 4:106–107.

Lives,"[182] written by Lo Erh-kang (1907–1997) showed this kind of change. It was hoped that scholars, as professional historians, would be value free, refrain from judgment, and be detached. But, in a tumultuous time, practical use and meaning were two major concerns that became nagging problems for most scholars.

Scholars educated in the West, such as Ho Ping-sung (1890–1946), who studied at Princeton and was heavily influenced by James Harvey Robinson's (1863–1936) historiography,[183] believed that historical study is always subjective and for practical use, and that there is no such thing as historical "fact." Ho also maintained that historians should focus on general trends rather than on particular facts. In the eyes of many, the focus of the style of history championed by Hu Shih, Fu Ssu-nien, and the IHP was precisely an obsession with particular facts divorced from any relevance to the present. Fu, however, ignored these people and had nothing but disdain for their criticisms.[184] The apathetic relationship between Fu and his critics is attested to in Fu's papers. Among the thousands of letters, only one relates to Ho Ping-sung,[185] only two relate to Ch'ien Mu,[186] and almost none came from any leftist historian.[187] Differences in their historical views also influenced personal relationships. In historical studies, a division between the center and periphery gradually formed. Hu Shih and Fu Ssu-nien, as the leaders of the "New Han

---

182 Lo Erh-kang, "Liang-ko jen-sheng," in Sheng-huo Tu-shu Hsing-chih San-lien shu-tien, ed., *Hu Shih ssu-hsiang p'i-p'an* (Peking, 1955), 7 vols., 2:183–188.
183 See Chou Ch'ao-min, "Ho Ping-sung shih-hsüeh li-lun ch'u-t'an," in Liu Yin-sheng, ed., *Ho Ping-sung chi-nien wen-chi* (Shanghai, 1990), 87, 92. Ch'iu Yung-ming, "Ho Ping-sung Li-shih chiao-hsüeh-fa shu-lun," in ibid., 203; Fang Hsin-liang, "Ho Ping-sung p'ing-chuan," in ibid., 417; and Hu Feng-hsiang, "Ho Ping-sung yü Lu-pin-sun (J. H. Robinson) te hsin-shih-hsüeh," *Shih-hsüeh-shih yen-chiu*, no. 3 (1987), 31–37.
184 There was tension between Fu's group and leftist historians. An example is Ko I-ch'ing's confrontation with Li Ho-lin (1904–1988). See FSNP, II-502. Fu was almost apathetic toward the debate on social history. My interview with the late Kao Ch'ü-hsün (1910–1991) in the winter of 1990 revealed that Fu hardly mentioned this event.
185 FSNP, III-1215, a letter from Ho Ping-sung to Chu Chia-hua in which Ho asked Chu to recommend one of his students to Fu.
186 One was written by Ch'ien and Yao Ts'ung-wu to solicit financial aid for their students. See FSNP, IV-793. The other one was from Ch'en Yüan (Hsi-ying, 1896–1970) to Fu to criticize Ch'ien's personality. See FSNP, II-570. Ch'ien Mu's name did not even appear on the list of possible candidates for academician of Academia Sinica. Hu Shih, Fu Ssu-nien, and members of the IHP made considerable contributions to the preparation of that list. Ch'ien Mu's hostility toward Fu is evident in his memoirs. See Ch'ien Mu, *Pa-shih i shuang-ch'in, Shih-yu tsa-i*, 202.
187 There was one letter from Yin Ta (Liu Yao, 1906–1983) to Fu Ssu-nien. See Wang Fan-sen and Tu Cheng-sheng, *Fu Ssu-nien wen-wu tzu-liao hsuan-chi*, 222. However, Kuo Mo-jo was nominated by Hu Shih and Fu Ssu-nien for the status of academician to Academia Sinica because of his contributions to the study of bronze inscriptions.

learning," at least in the eyes of the academic world, were the leaders of the core, while their foes were relegated to the periphery.[188] But after 1950 the periphery became the center, and the core was relegated to the periphery.

188 I define center and periphery in terms of (1) their accessibility to government financial aid and funds, (2) their power in academic appointments, and (3) their status in the academic world. As for their influence on young students, the periphery was greater than the center. The animosity of the periphery to the center was illustrated by Kuo Mo-jo, who once planned to use eight newspaper literary supplements to criticize Hu Shih. See FSNP, I-1306, Hu Shih to Fu Ssu-nien. For Fu Ssu-nien's animosity toward leftist scholars, see Ch'en Han-sheng, *Ch'en Han-sheng hui-i-lu* (Peking, 1988), 56–58.

3
Toward a Theory of Plural Origins of Chinese Civilization: Hypotheses on Ancient Chinese History

The scholars of the May Fouth generation, strongly influenced by the concepts of pluralism and the genetic method, came to embrace an amoral, nonethical approach to learning, seeing all things in a state of constant change and evolution. Their views on what had traditionally been considered orthodox and unorthodox writings were fundamentally shaken, giving way to completely different interpretations of China's past. Once the breach had been made, diverse viewpoints came pouring out, and this generation of scholars created a new interpretive tradition that remains influential in our own day. Fu Ssu-nien's explanation of the history of Chinese antiquity is an example of this major interpretive change.

The years between 1927 and 1937 were Fu's most productive years for studying the history of Chinese antiquity. During this period he developed several very challenging hypotheses in this field. Two traits are discernible: first, he dissolved the history of Chinese antiquity from one overarching system into distinct processes; and, second, he pieced together the ancient history that had been smashed into fragments by the Movement of Doubting Chinese Antiquity. Nevertheless, his reconstruction of the history of ancient China was not a return to the original thesis. Instead it was an attempt at a new synthesis in the light of new data.

Ku Chieh-kang was the first to become suspicious of the vertical, linear relationship of the Three Dynasties. In Ku's renowned article responding to two antagonists who criticized his radical skepticism at the beginning of the Movement of Doubting Chinese Antiquity in 1923, Ku maintained that he had decided "to destroy the single ethnic origin theory," "to destroy the assertion that in ancient China the whole territory was unitary," "to destroy the idea that ancient China was a golden society," and "to destroy the notion that the Three Dynasties were transmitted linearly."[1] Ku mailed copies of these articles to Fu Ssu-nien in Berlin, thereby inspiring Fu to break with his old beliefs.[2] It was Ku, therefore, who had torn the old mansion down; Fu's contribution was to reconstruct the fragmented bricks into his plural origins theory.

The first hypothesis Fu brought forward was the plural origins of Chinese civilization, which challenged the conventional idea of "Hua-Hsia." The impact of this plural theory on Fu's contemporaries is evident in Hsü Hsü-sheng's (1888–1976) observation that "From ancient times our country has called itself Hua-Hsia. This has been passed down for several thousand years without further distinction."[3] People were stunned by Fu's theory because the conventional idea of the origins of Chinese civilization was a monistic one.[4]

According to the traditional view, the history of Chinese antiquity involved battles between Hua-Hsia and the Miao. Hua-Hsia was viewed as one nation and the Miao as the other.[5] On the Hua-Hsia side, the Three Dynasties transmitted power linearly. For example, in the late Ch'ing, Ch'en Tu-hsiu began his "Chronological History of Chinese Antiquity" (Chung-kuo li-tai ta-shih) with the struggle between the Han and Miao people, followed by the transmission of power through the Three Dynasties.[6] In 1920 in Lü Ssu-mien's (1884–1957) *Vernacular History of China* (*Pai-hua pen-kuo-shih*), the Shang and Chou were regarded as Han people, with origins in western China. From the present Shansi area, they fought through Honan and proceeded east to

---

1 Wang Fan-sen, *Ku-shih pien yün-tung te hsing-ch'i*, 237.
2 According to Fu's memory. *FSNC*, 1504–1505. The Japanese scholar Uehara Tadamichi noticed that in this correspondence Fu treated Ku like a student. See Uehara Tadamichi, "Fu Shinen no kodaishi kenkyu ni tsuite," *Ko-dai-gaku*, 1:2 (1952), 125.
3 Hsü Hsü-sheng (Hsü Ping-ch'ang), *Chung-kuo ku-shih te ch'uan-shuo shih-tai* (Peking, 1960), 28.
4 For example, Wang Kuo-wei believed that the ancestors of Hsia, Shang, and Chou could all be traced to Huang-ti. See "Yin Chou chih-tu lun," in *Kuan-t'ang chi-lin* (Peking, 1959), 454.
5 This was a common idea in ancient Chinese texts. See Hsü Hsü-sheng's summary in *Chung-kuo ku-shih te ch'uan-shuo shih tai*, 101–109.
6 *An-hui su-hua pao*, no. 3 (1904), 11–14; no. 4 (1904), 9–12; no. 5 (1904), 9–12; no. 6 (1904), 9–12; no. 7 (1904), 11–16 (facsimile edition, Peking, 1983). Traditional historiography seldom touched on this problem. See, for example, *Erh-shih-erh shih tsuan-lüeh* (1803) and *Yü p'i li-tai t'ung-chien chi-lan* (1874).

Shantung, northern Anhwei, and Kiangsu.[7] The ethnic Han Chinese were, then, from the west and had gradually proceeded to the east.

In the traditional view, Chou culture was considered the first culmination if not the cradle of Chinese tradition. In the late Ch'ing, Hsia Tseng-yu (1863–1924) announced that "if not for the Chou people, the Chinese might still be at the stage of the primitives. All Chinese religion, ritual, politics, and literature were products of Chou. Chou was to China what Greece was to Western civilization."[8]

These propositions represent an unconscious "western" bias. In his *Records of the Grand Historian*, Ssu-ma Ch'ien (145–86 B.C.) held that dynasties with western origins always flourished, whereas those from the east always declined.[9] The T'ang scholar Chang Shou-chieh, an annotator of *Shih-chi*, implied that the Three Dynasties originated in the west.[10]

There was another traditional view concerning the relationship between the Three Dynasties. As described by Chang Kwang-chih,

> Two elements that have formed the cornerstone of our understanding of Sandai [San-tai] history are due for a basic overhaul. There are, first, the emphasis on the vertical relationship of the Three Dynasties and, second, the understanding of the developing sequence of the Three Dynasties as an island of civilization in a sea of barbarous contemporaries.[11]

This old view of the essential unity of the Three Dynasties was supported by the Classics.

Fu Ssu-nien challenged these conventional ideas; he suggested that the relationship among the Three Dynasties was a horizontal interrelationship and that there were, in fact, always wars between two competing ethnic groups. This hypothesis contradicted the old accounts of harmonious relations among Yao, Shun, and Yü and questioned Confucian traditions and dismantled the story of the "Sixteen-Character Transmission" (*shih-liu tzu hsin-ch'uan*). The story went that Shun had passed sixteen characters to Yü. The sixteen characters read, "The mind of man is restless; its affinity for the right way is small. Be discriminat-

---

7 Lü Ssu-mien, *Pai-hua pen-kuo-shih* (Shanghai, 1920), 109. Lü later modified his view. See Lü Ssu-mien, *Hsien Ch'in shih* (rpt., Taipei, 1967), 103.
8 Hsia Tseng-yu, *Chung-kuo ku-tai-shih* (Peking, 1955), 29. This view was widely held. See, for example, Wang Kuo-wei, "Yin Chou chih-tu lun," in *Kuan-t'ang chi-lin*, 453–480.
9 *Shih-chi* (Peking, 1973), 686.
10 See, for example, the T'ang historian Chang Shou-chieh's annotation of the placename of *Po*, the capital of King T'ang of the Shang Dynasty, in *Shih-chi* (Peking, 1982), 10 vols., 2:686.
11 See Chang Kwang-chih, "Sandai Archaeology and the Formation of States," in David Keightley, ed., *The Origins of Chinese Civilization* (Berkeley, 1983), 496.

ing, be undivided, that you may sincerely hold fast the mean."[12] The "Sixteen-Character Transmission" became one of the major teachings on which Sung and Ming Neo-Confucianism were based. According to Fu Ssu-nien's hypothesis, Shun belonged to the eastern group and Yü to the western group. Since the two groups were in conflict, how then could Shun transmit the sixteen characters to Yü?

Fu also challenged the traditional Chou culture centrists by arguing that the I and the Shang on the eastern coast, and not the Chou, were to China as the Greeks were to Western civilization. Fu also held that the direction of the spread of culture was from the eastern coastal areas to the west.

The Plural Origins of Chinese Antiquity

Three historians first advanced the theory of the plural origins of Chinese antiquity: Meng Wen-t'ung (1894–1968) in 1927, Fu Ssu-nien in 1934, and Hsü Hsü-sheng in 1943. Meng's work was the least influential. When Fu was gradually developing his hypothesis, from 1924 to 1934, he was unaware of Meng's book and thus never mentioned his work. Hsü Hsü-sheng made an identical discovery but, after learning that Meng and Fu had preceded him in it, digested their theories and incorporated them into his book.

The lack of influence of Meng's work needs to be discussed. In the wake of the Movement of Doubting Chinese Antiquity, Meng Wen-t'ung's work was based completely on textual evidence and was, therefore, considered too insubstantial for serious attention. Hsü Hsü-sheng's three-group theory was established through his sensitive studies of ancient myths, but its focus was less on the period of the Three Dynasties than on the period of the myths. Through a deft and cautious use of textual material combined with support from the newly discovered archaeological evidence, which was quite convincing, Fu Ssu-nien's hypothesis was the most influential.

Several lines of intellectual development in the late Ch'ing and early Republican periods led these scholars to this new awareness that there may have been plural ethnic and cultural groups in Chinese antiquity. I discuss these currents as follows: first, the discovery of the historical value of non-Confucian pre-Ch'in texts and their historical implications; second, the challenge of Ku Chieh-kang's suspicion toward the records of Chinese antiquity; and, third, the challenge to the theory of the Western origins of the Chinese.

---

12 The passage appears in *Book of Documents*. I use James Legge's translation; see *Chinese Classics* (Hong Kong, 1861), 3. 1:61–62.

The rise in status of non-Confucian ancient texts began gradually during the Chia-ch'ing (1796–1820) and Tao-kuang periods (1821–1850) of the Ch'ing Dynasty. By the late Ch'ing, scholars like Chang Ping-lin even held that "records kept in non-Confucian texts are more reliable [than those in Confucian Classics]."[13] Wang Kuo-wei was the first scholar to make fruitful use of non-Confucian texts to bear on a study of oracle bone inscriptions. Thus he was able to authenticate the royal genealogy of the Shang Dynasty by identifying some of the king's names recorded in the inscriptions with those in the *Shan-hai ching* (*Classics of Mountains and Seas*) and *Ch'u-tz'u* (*The Songs of the South*), two unorthodox texts whose value as historical evidence had never been recognized by Confucian scholars.[14] Fu Ssu-nien echoed Wang Kuo-wei and proclaimed that as far as Shang history was concerned, the "Basic Annals of Shang" (Yin pen-chi) of the *Records of the Grand Historian* was filled with mistakes and that the *Tso's Commentaries* and *Kuo-yü* (*Discourses of the States*) were ethicized to a considerable degree. "They are inferior to several texts with mythical stories of early antiquity, such as the *Shan-hai Ching* and the "T'ien-wen" chapters of the *Ch'u-tz'u*.[15] Fu Ssu-nien told his students at Peita that, because Confucians tended to humanize and rationalize ancient myths and legends in order to formulate an ethical system, "it is almost true that the farther those [texts] are from Confucianism ... the greater is their reliability. For example, the *Mencius* cannot [in this respect] be compared to the *Ch'u-tz'u*, nor the *Ch'u-tz'u* to the *Shan-hai-ching*."[16]

Meng Wen-t'ung also followed his mentor Liao P'ing (1852–1932) in taking unorthodox ancient texts seriously and pointing out discrepancies between these texts and orthodox texts.[17] Liao had, to a certain

13 On the rise of non-Confucian texts in the late Ch'ing, see Wang Fan-sen, *Chang T'ai-yen te ssu-hsiang*, 26–33. As for Chang Ping-lin's view, see his "Ta-sheng ch'i-hsin-lun yüan-ch'i," quoted in Wang Fan-sen, *Chang T'ai-yen te ssu-hsiang*, 184. Hu Shih perceptively summarized the new development as the breakdown of orthodoxy and the rise of heterodoxy. See Keng Yün-chih, *Hu Shih nien-p'u* (Hong Kong, 1986), 126.
14 See Wang Kuo-wei, "Yin pu-t'zu chung so chien hsien-kung hsien-wang k'ao," *Kuan-t'ang chi-lin*, 409–437, and "Yin pu-t'zu chung so chien hsien-kung hsien-wang hsü-k'ao," 437–450.
15 FSNP, I-807, a draft entitled "Chung-kuo shang-ku-shih yü k'ao-ku-hsüeh."
16 FSNP, II-945, a draft entitled "Chung-hsi shih-hsüeh kuan-tien chih pien-ch'ien."
17 When Liao encountered these texts, he was in the self-proclaimed "fourth phase" of his learning, the main characteristic of which was reverence for unorthodox texts. Liao claimed that during his life he experienced six major changes in intellectual orientation; these he called his "six changes" (*liu-pien*). Cf. Feng Yu-lan, *A History of Chinese Philosophy*, trans. Derk Bodde (Princeton, 1952), 2 vols., 2:715–717.

extent, detected discrepancies of historical records in various ancient texts. His unique view on the differences between the New Text School and the Old Text School was largely based on discrepancies in descriptions of certain identical institutions and rites.[18] Influenced by this tenet, Meng carefully compared ancient texts to find their discrepancies, which he then tried to interpret in terms of regional variations. Meng further reached the conclusion that "what Mencius stated is suspect, while what he reproached [as unreliable] turns out to be more believable."[19] Meng also sensed an ethicalizing tendency in the Confucian Classics, which led him to some radical conclusions – for example, that King Wu and the Duke of Chou were in fact the vicious men of Po I's description rather than the exemplars of the *Analects*. In this case only the ancient texts of the Three States of the Wei, Chao, and Han (*San-Chin*) regions kept reliable records; those of the states of Tsou and Lu (the birthplace of Confucius and Mencius) were less reliable.[20] These assertions were so iconoclastic that Meng later censured himself for "slandering Yao and Shun, mocking King T'ang and King Wu. What mad and perfidious propositions these were."[21]

Meng Wen-t'ung was dissatisfied with Ku Chieh-kang's radical skepticism toward ancient Chinese history. Ku's shortening of Chinese history struck at the nationalistic sentiments of Meng and his mentor Liao P'ing. Nationalistic feelings were crucial to Liao P'ing's drastic changes in his interpretation of the *Rites of Chou*. During his early years Liao was famous for his destructive hostility toward the *Rites of Chou*. But witnessing the iconoclasm of the late Ch'ing, he completely changed his view and praised the text as faithful to the Confucian ideal. According to Liao's unique interpretation of the *Rites of Chou*, the territory of ancient China was extremely wide and its history unbelievably long.[22] With the corroboration of various apocrypha (*wei-shu*), documents almost never taken seriously by historians, he asserted that in prehistorical periods there were several rulers (*ti*) who ruled simultaneously and that those houses lasted hundreds or thousands of years. It was at Liao's encouragement that in 1915 Meng Wen-t'ung had begun to probe into this issue. Liao might have wanted to dispute the theory of the Western origins of Chinese civilization, an extremely popular theory in late

---

18 Liang Ch'i-ch'ao, *Intellectual Trends in the Ch'ing Period*, trans. Immanuel Hsü (Cambridge, Mass., 1959), 51.
19 Meng Wen-t'ung, *Ku-shih chen-wei* (Shanghai, 1933), preface, 6.
20 Ibid., 15.   21 Ibid., 2.
22 On the change from denouncing the *Rites of Chou* to believing in it, see Wang Fan-sen, *Ku-shih pien yün-tung te hsing-ch'i*, 166–170.

Ch'ing, by bringing up the theory of the long, local, and plural origins of the Chinese.[23] With this, Liao believed, Western and other Oriental countries could not compare with the length of Chinese history, "something of which the Chinese can be proud."[24] It was not until 1927, one year after the publication of the first volume of Ku Chieh-kang's *Ku-shih pien* (which stunned the intellectual world), that Meng felt the urgency of finishing up the project suggested by Liao P'ing. We can be sure that Meng did not care as much about the Western origin theory as he did about refuting Ku's radical position. In doing this, Meng also based his work on apocryphal texts revived by the Ch'ing New Text School. Meng maintained that the "odd stories" (*ch'i-shuo*) of the apocrypha were sufficient to attest that there was a bulk of reliable historical data outside of Confucian texts.[25]

Liberated from the limited perspective of orthodox texts, Meng freely compared historical events recorded in various orthodox and unorthodox texts and found that, with regard to many identical events, three different modes of narrative were discernible. From this, Meng concluded that there were three parallel groups of people in ancient China who together formed ancient Chinese civilization.

Hsü Hsü-sheng's conclusions were similar to those of Fu and Meng: texts with confusing, tangled myths and stories were closer to ancient realities, while those with neat appearances were almost sure to have been "humanized" in a process Western scholars call "euhemerism."[26] Hsü Hsü-sheng's hypothesis was formulated after meticulous comparisons of various kinds of ancient texts. He found that there were enormous discrepancies (*pu-tou-t'ou*) with regard to the same historical events, and this inspired him to reinvestigate the reliability of the traditional unitary origins theory.[27] He believed that the unitary theory had its origins with the scholars of the Spring and Autumn Period and the Warring States Period, and that these scholars, unaware of the reality of plural origins, forged discrepancies together into a unitary sequence.

---

23 In late Ch'ing there was a popular theory championed by scholars of the National Essence group holding that the Chinese race came from western Asia and that China in high antiquity shared many cultural traits with the Greeks, Romans, Saxons, Franks, and Slavs. See Yü Ying-shih, "The Changing Conceptions of National History in Twentieth Century China," in Erik Lönnroth, Karl Molin, and Bagmar Björk, eds., *Conceptions of National History*, Proceedings of Nobel Symposium 78 (New York, 1994), 155–174.
24 Meng Wen-t'ung, *Ku-shih chen-wei*, 1.
25 Ibid., 3. That the histories recorded in Confucian Classics had been heavily modified, if not forged, by the ancient sages was a typical assumption of the scholars of the late Ch'ing New Text School.
26 Hsü Hsü-sheng, *Chung-kuo ku-shih te ch'uan-shuo shih-tai*, 303–304.
27 Ibid., 31.

This was not a matter of intentional forgery but of imperfect knowledge of antiquity.[28] The ancients were not, Hsü argued, as omnipotent as many Chinese believed.

Hsü Hsü-sheng was also responding to Ku Chieh-kang's works. What disappointed Hsü Hsü-sheng was the methodology Ku had applied in disproving the reliability of ancient history – namely, dismissing all mythical stories as deliberate forgeries. Although he was trained in France in philosophy, Hsü Hsü-sheng was familiar with contemporary French studies on myth and was well aware that ancients thought through myths. Mythical stories were, he thought, closer to historical reality than non-mythical history.[29] Comparing and analyzing various anecdotes and myths, Hsü concluded that the discrepancies had their origins in the differences among three ethnic groups in ancient China: the Hua-Hsia, Tung-I,[30] and Miao-Man.

The interesting coincidence about Meng, Fu, and Hsü is that they were all responding to the *Ku-shih pien* Movement and that they all viewed non-Confucian unorthodox texts as of better historical value than orthodox ones. The reversal in the evaluation of historical materials helped break up the frozen system of the history of antiquity.

But Fu Ssu-nien did not reach his hypotheses of the plural origins of ancient China through the same means of textual comparison. What particularly distinguished Fu from others was his conviction that there was an eastern local cultural tradition in China. In addition to this, two other sources of Fu's ideas should also be discussed here: the influence of European historiography, which reminded Fu that many European countries had multiethnic constituent groups; and the theory of a Western origin of Chinese civilization, which suggested to Fu that in antiquity there might have been an alien ethnic group in western China.

---

28 Ibid., 37, 304.
29 Ibid., 303. Ku Chieh-kang believed that attention to myth was harmful to the understanding of the history of antiquity. Hsü, on the other hand, asserted that myths were necessary for understanding Chinese antiquity.
30 Chang Kwang-chih states in his "Sandai Archaeology and the Formation of States" that "Prior to or during Shang and Western Chou periods, there was more than a single ethnic group living in the area that is now Shantung, eastern Honan, northern Kiangsu, the northeastern corner of Anhwei, and perhaps the coast of Hopei on the Gulf of Chihli, and across the Gulf, the two sides of the Liaotung peninsula and Korea. Those that we can find in textual records included such tribal units as T'ai Hao, Shao Hao, Yu Chi, and Hsü Fang, and such clan names as Feng, Ying, and Yen; all of them were referred to as Yi. . . . The major events during the Hsia dynasty were the conflicts with these Yi groups." See Chang Kwang-chih, "Sandai Archaeology and the Formation of States," in Keightley, *The Origins of Chinese Civilization*, 498.

Compared with Meng Wen-t'ung and Hsü Hsü-sheng, Fu Ssu-nien paid particular attention to ethnic differences when interpreting the history of Chinese antiquity. His equation went "History is the product of ethnicity [*chung-tsu*] multiplied by geography."[31] "Ethnicity," he continued, "is the most dominant element. When ethnic groups change, then history changes immediately."[32] Ethnic composition was a subject of the German historical schools. A great number of works were compiled to trace the origins of the German ethnicity and to recount how Germany was not caught up in the historical momentum that led many European countries to become nation-states.[33]

In Europe, Fu learned that India, southern Greece, and France had multiple ethnic groups and that conquering ethnic groups were usually culturally less advanced people who adopted the culture of the conquered people and became its protectors. Fu developed this proposition one step further by arguing that different social classes were in fact constituted by different ethnic groups.[34]

After returning to China from Berlin, Fu wrote that his future project would be the "Formation of the Chinese People."[35] The attention paid to ethnic differences led Fu to consider the Western origins theory discretely by taking notice of the ethnic differences in western China in ancient times.

In the 1920s Fu believed that the Chinese were originally from the Tarim basin of Sinkiang.[36] In his mature years he never reached any conclusion on the sustainability of this theory, but he did find that it could not be totally dismissed. Although Fu seldom publicly discussed the theory of the Western origins of Chinese civilization, he did express concern in private that there might have been many Indo-Europeans involved in ancient Chinese history. He believed that during the Western

---

31 *FSNC*, 1230.   32 Ibid.
33 On ethnic history as a major topic in German historical study, see, for example, Friedrich Meinecke, *Cosmopolitanism and the Nation State*, trans. Felix Gilbert (Princeton, 1963), 12–13, n. 8.
34 Fu Ssu-nien's "Eastern Extension of the Chou Feudal System and the Surviving Subjects of the Yin Dynasty" (Chou tung-feng yü Yin i-min) was based on this theory arguing that the Shang, though culturally more advanced, were subjugated by the Chou with the consequence of being suppressed into lower social groups. Fu also believed that tribal names became class names and that later the class names transformed into names denoting certain kinds of people. For example, I and Man were originally tribal names, but because they were ruled by other ethnic groups, I and Man eventually came to denote barbarian groups. These ideas appeared in many of Fu's writings. See, for example, *FSNC*, 643–644.
35 FSNP, II-627, a notebook of Fu.
36 Fu Ssu-nien, "Liu Ying chi-hsing," *Ch'en-pao* (August 6, 1920).

Chou, communication between China and the West was more extensive than we realize.[37] In his manuscripts Fu often speculated that the Chinese ideographs might not have developed indigenously. Following Western scholars, he speculated further that horse-drawn chariots might have been introduced to China from western Asia.[38] In a notebook he even remarked that the Pai-ti was in fact a white European group, some of whom were still active in the Tun-huang area in the medieval period.[39] In another unpublished draft he conceded that the Painted Pottery culture of western China must have been related to Indo-European peoples of the Neolithic period; this was especially apparent from the painted pottery found by Anderson.[40] But Fu Ssu-nien only suggested that there was considerable communication between China and the West. He did not endorse a Western origins theory.

All of this simply reminded Fu that in ancient times, in addition to local people, there might also have been "foreign people" who moved to western China and remained there. Because none of these hypotheses were published, it may well have been that Fu was very cautious, if not ambivalent, about their veracity. Fu's continuous interest in the relationship between China and the West and his hesitation to publish any writings on the topic show that deep in Fu's mind was the conviction that several different ethnic groups might have occupied western China continuously. His longtime conviction that in ancient times there had been a people on the eastern coastal area of China produced the idea that there had also been a cleavage between "western" and "eastern" groups. This was an important incentive for him to develop the hypothesis of the plural ethnic origins of Chinese antiquity.

The "indigenous" versus "foreign" thesis was not new to the Chinese. Hsia Tseng-yu, the first author of a general Chinese history, first recognized that Miao was not the name of a nation, as traditionally believed, but of people of certain ethnic groups, and he contended that the Miao people were native while the Han people were from western

---

37 FSNP, I-807, a draft entitled "Chung-kuo shang-ku-shih yü k'ao-ku-hsüeh." In this draft, Fu argued that painted pottery was introduced from Central Asia. He also believed that the so-called Hu people were Indo-Europeans. After Fu's death, Hu Shih pointed out in a memorial service that one of Fu's ambitions was to send an expedition following the route to western Asia to find relics that might relate to the history of the communication between China and the West. See FSNP, I-1695, an offprint entitled "Kuan-yü Fu Meng-chen hsien-sheng sheng-p'ing te pao-kao."
38 FSNP, I-807. The IHP tended to refute the Western origin theory. See, for example, Fu Ssu-nien et al., *Ch'eng-tzu-yai* (Nanking, 1934), 4; Yin Ta, *Hsin-shih-ch'i shih-tai* (Peking, 1955), 83–142.
39 FSNP, II-910, a notebook of Fu.
40 FSNP, II-637, a draft entitled "Yü kung Chiu-chou shih-ming."

Asia.[41] Fu Ssu-nien challenged the indigenous versus foreign thesis by drawing attention to the fact that along the eastern coast there had been another native group existing, and that this group constituted the cradle of Chinese culture. Fu concluded that there must have been a cleavage between eastern and western China.

Vague ideas about the cleavage between eastern and western China were one thing, but there was yet another piece to the puzzle: which group was in the east and which in the west? Given the traditional Chinese belief that Hsia, Shang, and Chou all originated from the west, it was extremely difficult to make any differentiations before these periods.

At the same time, Wang Kuo-wei and his student were developing a new interpretation of ancient China that was in some respects similar to Fu's ideas. Wang was a pioneer in differentiating the institutional differences between Shang and Chou. We cannot be sure if Fu Ssu-nien had read Wang's "On Yin and Chou Institutions" (Yin Chou chih-tu lun) (1917) before he went abroad. It was, however, not until 1927 that Fu read Wang's collection of historical studies, *Kuan-t'ang chi-lin*, for the first time "with excitement."[42] He was excited by Wang's geographical and ethnic approach to ancient history, an approach that coincided with his own concerns. He found Wang Kuo-wei's pathbreaking monograph "On Yin and Chou Institutions" fascinating, especially since it challenged the old assumption that the "Chou followed the Yin rites" and proclaimed that Yin and Chou institutions were two different systems. In the margin of Wang Kuo-wei's book, Fu Ssu-nien marked, "the various differences between Yin and Chou institutions were due to their different ethnicities."[43]

By tracing the geographical locations of the Shang capitals, Wang found that most of them were in eastern China, while the Chou capitals were in the west.[44] This observation triggered further investigation by Wang's brilliant student, Hsü Chung-shu (1898–1991). Hsü published a short essay in 1924 entitled "Extrapolating Yin and Chou Ethnicities on the Basis of Ancient Texts" (Ts'ung ku-shu chung t'ui-ts'e chih Yin Chou min-tsu). This essay interpreted the differences between Yin and Chou as resulting from different ethnic groups. He broke away from his mentor's proposition that Yin and Chou were from the same ancestor,[45]

---

41 Cf. Hsü Hsü-sheng, *Chung-kuo ku-shih te ch'uan-shuo shih-tai*, 53.
42 *FSNC*, 998.
43 See Fu's own collection of *Kuan-t'ang chi-lin*, now stored in the IHP.
44 Wang Kuo-wei, "Yin Chou chih-tu lun," in *Kuan-t'ang chi-lin* (Peking, 1959), 451–453.
  In this monograph, Wang held that Hsia and Yin were of the same origin.
45 Ibid., 454.

suggesting instead that Yin and Chou were two different ethnic groups and that there had been a great ethnic clash during the transition period of Yin and Chou. The institutional differences described by Wang Kuo-wei in fact reflected ethnic clashes, but the later Chou people covered this fact up, and Confucians invented the theory of "consoling the people and punishing the guilty [i.e., the Shang people]" (*tiao-min-fa-tsui*) to explain this dynastic shift.[46]

The views of Wang and Hsü confirmed what Fu had been suspecting for several years. In 1924 Fu wrote that "The grand enlightenment of Chinese culture in the transition period between Yin and Chou might have had something to do with ethnic [problems]. In sum, Chinese history and Chinese ethnic variation are very much worth studying."[47] In the letter responding to Ku Chieh-kang, started in January 1924 and not even finished in October 1926, Fu stated that the ancestors of the Chou people might have been the Jung or Ti, who were not native:

I suspect that Chinese culture gradually spread from the east to the west [and not vice versa]. The area of the Nine Rivers [Chiu-ho], the Chi and Huai Rivers, and the area between the Shantung and Liaotung Peninsulas connecting eastern Honan is the cradle of Chinese culture. Because of the rise of the Shang, this culture moved one step westward. Because of the rise of the Chou, [this culture] spread one step further westward. Otherwise, why were there so many ancient kingdoms in this area? Ch'i might also have been a strong ethnic group with origins outside China.[48]

Fu wondered: "After all, who were the Chu Hsia and who were the Jung and Ti?"[49] He concluded that historians should realize that the Chinese are not composed of one ethnic group or one culture.[50]

In 1927 Fu read Hsü Chung-shu's essay and learned that Hsü also contended that Yin and Chou were two different ethnic groups.[51] Hsü's article strengthened Fu's confidence in his hypothesis. In 1928, when he was lecturing in Kwangchow, Fu asserted in a printed syllabus that

---

46 Hsü Chung-shu, "Ts'ung ku-shu chung t'ui-ts'e chih Yin Chou min-tsu," *Ch'ing-hua kuo-hsüeh lun-ts'ung*, 1:1 (1927), 109–113.
47 *FSNC*, 1550.
48 *FSNC*, 1534. The ancient *Chiu-ho* was the hundreds of square miles of coastal area around Pohai.
49 *FSNC*, 1535. 50 Ibid.
51 *FSNC*, 998–999. Fu and Hsü came up with similar ideas almost simultaneously. But Fu's propositions were raised only in a hypothetical way, while Hsü expressed them with more confidence. Surprisingly, far away in Szechwan, Meng Wen-t'ung was undertaking similar investigations in 1927. See Meng Wen-t'ung, *Ku-shih chen-wei*, preface, 1.

"Yin and Chou were not of the same ethnicity."[52] Fu started writing his long article, the "East-West Theory of I and Hsia" (I Hsia tung hsi shuo), the next year.

During his work on this project Fu also produced an important article entitled "On the Greater and Lesser Eastern [China]" (Ta-tung hsiao-tung shuo), which strengthened Fu's conviction that Shang and Chou belonged to different ethnic groups. In this article he argued that it took several hundred years for the Chou people to thoroughly dominate the Shang; this was a painful process of conquering and employing cautious strategies to consolidate all newly acquired land. This painstaking task was evidenced by the fact that the seats of some enfeoffed kingdoms were moved step by step from the west to the east.[53] Fu even asserted that land east of Loyang was not totally "Chou-ized" (*Chou-hua*) until the end of the Western Chou.[54] This project led Fu to believe that the Chou must have been dealing with different ethnic groups.[55]

Although Fu and Hsü Chung-shu reached the same conclusion simultaneously, the latter produced only a short essay whereas the former presented his case with elaborate argumentation and extensive data. Fu did not, however, choose to publicize his hypothesis until archaeological findings could be obtained to substantiate it. The archaeological finding that supported Fu's hypothesis was the excavation at Ch'eng-tzu-yai, Shantung.

Fu's upbringing in Shantung exposed him to local traditions, customs, and modes of worship, all of which left him with the vivid impression that the ancient Shantung area must have been the center of an indigenous Chinese culture that differed much from that of western China, though western cultural elements had long been superimposed on the original local culture.[56] An archaeological team had been sent by Fu to

---

52 *FSNC*, 27. This point is still in dispute. One of the reasons why Fu believed that Shang and Chou were two different ethnic groups is that he found some grammatical problems in some early Chou texts and assumed that this was because the Chou people had only recently adopted the Shang language and had not yet mastered it. See FSNP, I-244, a notebook of 1930s. I believe that this was a preparatory outline for the *I Hsia tung hsi shuo*. According to these notes, the original title of this treatise was *Yü Hsia liang-hsi shuo*.

53 Wang Yü-ch'üan was inspired by Fu's theory that the states of Lu, Ch'i, and Yen were first enfeoffed in Honan and only later moved to Shantung and Hopei to date early Ch'i knife coins in the first part of the ninth century B.C. See Wang Yü-ch'üan, *Early Chinese Coinage* (New York, 1951), 150–153. On their correspondence concerning this topic, see FSNP, III-976, 977, 978, three letters from Wang to Fu.

54 FSNP, I-224, a notebook of the 1930s.   55 *FSNC*, 754–755.

56 Fu's hometown of Liao-ch'eng is very close to Ch'ü-fu, the ancient cultural center of K'ung-sang. Local worship also inspired Fu to make the distinction between Shang and Chou. Fu found in Shantung that the Shang general, Huang Fei-hu (Fei Lien), who

the coastal Shantung area to find the traces of this indigenous culture. The team worked especially in P'ing-ling and Lin-tzu areas.[57] He expected that these areas would have cultures that differed from those of Shansi and western Honan, where the Yang-shao painted pottery was found and which was suspected to be of western Asian provenance.

The thrilling moment came in 1930, when a major excavation at Ch'eng-tzu-yai in Lungshan, Shantung, went a long way toward substantiating his dream. For the first time a large amount of black pottery was found; the culture that produced this pottery proved to be different from the Painted Pottery culture of western China. It was named the Lungshan culture.[58] Fu's hypothesis, proposed in 1924, that there must be an indigenous culture originating in the area around Shantung and the Liaotung Peninsula was finally vindicated.

The findings at Ch'eng-tzu-yai included rampart walls, oracle bones, and black pottery.[59] The former two were the same as the findings at Yin-hsü and had not been found in any of the Yang-shao sites.[60] An assumption emerged in Fu's mind that oracle bone divination must have been a long-standing tradition in eastern China. In the Ch'eng-tzu-yai excavation it was also found that a Shang stratum was right on top of the Black Pottery stratum, and from this Fu concluded that there was a very close if not identical relationship between the Shang and the Black Pottery culture.[61] This finding must have thrilled Fu because he had assumed that the Shang people were from Manchuria and later conquered the I people; the cultural layers seemed to suggest a similar story.

In 1935 Fu Ssu-nien published the "East-West Theory of I and Hsia," in which he suggested that prior to the Chin Dynasty (266–316) there was only an east-west division and that the north-south division occurred

allegedly had been chased and killed by a Chou army in the Shantung area, was widely worshiped by the common people, while the worship of King Wen of Chou was only occasional and was only encouraged by the literati. See *FSNC*, 902.
57 *FSNC*, 944.
58 The investigation bore fruit by accident; when Wu Chin-ting (1901–1948) visited Lungshan, he came across some relics on the top of a city wall. Wu, Fu Ssu-nien, and other members of the IHP immediately sensed the meaning and significance of the scattered potsherds.
59 Fu Ssu-nien et al , *Ch'eng-tzu-yai*, 26–89. The publication of this archaeological report was, according to Hsia Nai, the most important event in the history of Chinese modern archaeology. See Hsia Nai, "Liang Ssu-yung chuan-lüeh," in *Chung-kuo hsien-tai she-hui k'o-hsüeh-chia chuan-lüeh* (Shansi, 1985), 7:377.
60 This assumption was proved wrong. In the 1950s black pottery was found in several Yang-shao culture sites. See Chang Kwang-chih, "Yin Shang wen-ming ch'i-yüan yen-chiu shang te i-ko kuan-chien wen-t'i," in Tu Cheng-sheng, ed., *Chung-kuo shang-ku-shih lun-wen hsüan-chi* (Taipei, 1979), 2 vols., 1:273.
61 "Shih-yü-so fa-chan-shih," 332, 334.

thereafter. The distinction roughly coincided with geographical variations, and a line could be drawn along the P'ing-Han Railway. East of it is a vast plain, while to the west is a vast mountainous area. Geography was seen as the key to understanding the formation of cultural differences.

The confrontation of the east and the west was thus the driving force behind the history of the Three Dynasties. During the Hsia Dynasty and the combat between I and Hsia, the I were in the east and the Hsia in the west. In the Shang Dynasty, the confrontation was between Shang in the east and Hsia in the west. Later, the Chou rose up in the west and conquered the Shang, again a confrontation between the east and the west.[62] In these confrontations there were vicissitudes of the east and west respectively, but in general the east seldom scored victories and the west usually prevailed. The reasons for this were many. Generally speaking, the economy of the east was robust, as was its culture. The west, however, was militarily stronger. After subjugation, the Chou became the guardian of the eastern culture. Fu reminded his readers that despite the vicissitudes of the east and the west, the cultural center was always in the east, in the Ch'i and Lu (Shantung) area.[63]

But Shang culture was, according to Fu, adopted from the local people, the subjugated Tung-I. Fu repeatedly asserted that the I people had made enormous contributions to Chinese civilization. He suggested that the most important place in ancient China was K'ung-sang or modern Ch'ü-fu, the headquarters of the ancient I people and the capital of Shao Hao and Hou-i. When the Duke of Chou dispatched his eastward expeditionary army, the enemy he pursued, the An, resided there. The native son I Yin cunningly used local wisdom to serve T'ang of Shang and help them to conquer successfully the Hsia. Hundreds of years later another native son, Confucius, skillfully wove the local traditions into Confucianism.[64]

Fu repeatedly emphasized that even down to the Ch'in and Han the dominant culture elements still emanated from this area. Both the Ch'i and Lu cultures dominated the Han Empire with systems of thought such as the Five Elements theory (*wu-hsing*) and Confucianism.[65] Fu believed that after the Chou conquest of eastern China the Chou excluded the I people from the Confucian records. The Chou people

---

62 *FSNC*, 887.   63 *FSNC*, 889.   64 *FSNC*, 882, 890, 892.
65 *FSNC*, 902–903. Fu seemed to have hoped to answer several nagging questions by tracing cultural origins back to the I. Why, for example, was there suddenly a pre-Ch'in period of cultural blossoming without any traceable origins?

Plural Origins of Chinese Civilization

ended up concluding that only Yü, Hsia, Shang, and Chou were legitimate dynasties. From an eastern point of view, the place of Hsia in the orthodox historical record might have been replaced by the I.[66]

Fu Ssu-nien was puzzled that scholars had, over the past two thousand years, ignored the cleavage between the eastern and western groups. He believed that scholars of the Warring States Period were inclined to ethicalize history. They amassed gods from different places and times together into a "pantheon" (*Ch'üan-sheng-t'ang*) as did the Greeks, thus erasing the differences between the two regions. The idea of different ethnic groups was applied by Fu to dissolve this pantheon into fragmentary pieces. The moral exhortations connected with the image of a peaceful harmonious world during the Three Dynasties were suddenly shattered; the Three Dynasties was an era of strife, plotting, and confrontation.[67]

Fu also promulgated several other controversial hypotheses. One was concerned with the origins of the Shang people. Fu asserted that they "were not I themselves, though they at times dominated the I people, adopted I culture, and were supported by the I people in their conquest and subjugation of the Hsia. The conquest can thus be said to be an I triumph over the Hsia."[68] As mentioned earlier, Fu even traced Shang origins to Manchuria. Owing to a paucity of materials, the origins of the Shang were so obscure that when Wang Kuo-wei suggested that the Shang arose in eastern China, Hu Shih scoffed.[69] Fu Ssu-nien further developed Wang Kuo-wei's hypothesis by suggesting that the Shang were originally from Manchuria and had conquered the culturally advanced I people who inhabited the eastern coastal area.[70]

The third hypothesis was that I-Shang was the cradle of Chinese civilization. In this, Fu disagreed with Wang Kuo-wei, who after comparing Shang and Chou cultures had asserted that the Chou culture was far higher than the Shang – that the Chou made itself into a "moral group." According to Wang Kuo-wei, the Chou's feudal and ethical codes, the major achievements of the Duke of Chou, were the most significant

---

66 *FSNC*, 883.   67 *FSNC*, 883, 887, 902.
68 Ibid., 864. I adopt Chang Kwang-chih's translation. See "Sandai Archaeology and the Formation of States," in Keightley, *The Origins of Chinese Civilization*, 498.
69 Hsü Kuan-san, *Hsin-shih-hsüeh chiu-shih-nien*, 1:163.
70 *FSNC*, 823–839. Fu's assumptions were supported by archaeological investigation. See, for example, Kan Chih-keng, Li Tien-fu, and Ch'en Lien-K'ai, "Shang hsien ch'i-yüan yü Yu Yen shuo," *Li-shih yen-chiu*, no. 5 (1985), 21–34. On the basis of textual evidence, scholars such as Chin Ching-fang also insisted that the Shang people were from Manchuria. See Chin Ching-fang, "Shang ch'i-yüan yü wo-kuo pei-fang shuo," *Chung-hua wen-shih lun-ts'ung*, 7 (1978), 65–70.

achievements in Chinese history – a conventional idea throughout Chinese history. But Fu disagreed with this conventional proposition and denounced the Chou culture; this was doubtless an attack on Confucianism, which consisted mostly of Chou culture. Fu contended that "All suspicion that Shang culture was not as high as the early Chou culture should be totally discarded."[71] Fu argued that historical figures such as Han-cho, Hou-i, and King Chou of Shang, considered ruffians in the traditional Confucian view, were in fact heroic figures.

Reconstructing Ancient Chinese History

With the notion of consistent forces at work throughout the Three Dynasties, Fu Ssu-nien and the IHP tried to pick up the fragments left by the Movement of Doubting Chinese Antiquity.[72]

During the May Fourth era Fu Ssu-nien was one of the forerunners who doubted the reliability of traditional accounts of ancient history. In 1918 Fu encouraged people to "suspect all that is above suspicion." Radical books such as Yao Chi-heng's (1647–?) *Forged Ancient and Modern Texts* (*Ku-chin wei-shu k'ao*) were singled out for attention, a sentiment later echoed by Ku Chieh-kang in 1923.[73] In 1918 Fu even asserted that only after King P'ing of the Eastern Chou was there reliable history.[74] This view was similar to that held by Fu's college roommate Ku Chieh-kang in the 1920s. But Fu gradually developed ideas and methodologies that were very different from Ku Chieh-kang's. First, Fu developed his genetic view of the formation of the ancient texts. Second, he argued that discrepancies in the ancient histories should largely be attributed to natural causes, such as ethnic or geographical variation. This second idea was clearly at odds with Ku Chieh-kang's belief that discrepancies in the ancient records were due to the fact that philosophers of the Spring and Autumn and Warring States periods substantially altered the historical records to suit their own purposes.[75]

---

71 *FSNC*, 621.
72 The formidable impact of this movement was best described by Hsü Hsü-sheng, who wrote that in the 1920s most history departments in China were in the hands of supporters of this school. Hsü Hsü-sheng, *Chung-kuo ku-shih te ch'uan-shuo shih-tai*, 26–27.
73 *FSNC*, 1417–1419. 74 *FSNC*, 1231.
75 Fu Ssu-nien criticized Ku in his handwritten remarks in his copy of the first volume of *Ku-shih pien* (1925). According to Fu, Ku took ancient myths so seriously that he worked assiduously to substantiate them; and if they were not verifiable, Ku then believed that they were fabricated by scholars of Warring States Period. The copy is now stored in the IHP, Academia Sinica. The growing divergence between Fu's and Ku's views also coincided with the deterioration of their friendship. In 1927 Ku was appointed by his

In 1928 in the lecture room of Chungshan University, Fu told his students that the term "fabrication" (*wei-tsao*) was not always applicable to historical discrepancies. If ancient texts were dissolved from a static system into a process, most discrepancies could be explained. This concept involved viewing texts not as unchanging objects but as entities with a history. In the evolutionary process, scholars sometimes added new paragraphs. Therefore, it was quite natural to find later events appearing in supposedly earlier texts. Fu complained that the doubters of antiquity did not allow for interpolations or mistakes in the transmission of texts. He said that the pre-Ch'in texts were passed down by Han scholars; because Han scholars were far removed in time from the ancients, they were not always able to be objective in compiling their works.[76] While Han scholars did make mistakes, Fu argued, they seldom engaged in deliberate fabrication.

Fu emphasized that it would have been impossible to fabricate many of the things that the doubters of antiquity believed to be fabrications. For example, literary forms should be viewed as the result of development over time. People who believed that a certain person created some literary forms were in fact unaware of the development of these literary forms.[77] Place-names also formed spontaneously and could not possibly

---

old friend Fu Ssu-nien to teach in Chungshan University. Mainly owing to Fu's overbearing personality, their disagreements over administrative and academic affairs escalated into personal conflicts. Fu's evident sense of competition also seriously damaged their friendship. According to Liu Ch'i-yü, the publication of the letter mailed by Fu to Ku in late 1926 was the direct cause of their quarrel. In that letter, Fu made a number of comments on Ku's articles and praised Ku's achievement, claiming that Ku's theory that the history of Chinese antiquity was made of many layers of fabrication (*ts'eng-lei tsao-cheng shuo*) had rendered him "the king of [Chinese] historiography." Without Fu's consent, Ku published this letter in January 1928, much to Fu's annoyance. See Liu Ch'i-yü, *Ku Chieh-kang hsien-sheng hsüeh-shu*, (Peking, 1986) 271. In the second volume of the *Ku-shih pien*, we find that only a curtailed version of that letter was included. Fu Ssu-nien, "T'an liang-chien Nu-li chou-pao shang te wu-shih," *Ku-shih pien* (Peking and Shanghai, 1926–1941), 7 vols., 2:288–301. It is worth noting that in that letter, after the sentence praising Ku as "the king of [Chinese] historiography," Fu said that he himself was lucky because he was not a historian and thus could avoid being a subject under Ku's "kingship." But later, when Fu decided that historical study would be his vocation, a sense of competition may have made him unhappy to remain as Ku's subject. The keen sense of competition was probably intensified after the publication of Arthur Hummel's "What Chinese Historians Are Doing in Their Own History" in the July 1929 issue of the *American Historical Review*, which brought considerable reputation for Ku even among Western historians. For more information on the quarrels between Fu and Ku, see two letters from Ku to Hu Shih dated June 15, 1928, and August 20, 1929, collected in *Hu Shih lai wang shu-hsin hsüan*, 1:482–483, 532–540. Arthur Hummel's article first appeared in the *American Historical Review*, 34:4 (July 1929), 715–724, and was included in the second volume of the *Ku-shih pien*, 421–443.

76 *FSNC*, 62–64.   77 *FSNC*, 178.

have been invented. Therefore, although the names of some Han places appeared in "Yü-kung" (A Modest Approach to the Tribute of Yü), a pre-Ch'in text, it was not necessarily true that "Yü-kung" was a fabrication by Han scholars because the Han place-names could have been passed down from a very early period. The authenticity of the term *Chiu-chou* (the nine divisions of China alledgedly under Yü the Great) has long been disputed because it appeared only in "Yü-kung," a rather late text. But Fu asserted that the *Chiu-chou* could be of very early origin while the "Yü-kung" could be very late. Fu believed that although the term *Chiu-chou* was not necessarily of Hsia or Shang origin (as many believed), it could be dated to no later than the Western Chou[78] and was certainly not invented by any Han scholar. The Five Elements theory, Fu believed, was not fabricated by Liu Hsin (?–A.D. 23) and Wang Mang (45 B.C.–A.D. 23), but rather evolved naturally over a long stretch of time.[79]

Fu also developed some methods for tackling complicated textual problems, most of which were developed in opposition to Ku Chieh-kang's methodologies. For example, authentic texts could contain false records, and false texts could contain genuine historical data.[80] Even if an earlier text was mingled with late records, it could still contain real histories.[81] Fu's most important point was that asking whether a text was authentic or false was in itself an illegitimate question because in ancient times the ideas of "book" and "authorship" were not developed. It was therefore absurd, Fu argued, to ask if an ancient text was written by someone in a certain time. Fu contended that to question the authenticity of a book was to suppose that rigorous ideas of authorship had appeared already in pre-Ch'in times. According to Fu, the proper question to ask in the history of Chinese philosophy was not what the thought of Kuan Chung was but what was the thought recorded in *Kuan-tzu*.[82] Fu pointed out that while from a modern perspective books such as the *Analects, Mencius, Mo-tzu,* and *Chuang-tzu* could all be construed as fakes, the ancients never asked questions in this way.[83] These concepts, for the most part presented by Fu in 1928, clearly contributed to Ku Chieh-kang's decision to redirect the orientation of the Movement of Doubting Antiquity from discussing authors of ancient texts to the texts themselves.[84]

78 *FSNC*, 84.   79 *FSNC*, 142.   80 *FSNC*, 189.
81 *FSNC*, 153. This opinion was shared by Wang Kuo-wei and Ch'en Yin-k'o. See Wang's *Ku-shih hsin-cheng* (Peking, 1935), chs. 1–2. Ch'en Yin-k'o, "Ch'ung-k'o Yüan Hsi-yü jen Hua-hua k'ao hsü," in *Ch'en Yin-k'o hsien-sheng lun-wen-chi* (Taipei, 1977), 2 vols., 1:683–684.
82 *FSNC*, 739–740.   83 *FSNC*, 740.
84 Hsü Kuan-san, *Hsin-shih-hsüeh chiu-shih-nien*, 1:183, n. 43.

Fu Ssu-nien believed that Confucianists modified ancient texts to fit Confucian teachings by trying to smooth over the discrepancies and contradictions and by sanitizing some of the "immoral" stories.[85] Crude and mythical texts were, then, "cleaned up" to fit Confucian teachings.[86] Original historical realities were twisted, rearranged, and systematized.[87] Political unification in later periods produced a major cover-up of the discrepancies in ancient history, and the bloody struggle among the ethnic groups I, Hsia,[88] and Chou was obscured.[89]

Another reason for the discrepancies in ancient texts is found in the historian's own limitations. Fu argued that Ssu-ma Ch'ien, for example, while doubtless an outstanding scholar of contemporary history, did not understand ancient history, as attested by the numerous errors he committed.[90] Fu held that the limitations of historians should be taken into account and that the theory of fabrications by Wang Mang's group should be reexamined.[91] When Han scholars wrote down the definitive version (*hsieh-ting*) of the Confucian Classics and texts of the pre-Ch'in philosophical schools, they made mistakes in their editing, producing many discrepancies, errors, and contradictions in accounts of ancient history.[92] Liu Hsiang (77–6 B.C.) and Liu Hsin were two major figures in this process, for, according to Fu, they twisted and excluded much data. Nevertheless, they were not, in Fu's view, fabricators.

Another of Fu's efforts to redeem ancient history was his search for the social origins of the pre-Ch'in philosophical schools. Perhaps partly influenced by K'ang Yu-wei, Hu Shih in his epoch-making *Outline of the History of Chinese Philosophy* dismissed the traditional theory that the major pre-Ch'in philosophical schools originated in the various royal offices of preclassical antiquity. This view contributed substantially to the rise of the radical suspicion that pre-Ch'in philosophical texts were mostly fabricated for political purposes. Fu did not agree with this proposition and contended that the differences among various professions (*chih-yeh*) constituted the social origins of these philosophical schools.

In the late Ch'ing and early Republican period, there was not enough archaeological evidence to support the view that prior to the Eastern Chou China had a cultural tradition long enough to produce such a philosophical breakthrough. Hence, at a time when the nation's

---

85 *FSNP*, I-807, an untitled draft about *Chi-chung Chou-shu*. Fu contended that the *Chi-chung Chou-shu* was excluded from the body of Confucian texts because it contained chapters held in disfavor by Confucians.
86 *FSNP*, II-630, a draft about the textual order of the *T'ien-wen* chapter of the *Ch'u-tz'u*.
87 *FSNC*, 860, 869, 875.   88 *FSNC*, 865.   89 *FSNC*, 883.
90 *FSNC*, 856.   91 Ibid.   92 For example, *FSNC*, 64.

self-confidence was at its nadir, people tended to believe that China's high culture must have been borrowed from another culture. Fu argued against this notion by contending that during the Eastern Chou there was no superior culture around China from which to borrow. "It is a gross fallacy on the part of the historian," he warned, "to mistake what we do not know for what never existed." "What we did not know has been translated into what never existed."[93] One year after Fu put forth his hypothesis, the findings at the Anyang excavations persuaded him that there was indeed a long, indigenous cultural tradition that accounted for the rise of the pre-Ch'in philosophical schools.

Fu's other studies in ancient history also show the character of dissolving unified systems into the development of multiple processes.[94] One of his most famous works traces the origins of the five ranks of nobility (*Wu-teng-chüeh*). Because Fu perceived that Hsia, Shang, and Chou came from different origins, he questioned the formation of this system and dissolved it into processes of different origins. Tracing the sources and original functions of the five ranks, Fu refuted the old assumption that the five ranks of nobility began as a system during the Shang Dynasty. In this he was certainly affected by his knowledge of the system of noble ranks in European countries.[95] With regard to the origins of the ancient Chinese language, Fu also showed that the usage of ancient ideographs differed in different regions, times, and classes.[96]

Two other famous articles by Fu, "Eastern Extension of the Chou Feudal System and the Surviving Subjects of the Yin Dynasty" and "On the Greater and Lesser Eastern [China]," display similar features. They discuss the process of the Chou colonization of Yin proper. Fu debunked the old belief that the Chou succeeded in conquering the Shang in a short time because of the virtues of the former and the shortcomings of the latter. His hypothesis was that before King P'ing of the early Eastern Chou, the Huai valley was not fully controlled by the Chou people. He pointed out that the political feudalism of the Chou Dynasty was basi-

---

93 *FSNC*, 435. In his memoir, Feng Yu-lan (1895–1990) acknowledged that he was heavily influenced by this point. See Feng Yu-lan, *San-sung-t'ang tzu-hsü*, 217–218.
94 *FSNC*, 959. The genetic method was introduced to the Chinese intellectual world by Hu Shih and soon became a welcome weapon during the New Culture period. See Feng Yu-lan, *San-sung-t'ang tzu-hsü*, 201, and also Chow Tse-tsung, *The May Fourth Movement*, 297–298. Cf. William James, *Pragmatism* (Cambridge, Mass., 1979), 37.
95 Fu made careful observations of the historical formation of the noble-rank system of European countries while in Germany. See *FSNC*, 799.
96 *FSNC*, 634.

cally a system of military colonization. It required several generations for the Chou to consolidate its power in central and eastern China. Therefore, the same political place-names did not necessarily refer to identical geographical places. For example, Lu, Ch'i, and Yen were first enfeoffed in Honan and later moved to Shantung and Hopei. This hypothesis proved useful in tackling some puzzling questions of the Chou period.[97] This long-term evolutionary view of Chou colonization grew rather naturally out of Fu's bent for genetic thinking.

The genetic method or perspective also helped Fu to tackle some textual problems. One of these points was that the basic textual unit in ancient China was not what we call "book" (*shu*) but "chapter" (*p'ien*). After long periods of development, texts in *p'ien* formed from various origins could be compiled in "book" form by people of a certain profession.[98] During the period of textual development, interpolation, abridgment, or rewriting was common, and texts remained open to changes even after compilation. Here, clearly, the genetic point of view is a built-in feature of Fu's methodology. At one time he had even planned to write a book on the evolutionary changes in pre-Ch'in philosophical texts.[99]

Fu's strategy to dissolve system into process did not call into question the historicity of preclassical antiquity as did Ku Chieh-kang's historical skepticism. In its own way, however, Fu's approach also undermined the very foundation of the Confucian conception of ancient history. In the Confucian account, the ruling elite in the last days of the Shang Dynasty is described as indulging in many vices, including licentiousness, drunkenness, addiction to sorcery, and heretical religious practices. On the other hand, the founding members of the Chou Dynasty are treated in early Confucian texts as either innovators or guardians of Chinese civilization. The *tsung-fa* (lineage) system, benevolent government, and the ritual order, for instance, were regarded as important contributions of the Chou. In modern times, the great Wang Kuo-wei still subscribed to this traditional view.[100] It was Fu who reversed this tradition by giving the Shang culture higher credit. For example, he praised King Chou,

---

97 For the influence of this hypothesis, see Yang Lien-sheng, review of *Fu Meng-chen hsien-sheng chi*, *Harvard Journal of Asiatic Studies*, 16:3–4 (1953), 488
98 Fu might in this regard be influenced by Chang Hsüeh-ch'eng's (1738–1801) *Wen-shih t'ung-i*. See *Chang Hsüeh-ch'eng i-shu* (1920; rpt., Peking, 1985), 6, 29.
99 "Hsien Ch'in wen-chi te yen-hua" (The evolution of pre-Ch'in texts) appears as a title in FSNP, I-433, a notebook datable to late 1926.
100 Wang Kuo-wei, "Yin Chou chih-tu lun," in *Kuan-t'ang chi-lin*, especially 477–478. In this treatise, Wang Kuo-wei describes the Shang people as vengeful, debauched, and perfidious; ibid., 479.

one of the most notorious "bad last rulers" in Chinese history, as one "capable of love, strength, and craving" – in sum, "a great hero."[101] But love, strength, and craving were not positive traditional values. This kind of reevaluation could only appear after the New Culture Movement. After studying the history of the confrontation between the Shang and Chou, Fu wrote: "As for the Chou, they had absolutely no virtue; father and son could not live harmoniously. But they were very good in calculating. It is no surprise that these north[western] barbarians had the special characteristic of north[western] barbarians."[102]

Fu's approach to history coincided with his political preferences. For example, as one who had stressed the cleavage between the east and west in ancient China, Fu always preferred the eastern tradition (Tung-I and Shang) over the western (Chou). In the same vein, Fu challenged a long-lasting nostalgia associated with reviving the nation by reviving northwestern China; politicians such as Chiang Kai-shek and scholars such as Ch'ien Mu and Hsiang Ta (1900–1966) were earnest in this endeavor right after the end of the Sino-Japanese War.[103] Fu asserted that even the area ten miles outside of Sian was as poor as a "field of ghosts" and that northwestern China was therefore unsuitable to be the center of the nation.[104] He emphasized that China should take the northeast as its center[105] and even proclaimed that if China failed to develop Manchuria, it would never become a first-class nation.[106] Somewhat surprisingly, these propositions coincided with the antinorthwestern ideas suggested in his historical studies. Similarly, Fu's famous attempts to locate the origins of a distinctly Chinese culture in Shantung seem to have stemmed in part from a romantic attachment to the place of his birth. Nevertheless, Fu's methodological integrity and his insistence on securing proof for his hypotheses gave his theories substance and earnestness that transcended the idiosyncratic motives behind much of his work.

The Influence of Fu's Hypotheses

Although Fu's working hypotheses on ancient Chinese history shed much new light on the field, some of them have now been challenged.[107]

---

101 *FSNC*, 1532.   102 *FSNC*, 1532–1533.
103 FSNP, IV-1246, a letter from Fu to Chu Chia-hua. As for Ch'ien Mu's view, see Ch'ien's "Chan-hou chien-tu te wen-t'i," in *Cheng hsüeh ssu-yen* (Chungking, 1945), 137–152.
104 In a debate on the location of China's capital after the Sino-Japanese War, Fu strongly opposed anyone who argued that the new capital should be in Sian or any place in northwestern China. See *FSNC*, 1809–1820.
105 *FSNC*, 1859.   106 *FSNC*, 1857.
107 Yang Lien-sheng made a preliminary assessment of the influence of Fu's hypotheses in his review of *Fu Meng-chen hsien sheng chi*, 487–490.

His plural origins theory has exerted the greatest influence in historical study.[108] After its publication, the hypothesis in the "East-West Theory of I and Hsia" was favorably received at home and abroad, as clearly shown in the works of Hsü Hsü-sheng, Wang Hsien-t'ang (1896–1960), and Owen Lattimore.[109] Hsü Hsü-sheng later carried out some further explorations along similar lines.

But in the mid-1950s, especially after the excavation of the Miao-ti-kou site in Honan, a Lungshan stratum of cultural relics was found superimposed upon that of the Yang-shao stratum with an intermediary stratum. This phenomenon led scholars such as Chang Kwang-chih to revive the unitary origins theory. But the three archaeologists Li Chi, Hsia Nai, and Kao Ch'ü-hsün (1909–1992), who had previously worked closely with Fu Ssu-nien, insisted that the eastern Lungshan culture had its own independent origin. During the past twenty years, the plural origins theory has resurged and expanded as a result of multitudinous new archaeological findings. These new developments have persuaded Chang Kwang-chih to forsake the Lungshan Expansion theory, which he held for about twenty years. This theory, first presented by Chang in 1959, ran through three editions (1963–1986) of his *Archaeology of Ancient China* but is explicitly abandoned in the fourth edition (1986) of the book.[110]

Fu's plural origins theory was also challenged from another angle. For example, Yang Hsiang-k'uei, who agreed with Fu's plural origins theory, disagreed with Fu's assertion that the Hsia belonged to the west. Yang believed that the Hsia had something to do with the eastern I people.[111] Because Hsia sites have not yet been located, settling the disagreement

---

108 Li Ling, "Ch'u-t'u fa-hsien yü ku-shu nien-tai te tsai jen-shih," *Chiu-chou hsüeh-k'an*, 3:1 (1988), 105–136.
109 *FSNC*, 2644. See also Owen Lattimore, *Inner Asian Frontiers of China* (New York, 1940), 308–312, 318–321, 324–325. In 1941 Chang Yin-lin (1905–1942) adopted the plural origins theory in his *Chung-kuo shih-kang* (1941; rpt. Taipei, 1963), 21. Yang K'uan, the historian whose "theory of differentiation of myths" (shen-hua fen-hua shuo) dominated the later development of *Ku-shih pien*, held that the different versions of Chinese ancient history were in fact the differentiation of myths originating from east and west ethnic groups. Yang was obviously influenced by Fu in forming this hypothesis. See Yang K'uan, "Chung-kuo shang-ku-shih tao-lun," in *Ku-shih pien*, 7:148–156
110 Chang stated that "rethinking both old and new archaeological data has led me to conclude that the Lungshan Expansion theory constitutes important barriers to a true understanding of the ancient history of China. I am convinced that the horizontal interrelationship of the Three Dynasties was crucial to the formation process of the ancient Chinese states." See Chang Kwang-chih, "Sandai Archaeology and the Formation of States," in Keightley, *The Origins of Chinese Civilization*, 496.
111 See Yang Hsiang-k'uei, *Ta-i-t'ung yü Ju-chia ssu-hsiang* (Chilin, 1989), 3–5, and his "P'ing Fu Meng-chen te I Hsia tung hsi shuo," in *Hsia-shih lun-ts'ung* (Shantung, 1985), 151–158.

between Fu and Yang will be crucial to future archaeological investigations.[112] However, there has as yet been no finding of Hsia culture in the Shantung area.

Fu Ssu-nien's contribution to the study of the I was also considerable. After the Western Chou, the I were reduced culturally to a very low status. In texts like the *Analects*, *Tso Commentary*, *Ku-liang* and *Kung-yang Commentaries*, and the *Records of the Grand Historian*, I is almost a synonym for barbarian.[113] Fu was probably the first modern historian to elevate the status of the I and to shed new light on the study of an obscure and mysterious culture. These efforts have continued to influence the work of contemporary historians.[114] Tsou Heng, a leading archaeologist, proclaimed that recent archaeological findings confirm that Shantung was basically of I culture, and this bears out Fu's east-west theory of I and Hsia.[115]

Fu's hypothesis on the formation of ancient texts was also widely adopted. For example, only in his memoirs did Feng Yu-lan (1895–1990) attest that several of his works were based on Fu's hypothesis concerning ancient authorship and textual forms.[116] The validity of this hypothesis has been substantiated by archaeological findings over the past twenty years.[117]

Fu's "The Eastern Extension of the Chou Feudal System and the Surviving Subjects of the Yin Dynasty" was the inspiration for Hu Shih's famous article "On the Origin of the 'Ju' and Their Relation with Lao-tzu and Confucius" (Shuo Ju).[118] Although their assertions have been

---

112 Hsü Hsü-sheng went along with Fu, insisting that the Hsia site should not be in the east. His attempt to find the Yen-shih site (in west Honan) was in accord with this hypothesis.
113 P'ang Cheng-hao, *Tung-I ku-kuo shih-lun* (Chengtu, 1989), 32–33.
114 For example, the basic argument in a recent study entitled *Tung-I ku-kuo shih-lu* was an exact duplication of Fu's perspectives, though it gives no credit or acknowledgment to him. This was partly due to political taboos. See the preface written by T'ang Chia-hung for P'ang Chen-hao's *Tung-I ku-kuo shih-lun*, 13, 15.
115 See Tsou Heng's preface for Wang Hsun, *Tung-i wen-hua yü Huai-i wen-hua yen-chiu* (Peking, 1994).
116 Feng Yu-lan acknowledged this in his autobiography; see *San-sung-t'ang tzu-hsü*, 207.
117 Li Ling, "Ch'u-t'u fa-hsien yü ku-shu nien-tai te tsai jen-shih," 108–113.
118 Hu Shih, "Shuo Ju," *Chung-yang yen-chiu yüan Li-shih yü-yen yen-chiu-so chi-k'an*, 4:3 (1934), 233–290. Hu acknowledged Fu's inspiration in this article. His letter to Fu also attested to this; see FSNP, II-644. Wing-tsit Chan has made a summary of Hu Shih and Fu Ssu-nien's studies, but seems to suggest that Fu's work was basically a follow-up of Hu's "Shuo Ju." See Chan Wing-tsit, *Religious Trends in Modern China* (New York, 1953), 27–30. This hypothesis had been widely adopted in many books. See, for example, Hsiao Kung-ch'üan, *Chung-kuo cheng-chih ssu-hsiang shih* (Taipei, 1954), 6 vols., 1:56–57.

disputed, the hypothesis itself nevertheless continued to attract the attention of historians.[119] It is impossible to set forth accurately the influence of Fu's works,[120] but it is interesting to point out that even his opponents, whether knowingly or unknowingly, often appropriated his ideas for their own purposes.[121]

But the most important contribution of Fu Ssu-nien lies in the rehabilitation of ancient history as a field of study. This was, needless to say, not a one-man mission but a task accomplished by a group of scholars. From the beginning of the Movement of Doubting Antiquity, university teachers, including Liu I-cheng and Miao Feng-lin at Tungnan University (later Chungyang University), criticized the movement from various perspectives. Wang Kuo-wei and Ch'en Yin-k'o also expressed dissatisfaction in their writings.[122] Since the opposition was largely based on controversial textual evidence, none of these critics truly succeeded in

---

119 Scholars such as Kuo Mo-jo, Ch'ien Mu, Jao Tsung-i, and Fan Wen-lan (1893–1969) all opposed Hu's "Shuo Ju." See, for example, Kuo Mo-jo, "Po 'Shuo Ju,'" in *Ch'ing-t'ung shih-tai* (Peking, 1954), 127–156; Ch'ien Mu, "Po Hu Shih chih 'Shuo Ju,'" in *Chung-kuo hsüeh-shu ssu-hsiang-shih lun-ts'ung* (Taipei, 1976–1980), 8 vols., 2:373–382.

120 For example, the article "Lun so-wei Wu-teng chüeh" (*FSNC*, 770–806) was followed by publications by Tung Tso-pin, Ch'en P'an, and others. See, for example, Tung Tso-pin, "Wu-teng-chüeh tsai Yin Shang," *Chung-yang yen-chiu yüan Li-shih yü-yen yen-chiu-so chi-k'an*, 6:3 (1936), 413–430, and Ch'en P'an, "Hou yü she-hou," ibid., 22 (1950), 121–128.

121 Fu Ssu-nien asserted that the more people sensed that they had control of their own fate, the less was their need for a belief in the power of Heaven. Fu's objective was to determine exactly when "the dawn of humanism" (*jen-wen te li-ming*) began in ancient China by tracing the changing proportion between "heaven" (*t'ien*) and "man" (*jen*) in pre-Ch'in philosophical schools. By "the dawn of humanism" he meant the period when people had a healthy and balanced view of what could be accomplished only by heaven and what could be decided by human effort. In primitive times people believed that human fate was all in the hands of an unknowable destiny; this was essentially fatalism. But by the early Chou, Fu argued, the efficiency of human effort was sensed, and this marked the dawn of Chinese civilization. Confucius was, according to Fu, in the middle of the spectrum; that is, Confucius encouraged people to do their utmost and then await heavenly destiny. Fu called this the "Awaiting Destiny Theory" (*ssu-ming shuo*). In Confucian doctrine heaven was powerful, but the voluntary force of human beings was recognized as well. See *FSNC* 636–640.

Hsü Fu-kuan was a exponent of New Confucianism and a frequent critic of Fu, but he also followed Fu's proposition that during the early Chou there was an incipient humanistic spirit. But it should be noted that he leveled a strong attack against Fu in the same book. See Hsü Fu-kuan, *Chung-kuo jen-hsing lun shih* (Taichung, 1963), 15–35.

122 See, for example, Wang Kuo-wei's *Ku-shih hsin-cheng*, especially ch. 1, *tsung-lun*, n.p., ch. 2, and also T'ang Lan's (1901–1979) preface for this book, n.p. On Ch'en Yin-k'o's opinion, see "Ta-ch'eng-ch'i-hsin-lun wei Chih-i hsü te chen-shih-liao," in *Ch'en Yin-k'o hsien-sheng lun-wen-chi*, 2:1343–1347.

silencing radically skeptical historians. Fu and his institute, however, provided powerful counterforces with their careful new archaeological investigations. It is a paradox that Fu, as a former supporter of the *Ku-shih pien*, changed his stand and ultimately became more influential than his former colleagues. In 1938 Fu pronounced that the history of not only the Shang but also the Hsia was believable. He asserted that if there had been no Anyang excavation,

> The theory that prevailed ten years ago (in the *Ku-shih pien*), including such views as "Shang culture was still at a very low level," "that the [Shang] was a nomadic period," "that the [Shang] was still in the Stone Age," and "that the genealogy recorded in 'Yin-pen-chi" [of the *Records of the Grand Historian*] was fabricated," would still have been popular. Although those who held such (radical) views were unable to establish their cases on clear evidence, their opponents also found it difficult to refute them in any decisive way. We are fortunate today because we now have a rough idea of how the "Chou inherited the Yin rites." We cannot, therefore, responsibly dismiss the authenticity of the proposition that "the Yin inherited the Hsia rites." . . . To what extent Hsia politics and society developed is difficult to grasp, but we may be sure that the Hsia Dynasty did exist, that its culture was fairly high, and that its culture figured into the cultural heritage of the Shang.[123]

Fu also tried to rescue the credibility of the *Tso's Commentaries*, *Kuo-yü*, and *Rites of Chou*, three controversial texts that had long been regarded as fabrications. Fu pronounced that "*Tso's Commentaries* and *Kuo-yü* are the most treasured books of the Eastern Chou. Although the final compilation of these texts was made during the Warring States Period, the material they adopted was very early and even included Western Chou data."[124] Fu's animosity toward the *Ku-shih pien* was manifested in a draft of a short comic tale he wrote to mock Ku Chieh-kang and Ch'ien Hsüan-t'ung, two major protagonists of the *Ku-shih pien* who had been Fu's close intellectual allies in the May Fourth era.[125]

However, after the Movement of the Doubting of Chinese Antiquity, nothing about the history of that period would remain the same. Although Fu Ssu-nien and the IHP tried to restore the Chinese historians' confidence in the reliability of a number of early documents, Fu was by no means rehabilitating traditional views of Chinese antiquity. After the dismantling of the old picture of ancient history, the new picture Fu pieced together was very different from the traditional one.

---

123 *FSNC*, 632–633.   124 *FSNC*, 561.
125 The draft has never been published and is undatable. For a translation of part of this draft, see Appendix 1.

Fu was antagonistic to the traditional views and tried to reconstruct what ancient China really was. Although he was not as agnostic toward Chinese antiquity as Ku Chieh-kang, his views were no less iconoclastic than those of Ku.

4
Contra-Introspective Moral Philosophy

Two years after the publication of his "East-West Theory of I and Hsia," Fu set out in 1937 to search for the dawn of Chinese humanism and the origins of Confucian moral philosophy. The project, "The Disputation and Vindication of the Ancient Glosses on 'Nature' and 'Destiny'" (Hsing ming ku-hsün pien-cheng) (1937) has been considered an illustration of the ideal combination of historical and philological approaches, an ideal incorporated in the name of the institute he established.[1] But below the surface of his rigorous study were modern concerns. In the wake of the New Culture Movement, people had lost faith in the traditional Chinese value system, especially its moral philosophy. Many members of the May Fourth generation believed that the weakness of the nation was deeply rooted in its subjective thinking, introspection, passivity, moralizing, and mysticism. For this reason they had a deep animosity toward traditional introspective moral philosophy and thought it the source of the nation's ills. They proposed a positivistic mentality as the fundamental solution to these problems.

Several measures were taken to renovate the introspective and moralistic tradition, and the Movement for Rearranging the National Heritage (Cheng-li kuo-ku yün-tung) contributed to this enterprise. In a famous slogan, Hu Shih proclaimed that what was needed was a systematic critical reexamination of the Chinese tradition "to apprehend demons and beat ghosts." A central purpose of this movement was to dispel romantic illusions about Chinese tradition by exposing its depraved state to the fullest extent. Only in this way, it was believed, could any association this

---

1 Upon its publication this treatise was welcomed by many scholars. In a letter to his son, Ch'en Yüan (1880–1971) expressed his admiration by saying that reading this treatise made him realize how backward his own scholarship was. See Ch'en Chih-ch'ao, ed., *Ch'en Yüan lai wang shu-hsin chi* (Shanghai, 1990), 661–662. Even Chao Chi-pin, a leftist historian, published an extremely favorable review, "Tu 'Hsing ming ku-hsün pien-cheng,'" in *Chao Chi-pin wen-chi* (Honan, 1985), 2 vols., 1:7–14.

tradition might still have with modern China be effectively severed. To use Fu Ssu-nien's expression, after this kind of effort conservatives like Liang Shu-ming would no longer be able to sustain a connection between Confucius and modern times.[2]

The work of this new generation was not only to exorcise demons from Chinese tradition. On the positive side, they wanted to revitalize Chinese tradition by reinterpreting it. Hu Shih singled out a group of Ch'ing "new philosophy" (*hsin che-hsüeh*) scholars as being particularly valuable in this respect.[3] In the same vein, Fu Ssu-nien reinterpreted the history of Confucian philosophy by emphasizing the importance of the Hsüntzu tradition on the one hand and denouncing the introspective moral philosophy of Mencius on the other. Fu Ssu-nien praised Hsün-tzu because he "never accepted any introspective moral theory."[4]

As late as 1928 Fu held that humanity (*jen*) and justice (*i*) were not innate in the human mind but were man-made.[5] Fu held that the human mind should not be considered a repository of truth and goodness and was not the source of moral consciousness. He chose to treat human nature in terms of physiological self, psychological self, and cognitive self rather than moral self.[6] To explicate this moral philosophy, Fu combined the two disciplines of "history" and "philology" in asserting that at the beginning of Confucianism there was no introspective connotation to moral terms such as *hsing* (human nature) and *ming* (destiny).

The Emergence of the Anti-Introspective Tradition

In moral philosophy the continuity between Fu and the Ch'ing evidential research tradition is evident. During the eighteenth century a group of Ch'ing evidential scholars began to develop a new line of interpretation to dispute the internal and axiomatic moral value of Chinese tradition. This trend was initiated by Tai Chen (1723–1777) and followed by Hung Pang, Tuan Yü-ts'ai (1735–1815), Ling T'ing-k'an (1755–1809), Chiao Hsün (1763–1820), and Juan Yüan (1764–1849). Juan's exegesis revived the Han commentary of *jen* as *hsiang-jen-ou*, which simply meant social intercourse between two persons; the internal moral feelings

---

2 FSNP, I-433, a notebook of Fus.
3 Hu Shih, *Tai Tung-yüan te che-hsüeh* (Taipei, 1975), 121.
4 *FSNC*, 697.   5 *FSNC*, 1314.
6 Here I adopt Chang Hao's terminology. See Chang, "New Confucianism and the Intellectual Crisis of Contemporary China," in Charlotte Furth, ed., *The Limits of Change: Essays on Conservative Alternatives in Republican China* (Cambridge, Mass., 1976), 276–302.

involved were left undiscussed.[7] Thanks to his high office as a governor-general, Juan Yüan was the most powerful advocate in this new movement, which he pushed to its peak. The purpose of the new thinking was to supplant the key ideas propounded by Sung and Ming Neo-Confucianists and restore the original meanings to the terms. Han classical studies were widely cited in an attempt to articulate a new moral vision.

When Tai Chen first published his magnum opus, *Evidential Analysis of the Meaning of Terms in the Mencius* (*Meng-tzu tzu-i shu-cheng*), among his friends and students only Hung Pang really appreciated it. But by Juan Yüan's time, Tai's style had gained popularity and was widely emulated by first-rate scholars. The new wave developed with such rapidity and force that it stunned many scholars sympathetic to Neo-Confucianism. Fang Tung-shu (1772–1851), Tseng Kuo-fan (1811–1872), Chu I-hsin (1846–1894), and many others criticized this new philosophy for replacing the meanings of *hsin* (mind), *hsing*, *jen*, and *i* given by Chu Hsi (1130–1200) with his own proponents, and also for its intolerance toward anyone who defended Neo-Confucian discourse on the moral quality of mind.[8]

The hostility toward introspective moral philosophy was not only continued but also intensified in the New Culture Movement. People rebelled against the idea of the sage and argued that the human mind was no different in kind from a monkey's.[9]

The Debate Over Science and the Philosophy of Life (K'o-hsüeh yü jen-sheng-kuan lun-chan) in 1923 was a showdown between two antagonistic groups. The "Scientist Group" armed itself with positivism, especially the brand of positivism propounded by Ernst Mach,[10] while the other group insisted on the need for a Neo-Confucian metaphysics as the basis of the moral interpretation of human life. As the debate raged, it soon became obvious that the "Scientist Group" had scored a landslide victory. Nevertheless, the introspective moral tradition still flourished in the 1920s. Hu Shih observed in 1924 that there was a rehabilitation of the traditional introspective moral philosophy. Hu found that the adherents of the philosophy were advocating "inner life,"

---

7 Juan Yüan, "Lun-yü lun jen lun," in *Yen-ching-shih chi* (Taipei, 1964), 3 vols., 1:173.
8 Chu I-hsin said that Tai Chen never forbade people to mention *hsin*, but he did admit that whoever touched upon the issue of *hsin* was quickly scolded. Ch'ien Mu has made a summary of Chu's ideas. See Ch'ien's *Chung-kuo chin san-pai-nien hsüeh-shu-shih*, 4th ed. (Taipei, 1968), 2 vols., 2:624–625.
9 For example, Wu Ching-heng, "I-ke hsin hsin-yang te yü-chou-kuan chi jen-sheng-kuan," in *Wu Ching-heng hsüan-chi* (Taipei, 1967), 10 vols., *che-hsüeh* volume, 11–128, especially 22–34. As mentioned in Chapter 1, Fu Ssu-nien also believed that the quality of the human mind was as low as that of any creature.
10 D. W. Y. Kwok, *Scientism in Chinese Thought, 1900–1950* (New Haven, 1965), especially ch. 6.

In Europe, Fu's antiintrospective attitude toward moral philosophy was reinforced. John Watson's (1878–1958) abhorrence of the subjectivism of introspective psychology reinforced Fu's distaste for the traditional Chinese philosophy of mind.[14]

What is more, Fu believed that savagism could be an alternative path for China's future. Ch'en Tu-hsiu had promoted animalism and savagism during the New Culture Movement,[15] and this made a deep impression on the young Fu Ssu-nien. Fu later constantly recollected that Ch'en Tu-hsiu's great contribution to modern China was his advocacy of an ethical revolution in China. This was based, however, on savagism. "What is savagism?" Fu quoted Ch'en's comments about a savage: "his will power is obstinate and fierce. He is a good fighter who never bends; his health is robust enough to confront [the challenges of] nature. [Savage people] only count on their instincts, and rely on no others for their judgments. They are loyal to their true selves and do not cover themselves up."[16] Ch'en Tu-hsiu believed that undue emphasis on humaneness had made China a decadent and degenerate nation.[17] The savagists called for the annihilation of the nation's introspective moral tradition because they believed it had produced the nation's weakness. The revival of Friedrich Nietzsche's (1844–1900) theory during his study in Germany must have strengthened Fu's belief in savagism. Thus, at the end of 1926 Fu even told Hu Shih in Paris that savagism could be a powerful medicine for the nation's ills. They both agreed that human history was ironic – when people live in a savage society, they need to develop a system of rules to define and prescribe their own activities, and this in turn helps to create a civilized society.[18] In a letter written the next year, Fu repeated to Wu Chih-hui and Tai Chi-t'ao (1891–1949) that his ultimate goal was to educate the students of the Humanities School at Chungshan University to follow "savagism" as an antidote to an overcivilized China. Fu's only goal as dean of the School of Letters was, as he himself admitted, to train several teachers of Chinese and not to encourage Chinese learning.[19]

14 Cf. Edwards, *The Encyclopedia of Philosophy*, 1:268. On Fu's exposure to Watson's work, see a letter from Fu to Chao Yüan-jen, FSNP, III-195.
15 Ch'en Tu-hsiu, "Chin-jih chih chiao-yü fang-cheng," in *Ch'en Tu-hsiu chu-tso hsüan*, 1:145–146.
16 *FSNC*, 1647.
17 Ch'en Tu-hsiu, "Chin-jih chih chiao-yü fang-chen," in *Ch'en Tu-hsiu chu-tso hsüan*, 1:146. In their conversation in 1926, Hu Shih also wholeheartedly agreed with Fu Ssu-nien's "savagism." See FSNP, I-1678, Hu Shih to Fu. It is worth noting that John Dewey also told Chinese students in 1924 that "China is overcivilized." See Hsiao Kung-ch'üan, *Wen-hsüeh chien-wang lu* (Taipei, 1972), 68.
18 FSNP, I 1678, Hu Shih to Fu Ssu nien.
19 *FSNC*, 2445.

"philosophy of innate knowledge," "pure-ideal theory," or interpreting *jen* as "intuitionism." The philosophies of Rudolf Eucken (1846–1926) and Henri Bergson (1859–1941) were introduced to reinforce the authority of the Lu Hsiang-shan–Wang Yang-ming philosophical school. Hu Shih viewed this as detrimental to the nation's future and said that it was the moment for those who cared about the future of Chinese thought to choose whether to "deceive themselves" with notions of "spiritual civilization" and "inner life" or to choose the more difficult approach of adopting pure reason, continuing the tradition of the past nine hundred years of investigating things, using the scientific method to modify the methodologies of the Ch'ing evidential research school, and employing scientific knowledge to modify the philosophy of Tai Chen and Juan Yüan.[11]

During the late Ch'ing and early Republican era, Chang Ping-lin and the National Essence (Kuo-ts'ui) group sympathized with the new philosophy advanced by Tai Chen and other evidential scholars. Educated mostly in Ch'ing learning and under the professors of Chang Ping-lin's group at Peita, Fu Ssu-nien was well versed in this topic. In particular, Fu had inherited the problem Juan Yüan dealt with in his article "Ancient Glosses on 'Nature' and 'Destiny'" (Hsing ming ku-hsün).[12] The continuity between Juan and Fu is very evident, especially in their hostility toward introspective philosophy.[13]

---

11 Hu Shih, *Tai Tung-yüan te che-hsüeh*, 196–197.
12 See Juan Yüan, *Yen-ching-shih chi*, 191–214.
13 On Fu's negative attitude toward Neo-Confucianism, see, for example, *FSNC*, 1215. In FSNP, I-433, a notebook of 1926, Fu also denounced Wang Yang-ming's (1472–1528) teaching. In FSNP, III-1112, a letter from Ho Ch'ang-ch'ün (1903–1973) to Fu, Ho Ch'ang-ch'ün quoted Lao Kan's words that Fu never accepted any writing concerning Neo-Confucianism to be published in the *Bulletin*. In FSNP, III-911 and III-914, two letters from Fu's student Sun Tz'u-chou to Fu showed that there was a new trend calling for saving the nation with Neo-Confucianism (*li-hsüeh chiu-kuo*). A comparison of the materials employed by Fu and Juan shows that Juan did not use data such as inscriptions or archaeological findings but only ancient texts to support his propositions; this approach reflected the limitation of his idea of "historical data." Juan's intention in writing "Hsing ming ku-hsün" was to read the minds of the ancients when they were writing ideographs like *hsing* and *ming*, whereas Fu's intention was to describe the development of these ideas genetically. As mentioned in Chapter 3, the genetic approach was a powerful thinking apparatus for pragmatist intellectuals like Hu Shih, Feng Yu-lan, and others and was also a sharp weapon for Fu to tackle various kinds of issues. Fu also used it to challenge the methodology of the Ch'ing scholars. Fu found that the approach of both Tai Chen and Juan Yüan was to "know what the ancient sages really thought" (*ch'iu-ch'i-shih*); they therefore insisted on knowing what the sages had in their minds while certain terms were created. According to Fu, Hui Tung (1697–1759) and Ch'ien Ta-hsin, who were always considered to have achieved less than Tai Chen, were aware of the idea of historical development and collected material according to time periods. Obsessed as they were with pursuing the real minds of the ancient sages, Tai and Juan confused texts and ideas from different periods. See *FSNC*, 501–502.

Deethicizing Ancient Moral Philosophy

Fu began his job by attempting to deethicize ancient Chinese history. Fu Ssu-nien and his school have been identified as major proponents of the Movement to Rearrange the National Heritage,[20] a movement that emphasized demystifying and deethicizing the Chinese tradition[21] and reflected a widely held attitude of the period.

Fu was keenly aware that objective historical study would be a powerful weapon that would help free himself from the grip of ethicized history.[22] Archaeological findings served to reinforce the deethicization of the world of the ancient sage-kings. Li Chi and Tung Tso-pin, two major leaders of the Anyang excavation, proclaimed after careful study of the new findings, especially inscriptions on oracle bones, that many moral ideas had never appeared in extant Shang materials and that *hsin* and *hsing* appeared only after middle Chou.[23] Hsü Chung-shu's study of benedictory words on bronze vessels fell into the same category.[24] It was Juan Yüan's dream to trace the "minds" of the ancient sages through etymological study.[25] Yet new archaeological findings turned out to be detrimental to some established moralized ideas, for through these archaeological findings it was found that the ancient sages did not live in an age of morality.

Textual analysis also led to demystification. For example, Fu's closest associate, Ch'en P'an (1905–1999), followed him in tackling the ques-

---

20 See Hsü Fu-kuan, "San-shih-nien lai Chung-kuo te wen-hua Ssu-hsiang wen-t'i," in *Hsüeh-shu yü cheng-chih chih-chien*, 2:143.
21 See *FSNC*, 1301. The deethicization of the ancient moral terminology was preceded by many Ch'ing evidential research works. Chang Ping-lin's works are most illustrative in this regard. For instance, the solemn ancient official titles were traced back to their most mundane origins; *tsai-hsiang* (prime minister), for example, originally meant, according to Chang, servant. Cf. Wang Fan-sen, *Chang T'ai-yen te ssu-hsiang*, 189–198.
22 Armed with Ch'ing philological training, reinforced by the comparative linguistics training he had received in Germany, Fu was intellectually well prepared for the movement. For example, based on his minimal knowledge of Burmese, Tibetan, and Thai, Fu suggested that acceptance of the commentary by Wang I of the Chin Dynasty on the work "T'ien-wen" was problematic. Wang had noted that this title went against Chinese grammar by putting the object before the verb. Fu denounced this as absurd and suggested that putting the object before the verb was a grammatical rule of Tibeto-Burmese languages, not Sino-Thai languages. Therefore, Fu suggested, the *Ch'u-tz'u*, being southern literature, might contain certain elements of the Burmese language. See FSNP, II-630, a draft about the textual order of the "T'ien-wen" chapter of *Ch'u-tz'u*.
23 Li Chi, "Anyang fa-chüeh yü Chung-kuo ku-shih wen-t'i," in *Li Chi k'ao-ku hsüeh lun-wen-chi*, 2:836.
24 Hsü Chung-shu, "Chin-wen ku-tz'u shih-li," *Chung-yang yen-chiu yüan Li-shih yü-yen yen-chiu-so chi-k'an*, 6:1 (1936), 1–44.
25 Ch'ien Mu, *Chung-kuo chin san-pai-nien hsüeh-shu shih*, 2:482–484.

tion of the moral principles (*i-li*) of the *Tso's Commentaries*. These principles had been the focal point of extensive debates from the late Han to the late Ch'ing. But through comprehensive studies, Ch'en P'an proclaimed that the *I-li* were nothing but grammatical rules of the Lu people in the Spring-Autumn Period.[26]

Several of Fu's unpublished manuscripts also attest to his intention to deethicize ancient tradition. For example, in one draft he argued out that many ancient rituals originated from primitive totem tribal practices, which were later idealized in the Spring-Autumn Period.[27] The Five Elements theory, which became mystical after the Han, was, according to Fu, very crude in its origin.[28] Fu's discussion of the *Book of Poetry* entry, "Heaven produced all people; there are various affairs and laws pertaining to them" (*yu-wu yu-tse*), also contained similar secular interpretations; the original meaning of *wu*, Fu argued, was not profound at all and was perhaps a sexual totem. It was therefore absurd to interpret the passage abstractly.[29] The work of demystification entailed reverting to naked facts, an approach that contributed much to the desacralization of the ancient tradition.

Ending the Introspective Moral Tradition

When Fu Ssu-nien began writing "Disputation and Vindication," deethicization was also one of his major goals. His intention was well expressed in a letter from Chang Cheng-lang (1912–). Chang was a member of the IHP who had assisted Fu in his study of bronze inscriptions; in this letter he supported Fu's conclusion that judging from his thorough study of related materials, Fu could be confident that there was no "mystical implication" in the original structure of the character *ling* (order) in the bronze inscription.[30] Chang also felt that the meaning of their work was to help to demystify the philosophical implications of ancient Chinese thought.[31]

Accordingly, Fu traced the origins of Chinese introspective moral philosophy and showed that the idea that "the physical process of living is what is meant by human nature" (*sheng chih wei hsing*) was originally a Confucian tenet, even though in practice it was opposed by Confucians throughout history.

---

26 Ch'en P'an, *Tso-shih-ch'un-ch'iu i-li pien* (Shanghai, 1947), preface, 1–2. The preface was written in 1935.
27 FSNP, II-641, a draft entitled "T'u-t'eng i-chi."
28 Ibid.   29 Ibid.
30 FSNP, IV-295, Chang Cheng-lang to Fu Ssu-nien.
31 FSNP, IV-291, Chang Cheng-lang to Fu Ssu-nien.

Fu held that the character *hsing* (human nature), as it appeared in ancient texts and inscriptions, was almost always in the form of the character *sheng* (the physical process of living), and from this he concluded that in original Confucianism there was only the concept of a physical nature and no notion of an innate moral nature. The origin of *ming* (destiny) was *ling* (order), meaning something ordered by heaven; it conveyed no sense of "destiny." Fu also reminded his readers that the general idea of *jen* (human being) was formed very late and was originally a tribal name.[32]

In a way, Fu was more radical than Juan Yüan. In his "Ancient Glosses on 'Nature' and 'Destiny,'" Juan recognized that the two characters *hsing* and *ming* were both already vital constituents of Confucian Classics, though with a rather mundane connotation. Fu argued that the words *hsing* and *ming* did not occur in the Western Chou texts. Although the ideas of these two words and their current forms might be safely dated to the Eastern Chou, the original writing graphs *ling* and *sheng* were not totally replaced by *ming* and *hsing* until the Han. It was, according to Fu, after the expansion of the availability of writing materials (especially silk and bamboo) in the Warring States Period that people could move easily to amass huge amounts of writing materials for rearranging and copying ancient texts. Fu believed that the copyists changed the former characters to the latter ones according to contemporary ways of thinking. The characters appearing in the present version of the Five Classics or pre-Ch'in texts do not represent the original forms of these texts, he argued.

Taking the character *hsing* as an example, Fu asserted that the forms of Chinese graphs underwent a major change with the addition of more radicals to many characters. He argued that this tendency or vogue led scribes to add the radical *hsin* (mind) to the original character *sheng*, thereby producing the character *hsing*.[33] This all showed that humanized moral philosophy began not during the times of the Six Classics but much later, in the Warring States Period.

Through this etymological investigation, Fu suggested that before the Eastern Chou, the later word *hsing* (human nature) was in the form of *sheng*, which meant the physical quality of the human life and was devoid of any necessary moral connotation; *ming* was in the form of *ling*, which meant nothing but the arbitrary order from heaven, or some other authority, with very little room for human destiny.

When Fu was tracing the development of language, he meant to trace the thought of respective periods. He had German comparative lin-

32 FSNC, 641–644.   33 FSNC, 507–596.

guistics theory in mind, especially the theory of Wilhelm von Humboldt (1767–1835).[34] Fu outlined in the opening pages of "Disputation and Vindication" several basic notions on which he based his study: a language expresses the character of the people who use it; language is a sign of human capacity; language is inner form; and thought and language form a close union. These ideas were repeatedly stated on several other occasions[35] and were possibly derived from von Humboldt.[36]

The philological rediscovery of *hsing* and *ming* led Fu to reinterpret Confucian teachings. Confucius laid a foundation for the growing humanistic spirit, Fu said, but because in the *Analects* only the graph *sheng* was used, Confucius had no idea that human nature was to be defined as a moral good. Fu thus asserted that Confucius never set forth the idea that human beings were born good. He even suggested that in view of Confucius's notions that "in natural disposition [*sheng*] they are similar but in practice they differ widely" and that one should "deny oneself and return to ritual," it was not farfetched to say that the theory of human nature advocated by Hsün-tzu was in fact an authentically Confucian teaching. He even suggested that authentic Confucian political theory centered not in the "kingly way" (*wang-tao*) but in "the way of hegemons" (*pa-tao*).[37]

After reevaluating Confucius's thought, Fu turned to Mencius, stating that "Mencius was a pantheist. . . . He interpreted the way of heaven via human beings in such a way . . . that [he in fact] pushed Confucian humanism to its culmination."[38] Mencius was less religious than Confucius.[39] Although the graph *hsing* (with the radical *hsin*) began to appear in the *Analects*, its connotation was close to *sheng* (physical quality). The connotations of introspective moral meaning in the character *hsing* were later developed by Mencius[40] and do not represent authentic Confucian teachings, he argued. Thus, Fu believed that Mencius's further interpretations of Confucian teachings were not sustainable. What mattered here was not whether Mencius or Hsün-tzu represented authentic Confucianism; the present concern was about what the Chinese cultural orientation was. Should China end its intro-

---

34 Cf. Lo Chia-lun, "Yüan-ch'i lin-li te Fu Meng-chen," in *Fu ku hsiao-chang ai-wan-lu*, 43.
35 *FSNC*, 417–421, 499–502.
36 These ideas can be seen in *FSNC*, 499–501. See also the opening pages of Fu's "Chan-kuo tzu-chia hsü-lun," *FSNC*, 417–420. As for Humboldt's notions, see the introduction written by Hans Aarsleff for the English translation of Wilhelm von Humboldt's *On Language* (Cambridge, 1988), trans. Peter Heath, xiv, xvi, xviii, xv, xxxiv.
37 *FSNC*, 660–667.   38 *FSNC*, 688.   39 *FSNC*, 678.   40 *FSNC*, 506.

spective moral tradition, and should Neo-Confucianism develop any further?

Fu Ssu-nien was about to reverse the tradition of establishing Mencius as the orthodox transmitter of Confucius's teaching. Han Yü (768–824) ardently held that after the death of Confucius it was Mencius who inherited his legacy,[41] and this represented the typical opinion of later centuries. After the triumph of Neo-Confucianism, Mencius's status and role as the heir of Confucian orthodoxy were hardly ever questioned.[42] Fu, however, startled many by denouncing the ideas of Mencius as a deviation from authentic Confucian doctrine. Fu traced the reasons for the deviation and asserted that owing to the fierce debate between Mencius and the followers of Mo-tzu, the former was finally forced by the logic of his enemies' argument to develop an extreme version of absolute free will.[43] Therefore, in every respect, be it disposition, rhetoric, or logic, Mencius did not represent the true Confucian heritage and sometimes was even diametrically opposed to the teachings of the *Analects*. In his theory of human nature, Fu argued, "Mencius was the absolute opposite of Confucius." This fact was well known to Sung scholars, Fu maintained, but they dared not make it widely known. Confucius's notion of human nature reflected the reality of the average person and emphasized that only after learning could people become virtuous. The theory that human beings were born good was foreign to Confucius; the teachings of Hsün-tzu were much more akin to Confucius. Fu denounced Mencius as an extremely illogical man who always "argued irrationally."[44] Although Mencius claimed that he hoped to follow Confucius's teachings, Fu argued that he was actually a product of the Warring States Period and a reactionary opponent of Mo-Tzu.[45]

Hsün-tzu was deemed an orthodox thinker by Fu Ssu-nien. The strengths of Hsün-tzu's teachings were many, Fu held. He believed that the ritual theory of Hsün-tzu was "learning from things outside-of-mind" (*wai-hsüeh*) and not internal learning; it was a learning of propriety and particularity, not vagueness.[46] He also believed that Mencius absurdly taught that "returning to inspect your inner self is most joyful," whereas Hsün-tzu held the opposite view, calling for investigation of all aspects of a case before forming a principle that accounts for all of these aspects.

---

41 Han Yu expressed this point in his essay "Yüan Tao." For a discussion, see Ch'en Yin-k'o, "Lun Han Yü," in *Ch'en Yin-k'o hsien-sheng lun-wen-chi*, 2:1281.
42 There were still some exceptions; cf. Ch'en Teng-yüan, *Kuo-shih chiu-wen* (Peking, 1958), 2 vols., 1:273–276.
43 *FSNC*, 679–680, 686–687.   44 *FSNC*, 675, 680.
45 *FSNC*, 680–681.   46 *FSNC*, 698.

In this way, the Ch'eng-Chu doctrine of *ko-wu* (investigating things) was a descendant of Hsün-tzu's teachings.

For moral transformation, Fu believed that Hsün-tzu's theory was more practical.[47] That explains why Fu appreciated Hsün-tzu's emphasis on "discipline" (*yüeh-lü chu-i*), which was exactly what Fu had called for during the May Fourth period. He said that Hsün-tzu called for restraining the self and reviving rituals, something "Mencius never dreamed of."[48] Fu also concurred with Hsün-tzu in educational theory because Hsün-tzu was an advocate of externalism (*wai-wu chu-i*) "who never based himself even slightly on internal theory."[49]

The pros and cons of the teachings of Hsün-tzu and Mencius reflect Fu's own belief. Fu asserted that the human mind contains only physical matter and no innate source of goodness. Physical elements were the substance of natural things, "while good or evil is the people's choice in the context of human relationships. . . . Nature precedes humanity." It was therefore absurd, Fu argued, to use a "man-made" (*jen-wei*) moral code to describe original nature.[50] Good (*shan*) and bad (*o*) were not, therefore, appropriate terms to describe human nature. "Generations of endeavor were required to transform natural man into civilized man." Because the transformation from the physiological self to the moral self requires immense and multiple efforts, the introspective moral philosophy of setting the mind at ease (*fang-hsin*) is not the right way to achieve moral goals; on the contrary, it is through self-control and external discipline that moral goals are achieved. This argument of Fu's was related to his ideal of "citizenship training" as proposed in the New Culture period.

For many centuries Hsün-tzu's teaching had been an alternative to the Mencian tradition. Whenever disappointment with orthodoxy loomed large, the Hsün-tzu alternative gained in stature and attractiveness. Like Chang Ping-lin, who attributed much merit to Hsün-tzu,[51] Fu Ssu-nien found his ideals in Hsün-tzu. Of all Hsün-tzu's tenets, Fu felt that the most urgent was to propagate the concept that, since learning is always "learning-outside-of-mind," paying special attention to conquering nature could lead to the learning based on things (*wu-hsüeh*).

At the inception of the project, Fu planned to devote only a treatise to argue this point with regard to the pre-Ch'in period,[52] the only period for which he could use the philological and statistical approaches

---

47 Ibid.   48 Ibid.   49 *FSNC*, 697.   50 *FSNC*, 695.
51 On Chang Ping-lin and the trend of reviving Hsün-tzu's tenets, see Wang Fan-sen, *Chang T'ai-yen te ssu-hsiang*, 31–32, 185.
52 *FSNC*, 493.

for solving problems of intellectual history.[53] But he soon came to realize that, in following his interpretation of early Confucianism, it was necessary to reinterpret Chinese intellectual history after the Han period. It is discernible that at the later stage of this writing project (1937) he began to develop a new understanding of Sung Neo-Confucianism.

In the concluding part of the "Disputation and Vindication," Fu discusses the teachings of Tung Chung-shu (176–104 B.C.), Yang Hsiung (53 B.C.–A.D. 18), Wang Ch'ung (27–91), Han Yü, Li Ao (772–841), Ch'eng I (1033–1107), and Chu Hsi, arguing that the dualistic views of human nature held by Han scholars, regardless of their ideas of "combinations of good and evil" or the "dual existence of good and evil," were in fact in agreement with the teachings of Confucius and Hsün-tzu. This was a Chinese tradition and was rediscovered by Li Ao, who developed the dualistic view that a man had it in his nature to become a sage and that the betrayal of this ability inherent in his nature was owing to feeling (ch'ing). This view of nature was later developed by Sung Neo-Confucians into "the nature as found in the physical elements" (ch'i-chih-chih-hsing) and "the nature of moral and ontological goodness" (i-li-chih-hsing). Fu said that the notion of "nature as found in the physical elements" was first raised by the Ch'eng brothers to complement "the nature of moral and ontological goodness" and was the greatest philosophical contribution after Confucius. He believed further that the Ch'eng brothers and Chu had, through this dualistic view of human nature, directly connected themselves to the orthodox legacy of Confucian thought. This new dualism, Fu believed, fully absorbed the pre-Ch'ing philosophers' views without their inner contradictions.[54] Fu disagreed with the conventional wisdom that Li Ao had adopted the doctrine of Ch'an Buddhism to construct his dualistic view of human nature and emphasized that this dualistic view was never found in Ch'an Buddhism.[55]

But Fu believed that there had long been a misunderstanding that had relegated Han Yü's and Chu Hsi's theory of human nature to the Mencian school. Fu pointed out that both Han Yü and Chu Hsi were most hesitant to accept the theory that human beings are born good.[56]

---

53 The statistical approach was employed by Fu Ssu-nien in his *Hsing ming ku-hsun pien-cheng*; see, for example, *FSNC*, 516–534, 539–547.
54 *FSNC*, 731, 727.
55 It was widely held that the dualistic view of human nature of Sung Neo-Confucianism was derived from Buddhism. See, for example, Feng Yu-lan, *A History of Chinese Philosophy*, 414.
56 *FSNC*, 731–732.

He found that Chu Hsi had secretly expressed his disappointment whenever he commented on Mencius's theory that human beings are innately good. Fu pointed out that most of Chu's exegesis seemed to demonstrate Mencian theory, yet in fact Chu was also modifying Mencian theory (*nei-wei-i erh wai-ch'ien-chiu*).[57]

Fu followed Hu Shih by emphasizing that Chu Hsi's interpretation of *ko-wu* as "investigation of things" represented a pathbreaking and significant development in explicating the learning from external things (*wu-hsüeh*). This approach, according to Fu, seriously influenced Ch'ing learning.

Fu's treatise strongly suggested that the long controversy between Han and Sung learning was absurd and that, in fact, Han moral philosophy was the predecessor of Ch'eng-Chu Neo-Confucianism.[58] Fu's view might have been preceded by some Ch'ing scholars such as Ch'en Li (1810–1882), who championed the fusion of Han and Sung learning as far as moral doctrine was concerned.[59] Ch'en's stand was typical of many intellectuals of his time, and it came into vogue in the late Ch'ing. Fu was, in a sense, following this trend. He was, however, critical of Tai Chen and Juan Yüan for their failure to recognize that the dualistic view of human nature had Han origins, a failure that had caused the controversy between Han and Sung learning in the Ch'ing.[60]

In his early years Fu was one of the May Fourth youths who always saw the "devil" (*kuei*) in Neo-Confucianism (*Li-hsüeh*). Twenty years later, when he recognized the value of the Ch'eng-Chu brand of Neo-Confucianism, he experienced a period of intellectual transition. At this time he seemed to have returned to the moral philosophy of the Ch'eng brothers and Chu Hsi, though with his own reinterpretations.

Hu Shih's works "The Methodology of Ch'ing Scholars" (Ch'ing-tai hsüeh-che te chih-hsüeh fang-fa), "Shuo Ju," and "The Indianization of Medieval China" are good examples of a historian's attempts to redirect the future development of the intellectual world through historical study.[61] Hu attributed the Chinese introspective and mystical orientation to the massive importation and assimilation of Indian thought. The tone of Hu's writings suggests that he took upon himself the task of freeing

---

57 *FSNC*, 732.   58 *FSNC*, 722.
59 The call for fusion of Han and Sung learning was very popular in the late Ch'ing intellectual world. Ch'en Li was one major representative of this trend; cf. Ch'ien Mu, *Chung-kuo chin san-pai-nien hsüeh-shu-shih*, 2:620.
60 *FSNC*, 736.
61 Hu Shih, "Ch'ing-tai hsüeh che te chih-hsüeh fang-fa," in *Hu Shih wen-ts'un*, 1:383–391. See also his "The Indianization of China: A Case Study in Cultural Borrowing," in *Independence, Convergence, and Borrowing in Institutions, Thought, and Art* (Cambridge, Mass., 1937), 219–247.

Chinese intellectuals from this non-Chinese intellectual system and urging them to continue the native tradition of less emphasis on mystical and introspective moral philosophy.[62] Fu Ssu-nien's "Disputation and Vindication" also sought to expose the history of the digression of Chinese moral philosophy and to redirect it. Fu inevitably projected his concept of human nature into his interpretation of Chinese moral philosophy. He wished to transform traditional Chinese moral philosophy and purge it of its disposition to quietude, introspection, passivity, and mental cultivation. In "Disputation and Vindication," Fu meant to shake the historical foundation of the "inward tradition" (*nei-pen lun*) by recognizing a more healthy tradition, a tradition that emphasized the investigation of things, effort, and discipline.[63] Thus, what matters is how intellectuals of this generation interpreted Confucians, not whether Mencius or Hsün-tzu deserved the label of "orthodox." To debate which one should be labeled "orthodox" does not advance our understanding of Chinese history. What is more important is to understand the past and present of Chinese intellectuals.[64]

It is, however, interesting to find that in some ways Fu, the harbinger of the New Culture Movement, later became less radical than Juan Yüan. Juan rejected, at least in writing, all of the Neo-Confucian tradition and held that the character *hsin* (mind) appeared in Confucian Classics only incidentally and had absolutely nothing to do with Confucian learning. Fu did not share this radical attitude at all.[65] At least by the 1940s he held, instead, that the Ch'eng-Chu moral philosophy deserves respect. When compared with the attitude of the May Fourth youths who rejected the entire Neo-Confucian tradition, Fu's respect for Ch'eng-Chu moral philosophy represents an important modification of his former stand and is associated with the intellectual transformation of his later life.[66]

---

62 Hu Shih, "The Indianization of China: A Case Study in Cultural Borrowing," *Independence, Convergence, and Borrowing in Institutions, Thought, and Art*, 225, 238, 242–243, 247.
63 *FSNC*, 721.   64 *FSNC*, 224.
65 Juan Yüan, "Hsing-ming ku-hsün," in *Yen-ching-shih chi*, 1:191–196.
66 The change of Fu's evaluation of the philosophy of the Ch'eng brothers and Chu Hsi is manifested in *Hsing ming ku-hsün pien-cheng*. See *FSNC*, 720–736.

5

The Burden of the May Fourth Mentality

The preceding chapters have considered Fu's role in the making of a new historical school, the challenging working hypotheses of Chinese ancient history he promulgated, and the moral philosophy he championed. These three pursuits represent Fu's major scholarly efforts from 1927 to 1937, or roughly the period from his return to China until the outbreak of the Sino-Japanese War.

But during these relatively peaceful ten years, Fu was also forced to attend to several nonacademic social and political matters. There were, in addition to the controversy over Chinese social history, three important developments that Fu confronted after the Japanese invasion in 1931: the rising tide of nationalism; the rise of political absolutism and a debate over dictatorship and democracy;[1] and the rise of cultural nativism, especially the proclamation of "The Declaration for Cultural Construction on a Chinese Basis" (Pen-wei-wen-hua chien-she hsüan-yen) of 1935. These events turned the May Fourth mentality into a burden for many thoughtful intellectuals.

The Debate on the Nature of Chinese Society began around 1928. The issue was how historians correlated their research with social and political events. The rising tide of nationalism and the urgent task of mobilizing the Chinese people to resist Japan after the Mukden Incident in 1931 required a sense of collective worth that challenged the iconoclastic May Fourth youths.

History and Politics

With their belief in linear historical sequence, it was difficult for modern Chinese historians to make a connection between the backward past and

---

1 On this debate, see Charlotte Furth, *Ting Wen-chiang: Science and China's New Culture* (Cambridge, Mass., 1970), 215–219.

a promising future. If the country developed at a normal speed, there would be no immediate bright future, given Chinese backwardness; a major upheaval would be required in order to cast away the rotten past and pave the way to a bright future. Explaining the obstructions away or at least bypassing them would be a serious challenge to a nation so obsessed with historical continuity. To the Chinese, history was like the shadow that followed them wherever they walked: it could not be left behind.

One way of explaining away the past was proposed by Lei Hai-tsung (1902–1962), Chu Ch'ien-chih (1899–1972), and others who argued that Chinese history had in fact developed in a cyclical or circular manner and that the nadir of the circle had almost been reached; soon thereafter, a new and buoyant start would be under way.[2]

Dialectic (*pien-cheng-fa*) was another way to explain the past away. In the debate over dialectics and formal logic in the 1930s, most supporters of the dialectical method were inclined to create momentum by means of offering a possible leap to ensure that China had the opportunity to transcend its predicament in one giant leap, just like the leap from thesis to antithesis. The opponents of dialectics were basically evolutionists who believed that the course of China's development was a linear one. The strength of the dialectical historical view in offering hope to the Chinese also accounted for the victory of dialectics, which satisfied the need for acquiring momentum to transcend the miserable present.[3]

Fu Ssu-nien's contemporaries were surprised that Fu and the IHP neglected to answer pressing contemporary questions. In fact, it was Fu's purpose to keep aloof. Writing history or forging any philosophy of history to answer immediate political questions was forbidden by Fu; only monographic investigation was encouraged.[4] Fu Ssu-nien prescribed that the purpose of the IHP was not to give bright hope to people intentionally but to reveal objectively the nation's past; it would not affect politics. It was his solemn mission to champion absolutely objective historical study and to establish autonomous areas of inquiry. Fu and his colleagues believed that utility was important, but that it should be a natural consequence of scholarly research and not a matter of intentionally twisting historical facts to serve current purposes. He felt that learning for practical use was always detrimental to the autonomy

---

2 Cf. Hsü Kuan-san, *Hsin-shih-hsüeh chiu-shih-nien*, 2:21–74. As for Lei Hai-tsung's view, see his "Periodization: Chinese History and World History," *Chinese Social and Political Science Review*, 20:4 (1937), 461–491, especially 489–491.
3 Cf. Kuo Chan-p'o, *Chin-tai Chung-kuo ssu-hsiang-shih* (n.p., n.d.), 478–479, 499–500.
4 FSNC, 1301, 1303.

of learning.⁵ Therefore, Fu's goal was as Ranke's "Wie es eigentlich gewesen" (narrate the events of the past as they actually happened) – absolute loyalty to historical objectivity and intentional avoidance of any entanglement with present problems. Fu also opposed the history of civilization (*wen-ming shih*) approach advocated by Liang Ch'i-ch'ao, who hoped to find the laws behind the development of Western history and then demand that China follow the same path.⁶

But at the same time, another group of historians strongly believed that history should relate itself to the grand revolution (*ta-ko-ming*). The leftist historians were most conspicuous in this regard. Their social background and attitude toward historical writing differed from those of Fu Ssu-nien and his school.

Kuo Mo-jo, a leftist who served the KMT propagandist organ in the Northern Expedition and then deserted to Japan after the purge, observed that the scholars of his time could be classified into three groups: the "gold-plated" group (those who had studied in Western countries), the "silver-plated" group (those who had studied in Japan), and, of course, the "nongilded" group. The leadership of the academic world was mainly in the hands of the gold-plated group,⁷ a group of historians who based themselves at the Academia Sinica, Peita, and Ch'inghua and were led by Hu Shih and Fu Ssu-nien.⁸ Peking was the power center of this group, which was sometimes called by its opponents the "New Han Learning" (Hsin Han-hsüeh), with the implication that its members advocated objective, monographical, and even trivial studies and published articles in major academic journals.⁹

Many radical teachers, journalists, and young students constituted the peripheral group who challenged the mainstream. Most of them lived in Shanghai and worked in the mass media, in bookstores, or at second- and third-rate universities. Although many of their works are subtle and meticulous, in general they published their studies in newspapers, mag-

---

5 *FSNC*, 1311.
6 Cf. Yü Ying-shih, "The Changing Conceptions of National History in Twentieth Century China," in Erik Lönnroth, Karl Molin, and Bagmar Björk, eds., *Conceptions of National History*, Proceedings of Nobel Symposium 78 (New York, 1994), 155–174. Hsü Kuan-san, *Hsin-shih-hsüeh chiu-shih-nien*, 1:14–20.
7 T'ao Hsi-sheng made similar arguments. See *Ch'ao-liu yü tien-ti* (Taipei, 1964), 64.
8 Ts'ao Chü-jen (1900–1976) observed that four KMT figures who had a hand in education, Wu Chih-hui, Li Shih-tseng, Ts'ai Yüan-p'ei, and Chu Chia-hua, reached an understanding with Chiang Kai-shek that appointments to Peita, Academia Sinica, and the Ministry of Education were to be arranged by the four elders and mainly manned by Peita graduates. See Ts'ao's *Wo yü wo te shih-chieh* (Peking, 1983), 485.
9 According to a survey, through the China Foundation, Hu Shih had considerable influence on thirty-seven academic institutions throughout China. See Hsü Kuan-san, *Hsin-shih-hsüeh chiu-shih-nien*, 1:169.

azines, and productions of the less prestigious publishing companies.[10] They made their commitment plain that they were contemporary-minded in their writing and more concerned with changing the present. They tended to present macrotheory instead of detailed studies of minor subjects and were attractive to enthusiastic young intellectuals who longed for an all-encompassing answer to the country's past and present problems.[11]

In sum, after 1927 two different attitudes toward history gradually formed. The leftists targeted a lay audience and were more prone to changing the present through historical writings, while the mainstream historians restricted their audience to the academic world and avoided involvement in politics.[12] Leftists like Chien Po-tsan (1898–1968) denounced the approach championed by Hu Shih and Fu Ssu-nien and argued that historical study should be rescued from the filthy hands of "slaves of erudition" and returned to the "masses" as a powerful weapon for revolutionary struggle.[13] In arousing the revolutionary spirit of the masses, they could not afford to carry on studies in an academic manner; they needed to play the role of prophets and offer sharp, clear guidelines for future action. That was why Chien openly confessed that his historical books were "field guides" (*chan-tou chih-nan*)[14] and that "the purpose of historical study is not to illustrate what has happened; on the contrary, it is to change history."[15] Diametrically opposed to the evidential research style of the IHP, many leftists published books after 1927 with the word "critique" (*p'i-p'an*) in their titles.[16] This word implies that these works were not meant merely to describe what happened, but to criticize what went wrong and to suggest what should be done.[17]

---

10 This is my impression from my reading of *Chung-kuo tang-tai she-hui k'o-hsüeh-chia* (Peking, 1982–1990 to date, 11 vols.) and *Chung-kuo she-hui-k'o-hsüeh-lien-meng ch'eng-li wu-shih chou-nien chi-nien chuan-chi* (Shanghai, 1986).
11 Cf. Li Tse-hou, *Chung-kuo hsien-tai ssu-hsiang shih-lun* (Peking, 1987), 73.
12 *FSNC*, 1311. Fu clearly sensed the distinction between the audiences of scholastic journals and popular magazines. See *FSNC*, 2452.
13 Chien Po-tsan, *Li-shih-che-hsüeh chiao-ch'eng* (1938; 2nd ed., Changchun, 1949), 4.
14 Ibid.   15 Ibid.
16 *P'i-p'an* was in the titles of many works of that time. Cf. Hsü Kuan-san, *Hsin-shih-hsüeh chiu-shih-nien*, 2:119, n. 21.
17 For historians who meant to change history by means of history or to use history to accomplish "an urgent political mission," the twisting of historical evidence was common. Ts'ai Shang-ssu recollected that in the 1930s Chi Wen-fu (1895–1963), then an important leftist historian of the CCP, privately told him that for the sake of the revolution, twisting history at times was not wrong. Kuo Mo-jo's works were illustrative of this. To prove that the Shang Dynasty was a slave society (a crucial point in showing the applicability of Marx's five-stage theory of historical development to China), Kuo bypassed three chapters of the "P'an keng" in the *Book of Documents* simply because

The different roles played by the "New Han Learning" group and the leftist historians during the Debate on the Nature of Chinese Society is illustrative of two different approaches toward the function of history.

When Fu established the IHP and published his manifesto, the KMT purges had already been carried out. After this bloody tragedy the CCP split into two groups. Partly inspired by Moscow, a large-scale debate on the nature of Chinese society was launched to determine what kind of society China was and with what class the CCP should ally itself.[18] Pro-KMT historians, the "New Life Group" (Hsin-sheng-ming p'ai), also joined in this vociferous debate. It is clear that during this debate all three groups had, to a certain extent, based their interpretations of Chinese social history on Marxist theories. To most observers it appeared as if only a Marxist framework could offer a grand theory for analyzing Chinese history. Fu's historiographical school remained aloof from this controversy.[19]

In the controversy over Chinese social history, most people favored macrohistory over microhistory, subjective study over objective study, and history for the sake of changing society over history for the sake of objectively describing society. In the task of mobilization, leftist historians clearly defeated the mainstream historians. The historical paradigms presented by Liang Ch'i-ch'ao, Hu Shih, and Fu Ssu-nien that had prevailed were outdated by the 1930s. Historical materialism soon became a popular theory.[20] The process is much like the story of the Rankean school in Germany; when political crises approached, demagogic historians such as Heinrich Treitschke (1834–1896) were far more powerful and popular than adherents to the Rankean school.[21]

> Shang society as reflected in these chapters was antithetical to Lewis Morgan's "clan society." Kuo also bypassed the oracle bone inscriptions that would have shown the Shang to be a very advanced agricultural society and not a slave society. See Chien Po-tsan, *Li-shih-che-hsüeh chiao-ch'eng*, 24; Ts'ai Shang-ssu, *Chung-kuo chin-tai hsüeh-shu ssu-hsiang shih lun* (Kwangtung, 1986), 586–589; and Hsü Kuan-san, *Hsin-shih-hsüeh chiu-shih-nien*, 75.

18 Cf. Dirlik, *Revolution and History*, 57–94.
19 Hu Shih published only a few remarks during this controversy. He felt that many of the participants did not even understand the terminology they used. For example, he repudiated Chou Ku-ch'eng (1898–1996) for misunderstanding "feudalism." See Hu Shih, "Wo-men tsou na t'iao lu," *Hsin-yüeh*, 2:10 (1939), 11–12. As for the exchanges between Hu and Chou, see *Hu Shih te jih-chi*, July 30, 1940, n.p. Fu Ssu-nien never mentioned this controversy publicly. However, Fu was not unique in this; for example, Liang Fang-chung (1908–1970), an eminent economic historian, considered the debate worthless. See *Chung-kuo tang-tai she-hui k'o-hsüeh-chia*, 4:261.
20 Dirlik, *Revolution and History*, 41–43, 90.
21 Georg Iggers, *The German Conception of History* (Middletown, Conn., 1969), 197–200, and his "The Crisis of the Rankean Paradigm in the Nineteenth Century," in Georg Iggers and Konard von Moltke, eds., *The Theory and Practice of History: Leopold von Ranke* (Indianapolis and New York, 1973), 170–179.

Historians who boldly answered pressing political questions in simplified, clear-cut, and comprehensive terms enjoyed widespread popularity and acclaim.

In China such pressing political questions included the nature of the revolution, the moving force behind it, and the future of the revolution. These questions came hand in hand. Once the nature of Chinese society was discerned, the last question would also be answered. Many young intellectuals were attracted to the systematic schemes of the leftists and decided to follow their program for Communist revolution.

The success of the leftist historians in mobilizing the youth was not owing completely to their bridging of history and politics. The Marxist five-stage theory of historical development – that is, from primitive communism, to slavery, to feudalism, to capitalism, and finally to socialism – was also a powerful formulation that transformed despair with China's past into hope.[22] In this scheme a backward past is not detrimental to the future at all; on the contrary, a dark feudal past turns out to be a guarantee of a promising capitalist and finally socialist society. The historian's task was first to discern when each period began and ended and in what period China was in at that time. According to the Chinese Trotskyites, China had entered the capitalistic phase, and the feudalistic remnants were of no importance. Thus their current agenda was to strive for implementing a parliamentary system and to wait until China became fully capitalistic to launch a socialist revolution. According to the Chinese Stalinists, however, China was still in a semifeudal and semicolonial stage, and the urgent task was to mobilize peasants and start village riots against imperialists and feudalists.[23]

But the attractiveness of this five-stage theory transcended Trotskyism and Stalinism; it implied that no matter how dark and backward China's past had been, the next stage would be at worst a capitalist society and at best a socialist one. In sum, a backward past was almost deemed necessary for a bright future. Of course, in order for a better future to be achieved, the backwardness of the past needed to be eradicated. In modern China no philosophy of history had ever offered such optimism to such a desperate nation. This theory accounted for the emergence of the theory of the indigenous growth of capitalism, which saved Chinese national pride in a very peculiar way. According to the five-stage theory, a capitalist society would develop after the decline of a feudal society. Some leftist economic historians took great pride in announc-

22 Dirlik, *Revolution and History*, 224.
23 Kao Chün, *Chung-kuo she-hui hsing-chih lun-chan* (Peking, 1984), 2 vols., 1:1–26. Chou Tzu-tung et al., *San-shih nien-tai Chung-kuo she-hui hsing-chih lun-chan* (Shanghai, 1987), 18–20.

ing to the world that China had, without any contact from the outside, witnessed the development of incipient sprouts of capitalism.[24]

But part of the price for adopting the five-stage theory was to sacrifice the uniqueness of Chinese history, and this triggered much controversy among leftist historians. The opponents of the five-stage theory argued that explaining what had happened in Chinese history in terms of historical categories derived from European experience[25] amounted to a betrayal of the nation.[26] But for others this theory represented the only hope for the nation's future.

One of the thorniest problems in assessing the applicability of the five-stage theory to Chinese history was the question of whether the Shang was indeed a slave society. Because of the recent successes of the Shang archaeological excavations, Fu Ssu-nien and the IHP were expected by many to participate in this politically relevant controversy. But to the surprise of many, they kept their silence. Fu insisted that the historian's vocation was "to arrange materials in order for the facts to become naturally revealed."

It was also the government's hope that Fu and his colleagues would, as the leading authorities on the Shang, rebut the leftist historiography. Thus, years later when appeals were made to the Nationalist government to stifle the debate because it was potentially harmful to the KMT, their letters were referred by government officials to Fu.[27] Some of Fu's associates did stand up to dispute the "leftist hokum,"[28] but Fu himself did not respond. In his view, the amount of material available on Shang history was not sufficient to resolve the question, and he maintained that the IHP would never discuss the "historical view" (*shih-kuan*) or "phi-

---

24 For example, Fu I-ling (1911–1988) admitted that nationalistic feelings were intertwined in the formation of his important thesis of the sprouts of capitalism in China. Fu recalled that by means of this theory he could persuade his compatriots that, even without the influence of Western imperialists, China could still have developed capitalism. Fu's work began in 1940. See Fu I-ling, "Wo shih tsen-yang yen-chiu Ming Ch'ing tzu-pen-chu-i meng-ya te," in *Fu I-ling chih-shih wu-shih nien wen-pien* (Fukien, 1989), 47.
25 Dirlik, *Revolution and History*, 81.
26 The debate over the five-stage formulation, especially the question of whether the Shang was a slave society, was continuous among historians in China. National feeling was also seriously involved. For example, Fan Wen-lan, a major leftist historian, was opposed to this formulation for reasons related to national pride. Cf. Hsü Kuan-san, *Hsin-shih-hsüeh chiu-shih-nien*, 1:81–159.
27 When the people asked the government what Chinese society was, letters were referred to Fu Ssu-nien. See, for example, FSNP, I-509, T'ao Pai-ch'uan (1903–) to Fu; I-510, Liu I-ho to T'ao Pai-ch'uan.
28 Hu Hou-hsüan "Yin fei nu-li she-hui lun," included in Hu's *Chia-ku-hsüeh Shang-shih lun-ts'ung ch'u-pien* (1944), 2 vols., 1:1–14. Fu Ssu-nien also kept an offprint of this article. See FSNP, I-1699. As for the importance of Hu's article in this debate, see Lin Kan-ch'üan, *Chung-kuo ku-tai-shih fen-ch'i t'ao-lun wu-shih nien* (Shanghai, 1982), 108–112.

The Burden of the May Fourth Mentality

losophy of history";[29] it would describe history only as the data permitted. When questioned about whether the Marxist theory was sustainable, Fu replied that blindly following or denying the materialistic view of history would be inappropriate; what was necessary was to await more data and studies to ascertain whether it was applicable to Chinese history.[30] When Fu was asked to write a preface for a book refuting the Marxist historical view, he was hesitant to do so[31] because writing such a preface would have compromised his belief that history should be an autonomous description free of political or moral implication. In this he was similar to the view of Kume Kunitake (1839–1931), a forerunner of modern Japanese historiography: "Let us see history purged of the old usage of exhortation."[32]

The Debate on the Nature of Chinese Society, which required overall theory or perspective, was a challenge to Fu because he aimed at establishing an objective historiography that emphasized step-by-step study and avoided jumping to any grand generalizations. Fu's proposal to cut off any connection between historiography and politics became impractical in the face of the oft-asked question, What is the use of history?

Although Fu never participated in the Shang debate, the nature of Shang society was a latent concern of his. From 1931 on he repeatedly mentioned in passing that the Shang had a very high culture, an indirect refutation of the leftist tenet that the Shang was a slave society with very primitive agriculture,[33] but this was too implicit to be noticed. Cautious historical study always lagged far behind pressing political events. Only in the 1940s did Fu's associates such as Tung Tso-pin (1895–1963) and Hu Fu-lin feel confident enough to refute the leftist historians. Tung based his argument on the same oracle bones Kuo Mo-jo had used in the latter's attempt to show that the Shang was a slave society.[34] In his "The Shang Was Not a Slave Society" (yin fei nu-li she-hui lun), Hu Fu-lin remarks that Kuo's assertion, though ridiculous and unworthy of a refutation, had nevertheless thrived over the years. He complained to Fu that while Kuo had studied the oracle bones, he twisted the evidence that lay before him.[35] However, these works were not published until the

---

29 *FSNC*, 337, 1338, 1404.
30 FSNP, IV-8, a letter from Fu to Chou Mei-sun (1892–1963).
31 FSNP, IV-14, a letter from Wu Wei-p'ing asking Fu to write a preface for his book.
32 Jiro Numata, "Shigeno Yasutsugu and the Modern Tokyo Tradition of Historical Writing," in W. G. Beasley and E. G. Pulleyblank, eds., *Historians of China and Japan* (London, 1971), 271–272. Kume was known as "Doctor Expunger."
33 *FSNC*, 632–634.
34 Tung Tso-pin, *Yin-hsü wen tzu chia-pien* (Shanghai, 1948), preface, 11–12.
35 FSNP, IV-833, Hu Fu-lin to Fu Ssu-nien.

1940s – too late to check the momentum that the flourishing CCP had gathered.

It is not farfetched to say that from 1928 on, if the value of historical study is to be judged by its ability to mobilize people to transform contemporary society, Fu Ssu-nien and the mainstream historians were failures. If the function of history is to mobilize young students as the agents of revolution, the leftist historians were obvious victors. This was also the predicament of Hu Shih. Hu's ideal was to "aggregate the intellectual and human power of the whole country, fully adopt the scientific knowledge and methodology of the modern world, and consciously reform step by step. Working consciously, bit by bit, we can gradually achieve the full task of reform."[36] But "step by step" and "bit by bit" were not what people wanted. Liang Shu-ming commented to Hu Shih:

Your propositions stand in stark contrast to the "revolutionary wave" [*ko-ming-ch'ao-liu*] of recent years.... How can you counterattack the "Great Revolutionary Theory" held by many ingenious, knowledgeable, and experienced people? Upon what do you base your "step-by-step, conscious revolution" theory? If you cannot point out specific mistakes in the "Revolutionary Theory" and cannot substantially demonstrate that your gradual reformation theory is more efficient than the Revolutionary Theory, you are not qualified to negate [the propositions of] others and raise new propositions.

You... never present your own observations and judgment of the [nature] of Chinese society.... What kind of society is Chinese society? Do feudal systems and feudal powers still exist? These are the most enthusiastically debated issues. ... You are fond of historical study; you should have some contributions to make concerning these issues. We cannot help but ask you about this. The mistakes committed by revolutionaries represent their misunderstandings of Chinese society; therefore, if we cannot indicate and explain the structure of Chinese society, it will be impossible to get rid of false revolutionaries.[37]

Liang's challenge applied equally to Fu and the IHP. Similar challenges were often issued, and the outcome was always that the immediate demands of social and political reality inevitably overshadowed the more abstract commitment to objectivity in historical research.[38]

---

36 Hu Shih, "Wo-men tsou na t'iao lu," 15.
37 Liang's article "Ching i ch'ing-chiao Hu Shih-chih hsien-sheng" was included in *Hu Shih lun-hsüeh chin-chu* (Shanghai, 1935), appendix 1, 456.
38 For an excellent discussion of this, see Yü Ying-shih, *Chung-kuo ssu-hsiang ch'uan-t'ung te hsien-tai ch'üan-shih*, 566–571. It is worth noting that about forty years later, T'ang Chün-i (1909–1978), a New Confucianist, still held that the New Han learning style of studies made a contribution to the academic world, but failed to cope with general cultural and intellectual challenges. See T'ang Chün-i, *Shuo Chung-hua min-tsu chih hua-kuo p'iao-ling* (Taipei, 1974), 79.

An Outline History of Northeastern China

The Mukden Incident (1931) occurred immediately after the height of the controversy over Chinese social history and signaled that the subjugation of China by Japan was approaching. Right after this event, Fu asked his fellow intellectuals in Peking, "How should we intellectuals dedicate ourselves to the service of our country [*shu-sheng ho i pao-kuo*]?" Later, historians associated with Fu decided to compile a general history of China. But the exigencies of the time dictated that historical works be of immediate practical use. A letter from T'ao Hsi-sheng (1899–1988) to Fu Ssu-nien reflected this sense of urgency. T'ao argued that the Sino-Japanese War was a "cultural war"; when the Japanese army promoted books like *History of the People of Greater Asia* (*Dai Toa minzokushi*), the Chinese needed to have a similar book on the same topic.[39] Fu did undertake to organize a group of brilliant historians to write a general account of Chinese history, a project that would have been inimical to the historical approach he had promulgated in the manifesto of the IHP. In any event, the whole project did not come to fruition.[40] Fu was, however, prompted by the national crisis to write a short general history of Manchuria in order to prove to the Lytton Commission that Manchuria had been an integral part of China since ancient times. Because Fu refused to use the term "Manchuria," the project was termed a history of northeastern Chinese history. Together with Fu Ssu-nien, historians Yao Ts'ung-wu, Fang Chuang-yu (1902–1970), Hsü Chung-shu, Hsiao I-shan (1902–1978), and Chiang T'ing-fu (1895–1965) originally intended to contribute to the project. Owing to harsh criticisms from scholars like Miao Feng-lin on the first volume, *An Outline History of Northeastern China* (*Tung-pei shih-kang*) written by Fu Ssu-nien, the subsequent volumes that the other historians were supposed to write were never published.[41]

The volume written by Fu Ssu-nien ranged from ancient to medieval history and was in fact the first modern historical work done by a Chinese scholar on this area.[42] An abridged English translation by Li Chi

---

39 FSNP, I-1552, T'ao Hsi-sheng to Fu Ssu-nien. I have been unable to identify the book referred to in T'ao's letter.
40 T'ao Hsi-sheng, "Fu Meng-chen hsien-sheng," in *Fu ku hsiao-chang ai-wan-lu*, 51.
41 Because Fu was persona non grata for the Chinese Communist government, the authorship of *Tung-pei shih-kang* has been intentionally attributed to other scholars repeatedly. For example, it was attributed to Yü Hsün, Hsü Chung-shu, and Fang Chuang-yu; see *Chung-kuo tang-tai she-hui k'o-hsüeh-chia*, 5:14. This "mistake" provoked Hu Hou-hsüan to write "Tung-pei shih-kang ti-i-chüan tso-che shih Fu Ssu-nien," *Shih-hsüeh-shih yen-chiu*, no. 3 (1991), 48–49.
42 Cheng Ho-sheng, "Fu Ssu-nien teng pien-chu *Tung-pei shih-kang* ch'u-kao," *T'u-shu p'ing-lun*, 1:11 (1933), 18.

was sent to the Lytton Commission and aroused considerable discussion.[43] The main aim of this project was to refute a popular claim by Japanese scholars that Manchuria, Tibet, and Mongolia were originally not parts of the Chinese territory (*Man Mo Zo wa Shina no ryodo ni arazu ron*).[44] Confronted by this challenge to China's territorial integrity, Fu set out to prove three things. First, judging from mythology and ethnic and archaeological findings, the ancient inhabitants of Manchuria were identical to those of northern China and shared in the early Chinese civilization. Fu thus concluded that Manchuria was, in fact, one of the original cradles of Chinese civilization. Second, throughout recorded history northeastern China had been governed by a Chinese bureaucratic system. Third, in prehistoric and much of historic times, Manchuria and Korea maintained only minimal communication with Japan.[45]

In the wake of the Mukden Incident, Fu Ssu-nien's concern about the future destiny of Manchuria prompted him to express himself in his historical work. Although his treatise later drew much fire,[46] its structure and insights are still considered valuable.[47] The critics of the treatise were almost invariably associated with Chungyang University, the headquarters of a group of critics of the New Culture Movement. It is not surprising that two of the critics, Miao Feng-lin and Cheng Ho-sheng, were both students of Liu I-cheng, a respected conservative at Chungyang University. Miao's criticism was so harsh that even after fifty years, when Fu's associates were compiling Fu's collected works (*ch'üan-chi*), *An Outline History of Northeast China* was excluded on the grounds that it was not written by Fu alone. This was clearly incorrect.[48] Miao Feng-lin wrote satirically that although Fu's work was only several dozen pages long, the number of errors it contained could almost break the record for errors in any historical publication.[49] Miao found that Fu had only adopted materials from the "Tung-i monograph" ("Tung-i chuan") of the standard histories and

---

43 Fu Le-ch'eng, *Fu Meng-chen hsien-sheng nien-p'u*, in *FSNC*, 2631. Li Chi's translation entitled *Manchuria in History: A Summary*.
44 This was a popular opinion in Japan but was systematically proposed by Yano Jinichi in 1931 in an article entitled "Man-Mo-Zo wa Shina no ryodo ni arazu ron," *Gaiko jiho*, 35:412 (1931), 56–71.
45 Fu Ssu-nien, *Tung-pei shih-kang* (Peking, 1932), 31–32.
46 Miao Feng-lin, "P'ing Fu Ssu-nien chün *Tung-pei shih-kang* chüan-shou," *Wen-i ts'ung-k'an*, 2:2 (1934), 131–163. There is an offprint kept by Fu Ssu-nien in FSNP, II-604. Cheng Ho-sheng, "Fu Ssu-nien teng pien-chu *Tung-pei shih-kang* ch'u-kao," 7–18.
47 Ch'en P'an, "Huai ku en-shih Fu Meng-chen hsien-sheng yu-shu," *Hsin-shih-tai*, 3:3 (1963), 13–14.
48 *FSNC*, "Pien-chi fan-li," 1. The compilers were perhaps shocked that so many mistakes and distortions had been made by the "dean of objective history" and hence chose to believe that Fu was not the author.
49 Miao Feng-lin, "P'ing Fu Ssu-nien chün *Tung-pei shih-kang* chüan-shou," 1.

The Burden of the May Fourth Mentality

had neglected many scattered entries throughout the standard histories.[50] Why did Fu, who championed careful research, complete this treatise so hastily that he paid no heed to other available materials? And why did Fu sometimes even intentionally neglect accepted historical facts to fit his arguments? Why did Fu, a scholar with a fiery temper, never reply to Miao's criticisms?[51] Although these puzzles could perhaps be solved in many ways, the most convenient way is simply to note that Fu was a novice in this field and had insufficient preparation for taking on such a time-consuming task. But why did Fu, a scientific scholar, so hastily attempt this difficult task?

It turns out that a project on Manchurian history had originally been launched by the National Institute of Translation and Compilation (Kuo-li pien i kuan). The purpose of this project was to rebut the Japanese position that Manchuria and Mongolia had never been part of China proper. But owing to bureaucratic inertia and red tape, it was never published.[52] Fu, likely frustrated with this delay, decided to take it upon himself to write an impromptu refutation of the claims made by the Japanese militarists.

Fu was probably well aware of his inadequacy for the project, but for once his nationalistic feelings got the better of his academic principles. The mistakes and distortions he made are, again, attributable to his lack of knowledge in this area. But the tension between historical objectivity and urgent political needs must also be considered. It is unlikely that Fu was ignorant of the fact that in past dynasties China had not exercised complete control over Manchuria and that Manchuria had had extensive contact with Korea and Japan. But at a time when Japan had already annexed Korea and had made further claims on Manchuria, Fu decided to downplay the evidence favorable to the claims made in Japanese propaganda.[53] Fu's contention that China had exercised political control over Manchuria throughout its history would have been persuasive only if his readers were exclusively members of the Lytton Commission. But critical historians of China were also involved. Indeed, it would be unfair

50 Ibid., 28. See also Cheng Ho-sheng, "Fu Ssu-nien teng pien-chu *Tung-pei shih-kang* ch'u-kao," 13.
51 Fu's reply to a letter from Lu Mao-te to himself. See FSNP, no serial number, datable to 1941. Fu called Lu's attention to the fact that one of his arguments was mistaken and should not be quoted.
52 Cheng Ho-sheng, "Fu Ssu-nien teng pien-chu *Tung-pei shih-kang* ch'u-kao," 7.
53 J. Ferguson commented right after the publication of the English translation of Fu's treatise in a letter to Yüan T'ung-li (1895–1965) (on March 28, 1932) that "It is very interesting even though at this time it smacks more of politics than of scholarship. One might be led to believe after reading this pamphlet that during the earlier dynasties the central authority had organized control over such an outlying district as Manchuria, but we all know that this was not true." This letter was kept by Fu; see FSNP, II-890.

to say that Miao Feng-lin, the fierce critic of Fu's treatise, launched his attack to help the Japanese invasion. In addition to his animosity toward Fu,[54] Miao contended that, because Japanese scholars had paid serious attention to the history of Manchuria and had achieved much knowledge of it, it was incumbent for a Chinese historian to be on a level commensurate with that of the Japanese scholars.[55] Miao's nationalistic feelings led him to criticize the work of another patriot.

Fu was overwhelmed by the seemingly hopeless task of dealing with the current political crisis while at the same time remaining faithful to the principles of objective study and scientific rigor that he had espoused. The Fu who hastily published *An Outline History of Northeast China* was the same cautious historian of other projects. For example, after finishing several chapters of his *Ancient China and Ethnicity* (*Min-tsu yü ku-tai Chung-kuo shih*), he chose not to publish them until they could be more thoroughly corroborated.[56]

The Need for Cultural Identity

To the modern Chinese intellectual, the Mukden Incident was a most shocking event. Confronted with a foreign invasion, those invaded began to search for the soul of their nation. During a time when iconoclasm and westernization flourished, the first questions that arose from the national crisis were, Who are we and what is our nation? Many conservative scholars complained that the iconoclasm that flourished after the New Culture Movement had caused the disorder of Chinese society. This, in turn, over the long run had incurred the Japanese invasion.[57] Accompanying these questions was a revived interest in traditional learning. It was observed that after the Mukden Incident some began to think that "reading the ancient classics can save China."[58] Many intellectuals simply did not believe that it made sense to love one's mother country by denouncing its traditions. In 1934 the Nationalist government proclaimed its worship

---

54 This animosity had its origins mostly in the abhorrence by some faculty members of Chungyang University for the New Culture Movement and the new historiography championed by Fu.
55 Miao Feng-lin, "P'ing Fu Ssu-nien chün *Tung-pei shih-kang* chüan-shou," 35–36. Cheng Ho-sheng (1901–) knew that Fu's treatise was drawn up to serve the urgent political need to claim that Manchuria had absolutely no communication with Japan. But he felt, as a historian, that it should be as objective as possible. See Cheng Ho-sheng, "Fu Ssu-nien teng pien-chu *Tung-pei shih-kang* ch'u-kao," 17.
56 *FSNC*, 822.
57 For example, Yü Chia-hsi expressed this kind of criticism in his various writings. Cf. Mou Jun-sun, "Hsueh chien Han Sung te Yü Chi-yü (Yü Chia-hsi) hsien-sheng," in *Hai i tsa-chu* (Hong Kong, 1990), 133.
58 "Yeh Ch'ing hsien-sheng te i-chien," in *Tu-ching wen-ti* (Shanghai, 1935), 130.

of Confucius. In January 1935 ten university professors published a "Declaration for Cultural Construction on a Chinese Basis," which asked the acute question, Who are we? Their obvious target was May Fourth iconoclasm. The professors hoped to strengthen the connection between nationalism and the Chinese cultural legacy, combined with an implicit call for more political centralization. This declaration soon received widespread attention,[59] and the flourishing debate over classics reading followed immediately in March 1935.

The quest for a national identity also produced a flurry of terms beginning with *kuo* (national), such as *kuo-shu* (national martial arts), *kuo-i* (national medicine), and *kuo-hua* (national painting).[60] These terms were, of course, not new ones, but they flourished now as a reaction against increasing westernization. Several movements calling for cultural nativism also appeared: the Reading Classics Movement (Tu-ching yün-tung, 1935) and the Learning of the Classical Language Movement in elementary and junior middle schools (Chung hsiao-hsüeh wen-yen yün-tung, 1934). Meanwhile, Kuo-hsüeh-kuan (National Learning Academies) also sprang up in several places. A considerable number of old-style scholars who had been disparaged by the new scholars of the 1920s returned to national favor as transmitters and protectors of *kuo-hsüeh*.[61]

There was much that was ironic in the revival of *kuo-hsüeh*. The Movement for Rearranging the National Heritage was formally initiated by Hu Shih's "Opening Remarks" for the *Quarterly of National Learning* (*Kuo-hsüeh chi-k'an*) and was joined by many young intellectuals. This movement was considered by many of Hu's contemporaries to be unwise. Wu Chih-hui, Cheng Chen-to (1898–1958), and Ho Ping-sung predicted that this would lead to an unintended result: the revival of traditional learning. Wu Chih-hui criticized this movement as "westernized eight-legged essays" (*yang-pa-ku*) and said that it carried on the old learning in Western forms. Wu advised his fellow iconoclasts that the best way to cast off tradition was to be absolutely indifferent to it. Wu contended that as long as one kept one eye on tradition, the old rotten soul would

---

59 On the process of drafting this declaration, cf. Wang Hsin-ming, *Hsin-wen-ch'üan li ssu-shih-nien* (Taipei, 1957), 419–420. It is believed that the declaration was initiated by Ch'en Li-fu (1900–), a major leader of the KMT. See Feng Yu-lan, *San-sung-t'ang t'zu-hsü*, 237–238.
60 The origins of these terms can be traced back in Chinese history; however, they flourished chiefly in the early Republic, especially around the 1930s. Cf. Shih Ch'üan-sheng, ed., *Chung-hua-min-kuo wen-hua-shih* (Chilin, 1990), 3 vols., 2:630, 820–823, 856–858.
61 Cf. *Chung-kuo tang-tai she-hui k'o-hsüeh-chia*, 1:275, 2:310–311. Ironically, *kuo-hsüeh* was a term borrowed back from Japan (*kokugaku*) in the late Ch'ing. In the 1930s, however, most people were not aware of its origin.

come right back. They were all alarmed that this movement had helped to smuggle in the old soul of China under the new term *kuo-hsüeh*. Hu Shih and many others tried very hard to explain how *kuo-ku* differed from *kuo-hsüeh*, but to no avail.[62] In fact, once the new youths began working on exorcising the old evil from the Chinese heritage, they would find that a prerequisite for the task was good training in Chinese learning. This need was detected by a conservative who called for the reading of Confucian Classics and reminded people that one can only rearrange the national heritage if one has good classical training.[63] The unintended result was that in 1930s the old books that had been mostly neglected after the New Culture Movement flooded the market again under the sobriquet *kuo-hsüeh*.[64]

Still another factor ironically contributed to the revival of traditional learning. During the late Ch'ing and early Republican periods, people tended to believe that Western learning or scientific study, if adopted, would replace the old learning. But this was not always the case. For example, although the archaeological enterprises undertaken by the IHP were expected at their inception to contribute to the repudiation of many myths, the opposite result was achieved. Li Chi, the leader of these major excavations, noted on many occasions that much previously dismissed history was vindicated by archaeological findings; bronze inscriptions and oracle bones even bore out the records in many chapters of the *Book of Documents*.[65] When elephant skeletons were found at the Anyang site, the story recorded in various ancient texts that Shang people used elephants was borne out for the first time.[66]

---

62 Hu Shih, "Kuo-hsüeh-chi-k'an fa-k'an hsüan-yen," *Kuo-hsüeh chi-k'an*, 1:1 (1923), 1–26. How to distinguish between *kuo-ku*, *kuo-ts'ui*, and *kuo-hsüeh* puzzled many youths. For example, Ts'ao Chü-jen tried very hard to distinguish several confused definitions of these terms. See Ts'ao, "Kuo-ku-hsüeh chih i-i yü chia-chih," in Hsü Hsiao-t'ien, ed., *Kuo-ku-hsüeh t'ao-lun-chi* (Shanghai, 1927), 3 vols., 1:50–93.
63 Cheng Shih-hsü, "Cheng Shih-hsü hsien-sheng te i-chien," in *Tu-ching wen-t'i* (Hong Kong, 1966), 31–34.
64 It is helpful to take the publication activities of the Commercial Press as a test case. For the first time after the New Culture Movement, several large-scale projects for reprinting ancient Chinese texts were launched in the 1930s under the momentum of the *Cheng-li kuo-ku yün-tung*. See Wang Yün-wu, "Shih-nien lai te Chung-kuo ch'u-pan shih-yeh," in Chang Ching-lu, ed., *Chung-kuo hsien-tai ch'u-pan shih-liao* (Peking, 1954–1959), 5 vols., 2:343–344. Wang's article maps out the trends in Chinese publication between 1927 and 1936. On the revival of old learning, cf. Cheng Chen-to, "Ch'ieh man-t'an so-wei kuo-hsüeh," *Hsiao-shuo yüeh-pao*, 20:1 (1929), 8–13, and Ho Ping-sung, "Lun so-wei kuo-hsüeh," *Hsiao-shuo yüeh-pao*, 20:1 (1929), 1–7.
65 Li Chi, "Hua-pei Hsin-shih-ch'i-shih-tai wen-hua te lei-pieh, fen-pu yü pien-nien," in *Li Chi k'ao-ku-hsüeh lun-wen-chi*, 2:945.
66 Li Chi, "Anyang tsui-chin fa-chüeh pao-kao chi liu-tz'u kung-tso chih tsung ku-chi," in ibid., 1:138. The domestication of elephants by Shang people was referred to in *Lü-shih ch'un-ch'iu* and *Mencius*.

Archaeological investigations also confirmed that Chinese history was far longer than people had imagined and that the Three Dynasties were relatively late. These new findings encouraged Chinese to be proud of the length of their nation's history and to have confidence in the reliability of the traditional records.[67]

The revived interest in tradition even affected some of the May Fourth generation. For example, Yü P'ing-po, the former editor of the *New Tide*, claimed that there would be a promising future in reviving the old-style poetry.[68] A government policy to support an academy for national learning (*kuo-hsüeh-yüan*) was praised by some new intellectuals. Fu's closest associate, Chu Chia-hua, was also persuaded to patronize this movement to a certain extent.[69]

Fu's response to all of this was unique. Fu continued to denounce "national learning," "national medicine," and anything with the word "national" (*kuo*) in it.[70] His opposition came right after the publication of the "Declaration for Cultural Construction on a Chinese Basis" and the Debate on Classics Reading. Fu reminded his compatriots that the society from which the Six Classics had originated and the society of present China were very different and that reading the Classics was, therefore, of less relevance than was generally assumed. He even compiled a list of events to show how, in past dynasties, reverence for Confucianism had often preceded national catastrophe. Reading the Classics, he argued, never contributed to the making of any great dynasty.[71]

When the Nationalist government launched a moral exhortation movement in 1935, Fu promptly published an article entitled "On Government and the Championing of Morality" (Cheng-fu yü t'i-ch'ang tao-te) in which he publicly opposed the movement. He believed that after the transformation of the social structure, a coherent moral code would follow. The moral code the government called for was already outdated, Fu stated, and was thus essentially useless for society. In this famous article he continually stressed that Neo-Confucianism, by advocating "abstract morality," never brought any positive results. He believed that "citizenship training" (*kuo-min hsün-lien*) by means of law and politics was still the ultimate solution to arrest the deterioration of moral quality.[72]

---

67 Li Chi, "Chung-kuo ku ch'i-wu-hsüeh te hsin chi-ch'u," in *Li Chi k'ao-ku-hsüeh lun-wen-chi*, 2:870.
68 FSNP, I-438, Yü P'ing-po to Fu Ssu-nien.
69 FSNP, III-1253, Chu Chia-hua to Fu Ssu-nien.
70 FSNP, III-1251, a reply by Fu to Chu Chia-hua. See also III-1252, a reply by Chu to Fu.
71 *FSNC*, 2047–2053.
72 *FSNC*, 1694–1698. Fu repeatedly emphasized "citizen training" on various occasions. See *FSNC*, 1665, 2057.

In sum, at a time when the question, Who are we? haunted many, Fu adamantly opposed anything "national" and stubbornly called for abandoning national learning. He was known as an enthusiastic patriot who even risked his life to confront the Japanese in Peking, but his iconoclastic stands still puzzled many people.[73] Nevertheless, in Fu's view, there was no contradiction between his nationalistic enthusiasm and his desire to abandon traditional scholarship.

Patriotism and Iconoclasm

As a scholar, Fu perceived the challenge from Western scholars. Fu witnessed the achievements and development of European Sinology and argued that Chinese scholars should make their learning part of the international community and thereby move the center of Sinology from Paris back to Peking.[74]

The source of patriotism had changed in a very subtle way. When Westerners invaded with machine guns, China had to confront them with machine guns; otherwise, there would not be any justice between Western countries and China.[75] When Chinese scholars had to compete with the international community, the way they won international respect was to participate in the international game by the general rules. Edward Said severly criticized Western Orientalogists for interpreting the Orient through the skewed vision of their own prejudices.[76] Fu repeatedly emphasized that in modern times Chinese study should be undertaken with regard to the views of Westerners (*wai-kuo-jen te yen-kuang*). Chinese scholars should be free from the confinements of national learning to compete with Western scholars in a general way. Self-reproach and iconoclasm were, therefore, required. But to other patriotic scholars, Fu's group was measuring the value of Chinese

---

73 See, for example, Hsü Fu-kuan's "San-shih-nien lai Chung-kuo te wen-hua ssu-hsiang wen-t'i", in *Hsüeh-shu yü cheng-chih chih-chien*, 2:145.
74 This was expressed with regret in a letter from Fu to Ch'en Yüan in 1928. See *Shih-yü-so tang-an*, yüan 109, the file of "Ch'en Yüan." See also *FSNC*, 1314. Fu's desire to gain recognition of Chinese research work from the international community can be illustrated by the following event. The Anyang excavation was originally financed jointly by the Academia Sinica and the Smithsonian Institution. When the reports were going to be published, the Smithsonian asked to be coauthor. But Fu insisted that the work be undertaken solely by Chinese scholars, arguing that if the authorship were shared, Western Sinologists would not believe that Chinese scholars had accomplished this task by themselves. See FSNP, IV-378. The controversy resulted in some tough confrontations, but Fu did not yield because he believed that "we can certainly gain a good reputation for the academic world of our country." See "Shih-yü-so fa-chan-shih," 313.
75 Wu Ching-heng, "K'o-hsüeh-chou-pao pien-chi-hua," *Wu Ching-heng hsüan-chi, k'o-hsüeh* volume, 95.
76 Edward Said, *Orientalism* (New York, 1978).

civilization by Western standards and using the interpretations of Western Sinologists to probe China's past,[77] a perilous and treacherous enterprise.

Fu believed that science was the only standard with which to measure the value of learning, a measure that is "universal" and not "national." There is science, but no Chinese science. There is biology, but no Chinese biology. There is philosophy, but no Chinese philosophy. There is medicine, but no Chinese medicine. There is linguistics, but no Chinese linguistics. The Chinese raw materials should be reorganized and studied scientifically (*k'o-hsüeh-te*).[78] But this was not, according to Fu, to wipe out Chinese dignity. On the contrary, because the Chinese were very much at ease with their own native materials, they could make considerable achievements if they diligently applied Western methodology.

A famous example of Fu Ssu-nien's refutation of things national was his criticism of national medicine. In 1934 he published two famous essays denouncing Chinese medicine.[79] Fu wrote that he would rather die than consult a Chinese doctor; to do otherwise would, he said, "humiliate my education."[80] He even asserted that the flourishing of Chinese medicine was a sign of the gross failure of education.[81]

Private correspondence between Hu Shih and T'ao Hsi-sheng also illustrates the connection between patriotism and self-reproach. In 1935, when cultural nativism was running very high and Hu Shih was advocating self-reproach, T'ao Hsi-sheng, Hu's student back at Peita, could not help writing to Hu Shih and asking him why he still undervalued the Chinese tradition. T'ao suggested that Hu should change his attitude from "universalist" to "nationalist." Hu replied:

> I deeply believe that the way to save our country is to reproach ourselves deeply. ... We who advocate self-reproach are not unpatriotic at all; we are absolutely not antinationalistic. It is exactly because we love our country that we have decided to be its loyal remonstrators and friendly expostulators. We do not dare, nor can we bear to allow ourselves, to cover up the nation's disease and avoid seeking a physician for it.[82]

Hu Shih's attitude as represented here was typical of the concerns of many May Fourth youth and can also be illustrated by the comments

---

77 On using Western views to probe Chinese history, see *FSNC*, 1311. On viewing Fu and Hu Shih as treacherous, see, for example, Chou I-liang, "Hsi-yang Han-hsüeh yü Hu Shih," in *Hu Shih ssu-hsiang p'i-p'an*, 7:210.
78 *FSNC*, 1301, 1307, 1310.
79 *FSNC*, 2299–2310. These essays drew sarcastic responses; see *FSNC*, 2322–2329.
80 *FSNC*, 2303.   81 *FSNC*, 2309.   82 *Hu Shih te jih-chi*, June 12, 1935, n.p.

of Ch'ien Hsüan-t'ung, a zealous iconoclast of the New Culture Movement, in which he dared to announce that

[if we] want to prevent the conquest of China, and [if we] want our nation to be one among the civilized nations of the twentieth century, it is absolutely necessary to get rid of Confucianism and Taoism as a final solution. To destroy the Chinese language which stores the teachings of Confucianism and the magic spells of Taoism is the most fundamental solution.[83]

This attitude was shared by many others and had already been anticipated by K'ang Yu-wei's proposal to change all Chinese into Caucasians by various means.[84] T'ang Ts'ai-ts'ang (1867–1900), an activist of 1898 Reformation, also called for miscegenation (*t'ung-chung*).[85] Chao Sungnan, a diplomat in France, also argued that if China were to have a future, the only means was to romanize the Chinese language, and thus to transform all Chinese into "pseudo-Westerners" (*chia-yang-jen*). He called for sending children to study abroad and marrying them off to Westerners. He was proud that none of his children knew any Chinese. When Hu Shih met Chao in 1927, Hu noted that he sympathized with this crazy man; Hu believed that, in his own way, Chao was an enthusiastic patriot.[86]

In retrospect, during the May Fourth era Fu was an iconoclast as well as a patriot. On the one hand, he said that "the family is the source of all evils," "Confucian ethics and religion [*ming-chiao*] were meant to kill people," and "there are no ethics and religion that do not kill people."[87] He even adhered to the goal of "total westernization" (*ch'üan-p'an hsi-hua*), claiming that "It is not inappropriate to admire the West to excess. The difference between Chinese and Western cultures is the difference between right and wrong."[88] He emphasized that because evolutionary theory held true for the whole world, the East should follow exactly the Western evolutionary route.[89] China was climbing the same stairway, but China was still on a very low step; thus, when Fu was waiting to embark for Europe, he resented that he could not "fly to the West immediately" to acquire Western knowledge.[90]

But in 1925 Fu drew up a seal with the following inscription while

---

83 Ch'ien Hsüan-t'ung, "Chung-kuo chin-hou chih wen-tzu wen-t'i," *Hsin-ch'ing-nien*, 4:4 (1918), 354.
84 K'ang Yu-wei, *Ta-t'ung shu* (Peking, 1959), 121–122.
85 "T'ung-chung shuo," *T'ang Ts'ai-ch'ang chi* (Peking, 1980), 100–104.
86 *Hu Shih te jih-chi*, September 1, 1926, n.p.
87 *FSNC*, 1553–1558.   88 *FSNC*, 2412.   89 *FSNC*, 1457.
90 *FSNC*, 2568. Europeanizing the Chinese language was another of Fu's enterprises. He contended that Chinese grammar and syntax should be replaced by their English counterparts.

studying abroad: "I am a descendant of the heavenly Han" (*T'ien-Han chih hou*).⁹¹ And later, while drunk, he uttered his hopes of extinguishing and expelling Westerners (*yang-jen*) from China and expanding the Chinese territory to the Suez Canal.⁹² His hostility toward Westerners was quite similar to that of the Boxers in his hometown village. But his program for defeating the Westerners entailed learning from the West; patriotism and iconoclasm were, in effect, two sides of the same coin.

Political Choices

Politically, intellectuals had more choices before the collapse of the Peiyang warlord system than they did after the Northern Expedition. Before 1927, there were various political authorities, such as the Peiyang warlords and the Nationalist government in Kwangchow, to choose from.

Fu Ssu-nien returned to China and decided to side with the Nationalist government in Kwangchow.⁹³ Fu was attracted to the Nationalist government by the manifesto of the Second Convention of the KMT in 1924, which called for antiimperialism, anticomprador efforts, socialism, and democratic reform.⁹⁴ But following the unification of the nation in 1927–1928, the KMT's high-handed political, educational, and cultural policies seriously deviated from the manifesto. Fu Ssu-nien despaired at this because he lost the only choice available to him. His decision to side with the KMT turned from a choice of the greater good to a choice of the lesser evil.

Fu moved the IHP to Peking in 1929, and there he devoted his energy to academic work. Although he resided in Peking, the center of the former Peiyang warlords, he never recognized the remnants of the Peiyang warlords as possible candidates for leading China. Nevertheless, he continuously criticized and reprimanded Chiang Kai-shek and the Nanking government for its corruption and absolutistic rule.⁹⁵ Fu was very disappointed with Chiang and criticized him for appointing only his own cadets to govern newly annexed territories. He said young men became restless because they witnessed "stupid fellows" (*fan-t'ung*) and

---

91 The seal was drawn by Fu Ssu-nien in his copy of Otto Jespersen's *Philosophy of Grammar* (London, 1924). Fu noted that he bought this book in 1925
92 *FSNC*, 2376.
93 Fu also obtained two offers. One was from Chekiang University; see Lu Hsün, *Liang-ti-shu*, in *Lu Hsün ch'üan-chi*, 11:550. The other was from Ch'inghua University; see Wu Hsüeh-chao, *Wu Mi yü Ch'en Yin-k'o*, 39.
94 "Chung-kuo-kuo-min-tang ti-i-tz'u ch'üan-kuo tai-piao ta-hui hsüan-yen," in *Chung-kuo-kuo-min-tang ti-i-tz'u ch'üan-kuo tai-piao ta-hui shih-liao chuan-chi* (Taipei, 1984), 113–124.
95 *FSNC*, 1616, 1696, 1723, 1726.

"garbage" (*fei-wu*) cadets occupying almost all of the high positions. "Unless people are sages," Fu asked with a sigh, "how can they help but hide in a hermitage during such corrupt times?"

When the Central Plains Civil War broke out in 1931, he wrote with great dismay that it was an event that made middle-aged people feel disappointed and turned the youth into radical leftists. Fu admitted that he was also so extremely disappointed that he sought refuge and shelter in fields of learning utterly irrelevant to the modern world.[96] When the KMT introduced its period of tutelage (*hsün-cheng*) in 1928, Fu complained that the quality of the party was still so low that it could not presume to instruct (*hsün*) people.

Fu was especially dismayed at the way Chiang handled the Mukden Incident and the subsequent loss of Manchuria to the Japanese. Fu wrote painfully that the Nationalist government should apologize to the nation and that the warlords should shoulder more responsibility. Fu was especially unhappy with the KMT's foreign policy, which had conceded so much to Japan. In 1934, when the KMT government protested against Japan's establishment of a puppet regime in Manchuria, it did not even dare mention the name "Japan" in its official documents, for fear of irritating the aggressor nation.[97]

But in spite of all this, he still believed that the KMT represented the only viable leadership for China at that time. None of the remnants of the Peiyang League, Anfu League, Yenchiu League, or Chenghsüeh League were truly qualified for the difficult job of leading the country. For Fu, China's great tragedy was that the KMT could not improve itself, and no alternative to it existed.[98]

But limited political alternatives did not constitute an excuse for avoiding political choices altogether. Overwhelmed by the national crisis, Fu chose to side with a comparatively effective power to lead the nation in resisting foreign encroachments. He believed that "if China has a unified leadership, it will not necessarily guarantee that we will not be subjugated; but if we have no unified leadership at all, we will definitely be conquered."[99] Fu saw national unification as the top priority. In the event of the failure of the KMT government, the logic went, there would be no government in China and the nation would be conquered.[100] Fu reasoned that in the KMT there were only three powerful figures: Hu Han-min (1879–1936), Wang Ching-wei, and Chiang Kai-shek. But Hu and Wang were either unqualified or in positions of little power, so only Chiang Kai-shek could assume leadership. Based on this

---

96 *FSNC*, 1725–1726.   97 *FSNC*, 1681.   98 *FSNC*, 1613.
99 *FSNC*, 1612.   100 Ibid.

assumption, he placed his hopes in Chiang Kai-shek and objected to any form of separatism.[101]

Fu once confessed that in 1936 he would rather live under a dictatorship than see China subjugated by the Japanese.[102] This explains why in 1934 and 1935 during the Debate over Democracy or Absolutism, Fu supported neither his close friend Chiang T'ing-fu, who called for absolutism, nor Hu Shih, who called for democracy. As a cofounder of the journal *Tu-li p'ing-lun*, the major focus of this debate, Fu did not publish a single relevant essay. This unusual apathy indicates that Fu did not feel at ease with either of the two positions.

But why did Fu never consider the CCP as an alternative? It was not until the 1930s that Fu came to believe that the CCP would one day be a considerable political power. In addition to this, during his life Fu never abandoned his belief that the CCP was a tool of the Soviet Union for ultimately subjugating China. This was largely the result of his observation of Michael Borodin's (1884–1951) abuse of power in Kwangchow. As a strong nationalist, Fu vowed to resist exploitation by any foreign country. Fu's personal abhorrence of the CCP also resulted from the Kwangchow Riot launched by a Communist, Chang T'ai-lei, in late 1927. Thousands of people were killed during the turmoil and its aftermath, and Fu barely escaped execution by radical Communists.[103] Fu even claimed that he could not live with the CCP in the same society,[104] an impression based on the bloody experience he went through in Kwangchow. In late 1930 Fu even told his Communist friends that "it is easy for you to execute me, but it is absolutely impossible for me to respect you."[105] Fu also asserted that "class struggle" was only a pretense used by the CCP to mask its insatiable lust for power, and that this lust for power utilized the following eight varieties of hatred:

1 Chinese hatred of Westerners.
2 Hatred of the rich by the poor (Fu also hated the rich, but he rejected the cruel measures employed by the CCP to solve the problem of unequal distribution of wealth).
3 The common people's hatred of anyone superior to them.
4 The hatred of less competent people for their colleagues with superior ability (Fu said that this was common in the academic world but that the CCP offered an outlet for people so frustrated in other professions).
5 Hatred of high-salary employees by low-salary employees, and hatred of the more renowned by the less renowned.
6 The hatred of villagers for townspeople.

101 *FSNC*, 1724–1728.   102 *FSNC*, 1752.
103 Fu Le-ch'eng, "Meng li te tien-hsing," in *Shih-tai te chui-i lun-wen-chi*, 203.
104 *FSNC*, 2160, 2170.   105 *FSNC*, 2073.

7 Children's hatred of their parents.
8 The hatred of youth for their elders.

Fu believed that the CCP made good use of the subconscious feelings of people who were susceptible to any theory legitimizing their hatreds and desires for revenge. "Class struggle" theory, according to Fu, offered just such an outlet.[106]

But regardless of which side Fu Ssu-nien disliked the least, the traditional political role played by intellectuals was reduced in the wake of the marginalization of the intellectual.

During the reorganization of the KMT in 1925, and especially after its successful Northern Expedition, party members formed the core echelon of political power. The term "party" was in vogue, and most party members, themselves nonintellectuals or semiintellectuals, swiftly replaced the traditional literati as the center of political power. This occurred to such an extent that a low-level local party official was powerful enough to make much trouble even for Hu Shih, the most prominent intellectual of his time.[107]

Whether in politics or not, intellectuals became the most uprooted group in the political world. They were for the most part not well received by either the KMT or the CCP, two collectivistic parties. They had so little room to develop their power base that their political role in modern China radically clashed with Chinese tradition.

No matter how many May Fourth youths were recruited by Chiang Kai-shek or Mao Tse-tung, they were for the most part not welcomed by party members. In the KMT, many conservative party members believed that the New Culture Movement had sown and spread the seeds of Chinese communism. Even in 1950, when Fu was the president of T'aita, a former Communist, Jen Cho-hsüan (Yeh Ch'ing) (1896–1990), accused him of harboring Communists.[108] And when party members believed that only party dictatorship could mobilize the human and material resources necessary for saving the country, the May Fourth youths resisted their policies. The CCP, on the other hand, later maligned the New Culture Movement as a bourgeois movement and was disappointed that many May Fourth youths sided with Chiang Kai-shek. Therefore, after the 1920s the May Fourth youths were politically in an awkward position.

When the national crisis worsened, Fu's criticisms of Chiang Kai-shek

---

106 *FSNC*, 1992–1995.
107 Yü Ying-shih, "Chung-kuo chih-shih fen-tzu te pien-yüan hua," *Erh-shih-i shih-chi*, 6 (1991), 15–25.
108 *FSNC*, 2161–2162.

lessened. When the IHP was ordered by the Nanking government to move from Peking to Shanghai (1933) and later to Nanking (1934), Fu Ssu-nien remained in Peking for two more years and taught at Peita. Fu did not move to Nanking until 1936. But when Chiang was kidnapped by Chang Hsüeh-liang (1901–) in December 1936, a leaflet written by Fu marked the peak of his support of Chiang.

Upon hearing of the Sian Incident, Hu Shih and Fu Ssu-nien were prompted to write two enthusiastic articles denouncing Chang Hsüeh-liang. These were printed into leaflets and carried by airplanes for distribution over the Sian area. Fu emphasized in his leaflet that Chiang was now immeasurably important to the nation and that his safety was also the safety of the nation; rescuing Chiang was, therefore, the nation's highest priority.[109] The leaflet was written in the first-person plural "we," and Chang Hsüeh-liang was called a "bandit by blood" (*tsei-chung*).[110] But it should be noted that in this same leaflet Fu criticized Chiang for instituting military feudalism and dragging his feet on political reform.[111]

Japanese aggression forced both Hu Shih and Fu Ssu-nien to become more tolerant of the Nanking government, despite its failings. Hu Shih once remarked, perhaps partly in jest, that Chiang Kai-shek had never even dreamed of democracy and needed to be sent back to the village school to study again. But, Hu admitted in 1937 after the Marco Polo Bridge Incident, "Times have changed, and now there is no room for us to oppose the government."[112]

---

109 *FSNC*, 1754–1755.   110 Ibid.   111 *FSNC*, 1764.
112 Hu Shih, *Jen-ch'üan lun-chi* (Shanghai, 1930), 30. See also Keng Yün-chih, *Hu Shih nien-p'u*, 165.

6
Statism and the Later Days of a May Fourth Youth

After the Marco Polo Bridge Incident, foreign aggression accelerated and liberals lost their moral high ground for criticizing their government. Fu was immediately invited to advise Chiang in Nanking on foreign affairs and was later handpicked by Chiang as a representative in the People's Political Council.[1]

Maintaining a distance from politics was, as we have seen, a major feature of Chinese liberals of the May Fourth generation. Liberal members of this generation believed that culture and academic work should be given more importance in order to secure a more promising future for China. As the national crisis worsened, however, they soon found it difficult to maintain their earlier beliefs. Hu Shih lamented that the cultural ideals of the May Fourth movement were soon superseded by political realities as the danger of national subjugation approached. This change occurred despite Ts'ai Yüan-p'ei's insistence that "study is the way to save our country."[2] Many intellectuals agonized over whether they could make any substantial contribution to their imperiled country.[3] The Mukden Incident raised serious questions in the minds of these scholars, and the Marco Polo Bridge Incident made these questions and doubts even more pressing.

Fu Ssu-nien and the IHP had long been criticized as unresponsive to social needs, if not political realities. Fears that their research was meaningless frequently appeared in the private correspondence between fellow members of the IHP. In one such piece of correspondence, Li

---

1 Chiang Kai-shek asked Wang Shih-chieh to invite Fu to attend these meetings. See FSNP, III-1439, a letter from Wang Shih-chieh to Fu.
2 *Ts'ai Yüan-p'ei hsien-sheng chi-nien-chi* (Peking, 1984), 2.
3 On the tension between study and politics, cf. Yü Ying-shih, "Wu-ssu – i-ko wei-wan-ch'eng te wen-hua yün-tung," in *Wen-hua-p'ing-lun yü Chung-kuo ch'ing-huai* (Taipei, 1988), 65–72. Ch'ien Chi-po (1887–1957), a traditional scholar, even started to study Chinese traditional military strategy. See Wu Chung-k'uang, "Wu shih Ch'ien Chi-po hsien-sheng chuan-lüeh," *Chung-kuo wen-hua*, 4 (1991), 190–198.

Chi asked: "After the Mukden Incident, we always asked ourselves: in the present circumstances, is the kind of work we are doing a waste?"[4] But Li assured them that "Although the nation is now facing disaster [*kuo-nan*], we should continue working on our original projects. We think this is the most appropriate way to contribute to our country."[5] But "If needed," Li continued, "we can take up arms to fight the enemy at any time." Li's confession epitomized the common anxiety of many intellectuals. An archaeologist of the Anyang excavations, Kuo Pao-chün (1893–1971), confided that at this time research was only a "useless decoration."[6] Yin Ta (Liu Yao, 1906–1983), another participant in the Anyang excavations, even secretly fled to Yenan to participate directly in political action.[7]

Fu, like numerous intellectuals, could not relieve his pangs of guilt. He confided in a letter to a friend that he felt extremely guilty about staying home and reading ancient books during such a time of national emergency. But he was soon to find that he could not do anything more helpful than reading ancient books, because he was unable to take up arms the way young men could.[8] Weng Wen-hao (1889–1971), a prominent geologist and high official, also confided to Fu that he was disappointed with geological studies because they could contribute almost nothing to the nation. The desperate war forced scholars to ask themselves the most fundamental questions about the practical application of their work.[9]

The tension in Fu's mind during the last fifteen years of his life was a major motivation that almost drove him to give up academic work and occupy himself with various kinds of state affairs. Fu later recalled:

My personality is inclined to the enjoyment of pastoral comforts. If [I had lived] at a time of peace and prosperity, I would surely have excelled in learning.... I originally felt dissatisfied toward the political and social [situations], but could not discover a good way [out of this situation] – therefore, I thought of going into hiding in academics. Still, I cannot forget [the welfare of] the people. So I

---

4 Li Chi, "Anyang tsui-chin fa-chüeh pao-kao chi liu-tz'u kung-tso chih tsung-ku-chi," in *Li Chi k'ao-ku-hsüeh lun-wen-chi*, 1:139.
5 Ibid., 131. 6 FSNP, III-693, a letter from Kuo Pao-chün to Fu.
7 Yang Hsiang-k'uei and Chang Cheng-lang, "Tao-nien Yin Ta t'ung-chih," *Li-shih yen-chiu*, no. 5 (1983), 73–77. Yin later became an early leader of the Cultural Revolution.
8 FSNP, I-57.
9 A group of IHP members even planned to join guerrilla bands. But there were also other responses to the national crisis. For example, Li Fang-kuei, a distinguished fellow of the IHP, stated in a letter that "our country is about to be conquered; we should quickly throw ourselves into our research with all our energy." See FSNP, I-1656, a letter from Fu to Hu Shih.

run back and forth, in and out of the door of academics. [I am frustrated] to the point of roaring – for when I come out of [academics], I cannot go very far away; when I enter [academics], I cannot stay in very long.[10]

After this point, Fu never again published any serious academic research work.

As previously stated, at the outbreak of the Sino-Japanese War Fu Ssu-nien was immediately summoned by the government to participate in the Council of National Defense (Kuo-fang ts'an-i hui). The war forced the IHP to move with several thousand boxes of books, experimental instruments, archaeological findings, and anthropological data from Nanking to Changsha. Later, in an attempt to avoid Japanese air raids, the IHP proceeded with extreme difficulty to Kunming in Yünnan province via Vietnam. The IHP had only stayed in Kunming for about nine months before it was forced to relocate to suburban Kunming in October 1938.

In December 1940 Fu decided to relocate to a place whose name did not appear on the map so that Japanese aircraft could not drop bombs there.[11] He accordingly chose a remote village, Li-chuang of Nan-hsi district in Szechwan province. Li-chuang, situated in the middle of the mountains, is invisible from the air. Following Fu, two other institutions relocated to this place. Fu's knack for moving the institute's colossal assets over several thousand miles over a shabby transportation system earned him the nickname "Mr. Mover" (Pan-chia hsien-sheng).[12] Fu was able to accomplish these logistical tasks because of his own stamina and his personal connections (*kuan-hsi*), which enabled him to procure enough vehicles for transport.[13]

During the war years the collection of the IHP was the only large-scale library in the entire southwestern region, and this was of great help to many humanities scholars.[14] The story repeated itself ten years later when the same collection was successfully moved to Taiwan and became a major resource for historical study.

It was also Fu's proposal to organize and combine Peita, Ch'inghua, and Nan-k'ai, the three most prestigious universities in China, into the Southwest Associated University (Hsi-nan lien-ta),[15] the most important educational organ during the war years. Thousands of students and pro-

---

10 In a letter to Hu Shih, 1942, FSNP, I-1676. Fu Le-ch'eng, *Fu Meng-chen hsien-sheng nien-p'u*, in *FSNC*, 7:2647–2648.
11 Teng Kuang-ming, "Hui-i wo te lao-shih Fu Ssu-nien hsien-sheng," in *Fu Ssu-nien*, 5.
12 See "Shih-yü-so fa-chan-shih," 355–379, 406–423.   13 Ibid.
14 Ibid., 434.
15 FSNP, I-1130, a letter from Yang Chen-sheng (1890–1956) to Fu.

fessors walked or took vehicles from northern China to Kunming to resume their studies there.

Critic of Government Malpractice

During the eight war years, Fu was the director of the IHP and also a representative in the People's Political Council. In the council Fu was very active in fighting governmental corruption and malpractice, and he also obstructed any motion that ran counter to his notions of the "modern scientific spirit," such as reviving traditional Chinese medicine.[16] These motions were motivated by the national crisis and sought to revive the value of the national past in order to affirm the value of Chineseness.[17] His fiery criticism of governmental malpractice during his tenure in the Assembly won him the nickname "Cannon Fu" (Fu Ta-p'ao).

Cannon Fu was especially famous for his attack on two premiers and his contributions to their ultimate resignations. H. H. Kung and Chiang Kai-shek had both married daughters of Charlie Soong (Sung Chia-shu, 1864–1918). The two men thus became related, and Kung became Chiang Kai-shek's protégé. Although Kung had a thoroughgoing Western education, he was still quite successful in expanding his power base by cultivating traditional personal relations, and he appointed his henchmen in disregard of formal procedure. In October 1933 Kung succeeded his brother-in-law, T. V. Soong (1894–1971) (the son of Charlie Soong), to the top financial post of the Nationalist government. This was a post that Soong himself had occupied almost continuously since 1926. During his tenure, Kung undertook several major financial reforms. He was appointed premier in 1938, thus succeeding Chiang Kai-shek. Several months after his appointment, Fu began to communicate with Chiang Kai-shek privately, expressing his contention that Kung was absolutely not qualified for his current position. Two long memos accused Kung of various sorts of corruption, malpractice, illegal appointments, abuse of power, and self-aggrandizement.[18] Kung soon became aware of Fu's impeachments, and the resulting tension between Kung

---

16 One well-known case is his opposition to K'ung Keng's (1871–1950) motion that traditional Chinese medicine should be esteemed. K'ung was infuriated by Fu's opposition and berated him with filthy language. The incident almost ended in fisticuffs. See Fu Le-ch'eng, *Fu Meng-chen hsien-sheng nien-p'u*, in *FSNC*, 7:2652.
17 For example, in Chungking Chiang Kai-shek was proclaiming Sung-Ming Neo-Confucianism. See Ch'ien Mu, *Pa-shih i shuang-ch'in, Shih-yu tsa-i*, 218.
18 The manuscripts of the two letters are in FSNP, I-45, I-48, both written in 1944. These two letters were sent by Fu to Hu Shih and are printed in *Hu Shih lai wang shu-hsin hsüan*, 3:604–612.

and Fu was so high that at one point Kung even tried to exact revenge against Fu by curtailing the budget of the Academia Sinica and lowering its status from an organ of the Presidential Office to that of the Executive Yüan, headed by Kung.[19] Only when Chu Chia-hua, another powerful figure in the Nationalist government, took the post of secretary-general of the Academia Sinica did the academy escape from this danger.

Kung's cultural policies also greatly irritated Fu. Upon assuming the premiership, Kung attempted to extend his reach into the cultural sphere. He once delivered a lecture to a gathering of professors in which he argued that various ideas held by intellectuals contradicted government policy and were thus inappropriate. Fu found the speech perplexing.[20]

Kung's corruption, although widely known and discussed throughout the nation, went unopposed; no one dared do anything about it.[21] But Fu was an exception; he continuously sent memos to Chiang reminding him that Kung's practices were damaging Chiang's reputation and the nation's strength. He told Hu Shih, "To protect Mr. Chiang's [reputation], I dare to rise against him [H. H. Kung]."[22] Fu Ssu-nien mentally came to feel that the Nationalist government was like a giant who could not lift himself up and that Chiang and his party had no potential for reform and rejuvenation. No private memorial from Fu could persuade Chiang and his party to cut off the tumor that was H. H. Kung. Extremely dismayed, Fu decided to attack Kung publicly.

In 1943 the Ministry of Finance decided to sell U.S. $100 million, which were part of a $500 million American loan, to the public. This was a colossal amount of money to an impoverished nation like China, and the American dollar constituted a guarantee of stability that would enable people to retain their wealth during a period of hyperinflation. But before long, Kung and his group announced to the public that the funds had already been sold. It was believed that Kung and his group had secretly bought up half of the money and sold it out at more than five times the original asking price. Many people knew that this had happened but could prove little or nothing. Finally, certain lower officials of the Bureau of the National Treasury, which was then in charge of

---

19 Several letters concerning this episode are in FSNP, I-92, IV-219, two letters from Wang Shih-chieh to Fu, and IV-169, one letter from Ts'ai Yüan-p'ei to Fu.
20 Feng Yu-lan, *San-sung-t'ang tzu-hsü*, in *San-sung-t'ang chüan-chi*, 1:102–103.
21 Ma Yin-ch'u (1882–1982) once spelled out his disappointment with Kung, which caused him trouble. See Yeh Yüan-lung, "Ch'ung-ta hsiao-chang Yeh Yüan-lung ch'ing-li Ma Yin-ch'u shih-chien," *Chuan-chi wen-hsüeh*, no. 3 (1992), 67–70.
22 See FSNP, I-48, a letter from Fu to Hu Shih.

selling the funds, mailed Fu several leaves from the account book of the bureau that showed that Lü Hsien, a henchman of H. H. Kung and the director of this bureau, was seriously corrupt and had been involved in "swallowing up" the U.S. dollars.[23] Fu Ssu-nien jumped at this rare chance. He proposed a motion in a session of the People's Political Council in July 1945. On hearing this, Ch'en Pu-lei (1890–1948), chief of staff to Chiang Kai-shek, and Wang Shih-chieh (1891–1981), general secretary of the People's Political Council (both of whom were good friends of Fu), endeavored to block the motion. They advised Fu that instead of going public with the scandal and incurring criticism from America and the CCP, he should send a personal memo to Chiang Kai-shek.[24] Ch'en Pu-lei and Wang Shih-chieh might also have tried to ask Hu Shih, who was in the United States during this time, to persuade Fu to withdraw his motion. Fu soon got a telegram from Hu advising him to stop his attack, but this was to no avail.[25] Fu was keenly aware of Chiang's congenial relationship with Kung and bore in mind his own unsuccessful experience in impeaching Kung privately to Chiang in past years. He criticized Kung publicly in an open session of the People's Political Council and challenged Lü Hsien to meet with him in the courtroom. Fearing that the evidence would be stolen by Kung's clique, Fu put it in a small suitcase, which he carried with him during the day and used as a pillow at night.[26] The whole nation was stunned by Fu's announcement, and Attorney General Cheng Lieh (1888–1958) even asked Fu to offer him evidence for further investigation.[27] Much hard evidence concerning the corruption of Kung's group continued to flood into Fu's mailbox,[28] allowing him to make several further motions.

Upon learning that H. H. Kung's corruption had incurred the anger of the American government, Chiang Kai-shek finally decided to fire Kung. He even informed Fu Ssu-nien that he was pleased with his courageous actions.[29] "I am happy that, at long last, I have caused Kung

---

23 Several leaves of the account book that showed Lü Hsien's corruption were kept in FSNP, no serial number.
24 Yüeh Yü-hsi, "Kuo-min ts'an-cheng hui ch'i-chien te liang-chien-shih," in *Fu Ssu-nien*, 164–165.
25 FSNP, I-1665. Hu Shih also noted this event in his diary. See *Hu Shih te jih-chi*, November 26, 1939, n.p.
26 See Fu Le-ch'eng, *Fu Meng-chen hsien-sheng nien-p'u*, in *FSNC*, 2653.
27 FSNP, I-688, a letter from Cheng Lieh to Fu.
28 For example, FSNP, I-628, a letter from the employees of the Bureau of the National Treasury; FSNP, I-617, a letter from someone with the alias Wang Yin-ming; FSNP, I-616, a letter from another anonymous person; FSNP, I-614, a letter from one who called himself Jung Fang; FSNP, I-626, a letter from Chu Chih-ch'ing (1898–1948).
29 In a letter to his wife, Yü Ta-ts'ai, Fu said that when he later met with Chiang K'ai-shek, Chiang expressed his agreement with Fu's actions. FSNP, I-1298.

enough troubles to force him to resign," Fu wrote to his wife. "I have tried to hamper Kung for about eight years but to no avail. This time I finally knocked him down, but the nation has already been damaged by him to a great extent. I am extremely grieved about the destiny of my people."[30]

Finally H. H. Kung resigned from three jobs: president of the Central Bank (which he had held for twelve years), secretary of finance (eleven years), and premier or vice-premier (eleven years).

In May 1945 the Nationalist government's announcement of its unilateral decision to summon the National Assembly (Kuo-min ta-hui) produced great tension between the KMT and the CCP. Foreseeing the immediate end of the war, Fu Ssu-nien, Huang Yen-p'ei (1877–1965), and four other representatives of the People's Political Council suggested that Chiang Kai-shek summon the Political Consultative Conference (Cheng-chih hsieh-shang hui-i), a suggestion that he accepted.

To secure consent from the CCP for participating in this council, Fu and the other representatives paid a visit to Yenan, then the base of the CCP. Upon the arrival of an invitation from Yenan, they flew to the town on July 1, 1945, for a five-day visit. There they reached two agreements with Mao Tse-tung, the first to stop the unilateral National Assembly, and the second to convene a political consultative conference. The mission successfully brought the two parties to the Chungking Conciliation Meeting. After the surrender of Japan, the leaders of the KMT and the CCP held a conference for thirteen days.[31]

Fu was personally acquainted with Mao Tse-tung from his student days at Peita. At that time Fu had been a prominent leader of the student movement, while Mao, a library assistant, had always been denied inclusion in discussion groups with Fu and Lo Chia-lun. But when they met

30 FSNP, I-1298. The heroic action was applauded by many people. For example, a letter from Wu Ming-ta praised Fu as "speaking for the four hundred fifty million people." FSNP, I-387, a letter from someone who called himself Ming Hsin compared Fu with Hai Jui (1514–1587), a famous remonstrator of the Ming Dynasty. See FSNP, I-723.

31 For a short sketch of this conference, see Kuo T'ing-i, *Chin-tai Chung-kuo shih-kang* (Hong Kong, 1986), 2 vols., 2:720–726. See also Yü Chan-pang, "Mao Tse-tung chu-hsi tsai Ch'ung-ch'ing t'an-p'an ch'i-chien," *Ch'ung-ch'ing wen-shih tzu-liao*, 24 (1985), 152–174. Before the visit, on June 2, 1945, Fu Ssu-nien, along with six other political leaders, urged Hurley, then American ambassador to China, to assist the Chinese to unify the country. See "The Ambassador in China (Hurley) to the Secretary of State, June 28, 1945," *Foreign Relations of the United States, 1945*, vol. 7 (Washington, D.C., 1969), 424–425. After Fu's visit to Yenan, it was reported by Hurley that Fu informed the American personnel that the situation was "hopeful," "but he was neither pessimistic nor optimistic." See "The Ambassador in China (Hurley) to the Secretary of State, July 7, 1945," in ibid., 428–429.

again, perhaps for the first time in thirty years, Mao had become the leader of the major power opposing the Nationalist government. At Mao's invitation, they stayed up talking the whole night. Fu found that Mao was very familiar with various low-brow novels, which, Fu believed, had helped him to understand the mentality of people in the lower social strata and to manipulate mass sentiment. He felt that Mao was a rebel leader like Sung Chiang, the major figure in the novel *Water Margin* (*Shui-hu chuan*).[32] In a way, both Fu and Mao had rebellious natures. During the May Fourth era, Fu had been the leader in rebelling against warlords, but Mao had been the leader in rebelling against the KMT. Fu conceded that he was only a small rebel like Ch'en Sheng (?–208 B.C.) or Wu Kuang (?–208 B.C.), whereas Mao was a major rebel like Liu Pang (r. 206–196 B.C.) or Hsiang Yü (232–202 B.C.). Inspired by this, Mao, on Fu's departure from Yenan, wrote a poem of the T'ang poet Chang Chieh (fl. 870s) for Fu in his own calligraphy. The last sentence of the poem was a description of Mao himself: "Liu Pang and Hsiang Yü did not read books."[33]

Two May Fourth youths had chosen different paths. One became a scholar, and the other chose "not to read books" but to become a political opponent of the Nationalist government. The divergence between them was complete three years later, when Mao denounced Fu as a war criminal.[34]

Ambivalence toward the Nation's Past

Fu was most reluctant to give up his iconoclastic ideals. During the Sino-Japanese War, some of the May Fourth youths praised their nation's past, and one even entitled a book "I Believe in China."[35] Fu was still torn between two opposite poles: patriotism and iconoclastic ideals. He seems to have alternated constantly between these two poles, unable to free himself from the resultant anguish. He sometimes conceded in public lectures that China had a glorious past, yet he never published these

---

32 Fu kept some documentation of this visit. See FSNP, I-156, I-158, I-164, I-165, I-175, I-627, I-633, IV-379. But those notes are rather fragmentary. For a description of this trip, see Huang Yen-p'ei, "Yen-an kuei-lai," in *Kuo-min ts'an-cheng hui tzu-liao* (Szechuan, 1984), 463–506. For some of Fu's other activities in Yenan, see Tso Shun-sheng, *Chin san-shih-nien chien-wen tsa-chi* (Hong Kong, 1954), 87. For some other documents concerning this visit, see *Kuo-min ts'an-cheng hui tzu-liao*, 451–462.
33 FSNP, I-38. This poem, together with a short letter, was written on July 5, 1945. Chang Chieh's poem was included in *Ch'üan T'ang shih* (Peking, 1960), 12 vols., 10:2650.
34 In "Tiu-tiao huan-hsiang, chun-pei tou-cheng," Mao announced that Fu, among others, was a war criminal. See *Mao Tse-tung hsüan-chi* (Peking, 1966), 1374.
35 See Schwarcz, *The Chinese Enlightenment: Intellectuals and Legacy of the May Fourth Movement of 1919*, 233.

lecture notes.³⁶ Fu Ssu-nien was periodically asked to deliver lectures to arouse the spirits of his compatriots by appealing to the nation's sense of dignity. We find that on several occasions Fu addressed the public with a certain confidence in China's past, whereas he scarcely mentioned modern Chinese history because of its perceived lack of glory. He always concluded his lectures with discussions of several memorable events or heroic figures to encourage his audience to wage a "holy war" (*sheng-chan*) against Japan. Although Fu could convince himself intellectually that iconoclasm ultimately served patriotism, his inner tension still ran high. The need for a national identity was heightened when the battlefield was full of munitions and blood. The issue of "Chineseness," which had been a rather academic issue prior to the war, was transformed into a weapon for mobilizing people to fight for the survival of their nation.

Fu was once commissioned by the Nationalist government's propaganda organ to draft a "History of the Chinese Revolution" (Chung-kuo min-tsu ko-ming shih-kao, ca. 1938–1939). In this work he wrote that "The Han Chinese are not a weak race; they are sometimes unfortunately weakened by dark politics. . . . They become stronger whenever they are challenged."³⁷ Fu did, however, discipline himself against hyperbole. Despite repeated requests, Fu never finished this treatise.³⁸ When these remarks are contrasted with those he jotted down in a notebook in 1927, it is evident that Fu had changed considerably. His 1927 remark read: "China is not a civilized country."³⁹ Yet in the mid 1940s, when the prominent scholar T'ang Yung-t'ung (1893–1964), who sympathized with *Hsüeh-heng*, an anti–New Culture journal, wrote to Fu that he was terribly worried about the deaths of learned old men and the discontinuity of Chinese traditional learning that would probably result, Fu expressed sympathy for T'ang's sentiments.⁴⁰ Less than twenty years earlier, Fu had every intention to put a stop to traditional learning, but now its very continuance was a great concern of his.

But relaxation did not mean abandonment, and Fu Ssu-nien was still acutely aware of the rising tide of a sense of "national essence" that accompanied the Sino-Japanese War. In various essays Fu reminded people not to exaggerate the glories of the nation's past. He conceded

---

36 FSNP, I-708, a set of lecture notes entitled "Chung-kuo chin san-pai-nien lai tui wai-lai wen-hua chih fan-ying."
37 FSNP, I-701.
38 Fu only finished two chapters of this book, which contained about twenty thousand words. He was drafting this book during the darkest days of the Sino-Japanese War.
39 FSNP, I-433.
40 FSNP, III-917, T'ang Yung-t'ung's letter to Fu.

that given this war, national confidence was a must. "But," he added, "it would be better to believe in our future endeavors than in the nation's past." He warned people not to "fabricate some nonexistent historical miracles in order to give a cover for [our] megalomania."[41] National essence could make some positive contributions to the national feeling, but it should not be abused, he added.[42]

During the war years, the tension between history and politics also surfaced in Fu Ssu-nien's mind from time to time. I raise one case as an example. During the Japanese occupation of Indochina, the Japanese had sought to convince the ethnic minorities of southwest China that they were actually Thai people who had little to do ethnically with the Han Chinese, and they were encouraged to separate themselves from the Chinese government. In the late 1930s many intellectuals who followed the government on its retreat into southwest China found themselves in an excellent environment for ethnic studies. Many of them observed these minorities for the first time and decided to explore the new field of ethnology. The Southwest Ethnic Research Association (Hsi-nan min-tsu hsüeh-hui) was organized by Fei Hsiao-t'ung (1910–). Ku Chieh-kang did several studies on the history of these minorities, while Fei Hsiao-t'ung and Wu Ching-ch'ao (1901–1968) conducted anthropological surveys. They published a number of articles revealing the ethnic diversities among these minorities and their differences with the Han Chinese.

Fu Ssu-nien soon instigated a debate with Ku Chieh-kang, Fei Hsiao-t'ung, and Wu Ching-ch'ao on their studies. During the debates, Fu criticized them as "purposeless scholars" (*wu-liao hsüeh-che*) who, "under the pretext of academic work" (*chia hsüeh-shu chih ming*), "were attempting to dismantle the nation's identity." Fu argued that when the entire nation was severely threatened by its enemy and southwest China was being egged on to sever itself from China, all the people of China proper should band together to fight the Japanese, and scholars should not supply the enemy so much as a single shred of evidence to persuade the southwest minorities to rebel under the banner of "Great Thaism" (*Ta Tai chu-i*).[43] He demanded to know why, while the Japanese were proclaiming that Kwangsi and Yünnan were originally the habitations of Thai peoples and while the British were encouraging the separatist tendencies of the chiefs of local tribes in Yünnan, some Chinese scholars

---

41 *FSNC*, 1829–1830.
42 *FSNC*, 1830.
43 *FSNC*, 2451–2452, a letter from Fu to Ku Chieh-kang; the original manuscript of this letter is in FSNP, II-143. *FSNC*, 2449–2450, a letter from Fu to Chu Chia-hua and Hang Li-wu (1904–1991); the original manuscript of this letter is in FSNP, III-1197.

were still exiling themselves to these places and tracing the ethnic origins of these peoples. Fu therefore wrote to Ku Chieh-kang that what he should do at this moment was prove that the *Hu* (non-Chinese "barbarians") and *Han* Chinese had already become integrated.[44] He said that it would not be inappropriate to publish their articles in virtually noncirculating academic journals (*hsüeh-shu k'an-wu*), but that it would be most improper to publish them in popular journals.[45]

Pacifying Student Unrest in Kunming and Punishing Turncoats

After the Japanese surrender, Chiang Kai-shek considered appointing Fu as the new president of Peita. At Fu's request, Chiang changed his mind and appointed Hu Shih in his stead. For various reasons Hu Shih, who by then had been relieved of his ambassadorship and had remained in the United States, was not sworn in immediately.[46] Fu Ssu-nien, who enthusiastically persuaded Hu Shih to accept the presidency of Peita, was appointed acting president of Peita during the interregnum. Peita was, by then, still a constituent of the Southwest Associate University in Kunming and was awaiting relocation to its Peking campus. Before long, Fu was traumatized by a large-scale student movement in Kunming.

The Kunming Student Movement was considered a major event that contributed to the success of the CCP. This event marked a longstanding confrontation between liberal leftists and the government's high-handed cultural policies.[47]

KMT policy toward intellectuals changed drastically after the United States joined in the Pacific War in 1941. Before then, intellectuals

---

44 Concurrently, Hsiung Shih-li was undertaking a project to prove that the Han Chinese and the Uighurs were originally the same ethnic group. See *Hsüan-p'u lun-hsüeh-chi* (Peking, 1990), 39.
45 FSNP, II-147. This brings us to an interesting issue: whether historians should, during times of national crisis, obscure unfavorable facts. T'ao Hsi-sheng believed that, in view of the present political situation, scholars should carefully hide some historical realities. For example, even though scholars might believe that China was a most backward country, it was still their mission to inform the people of their nation's glorious past in order to arouse nationalistic feelings among them. See *Hu Shih te jih-chi*, August 12, 1935, n.p.
46 After being dismissed from his ambassadorship, Hu Shih became angry at top governmental officials. He therefore refused to take up any government-appointed position. As for the presidency of Peita, Chiang Kai-shek first hoped to appoint Fu Ssu-nien, but Fu believed that Hu Shih was the best appointee, and he promised to be the acting president until Hu's return to China. Cf. Keng Yün-chih, *Hu Shih nien-p'u*, 181–184.
47 Cf. Feng Yu-lan, *San-sung-t'ang tzu-hsü*, in *San-sung-t'ang ch'üan chi*, 1:102–107.

wholeheartedly cooperated with the government in resisting foreign invasion. During the nation's life-and-death crisis, the government also endeavored to group everyone together to fight the Japanese. Democracy was for several years very much in vogue. The participation of America in the Pacific War was viewed by the Chinese people as assurance of the ultimate victory of the Allies and the survival of the Chinese nation. With this assurance, the government tightened its cultural controls and the intellectuals resumed their criticisms of the government. KMT's thought control policy was an important factor alienating intellectuals and thereby driving them to the left. Disputes between Chiang Kai-shek's government and the intellectuals led to numerous upheavals. Chiang perceived the government's policy toward intellectuals as too lenient, whereas the intellectuals saw the government as excessively strict. Although the government's cultural policies were inefficiently implemented and never successfully carried out, they still incurred enormous hostility from intellectuals and young students.[48]

Kunming, with its American air base and location remote from Chungking, retained a democratic atmosphere. Intellectuals there were relatively free to express their discontent. At the end of the war, students felt relieved that they could finally return to Peking. But the civil war erupted soon after the end of the Sino-Japanese War, and students of the Southwest Associated University were forced to wait in Kunming for another eighteen months for repatriation. They were extremely disappointed with the political situation when the local garrison extended its control to the campus, and a clash immediately broke out.

On December 1, 1945, a tragic event occurred while leftist students were holding a public meeting denouncing the KMT for its corruption and misgovernment, as well as for the responsibility they felt it should shoulder for the outbreak of the civil war. The local garrison commander, Ch'iu Ch'ing-ch'üan (1902–1949), dispatched a squad to the lecture hall. The agents stormed the hall with pistols and grenades, killing four students and wounding twenty-five others.[49] Students and professors immediately went into an uproar; they decided to boycott all classes, call for the punishment of the ringleaders in this slaughter, and publicize the true story of the tragedy. Because the government gave only slight concessions thereafter, a stalemate formed between the two sides. As the acting president of Peita, Fu was naturally one of the three executive members of the Southwest Associated University. Con-

---

48 Hsü Fu-kuan, *Chung-kuo ssu-hsiang-shih lun-chi* (Taichung, 1968), 230–231, 247–249.
49 On the event and its causes and casualties, see Hsiao Ch'ao-jan, *Pei-ching ta-hsüeh hsiao-shih*, 364–378.

sequently, he was invited by Chiang to settle this unrest, a difficult job requiring the most sophisticated talents.[50]

While negotiating with students to go back to their classrooms, Fu confessed to his wife that this mission was a leap into fire.[51] As the former marshal of the May Fourth demonstrations, Fu was ribbed by his friend with the saying: "He who cuts others' hair will someday have his own hair cut by others."[52] The implication was that after thirty years, the former rebel had become an authority charged with quelling a student movement. Fu became, at least in the eyes of the leftists, a tool of the KMT, and slander from leftist elements abounded.[53]

Fu persuaded the students to stop boycotting their classes by finally promising further concessions from the government. Fu's heroic denunciation of H. H. Kung had given him credentials as an impartial and upright negotiator. He blamed local party and military leaders and successfully appealed to Chiang Kai-shek to punish several of the ringleaders. As a result, students promised to resume their classwork. But different opinions among students delayed the negotiations, and the decisions of the student committee changed swiftly. Fu confided to a friend that he suspected that CCP students were behind the scenes impeding the negotiations.[54] During the repeated stalemates, Chiang Kai-shek once planned to resort to mass arrests.[55] Aware of this, Fu Ssu-nien and Mei I-ch'i (1889–1962), president of Ch'inghua University, announced that they would resign immediately if students did not accept the settlement terms. Fu also managed to have a faculty meeting decide that all faculty members would also resign.[56] The students agreed to end their protests, and classes resumed. A report from the American consul to the State Department stated that Fu had finally stabilized the situation. In the report, the American consul expressed relief that Fu had intervened, because, although Fu was not a government official, he had the power necessary to handle the situation.[57]

Fu was highly distressed by this incident. He wrote with sorrow that

---

50 A letter from Chiang Kai-shek to Fu and the manuscript of Fu's reply, FSNP, no serial number. Chiang's letter was written on December 7, 1945.
51 FSNP, I-1297, a letter from Fu to his wife.
52 Feng's words were quoted by Fu. See *FSNC,* 2061. See also Feng's *San-sung-t'ang tzu-hsü,* in *San-sung-t'ang chüan-chi,* 1:328.
53 See, for example, Ching Yen, "Wei 'kuan yü Fu Ssu-nien' pu-i," *Wen-hui-pao* (November 10, 1946).
54 FSNP, I-1332. A confidential letter from Fu to Chu Chia-hua expressed this suspicion. It turned out that from its beginning to its settlement, the CCP had in fact had a hand in this incident. On direction from the CCP in this event, see Hsiao Ch'ao-jan, *Pei-ching ta-hsüeh hsiao-shih,* 373, 376.
55 Ma Liang-k'uan, "Ch'ing k'an t'i-t'ou-che, jen i t'i ch'i t'ou," *Fu Ssu-nien,* 172.
56 Ibid.   57 Ibid., 174.

during the May Fourth movement it was out of nationalism that students stood up to demonstrate, whereas the students in Kunming were egged on by the CCP and patronized by the Soviet Union. But Fu also harbored some abhorrence toward the KMT ringleaders. He proclaimed that "Li Tsung-huang (1888–1978) and Ch'iu Ch'ing-ch'üan should be summarily executed.... My resentment toward Li Tsung-huang is no less than that toward anybody else."[58] He lamented the destiny of the nation and predicted that a blazing inferno would soon "burn rock and jade together." Although he had successfully solved a political debacle, he felt powerless and was pessimistic about the future of the nation.

Punishing the Turncoats

It is said that, upon learning of Japan's surrender, Fu Ssu-nien got himself drunk and roamed the streets of Chungking, kissing everyone he met. This brief period of celebration was followed by one of vengeance, as Fu took action to ferret out traitors who had served under Japanese control. Fu's hatred of turncoats was the result of a traditional concept of "loyalty," which, though hardly mentioned by Fu himself in any of his writings, was nevertheless a dominant factor in the world of his thought. Foreseeing the end of the war, in 1945 he wrote in a notebook under the heading of "Black List" the following comment: "Hsieh Kuo-chen [1901–1982] is a traitor." This was because Hsieh had worked for a compilation project led by the Japanese.[59] Fu seemed to have little sympathy for people who were forced to live and work under Japanese control after the legitimate Chinese government had retreated into southwest China.

During the war years Peita was reorganized by the Japanese military with the help of some Chinese intellectuals. It became Fu's policy to exclude all formerly pro-Japanese faculty members from Peita. Chou Tso-jen, who once served as the president of Peita, immediately wrote to plea with his former student Fu Ssu-nien to let bygones be bygones, but to no avail.[60] Fu also insisted that teachers and students who lived in the areas under Japanese occupation should be reeducated to learn to become real Chinese again. Yet there was a serious conflict between

---

58 Ibid., 175–176. Fu's anger toward Li Tsung-huang and Ch'iu Ch'ing-ch'üan was also expressed in two confidential letters to Chu Chia-hua; see FSNP, I-1326, I-1329. In FSNP, I-1326, Fu contended that the garrison commander Kuan Lin-cheng (1905–1980) was innocent.
59 FSNP, V-8, a notebook of 1945.
60 Ch'ien Li-ch'ün, *Fan-jen te pei-ai: Chou Tso-jen chuan* (Taipei, 1991), 210–211.

nationalism and political reality. Although the Nationalist government and some intellectual leaders, such as Fu Ssu-nien, felt it necessary to screen unloyal people and to reeducate all who had taught and studied in universities and professional schools, this demand, insisted on right after the war, was gradually softened. If teachers in the higher schools were suspended from their jobs, there would be no teachers left to fill the vacancies. The number of students who according to Fu needed to be reeducated was also too large. In a time when the KMT and CCP were struggling with each other, it was important to gain support from students; with so many student movements already opposed to the KMT government, it became unrealistic to insist on loyalty or national integrity. Fewer and fewer people therefore sided with Fu Ssu-nien, and he became isolated.

Similarly, when the government implemented a policy to set up continuation schools to educate the students who had once studied in schools controlled by the Japanese during the war years, many professors from the Japanese-run schools were retained to teach at these schools because there were not enough faculty members. But Fu insisted that they all had to leave. His stubbornness not only irritated the "turncoats" but also the many government officials who were in charge of reestablishing Chinese rule.

This expulsion policy also extended to his friends, such as Yü P'ing-po and Jung Keng (1894–1984). After being berated and shouted at by Fu, Jung Keng published a plea in a newspaper for leniency for faculty members who had served in the Japanese-dominated Peita. Fu immediately published two public announcements defending his policy, arguing that in 1937 Peita had instituted a policy encouraging its entire faculty to move to the south. And, Fu continued, almost all faculty members of the "bogus Peita" had not originally taught at the university, and it was therefore absolutely wrong to retain them. On top of that, Fu believed it was his responsibility to guard staunchly the principle of loyalty and thereby set a good example for future generations.[61] In doing this he might have had in mind the words he had once uttered: because of the lack of "citizenship training," there have been "many turncoats in Chinese history."[62] Hundreds of faculty members who had served in the Japanese-run Peita were finally fired. Fu believed that if Hu Shih had taken over the presidency of Peita right after the war, he would not have been resolute enough to expel these disloyal professors.[63]

61 Fu Le-ch'eng, "Fu Meng-chen hsien-sheng te min-tsu ssu-hsiang," in *Shih-tai te chui-i lun-wen-chi*, 158.
62 *FSNC*, 2056.   63 Wang Yün, "Fu Ssu-nien yü Pei-ching ta-hsüeh," in *Fu Ssu-nien*, 99.

Fu's purges also extended to powerful political figures. Angered by the ineffectiveness of political reform, Fu, as a university president, personally sued Pao Chien-ch'ing (1893–?), the president of Peita under Japanese occupation, and Chang Yen-ch'ing (1898–?), the vice-president of Hsin-min Society, an organization supporting the puppet regime. The lawsuit attracted enormous attention in northern China. Fu's reputation for punishing turncoats led people to believe that he was the man to whom custody of traitors should be remanded.[64]

In the summer of 1946, when Hu Shih returned to China for swearing in as president of Peita, Fu was relieved from the job. During his brief tenure at Peita, Fu had added the Colleges of Engineering, Agriculture, and Medicine to the existing Colleges of Arts, Science, and Law. After this, in the winter of 1945, "Mr. Mover" made preparations to move the IHP from Szechwan to Nanking.

The lives of members of the IHP in Li-chuang during the war years were miserable due to the humid climate and hyperinflation. The cost of living, however, was cheaper in Li-chuang than in the coastal areas. In 1946, after more than one year of waiting, the IHP was the first institute of the Academia Sinica to load its people in two ships to go downriver to Nanking.[65] Six years previous, when the IHP had relocated to Szechwan, it was heading for a less expensive area. But this time it was bound for the expensive city of Nanking. The "demobilization aid" from the government was not enough for members to buy even basic kitchen utensils and bedding. Witnessing this, Fu was extremely pessimistic about the future of the IHP and perceived that total political and economic collapse was imminent.[66]

Because of the shortage of paper for printing during the war years, only a few items of research by IHP members had been published. The IHP had been almost forgotten by its colleagues and the world at large. In 1947 and 1948, despite the impact of hyperinflation, Fu secured a large amount of paper with which to publish an impressive number of works by members of the IHP.[67]

64 For example, there is a letter from Nieh Yün-t'ai (1880–1953), an industrialist, to Fu reporting that his relative Ch'ü Hsüan-ying (1892–?), a famous historian who served in the puppet government, was hiding in his home. See FSNP, III-1123. Later Fu managed to get a copy of the record of Ch'ü's service under Japanese control. See FSNP, I-1265, a draft of written appeal for suing Pao Chien-ch'ing is still kept. See FSNP, IV-525.
65 "Shih-yü-so fa-chan-shih," ch. 8, 1–24.   66 Ibid.
67 This included thirteen issues of the *Bulletin*, thirteen monographs, four linguistic investigation reports, and two archaeological reports. See ibid., ch. 8, 39–46.

The "Pure Stream"

In 1947 the civil war and skyrocketing inflation both reached new heights. T. V. Soong, who had succeeded H. H. Kung as premier in 1945, was believed to be contributing to the economic deterioration by virtue of his bad policies and the immense corruption of his coterie. Soong was Kung's relative and enemy and also "the emperor's brother-in-law" (*kuo-chiu*). It is worth noting that in the history of the Nationalist government, excluding Chiang Kai-shek and Wang Ching-wei, there had been only two important premiers up to 1947: H. H. Kung and T. V. Soong. Both men were financial giants who had helped Chiang considerably in financing his cadets before and after the Northern Expedition. But malpractice and the prevalence of corruption irritated their compatriots. The CCP published many books denouncing them, and these proved to be extremely effective as propaganda.[68] Even in the 1960s, a supporter of the Nationalist government still believed that the Kung and Soong coteries had destroyed the entire Chinese middle class.[69]

Fu's attack on Kung and Soong unintentionally coincided with those of the leftists. The "loyalists" under the Nationalist government were echoed by Chiang's enemies, and this proved to be detrimental to Chiang's reputation.

Soong was a thoroughly Western-educated banker, as was Kung before him. Fu claimed that no more than one ten-thousandth of Soong's blood was Chinese. Contrary to Chiang's relationship with Kung, Soong was never congenial to Chiang.[70] There was much euphoria when Soong returned from the United States for swearing in as premier. People were expecting him to cure the economic woes created during Kung's tenures as minister of finance and premier. When Soong announced his policy of purchasing gold from people at lower prices and thereby elicited much criticism, Fu stood alone and wrote a powerful article to endorse Soong's policy.[71] Fu's belief was that during periods of national crisis, people should contribute their fair share to help the country. Yet before

---

68 See, for example, Ch'en Po-ta's *Chung-kuo te ssu-ta-chia-tsu* (Hong Kong, 1947); K'ang Chung-p'ing's "Lun Chung-kuo kuan-liao tzu-pen-chu-i," *Ch'ün-chung*, 38 (1948), 14–16; 39 (1948), 14–15, and Ching-chi tzu-liao she, ed., *T. V. Soong hao-men tzu-pen nei-mu* (Hong Kong, 1948).
69 Hsü Fu-kuan, "Shih shei chi-k'uei le Chung-kuo she-hui fan-kung te li-liang," in *Hsüeh-shu yü cheng-chih chih chien*, 2:1–14. This is the most widely read criticism of T. V. Soong and H. H. K'ung in Taiwan.
70 The tension between Soong and Chiang was widely discussed. See, for example, Parks M. Coble, *The Shanghai Capitalists and the Nationalist Government, 1927–1937* (Cambridge, Mass., 1980), 109–115.
71 *FSNC*, 1848–1855. Cf. Ch'eng Ai-ch'in and Li Hui-ling, "Tao-Sung-yün-tung te chu-chiang," in *Fu Ssu-nien*, 188–189.

long, corruption, malpractice, and unruly conduct by members of Soong's coterie irritated and provoked many people. In August 1946 Soong decided to sell U.S. $380 million from the Central Bank to the public to stabilize the inflation-ridden economy. It was contended that Soong's coterie bought up about $151 million of the total and that Kung's group purchased about $180 million. People believed that these two groups had gobbled up fully 89 percent of the entire sum.[72]

In addition, Soong implemented a new policy of issuing certificates for importing crucial resources. Because the Soong and Kung coteries controlled the certificates, they monopolized the importation of resources to the extent that, as Chiang Kai-shek complained, one pound of tobacco cost ten thousand *yüan* (Chinese currency) in February 1947. These two policies caused an economic disaster ("gold peril" in Shanghai and other cities), but the government made no move. Fu could endure this no more, and right after the "gold peril" he published his "This Kind of T. V. Soong Should Step Down" (Che-yang te Sung Tzu-wen fei-tso-k'ai pu-k'o) and two other vitriolic articles.[73] Headlines like "Fu Ssu-nien Would Launch a Revolution" appeared in newspapers.[74] The three courageous articles were widely hailed by the general public and also led Chiang Kai-shek to change Soong's policies immediately. Although Chiang blamed the CCP for the inflation, Soong stepped down in fifteen days.[75]

Letters of support mailed to Fu Ssu-nien began to accumulate. "Cannon Fu" became a modern remonstrator. Fu's action was followed by the party members of the KMT. One hundred core members of the KMT were motivated to call for punishing Soong's coterie. Even the *Central Daily News* (*Chung-yang jih-pao*), the major party newspaper of the KMT, called for the destruction of the Kung and Soong coteries.[76]

In retrospect, it is worth noting that among the KMT's numerous internecine struggles, there was at least one constant confrontation between those with intellectual backgrounds and those of the comprador (*mai-pan*) class.[77] Although mapping out the members of these two groups is very difficult, it is agreed that T. V. Soong and H. H. Kung

---

72 The numbers are impossible to ascertain. Here I adopt the numbers people tended to believe at the time. See *Chung-yang jih-pao* (Nanking), July 1, 1947.
73 The two other articles are "Sung Tzu-wen te shih-pai," *Shih-chi p'ing-lun*, 1:8 (1947), 5–7; and "Lun hao-meng tzu-pen chih pi-hsü ch'an-ch'u," *Kuan-ch'a*, 2:1 (1947), 6–9.
74 This headline led the *Shih-chieh jih-pao* (February 15, 1947). See *Hu Shih te jih-chi*, February 15, 1947, n.p.
75 See *Hu Shih te jih-chi*, February 17, 1947, n.p.
76 Cf. Ch'eng Ai-ch'in et al., "Tao-Sung-yün-tung te chu-chiang," in *Fu Ssu-nien*, 192.
77 This is an observation made by a high official, Ch'eng Ts'ang-p'o. See Ch'eng's "Tsai chi Fu Meng-chen hsien-sheng," in *Fu Ku hsiao-chang ai-wan-lu*, 50.

were the two heads of the comprador class, while Chu Chia-hua, Hu Shih, Fu Ssu-nien, Chiang T'ing-fu, Wang Shih-chieh, Weng Wen-hao, Ch'ien Tuan-sheng (1900–1990), Wu Ching-ch'ao, and others were in the intellectual group. Kung and Soong constantly put pressure on the intellectual group. Although members of the intellectual group occupied a number of high posts, they were constantly overwhelmed by various cliques inside the KMT party.

For example, during Hu Shih's tenure as China's ambassador to the United States, Soong was actually the real representative of the Nationalist government in America. Soong took every opportunity to deprecate Hu Shih, always bypassing him in negotiations between Chungking and Washington. Kung, Soong, and Wang Cheng-t'ing (1882–1961) were three major saboteurs who complained about Hu's "nondiplomatic" activities in America,[78] complaints that ultimately led to Hu's dismissal.[79] Chiang T'ing-fu was also harassed by Soong, and his letters of complaint to Fu were many.[80] Weng Wen-hao, as Hu Shih told Fu, was occupying the office of general secretary of the Executive Yüan without receiving any assignment from Soong, the premier.[81] The impression Fu got from their complaints was that Soong had gathered all power to his own clique and had neglected all other cabinet members.[82] Chu Chia-hua, the minister of education and later head of KMT organization and the major patron of Fu and the Academia Sinica, was also overwhelmed by Soong and Kung.[83] Fu did not actually serve in the government and so was not constrained by any official regulation, yet he was closely associated with all of the people who felt the sting of Soong's high-handed tactics, and he had the audacious character to stand up and resist even someone of Soong's standing. After these attacks, Fu became in the Chinese mind a representative of the "pure stream" (*ch'ing-liu*),[84] that is, the incorruptible element in public life.

78 Fu was well aware that T. V. Soong played the crucial role in dismissing Hu Shih from his ambassadorship in the United States. Fu was also well aware that Soong, then in America, was the real ambassador to the United States. For example, in a letter to Fu from Ch'ien Tuan-sheng, then Hu Shih's assistant, Ch'ien complained that Hu received no direct information from the central government. See FSNP, IV-63. In his diary, Hu Shih complained repeatedly of the ways in which Soong dishonored his ambassadorship. See *Hu Shih te jih-chi*, February 11, 1942, and May 19, 1942, n.p.
79 Cf. *Hu Shih te jih-chi*, November 5, 1945.
80 Chiang T'ing-fu's letters of complaint were many. See FSNP, I-457, I-461, I-464.
81 FSNP, I-1669, a letter from Hu Shih to Fu. In this letter Hu Shih severely criticized Soong.
82 Ibid.
83 On the struggle between Soong and Chu, see Fu's letter to his wife, FSNP, I-1300.
84 Several dimensions should be added to the understanding of the "pure stream." In Fu's case, the "pure stream" was not without personal preference. To be a member of the pure stream without becoming a martyr required a powerful patron. It is worth

To be a member of the "pure stream" was by no means to be a professional politician. Fu said that the reason he jumped into politics was simply because he could not forget the welfare of the people, so he "ran back and forth, in and out of the door of academics." But he confided that he could not go very far away and could not stay in very long.[85] And Fu knew that the only job he was truly fit for was that of a remonstrator rather than a high bureaucrat.[86] It is paradoxical that, at a time when the government was losing its legitimacy, the liberal intellectuals who joined the KMT government soon lost their credibility with the youth. When they were not in office, they were better trusted. That was why many of them accepted government appointments only reluctantly. After Hu Shih was relieved of his ambassadorship, he refused to be appointed to any government position.[87] Fu Ssu-nien also declined offers for positions as National Council member (*Kuo-fu wei-yüan*), minister of education, and president of the examination *Yüan*.[88] The best position for them to help the government was to be outside of the government. In the 1940s liberals were destined to occupy positions of little power.

Exhausted by his wartime and postwar activities, Fu's chronic high blood pressure worsened. In June 1947, after his flamboyant criticism of Soong, Fu went with his family to the United States for medical treatment. He stayed in New Haven most of the time, but he also received treatment at the Brigham Hospital at Harvard University. This was his only year of leisure since his return to China in 1926. He drew up a plan to read whatever works he had not had time to read over the years, and he always stayed up until two or three in the morning reading. Most of his attention was on Marxism and the revolutionary strategy of Lenin, a topic he had neglected and which had become most relevant during the 1940s. He might have felt that his negligence in repudiating

---

noting that Ma Yin-ch'u, the first to attack H. H. Kung, was later arrested. But Fu successfully avoided becoming a martyr. In addition to being Chiang Kai-shek's personal favorite, Fu was very skilled in handling his job. For example, he praised and criticized Chiang simultaneously.

85 In a letter to Hu Shih, 1942. FSNP, I-1676.
86 In a letter to his wife, Fu explained why he firmly rejected this appointment: "Only when I can have a great contribution to make shall I take up any position. But it seems difficult to do anything now.... Working with those nasty officials is not something I am willing to do." FSNP, I-1302.
87 Hu Shih to Fu Ssu-nien, FSNP, I-1668. Cf. FSNP, II-89, a letter from Wang Shih-chieh to Fu Ssu-nien and Ch'ien Tuan-sheng.
88 When Chiang Kai-shek hoped to appoint him to the *kuo-fu wei-yuan*, Hu Shih wavered a bit. Fu's outspoken opposition to the appointment caused some tension in their longtime congenial friendship. But they did not consider Peita an affiliate organ of the government, partly because it was in the north and was almost beyond the reach of the KMT. See FSNP, I-1681, a letter from Hu to Fu.

Marxism had somewhat contributed to the younger generation's attraction to the CCP. He decided that after returning to China most of his efforts would be directed toward connecting academic study with the practical world. On May 7, 1947, Fu wrote that he should edit a sociological review, write a general history of China, and establish the "Fu Ssu-nien Tribune."[89]

In the spring of 1948, Fu was elected to the Legislative *Yüan* in absentia. Without being notified, Fu was supported in a motion by more than three hundred legislators to run for vice-president of that organ.[90] The motion, however, failed.

Fu did not receive an operation as had been formerly planned; he was given a rather optimistic evaluation of his health.[91] Against his relatives' repeated advice, Fu chose to return to China instead of staying in the United States as a refugee. In August 1948, when the Nationalist government was in serious danger, returning to China was a very rare act.[92] He was, however, persuaded by his wife to leave their only son in America.[93]

The year Fu stayed in America was the period during which the CCP achieved tremendous momentum in the civil war. In mid-1948 the CCP forces were already almost equal to those of the KMT in number. At the end of that year, Manchuria and northern China were taken over by the CCP. The northwest also fell under its control. Upon his return to Nanking, Fu agonized over the deteriorating political situation. In December 1948, when Peking was about to be overrun by Chinese Communist forces, Fu Ssu-nien secured permission from the government to send two airplanes to rescue eminent scholars in Peking who wished to flee to the south. However, most scholars whose names were on the rescue list responded very passively to the invitation to flee, and only a

---

89 FSNP, I-1682.
90 FSNP, I-352, a newspaper clipping collected by Fu Ssu-nien. According to American Ambassador Stuart's observation, legislators were opposed to party domination, so they aimed at defeating another candidate for the vice-presidency, Ch'en Li-fu (1900–), the leader of the most powerful clique of the KMT. However, "Chen was elected on first ballot by 343 votes to 236 for nonparty candidate Fu Ssu-nien. Fu's authorship of articles offensive to Mongols was reportedly an important factor in his defeat, causing border people to vote solidly against him." See "The Ambassador in China (Stuart) to the Secretary of State, May 18, 1948," *Foreign Relations of the United States, 1948*, vol. 7 (Washington, D.C., 1973), 239–240.
91 FSNP, I-988, a summary of a medical record signed by Wang Herngwen. However, Fu was advised not to take any administrative job.
92 His only brother, Fu Meng-po, wrote Fu and advised him not to return to China. FSNP, IV-234.
93 Yü Ta-ts'ai, "I Meng-chen," in *FSNC*, 2583.

very few of them actually boarded the planes. It is recalled that when Fu received the planes at the Nanking airport and saw how few passengers their cabins held, he wailed in disappointment.[94] Knowing that Nanking would also soon fall to the Communists, Fu took with him a large number of sleeping pills. Upon hearing of the suicide of Ch'en Pu-lei and Tuan Hsi-p'eng (1897–1948), two old friends, Fu decided to die for the "old dynasty." Only his wife's intervention, it is believed, saved him from suicide.[95] He locked himself in a small room for three days and repeatedly recited a poem by T'ao Yüan-ming (365–427). This poem came to the minds of both Fu and Hu Shih as they witnessed the fall of their nation:

I planted mulberry trees by the river bank
And hoped to have a harvest three years hence,
But just when leaves began to deck the boughs
A sudden landslide changed the river's course.
The leaves were stripped, the branches all broken
Roots and trunk floated off to the blue sea.
The silkworms will have nothing to eat this spring
And who will furnish clothes against the cold?
I failed to plant them on the high plateau
And now today what have I to regret?[96]

In addition to the agony over the change of regime, it was recorded that Hu Shih recited this poem to reprimand himself for having neglected the work of guiding the youth. This reprimand was expressed in the two sentences: "I failed to plant them on the high plateau / And now today what have I to regret?" Hu believed that if in years past he had not been so obsessed with evidential research and had paid more attention to general issues, the youth would not have been taken in by Communist propaganda.[97]

During these three long days, while Fu was reciting this poem, he also felt as though all he had endeavored to achieve in the past was being

---

94 Li Hsiao-ting, *Shih che ju ssu* (Taipei, 1996), 65.
95 Fu Le-ch'eng, *Fu Meng-chen hsien-sheng nien-p'u*, in *FSNC*, 2667.
96 This poem is one of T'ao Yüan-ming's "Imitations" (*ni-ku*). James Hightower, *The Poetry of T'ao Ch'ien* (Oxford, 1970), 184. Hu Shih also wrote down this poem in his diary, see *Hu Shih te jih-chi*, January 2, 1949, n.p.
97 Hu Sung-p'ing, *Hu Shih nien-p'u ch'ang-pien ch'u-kao* (Taipei, 1984), 10 vols., 6: 2065–2066. At about the same time he was reciting this poem, Hu Shih admitted to the U.S. ambassador in China and former president of Yenching University Leighton Stuart his negligence in combatting communism and his excessive indulgence in research.

dismantled, which led him to rethink many of the values he had once espoused. But since he had "failed to plant them on the high plateau," what did he now have to regret?[98]

In late 1948, when Nanking was in great danger, Fu announced the disbanding of the IHP. He lamented that although he had hoped to remove the institute to a safer place to continue the nation's scholastic tradition, his deteriorating health had prevented him from undertaking such a burdensome task. But when the members of the IHP decided to carry on their work, Fu chose to move the IHP to Taiwan rather than to other proposed locations. The institute was safely relocated to Taiwan in late 1948. Fu was appointed president of T'aita in January 1949, almost at the same time that a large force of the Nationalist government was surrounded on the Hsüchow Plain. Later, when the capital of the Nationalist government was "moving on foot," Fu was already in Taiwan devoting his energies to T'aita.

During the last years of the Nationalist regime, Fu was singled out by CCP propaganda organs as a target of attack. Fu's bitter criticism of the CCP and his role in settling the Kunming student demonstration infuriated the CCP, which labeled him "anti-CCP and anti–Soviet Union." "The name suits me,"[99] Fu retorted. Fu also became a major target of the *Wen-hui pao*, a CCP organ.[100] In August 1949 he was even denounced by Mao Tse-tung as a war criminal.[101]

An Intellectual in Times of Uncertainty: In Taiwan and at T'aita

Fu is known in Taiwan more for his presidency of T'aita than as a historian. Fu today remains the most memorable T'aita figure in any poll.[102] The Fu Ssu-nien Gardens, the Fu Ssu-nien Hall, and the Fu Ssu-nien Bell, which rings hourly in commemoration of Fu's name, all remind T'aita students that there was once a Fu Ssu-nien. But Fu served at T'aita for less than two years.

---

98 Fu's disappointment was apparent in an article complaining that the works of leftist scholars intentionally appealed to common people and thus reached an unusually wide audience outside academia, whereas more-objective academic works did not attract a wide audience. See *FSNC*, 2089.
99 *FSNC*, 2160.   100 *FSNC*, 2072.
101 Ma Liang-k'uan, "P'ang-huang p'ai-huai nien ku-t'u," in *Fu Ssu-nien*, 197.
102 Li Ch'üan, "Fu-hai shuo san-ch'ien ti-tzu," in *Fu Ssu-nien*, 206. After Fu's death, commemorative articles multiplied. See *Fu ku hsiao-chang ai-wan-lu*, 81–97. During my undergraduate years at T'aita in the late 1970s, Fu remained a symbol of the university in the minds of most students and was the most memorable figure in the university's history.

Fu Ssu-nien arrived at T'aita when the KMT regime and T'aita were in great trouble. When he took over the president's office, Nanking was under attack by the Red Army. As for T'aita, it was undergoing serious difficulties.

Under Japanese occupation, T'aita was set up to train scholars specializing in tropical and subtropical (South Pacific) studies. Its other mission was to educate subjects loyal to the Japanese Empire. After T'aita was taken over by the KMT government, its purpose changed from training Japanese Taiwanese to training Chinese Taiwanese.[103]

The university imitated the German system and had 114 chaired professors. The university was a loosely confederated body with rather weak presidential power. After 1945, however, the presidency became the power center. This was the common practice in mainland China but was a new system for Taiwan. All of this resulted in some chaos. But the major cause of instability was the tension between native faculty, grouped in the medical school of the university, and the mainlanders who came to take over the university. This led to the exaggerated hunting of Communist students on the campus. The native group of faculty, especially some of the faculty of the medical school, were arrested or executed in the course of the February 28 Massacre of 1947.[104]

When Fu Ssu-nien came to T'aita, he tried to obtain as many good professors as possible from the mainland to fill the vacancies left by Japanese faculty members, who had originally constituted 88 percent of the body of the faculty. When Fu arrived, less than 1 percent was left.[105] Fu considered his mission at T'aita to be to heighten the academic quality of the university so that it could one day be comparable with Berlin University, Cambridge, or Oxford.

Fu Ssu-nien appreciated the chaired professor system of German universities. He emphasized that during the Japanese occupation, due to its chaired professor system, the university had advanced in its academic quality. He lamented that the chair system was replaced after 1945 when the mainland university system was introduced.[106]

Fu made considerable contributions to reviving and reinforcing the faculty of T'aita after the departure of the Japanese. Thereafter, in terms of the quality of teaching T'aita became one of the best universities in all of China. When the Nationalist government withdrew to Taiwan, millions of mainlanders followed and university enrollment suddenly increased by several times. T'aita was immediately overbur-

---

103 Tseng Shih-jung, "Chan-hou T'ai-wan chih wen-hua ch'ung-pien yü tsu-ch'ün kuan-hsi" (M.A. thesis, National Taiwan University, 1994), 134–136.
104 Ibid., 138–142, 150–152. 105 Ibid., 143–147. 106 *FSNC*, 2166, 2196.

dened by the unexpected expansion in enrollment, and T'aita's facility was strained to the breaking point. If all the students went to their classes, there were not enough chairs for them to sit in. Some students even lived in the patient rooms of the T'aita Hospital. During this initial crisis period, Fu used his extensive personal connections to "plunder" money from the cash-strapped Nationalist government for the benefit of the university.

Fu is also remembered for his staunch stance in favor of human rights. When Fu foresaw the white terror that would prevail in Taiwan during the 1950s, he strove to maintain academic dignity and resisted police intrusion onto the T'aita campus. His efforts to protect the independence of the academic world were hailed whenever students were arrested. Fu is well remembered for his statement: "I am running a university, not a police station."[107] He resisted the arrest of students carried out without hard evidence and successfully secured the release of many innocent students.[108] But because he was staunchly opposed to the CCP, Fu also helped the Nationalist government expel students accused of being Communists and sent a good number of them back to the mainland.[109]

On the other hand, Fu also envisioned that T'aita would eventually be nativized. He insisted on paying special attention to Taiwanese students and sent them to study abroad.[110]

Fu Ssu-nien was remembered not only for obtaining many prestigious teachers from the mainland but also for not allowing high government officials to get professorships. This was an uncommon action in an era during which political power was exercised on academic affairs. After 1950, whenever high officials used their political influence to secure their own professorial appointments, Fu was mentioned repeatedly as a bastion of resistance.

---

107 *FSNC*, 2159.
108 But during abnormal times only those with powerful personalities could be heroic without risking their own lives. Fu happened to have a heroic personality, democratic attitude, and personal relationships for curbing the white terror at T'aita, all of which allowed him to achieve a good reputation. As for protecting students, see, for example, FSNP, IV-264, a letter from a secret agent, Chao Kung-ch'ia, refusing Fu's request to release a T'aita student. Fu repeatedly announced publicly that he was running not a secret police office but a university. See *FSNC*, 2072, 2159. He was repeatedly denounced by KMT members for "not being anti-Communist" and for housing "Communist" professors. See *FSNC*, 2162–2163.
109 On sending Communist students back to the mainland, see Wang Shih-chieh's speech in a conference for the special commemorative issue of *Chuan-chi wen-hsüeh* in honor of Fu: Wang Shih-chieh, "Fu hsien-sheng tsai cheng-chih shang te erh-san shih," *Chuan-chi wen-hsüeh*, 28:1 (1976), 13.
110 P'eng Ming-min, *Tzu-yu te tzu-wei* (Taipei, 1995), 86.

During the last stage of his life Fu once again came to be very much concerned with educational issues, and his last articles were on this topic. While studying in Europe, he paid considerable attention to university education. His ideal was to establish a research-oriented university. Fu retained the old research orientation of T'aita but also paid particular attention to introductory courses. He required the most prominent and senior professors to teach freshmen classes.

Fu Ssu-nien lived in Taiwan for less than two years. During the last stage of his life Fu reflected on some of his convictions and the victory of the CCP. Some drastic changes are discernible in this period of his life.

Fu had always been labeled a liberal, but his political essays focused less on democratic ideas and more on the construction of a modern political culture. Until the mid-1940s he was fond of frequently making the following points: throughout Chinese history there was only central government and no local government;[111] China had masses but no society;[112] politics should be the business of the people, and it was absurd to count on the government to do everything;[113] and, finally, the Chinese upheld no political cause.[114]

For May Fourth youth, liberalism and egalitarianism were political ideas – ideas that preoccupied Fu's and other intellectuals' minds. Fu sometimes had difficulty keeping the balance between these two values. On many occasions, Fu strongly complained about the existence of social inequality. In 1919 he even wrote that all who owned cars should be sentenced to death.[115] In his late forties, he sometimes complained that, due to serious inequality, Chinese peasants led an animal-like life. He even regretted that new students who wanted to enlighten peasants never really understood them.

Fu had always believed that economic equality and individual freedom should be joined. Being keenly aware of the plight of the poor, Fu throughout his life maintained economic equality as his primary political concern. Fu constantly repeated that the ideal state would be one in which freedom as well as economic equality existed. For a state to have only one of these qualities without the other was unacceptable. A state of mild socialism and liberalism was Fu's utopia. Roosevelt and the platform of the Labor Party in England were his political models. Fu believed that Roosevelt's socialist policies imbued a new spirit into liberalism. He asserted that capitalism had been abusing liberalism to exploit the people and had produced extreme economic inequality.

---

111 *FSNC*, 1720.   112 *FSNC*, 1578.   113 *FSNC*, 1655.
114 *FSNC*, 1572–1575.   115 *FSNC*, 1590.

Imperialism was its natural product. It was a must for a liberal to be mindful of economic equality; without it, liberalism was not real liberalism.[116]

Socialism is one of the most ill-defined terms in modern China. Fu and a group of liberal intellectuals entertained similar ideals of socialism and longed for a world of liberalism without capitalism. They believed that through government power, economic inequalities could be corrected and that state-owned enterprises could bring material progress.

It is, however, interesting to note that with the victory of the CCP in mainland China forcing many of these liberal intellectuals to flee to Taiwan, the resultant political crisis dashed their dreams. The success of the CCP signaled the victory of economic egalitarianism by means of class struggle. Consequently, many intellectuals became aware that they could not ask for both freedom and economic equality at that time in China. Many people, including Hu Shih, Fu Ssu-nien, Lei Chen (1897–1979), and Yin Hai-kuang (1919–1969), gradually gave up socialist ideals in favor of liberalism.[117] The change in Fu Ssu-nien's attitudes was very evident. He decided that if there was no liberty, there was no equality either. Liberty should be esteemed above equality. In 1949 he changed his stand by writing that in order to acquire freedom, it would be legitimate to give up economic equality temporarily.[118]

Of those who fled the mainland and lived in Taiwan during the white terror, Fu and a group of intellectuals were unique in defending liberalism. Many of them became staunch advocates of liberalism and later suffered for it during the KMT's crackdowns in the 1960s.[119]

Searching for a Moral Source

In Fu's late life, his abandonment of crude materialism and positivism is readily observable, as is his return to the Mencian tradition. During his year-long stay in America, Fu had time to reflect on many things. First of all, he noticed that during the preceding twenty years, "Western learning" had changed considerably. Positivism was no longer as popular as he had once imagined. Fu found that his hostility toward Kantian

---

116 *FSNC*, 1939–1953.
117 Chang Chung-tung, "Hu Shih yü Yin Hai-kuang," *Kuo-li T'ai-wan ta-hsüeh wen shih che hsüeh-pao*, 37 (1989), 130–138.
118 *FSNC*, 1970.
119 Typical of these crackdowns was the arrest of Lei Chen, the proscription of the journal *Tzu-yu Chung-kuo*, and the treatment of Yin Hai-kuang.

philosophy and his appreciation of positivism and behaviorism had all changed. He wrote in 1947:

When I was in Europe, I was originally a crude materialist of the physiological type (in philosophy, not in other spheres). I therefore appreciated Pavlov, J. B. Watson, William James and his language theory of emotions, R. Carnarp, and Freud and his works. During the year of illness (1941), I constantly reflected on the meaning of human life. Sometimes these reflections seemed mystic, but they were not. I finally became aware that "the cosmos" is a grand deduction and that we have to make some assumptions, and take these assumptions as bases to deduce others.[120]

Fu did not fully express what these assumptions were. However, we know he "became disgusted with J. B. Watson's theory [of behaviorism]." He believed that in dealing with human problems, "behaviorism is too crude. [More spiritual elements] can help people avoid neglecting important facts."[121]

Fu also realized that human beings should be distinguished from other creatures and that they were not governed by the same rules of behavior, an idea that originated in the mid-1920s and grew stronger in Fu's later years. He said that in comparing animal behavior to human behavior, we should bear in mind that "man is one species of animal" but that "an animal is not a man." Fu believed that behaviorism and many Darwinists often unconsciously failed to distinguish animals from human beings.[122] In 1947 he said, "Believing in crude materialism and pragmatism is equivalent to saying 'I am always lying.' . . . I think I was naive before. To use the Kantian terminology, I was in my precritical period. This time, during my stay in America, I found that there has been little progress in behaviorism. I feel that Pavlov's experiments were very crude, and of Watson's contributions only the implicit language theory is valuable."[123]

Fu was no longer as optimistic as he had once been about the possibility of applying scientific methods to human affairs. He sympathized with Poincaré's theory that human feelings can be dealt with by models of natural science, but felt that we should recognize the limitations of such an approach. He admitted that he had become sympathetic with the "mentalistic" point of view and regretted his former materialistic leanings.[124]

This mentalistic turn led Fu to reappraise Mencius thought. During Fu's later years, his hostility toward Mencian philosophy changed. The most obvious signal of this came in 1949, when he required T'aita fresh-

120 FSNP, III-195, Fu to Chao Yüan-jen, ca. 1948. 121 Ibid. 122 FSNP, III-196.
123 Ibid. 124 Ibid. "Mentalistic" was Fu's own term.

men to read the *Mencius*. A "Mencius prize" (*Meng-tzu hsin-te chiang*) was instituted to reward fine essays on the text.[125] Traditional moral cultivation again came to Fu's attention. Ho Ting-sheng, a former colleague of Fu's in Chungshan University, noted that Fu visited him at T'aita for the sole purpose of discussing the concept of moral cultivation in the *Mencius*.[126] Hsü Fu-kuan, a critic of Fu, also noticed this drastic change.[127] This change was comparable with his switch to the New Culture group in 1917 and is another milestone along the lifelong journey of a May Fourth mind. Was this change due to the loss of China to the CCP or to some personal reason?

Fu was among the earliest of the May Fourth youths to face a serious threat of deteriorated health. His inherited hypertension almost cost him his life in 1941, an extremely busy year during which Fu was jointly appointed secretary-general of the Academia Sinica, director of the IHP, and a representative in the People's Political Council. He collapsed and was treated in an emergency room in Chungking by a prominent physician.[128] Lying on his hospital bed, Fu reflected on his life over the past forty-five years. He reevaluated Mencian philosophy, which was familiar to him thanks to his grandfather's instruction, although he had later come to despise it during the New Culture era.[129] We are unable to know if this constituted a return to a long-suppressed self. But we do know that after his recovery Hu Shih, then China's ambassador to the United States, advised Fu in a letter that, in the final analysis, *Lao-tzu* and *Chuang-tzu* were all useless to bring him peace of mind. "Why don't you read the works of your fellow Shantung provincials – Confucius and Mencius?" Hu suggested. "Come to think of it . . . they are so common, so plain in reflecting common feelings . . . that they can ease your hypertension by several tens of degrees."[130] Hu emphasized that "this is no joke; it is what I have felt intimately during my personal experiences in recent years. The greatness of Confucius is his insipidity, with nothing extraordinary or remarkable. He is really reasonable and sensible. Recently I read the *Mencius* and have also felt that he is quite delightful. Among the intellectuals of the past two thousand years, those who have had outstanding achievements and positive outlooks on life mostly benefited from the *Lun-yü* and the teachings of Mencius."[131] Compared

125 *FSNC*, 2290.
126 Ho Ting-sheng, "Sun-shih t'ai ta le," in *Fu ku hsiao-chang ai-wan-lu*, 76.
127 Hsü Fu-kuan, *Chung-kuo ssu-hsiang-shih lun-chi*, 232.
128 Fu Le-ch'eng, *Fu Meng-chen hsien-sheng nien-p'u*, in *FSNC*, 2644.
129 FSNP, III-195, Fu to Chao Yüan-jen.
130 Hu Shih to Fu Ssu-nien, FSNP, I-1649.   131 Ibid.

with the early Hu Shih, who championed the scientific outlook on life, this was a tremendous change.

But both Hu and Fu sensed that during life crises the positivistic mindset to which they had been espoused in their youths was so dry and unconcerned with private, innermost feelings that it was no longer a source of sustenance to them. Fu confessed that after his life-and-death experience in 1941, he was converted somewhat to the premodern Chinese moral tradition.[132]

When Fu was in the United States, the original plan for his operation was the surgical interruption of sympathetic nerve pathways.[133] It was reported that the factor worsening Fu's hypertension was his sensitive and anxious nature. Fu did admit that people always called him Cannon Fu, but the term "cannon" did not accurately characterize his entire personality because he was in fact very timid when confronting serious difficulties. He admitted that he always thought through the most complicated parts of things to the extent of frightening himself. He personally believed that this was extremely conducive to his hypertension. Later, he discovered Mencian moral philosophy as useful for stress management.

Fu noted in his 1946 notebook that "Mencius is the patriarch of liberalism and idealism."[134] The meaning of this is very ambiguous. It seems to denote a recognition of the indispensability of a moral foundation to liberalism. *Mencius* was useful for liberal preoccupation as a check on the government, which would be necessary if all individuals were to be allowed to develop political rights in an increasingly pluralistic society.

Mencius was also useful in cultivating the great spirit (*hao-jan-chih-ch'i*) while the CCP's threat was imminent. Fu resorted to *Mencius* to cultivate the students' moral courage while the nation was in crisis. The assignment of the *Mencius* as required reading for all first-year T'aita students was unusual for a staunch supporter of the New Culture Movement.[135] This requirement marked a drastic transition in Fu's evaluation of the Confucian philosophy of mind.

In the IHP, studying Neo-Confucianism was not only allowed but even

---

132 FSNP, III-195.
133 The surgery he expected to receive was described in a clipping entitled "Medical Forum," which was kept by Fu. See FSNP, I-351.
134 FSNP, V-82.
135 See Fu Le-ch'eng, *Fu Meng-chen hsien-sheng nien-p'u*, in *FSNC*, 2643–2644. Hsü Fu-kuan noticed that Fu himself was undergoing immense changes in 1947 and 1948, and he lamented that Fu did not get enough time to appreciate fully traditional Chinese moral values.

encouraged.¹³⁶ Fu himself was also reported to have devoted considerable time in expounding on Chu Hsi's philosophy.¹³⁷ In Taipei, Fu even argued that the term "New Culture Movement" did not make sense (*pu-t'ung*).¹³⁸ In fact, early in the 1943 commemoration of the May Fourth Movement, he had already called for cultural accumulation (*wen-hua chi-lei*).¹³⁹ As for student movements, Fu opposed them vehemently. Of them he said in 1932, "Therefore the most basic impulses burst out at the place of greatest weakness and least resistance. For this reason, the students [all engage in] either student movements or romantic affairs. The Communist Party opens widely the door of convenience [for such things], and from this it [gains] power."¹⁴⁰ Fu seemed to want to extirpate the seeds he had planted during his youth.

During his later years Fu also came to recognize that objectivity was not always possible, especially in the field of social science and historical study.¹⁴¹ His optimism about the attainability of objective knowledge changed greatly. As early as 1931, after the Mukden Incident, in an article entitled "Informal Discussion of Historical Textbooks" (Hsien-t'an li-shih chiao-k'o-shu), Fu had written that he no longer believed historiography was essentially of one nature with natural science.¹⁴² At T'aita, his confidence in historical objectivity decreased still further, and he held that "absolute objectivity is only an ideal."¹⁴³

Even more significantly, Fu's thinking on the relationship between tradition and modernity had changed. During the May Fourth era Fu was confident that tradition could be washed away overnight. But in 1949 he attacked the New Culture Movement and the May Fourth slogan of "total westernization" as absurd and contended that a nation's culture could not be changed unless its language was also totally changed.¹⁴⁴ The five thousand years of Chinese culture, Fu maintained, "shall never vanish.... There is no nation like China with an uninterrupted cultural tradition.... Now is the time to think of our ancestors and treasure our cultural tradition.... We are now becoming the carriers of a nonwhite culture...."¹⁴⁵ "Tradition will never die. It is impossible to erase tradition," he concluded.¹⁴⁶

136 This is according to an interview with Huang Chang-chien, a senior member of the IHP, November 20, 1990.
137 Lao Kan, "Fu Meng-chen hsien-sheng yü chin erh-shih-nien lai Chung-kuo li-shih hsüeh te fa-chan," in *Fu ku hsiao-chang ai-wan-lu*, 71.
138 *FSNC*, 2003. 139 *FSNC*, 1808. 140 *FSNC*, 2006.
141 Hsü Kuan-san, *Hsin-shih-hsüeh chiu-shih-nien*, 1:218.
142 *FSNC*, 1359. 143 *FSNC*, 1410–1413.
144 *FSNC*, 2120–2122. 145 *FSNC*, 2226.
146 *FSNC*, 2121. Similar ideas appeared repeatedly. See *FSNC*, 2122, 2223, 2225.

But Fu continued to maintain that Chinese tradition was in need of reform. "China's nonindustrial education should be rectified," he said. "Chinese traditions that have always neglected the masses should be corrected. Rectification, however, is not to erase but to broaden."[147]

Yin Hai-kuang observed that while most May Fourth youths became "worn out" (*yung-chiu le*), Fu Ssu-nien did not.[148] But Yin's characterization of Fu's mental attitude is a bit exaggerated. The older Fu never systematically discussed his convictions, but he seemed to reconcile the early tension between modern and traditional values. He had once, like most New Culture proponents, believed that destroying tradition was the prerequisite for introducing new things, but now he seemed to believe that old and new could coexist.

"Lay My Bones on This Tien Heng's Island"

Deep involvement in administrative matters was always detrimental to Fu's health. During the eight years of war with Japan, his deep worries about the potential subjugation of his native land and the poor environment he lived in also seriously damaged his health.[149] He even said that during those years he "suddenly jumped from a youth to an old man."[150] The old man did not live much longer. Fu suddenly died of hypertension on December 20, 1950, after being queried by Kuo Kuo-chi (1900–1970), a representative of the Taiwan Provincial Assembly nicknamed "Cannon Kuo," about the administration of T'aita. "Cannon Fu," who had gained his reputation for remonstrating against officials, died under another cannon's fire.

The speaker of the Taiwan Provincial Assembly announced to the public that "President Fu has passed away [*ch'i-shih*]." Because *ch'i-shih* is phonetically similar to *ch'i-ssu* (died of anger), T'aita students immediately perceived the insulting phonetic pun on Fu's death. The next morning, thousands of students stormed the Assembly and shouted "Out! Out! Out with Kuo Kuo-chi!" Students began throwing rocks at the Assembly, and a riot appeared imminent. Kuo fled through the back door. The students began to disband only after being persuaded that President Fu would have encouraged them to go back to their

---

147 *FSNC*, 2124–2125.
148 Yin Hai-kuang, "Wo i Meng-chen hsien-sheng," *Tzu-yu Chung-kuo*, 4:2 (1951), 79.
149 Fu to Hu Shih. FSNP, I-1676.
150 Fu Le-ch'eng, "Hsien-po Meng-chen hsien-sheng te jih-ch'ang sheng-huo," in *Fu ku hsiao-chang ai-wan-lu*, 13.

studies if he were still alive.[151] Approximately five thousand people attended Fu's funeral services. Fu once wrote on a scroll in 1949 to "lay my bones on this T'ien Heng's island,"[152] a request that turned out to be prophetic.

151 *Hsin-sheng-pao*, December 22, 1950.
152 *Fu ku hsiao-chang ai-wan-lu*, illustration, n.p. The character on this scroll read "Kuei-ku yü T'ien Heng chih tao," literally meaning to die on the island as did T'ien Heng, a loyalist of late Ch'in period who led five hundred subordinates to a small island and refused to recognize the newly founded Han government. All of them later committed suicide.

Conclusion: The Defeat of a May Fourth Youth

The fall of modern China from its position (at least in its own eyes) as the center of the civilized world to its new low as the most humiliated, hurt, and frustrated nation on earth produced festering nationalistic feelings. In the name of patriotism, a nationalist can bounce back and forth between conservatism and radicalism, between right-wing fanaticism and left-wing extremism. For such a figure, beneath the swift current of massive and unexpected change, patriotism is always the ultimate moving force.

This was especially true for Fu Ssu-nien's thought throughout his life. Born in a most conservative area and raised in a very traditional manner, Fu was expected to be a transmitter of traditional Chinese learning. Fu's surprise switch to the New Culture group in 1918 was mostly motivated by strong patriotic feelings and his search for an effective medicine to cure the nation's ills. Fu's patriotic enthusiasm expressed itself not by glorifying China's past, but through self-reproachment. His cultural iconoclasm was so thoroughgoing that he claimed that only Western learning could be called learning, whereas Chinese tradition should be completely discarded. But in his innermost self, he was torn between two extremes. He called for the complete abandonment of that with which he was most familiar and criticized the things with which he had previously been the most at ease. Dilemmas, discrepancies, and contradictions are evident in Fu's mind and writings. He was given the epithet "a bundle of contradictions" and led a life fraught with tension.

The two most important idols of May Fourth, Mr. Democracy and Mr. Science, did not come hand in hand. In his early writings, Fu did not use the term *min-chu* (democracy) often. His early concerns focused more on science and citizenship training. For Fu, the problem with Chinese politics was that there had never existed a "society," an entity that could only be created through citizenship training. In sum, three major concerns loomed large in Fu's mind during the May Fourth period: bridging the discrepancies between various cultural forms and Chinese social realities; avoiding harmful traditional mental attitudes, identified by Fu as introspection, moralization, and vagueness; and transforming the Chinese people from "masses" to "society" through "citizenship training."

Although his studies touched on many subjects, the main subjects Fu studied while a student in Europe were the natural sciences. In Europe his interests changed swiftly from psychology to mathematics to physics and finally to philology and history. When he finally found himself in the field of history, the methodology he introduced into Chinese historiography was a hybrid of positivism and Rankean historiography. The result was a methodology that made much of objectivity and scientific rigor. Fu Ssu-nien called for monographic study. He championed ordering historical materials so that the facts become naturally evident; he opposed excessive interpretation and generalization.

The establishment of the IHP was an enterprise for realizing Fu's new ideal of historical study. In this institute Fu insisted that historical study be a collective enterprise and that the creation of an institutional legacy be a prime goal of modern scholarship. His entrepreneurial style of management and his personal ties made the IHP a great success. Fu rang the bell, and productive scholars responded by coming to work together in this institute. The IHP became a leading institute for scholarship in Chinese historical study and trained a great many professional historians, archaeologists, philologists, and anthropologists. Two random cases are highly illustrative of this: when Chang Kwang-chih lists the six most important modern Chinese archaeologists, four of them are from the IHP, and when he lists the four most important leaders in the study of Shang history, all of them are from the IHP.[1]

Fu's emphasis on primary sources and his methods for collecting them also produced new styles of scholarship in the Republican period. He sent teams to open up archives, undertake anthropological investigations, conduct large-scale archaeological excavations, and engage in many other cooperative historical projects that led to much progress in many fields. The research methods he championed (using instruments, shovels, and one's feet) opened up new directions for research. In the wake of these successes, China witnessed the rise of a great number of associations as well as team projects in archaeology and history.[2]

But Fu's new history opposed general history. Its avoidance of any ethical or political commentary was criticized as being apathetic toward present realities, its placing of individual facts above theory was opposed

---

[1] See Chang Kwang-chih, *The Archaeology of Ancient China*, 3d ed. (New Haven, 1977), 6, and *Shang Civilization*, 46. Tung Tso-pin and Li Chi appeared in both lists.
[2] Shih Ch'üan-sheng, ed., *Chung-hua-min-kuo wen-hua-shih*, 2:720.

for failing to offer any simple general theory to answer urgent questions, and its antipathy toward philosophy and moral exhortation was sharply censured.

As a historian, Fu excelled in the history of Chinese antiquity. Viewing historical events plurally and genetically was definitely a methodological feature of his scholarship, and it was also part of the May Fourth universe of ideas. Fu Ssu-nien successfully pictured some significant junctures in the history of Chinese antiquity. Especially important was his hypothesis on the plural origins of Chinese antiquity. Several other working hypotheses also shed significant light on the field of ancient Chinese history. The major characteristic of these projects was the dissolution of systems into multievolutionary processes. Many traditional Chinese historical descriptions were dissolved into unrelated clusters that no longer supported Confucian moral teachings. For example, the morally constituted Three Dynasties were dissolved into a history of struggles between eastern and western ethnic groups. Doubting antiquity was an important part of the New Culture Movement, but Fu Ssu-nien, also a May Fourth youth, later was intent on dismantling Ku's radical hypotheses, gathering up the fragments of Chinese antiquity, and reconstructing it. Fu Ssu-nien was at the same time a destroyer and a builder.

Fu Ssu-nien was also known for his study of the origin of ancient Chinese moral philosophy. He believed that various traits of Chinese backwardness were deeply rooted in Chinese introspective moral philosophy. In Europe he was attracted to any antiintrospective philosophy, even crude materialism. Fu later traced the etymological origins of several key terms in Chinese moral philosophy and asserted that in orthodox Confucianism "there is neither good nor bad in our nature." Fu saw the Mencian moral tradition as a deviation from primordial Confucianism and took the tradition of emphasizing the spirit of investigating the external world and disciplining behavior as the true vision of Confucian teaching. This led to one of Fu's dilemmas. He was raised under the strong bearing of Mencian teaching, but to rescue China from its "liability" of introspective moral attitudes, he denounced the Mencian tradition and came to believe even in naive positivism.

May Fourth ideals gradually became a burden after the Mukden Incident in 1931. Fu, along with many other May Fourth youth, had called for cultural revolution prior to political revolution. Their abhorrence of warlord politics and their disappointment with the failure of the 1911 Revolution kept them away from politics and led them to the conviction that a cultural transformation was a necessary prerequisite to political order. The first step, they argued, was to establish an "academic society."

Therefore, they coined such slogans as "no talk of politics for twenty years," "do research regardless of its practical use," and "the only way to save our nation is to have young scholars devoting themselves for twenty or thirty years to profound learning."³ Fu tried at first to uphold precisely these ideals. But few of these values survived the challenges of immediate political needs, especially the confrontation between the KMT and the CCP and the life-and-death struggle with Japanese aggression. The autonomy of learning, a major goal of the New Culture Movement, proved a luxury. The dicta "truth for truth's sake" and "discovering the original meaning of one character is equal in value to discovering a fixed star" struck many young intellectuals as absurd. The pressing questions on the minds of many youth were rather where to go, what kind of society China is, and what is to be done – questions that required clear and simple answers. Study needed to be relevant to politics. The ideals of "suspending judgment" and "no talk of politics" were perceived as being blithely unconcerned with present realities and became a heavy burden to a generation of Chinese intellectuals.

Cultural iconoclasm, another feature of the May Fourth mentality, faced challenges as well. Fu Ssu-nien relentlessly called for criticism of Chinese tradition even after many of his fellows had softened their stances. But the revival of cultural conservatism in the 1930s and the pressing need to protect the nation from foreign encroachment required the concepts of collective worth and national identity. It was especially necessary to glorify the nation's past in order to persuade people that it was worthwhile to defend their country. For these and other reasons, cultural iconoclasm was severely challenged from various angles. In addition, the contempt for or neglect of the values and meanings of Chinese tradition also drew fire from New-Confucian scholars, who believed that moral values, especially those of the Mencian school, were essential for the people. They implied that the loss of these moral values had produced the moral anomie of the youth that later contributed tremendously to the success of the CCP.⁴ New Confucianists such as Hsiung Shih-li, and the philosophical school he helped to found, which is still active toady, insisted on the primacy of introspective moral philosophy. This was, in fact, a response to Hu shih and Fu Ssu-nien.

Individualism, another May Fourth value, was also challenged from both the right and left. Leftists maligned individualism as a capitalistic

---

3 Wu Ching-heng, "Ssu-shih-sui jih-chi hsüan-lu," in *Wu Ching-heng hsüan-chi*, hsü-pa, yu-chi, tsa-wen volume, 221.

4 See, for example, T'ang Chün-i, "Chung-kuo chin-tai hsüeh-shu wen-hua ching-shen chih fan-hsing," *Ming-chu p'ing-lun*, 1:24 (1950), 3–10, and Hsü Fu-kuan, *Chung-kuo ssu-hsiang-shih lun-chi*, 228.

value,[5] and in most party propaganda organs antiindividualism flourished.[6] Ch'en Ch'i-t'ien (1893–1984), a middle-of-the-roader and leader of the Youth Party, called for a revival of ancient legalism,[7] which was hostile to individualism. The rightists believed that individualism was harmful to the collective will so desperately needed by the nation during its time of crisis.

Vernacular language also came under severe criticism from the right and left. The KMT favored reading the Classics and prescribed the ancient language as a necessary part of the school curriculum, while the leftists criticized the new vernacular language advocated by the May Fourth youths as being impossible for the common people to command and denounced it as a Europeanized language (*Ou-hua yü-yen*) or new literary language (*hsin wen-yen*) and as capitalistic.[8]

Despite the fact that leftist ideals were in many respects rooted in the May Fourth movement, when "class" became a major concern, the May Fourth values were soon denounced as "urban," "capitalist," and "comprador." Many leftists had argued that May Fourth ideas could not serve the needs of the proletariat, and the work of transforming and enlightening the people was soon perceived as being apathetic to the masses. For adjusting to the needs of the proletariat, "native cultural forms" (especially those of the common people) were revived. When the roles of cultural forms were seen as mobilizing the masses to participate in the proletariat revolution or to resist Japanese aggression, May Fourth values were denigrated as especially irrelevant to social realities. In Mao Tse-tung's words, it was no longer the mission of the intellectual to enlighten the people: "the intelligentsia should make their own works welcomed by the masses and must transform and completely reconstruct their own thoughts and feelings."[9]

Confronting these challenges, May Fourth youths changed considerably. Some even abandoned their old convictions. The changes of two men most clearly illustrate this transformation. Ch'ü Ch'iu-pai (1899–1935), a leftist leader and formerly an enthusiastic participant in the May Fourth demonstrations, related in his outline for leftist

---

5 P'eng K'ang, "Hsin-wen-hua yün-tung yü jen-ch'üan yün-tung," in Ts'ai Shang-ssu, ed., *Chung-kuo hsien-tai ssu-hsiang-shih tzu-liao chien-pien* (Chekiang, 1982–1983), 5 vols., 3:107.
6 Hsü Yüan, "Fa-hsi-ssu-ti (Fascism) yü San-min-chu-i," in ibid., 3:690–696.
7 Ch'en Ch'i-t'ien, "Fa-chia te fu-hsing," in ibid., 3:835–844.
8 Ch'ü Ch'iu-pai, "P'u-lo (Proletariat) ta-chung wen-i te hsien-shih wen-t'i," in *Ch'ü Ch'iu-pai wen-chi* (Peking, 1985), "wen-hsüeh-pien," 6 vols., 1:461–483. See also "Ou-hua wen-i," in ibid., 1:491–497.
9 Mao Tse-tung, "Speech Made at the Yenan Forum on Literature and Art," May 2, 1942, in Conrad Brandt, ed., *A Documentary History of Chinese Communism* (Cambridge, Mass., 1952), 411.

associations that people should "bury" the May Fourth Movement. Mao Tun, a classmate of Fu, once courageously announced that he would stand by the May Fourth ideals, but in 1930 he changed his mind and called for the repudiation of remaining elements of the May Fourth Movement.[10]

Fu Ssu-nien obviously changed some of his views, especially after 1931. He never completely abandoned his May Fourth values but was constantly torn by them. In historical study he stuck closely to his ideal of objectivity. But in responding to the national crisis after the Mukden Incident, he hastily compiled his rather flimsy and subjective *Outline of the History of Northeastern China* to refute Japanese propaganda that Manchuria was not an integral part of China proper. The book was excessively general and broad and represented an aberration of his ideals, but the acute national crisis had compelled him to publish it. Although he championed the principle of remaining "true to the facts," during the Sino-Japanese War he denounced other scholars' studies on the ethnic history of southwest China and suggested that they should be stopped because the historical fact that the southwest minorities were of different ethnic origins would be detrimental to national unity. He denounced vehemently the so-called national learning, while in the eyes of outsiders many works of the IHP fell squarely into that category. He upheld iconoclasm as an effective medicine for curing China's cultural illness, but on certain occasions praised the nation's past to arouse patriotic feeling. He was indeed "a bundle of contradictions."

Fu Ssu-nien was famous for his support of the Nationalist government. It is noteworthy that in 1927 a good number of intellectuals moved from the north to Kwangchow to join the KMT, such as Lu Hsün, Kuo Mo-jo, and Yü Ta-fu. Fu was also attracted by the manifesto of the First National Convention of the KMT, a socialistic, anticomprador, and antiimperialistic platform. Later, however, the dictatorship of Chiang Kai-shek alienated them. In the early 1930s Fu harshly criticized Chiang and his party. This led to another dilemma. Given his hostility toward the CCP, politically Fu had to choose between the two parties he disliked the most. The Japanese encroachment forced him to support a powerful leader who, he believed, could save the country. Fu worried that even with a

10 Ch'ü Ch'iu-pai called for "taking off the May Fourth clothing." See, for example, Ch'ü's "Tzu-yu-jen te wen-hua yün-tung," in *Ch'ü Ch'iu-pai wen-chi*, 1:498–503. Cf. Paul G. Pickowicz, "Qu Qiubai's Critique of the May Fourth Generation: Early Chinese Marxist Literary Criticism," in Goldman, *Modern Chinese Literature in the May Fourth Era*, 351–384. As for Mao Tun, see Mao Tun (Shen Yen-ping), "Wu-ssu yün-tung te chien-t'ao – Ma-k'o-ssu-chu-i (Marxism) wen-i yen-chiu hui pao-kao," *Wen-hsüeh tao-pao*, 1:2 (1931), 14.

good government, China was still in grave danger of being subjugated by the Japanese; without any government at all, he concluded, China would certainly be conquered. He viewed Chiang Kai-shek as the only possible leader for China at that time. While denouncing Chiang, he also tried very hard to protect Chiang.

As an academic leader in a chaotic nation with limited resources for scholastic study, however, personal ties with the government were the only way of accruing funds for his enterprise. His political choice was, then, not only an ideological choice but also an administrative one.

But liberals had no real power base in China, especially after the success of the Northern Expedition. They could not twist their liberal ideals to conform to the KMT or the CCP, two collectivistic parties, and they were never really established in, or welcomed by, either party. They became, in fact, a "third kind of men" in modern Chinese politics.[11]

During the Sino-Japanese War, Fu Ssu-nien served seven consecutive years as a representative in the People's Political Council. In that organ Fu heroically criticized the corruption and malpractice of Premier H. H. Kung's clique and contributed to his resignation. Later, in 1947, witnessing the chaotic economy and corruption, in three famous articles Fu publicly denounced another premier, T. V. Soong, and contributed to his resignation as well. His efforts in bringing down two premiers brought Fu enormous prestige. But Fu was a traditional remonstrator and was by no means a career politician. Fu's criticism of the two premiers is obvious. On the one hand, in the increasing polarization of Chinese politics between the left and the right in post–May Fourth decades, the reformist orientation of the KMT regime during the Northern Expedition period provided the only space for a liberal like Fu to get involved in politics and to render some public service. On the other hand, the heavy authoritarianism of the KMT left little room for a liberal to exercise his rights to criticize and protest. The institutional and ideological basis of its party dictatorship were certainly off limits to discussion and criticism. Under these circumstances Fu could only attack the personages in politics and leave the political framework intact. This made him look more like a traditional Chinese scholar-official who protested despotism by attacking the chancellor (*tsai-hsiang*) while leaving the imperial center alone and less like a modern liberal who plays the politics of loyal opposition. Thus, in Fu's sensational denunciations of Kung and Soong we can see something of the predicament of the Chinese intellectual caught between traditional ideas and modern politics.

11 FSNP, III-886, a letter from Ch'u An-p'ing (1909–1966) to Fu Ssu-nien.

Fu refused repeatedly to become a cabinet member in the government. He did, however, serve as acting president of Peita and later, in the early 1949, as president of T'aita. At T'aita, Fu had considerable achievements in academic administration and became the most memorable figure in the educational history of Taiwan.

The fall of mainland China to the Chinese Communists was a tremendous blow to Fu Ssu-nien. As a nationalist, Fu's call to his compatriots to discard their traditions and embrace Western values made his conscience uneasy. His iconoclastic attitude toward traditional culture, especially his call for dispelling introspective moral values from the Chinese cultural heritage, was believed both by Fu Ssu-nien and others to have helped pave the way for Marxism in China. To them, however, the victory of the CCP to a large extent discredited their ideas.

Fu gradually turned back to the Mencian moral philosophy, and in his later years he required all T'aita freshmen to read the *Mencius*. He also denounced the slogan of "total westernization" as absurd. He believed that the Chinese tradition was of intrinsic humanistic value and even urged students to be propagators and transmitters of nonwhite culture. It would, however, be inaccurate to say that Fu in the end rejected all May Fourth ideals. At a time when most of Fu's old May Fourth friends had became senile, Fu was recognizable as a strong proponent of science and liberalism, two key May Fourth values.

The victory of the CCP also caused Fu to hold fast to liberalism. Although Fu said that liberalism should not be called an "ism" and denied that he himself was a liberal,[12] in his early life he was in fact a hybrid liberal and socialist. He paid equal attention to economic equality and political freedom. But when he finally found that the CCP encouraged violent class struggle in order to achieve economic equality, he and many others came to think that economic equality could not go hand in hand with liberty. There was an obvious shift in his later life: he no longer called for economic equality; instead, he held fast to liberalism.

Yet Fu's thought changed so rapidly in his later years that he was unable to articulate in any systematic way his numerous entangled ideas, ideas that unfortunately were buried with him when he died suddenly in 1950.

---

12 See Chin Yao, "I Fu Ssu-nien hsien-sheng," in *Fu ku hsiao-chang ai-wan-lu*, 59.

Appendix I
A Fragment from a Short Story Attacking Ku Chieh-kang

The following is a fragment from a short novel written by Fu Ssu-nien, in which he satirizes the methodology used by Ku Chieh-kang to dismiss the authenticity of ancient Chinese history.[1] Ku was Fu's roommate at Peita and later became one of China's foremost historians, known for his iconoclastic analytical investigations into Chinese antiquity.

A Jocular Essay (Hsi-lun)

The First Act

... This half of the letter I found in an antique shop yesterday. It was written by a certain *Li-pi-yu-che* (a person who believes as a matter of course). When I returned home I consulted the Dictionary of Worthies, and found that "Mr. *Li-pi-yu* was a person of the thirty-third century who systematically doubted history of antiquity; he wrote ten large volumes entitled *Ku-shih hsü-pien* (a continuation of *Ku-shih pien*, Ku Chieh-Kang's representative work) ... in which he argued that at the inception of Republican China many people's names were in fact forged by their contemporaries. Some were several different persons with the same names, others were one person with several names and still others were simply names not associated with real persons. All of these names were forgeries following the practice of Han scholars who set bewildering traps to confuse latecomers. He even claimed that Sun Yat-sen was simply a reincarnation of Sun Hsing-che of the *Hsi-yu-chi* (*The Journey to the West*) and was not a real person. Huang Hsing was but a reincarnation of the myth *Huang-lung hsien* (the appearance of the Yellow Dragon). They originated from popular beliefs and later fell into the hands of scholars [who forged them into personal names]. They polished the

---

1 FSNP, II-910, undatable.

Appendix I

stories [of popular beliefs] and also utilized popular motifs to elaborate their ideals.

This kind of rhetoric flourished for a certain period, and for generations people were shocked and considered him (*Li-pi-yu-che*) a profound thinker.

Here is the content of the letter:

On June 10, 5175, the 3214th year of the Republic of China, *Li-pi-yu* respectfully replies,

Mr. Ku Lo, I humbly received your letter stating your findings concerning historical materials of the early Republican period. My appreciation is hard to express. I have carefully read your letter over and over again and admire your scholarship very much. I have also spent some time studying the history of this period. At the beginning, I thought that this phenomenon [that the names of many people of Republic of China were in fact forged by their contemporaries] was only one facet of the activities of the literati of that time. Years later I suddenly came to the conclusion that this is in fact a clue to tackle all history of that period. As for the fabrications of these characters according to the literati's own ideals, I have published a book on it. I will now mention two or three examples to illustrate this. I wrote *The Chronological History of Hu Shih* (*Hu Shih nien-p'u*) to verify that many articles in *Hu Shih wen-ts'un* were in fact added after Hu's death. I also wrote in my "Study on Mr. Ku" (Ku chün k'ao) that many parts of Ku's *Ku-shih-chieh* were also interpolations or later changes, but this should come as no surprise to anyone. The case worth most concern is [the name of] Ch'ien Hsüan-t'ung. People have always believed that Ch'ien Hsüan-t'ung and I-ku Hsüan-t'ung were two names for one person. Actually, it is very stupid [to believe so].... In my investigations I have found that *hsüan* is part of the name of the K'ang-hsi emperor; thus, the name Ch'ien Hsüan-t'ung could not be dated any earlier than the first year of the Republic of China. [Ch'ien Hsüan-t'ung could not have] changed his name in the first year of the Republic because Mr. Ch'ien was most contemptuous of traditional Chinese culture. One of his dispositions definitely would not choose the character *hsüan* [as part of his name], because [the meaning of *hsüan*] is one hundred percent pertinent to Taoism. Thus, if we assume that Hsüan-t'ung was the *tzu* [alias name] of Wang Ching-hsüan, it is possible.[2] ... After careful consideration, one finds that the name Ch'ien Hsüan-t'ung is an empty name of nobody...

2 To show his endorsement to the Movement of Doubting Chinese Ancient History, Ch'ien Hsüan-t'ung changed his name to I-ku Hsüan-t'ung (i.e., the Hsüan-t'ung who suspects ancient history). Wang Ching-hsüan was an alias of Ch'ien Hsüan-t'ung, an advocate of the New Culture Movement. To distinguish New Culture ideals, Ch'ien used the alias Wang Ching-hsüan to publish an extremely conservative article in *Hsin-ch'ing-nien* to burlesque the conservatives. See Wang Ching-hsüan, "Wen-hsüeh ko-ming chih fan-hsiang," *Hsin-ch'ing-nien*, 4:3 (1918), 265–268.

Appendix II
A Transcript of a Conversation between Fu Ssu-nien and Ch'en Pu-lei

The following is a transcript of a conversation between Fu Ssu-nien and Ch'en Pu-lei, then Chiang Kai-shek's chief of staff, during a session of the Political Consultative Conference in Nanking in 1945 in which the character of Chiang Kai-shek was discussed.[1]

Fu: [Recently] Mr. Chiang exhorted the citizens of Shanghai to understand fully propriety and duty, to have a sense of frugality and shame, to be responsible, and to observe discipline [*ming li i, chih lien ch'ih*]. These are admonitions that the nation's highest leader should make to bureaucrats, not to the common citizens.

Ch'en: I agree with most of what you say. Mr. Chiang always speaks as if he were a teacher. He imagines that the audiences to which he speaks are composed of students, not officials or common people. I advised him on this before, but he read my comments without much interest. He is aware [of this], but he does not put [this awareness] into practice. For example, he often says "compare duty with performance," but his attention is always limited to the organs responsible for accessing and scrutinizing government organs. Although he has often said "due rewards and punishments will be meted out without fail," he seldom punishes people and often rewards in excess. (To him, so-called punishment is invariably oral remonstration, as if he were a teacher lecturing his students. This is due to his personality and his experiences in his early years.) He originally served as a military staff member, and thus he always worries excessively. (But in national affairs, he is very decisive.) He was also a school head for many years, so he is prone to act more like an educator than a politician.

---

1 FSNP, I-29, February 1946, written on a page of the Political Consultative Conference memo paper.

Glossary

ai	愛
An	奄
Anfu	安福
Anyang	安陽
chan-tou chih-nan	戰鬥指南
Chang Cheng-lang	張政烺
Chang Chieh	章碣
Chang Chih-tung	張之洞
Chang Ching-chiang	張靜江
Chang Hsüan	張煊
Chang Hsün	張勳
Chang Hsüeh-liang	張學良
chang-ku	掌故
Chang Kwang-chih	張光直
Chang Ping-lin (Chang T'ai-yen)	章炳麟（章太炎）
Chang Shen-fu	張申府
Chang Shih-chao	章士釗
Chang Shou-chieh	張守節
Chang T'ai-lei	張太雷
Chang Tso-lin	張作霖
Chang Yen-ch'ing	張燕卿
Chang Yin-lin	張蔭麟
ch'ang-jen	常人
Chao	趙
Chao Kung-ch'ia	趙公洽
Chao-ming wen-hsüan	昭明文選
Chao Sung-nan	趙頌南
Chao Yüan-jen	趙元任
ch'ao chieh-chi	超階級

Glossary

"Che-yang te Sung Tzu-wen fei tsou-k'ai pu-k'o"	這樣的宋子文非走開不可
chen	真
chen-hsüeh-wen	真學問
Chen-kuan cheng-yao	貞觀政要
Ch'en Ch'eng	陳誠
Ch'en Ch'i-t'ien	陳啟天
Ch'en Han-chang	陳漢章
Ch'en Li	陳澧
Ch'en Li-fu	陳立夫
Ch'en P'an	陳槃
Ch'en Pu-lei	陳布雷
Ch'en Sheng	陳勝
Ch'en Shou-i	陳受頤
Ch'en Tu-hsiu	陳獨秀
Ch'en Yen	陳衍
Ch'en Yin-k'o	陳寅恪
Ch'en Yüan	陳垣
Ch'en Yüan	陳源
Cheng Chen-to	鄭振鐸
Cheng-ch'i ko	正氣歌
Cheng-chih hsieh-shang hui-i	政治協商會議
cheng erh pu shu	證而不疏
"Cheng-fu yü t'i-ch'ang tao-te"	政府與提倡道德
Cheng Ho-sheng	鄭鶴聲
cheng-li kuo-ku	整理國故
Cheng-li kuo-ku yün-tung	整理國故運動
Cheng Lieh	鄭烈
Ch'eng Chin-fang	程晉芳
Ch'eng Hao	程顥
Ch'eng I	程頤
Ch'eng-shih chia-shu fen-nien jih-ch'eng	程氏家塾分年日程
Ch'eng Ts'ang-p'o	程滄波
Ch'eng-tzu-yai	城子崖
Chi	濟
Chi-chung Chou-shu	汲冢周書
Chi-ku-lu pa-wei	汲古錄跋尾
Chi Wen-fu	嵇文甫
Ch'i	齊
ch'i-chia	齊家
ch'i-chih-chih-hsing	氣質之性

210

Ch'i Lu	齊魯
ch'i-shih	棄世
ch'i-shuo	奇說
ch'i-ssu	氣死
chia-hsüeh-shu-chih-ming	假學術之名
"chia wei wan-o-chih-yüan"	家為萬惡之源
chia-yang-jen	假洋人
Chiang Kai-shek	蔣介石
Chiang T'ing-fu	蔣廷黻
Chiao Hsün	焦循
Chiao Chou	譙周
chieh	節
"chien-li hsüeh-shu she-hui"	建立學術社會
Chien Po-tsan	翦伯贊
Ch'ien Chi-po	錢基博
Ch'ien Hsüan-t'ung	錢玄同
Ch'ien Mu	錢穆
Ch'ien Ta-hsin	錢大昕
Ch'ien Tuan-sheng	錢端升
chih chieh K'ung Meng cheng-t'ung	直接孔孟正統
Chih-chia ko-yen	治家格言
chih-chüeh	直覺
chih-shih	知識
chih-yeh	職業
Chin	晉
Chin-pu tang	進步黨
chin-shih	進士
chin-shih	金石
chin-shih-hsüeh	金石學
Chin-ssu-lu	近思錄
chin-te hui	進德會
Ching-shih-ta-hsüeh-t'ang	京師大學堂
"Ching-tai hsüeh-che te chih-hsüeh fang-fa"	清代學者的治學方法
ch'ing	情
ch'ing-chen	情真
ch'ing-liu	清流
ch'ing ming	清明
Ch'ing-nien	青年
ch'ing-tang	清黨
Ch'inghua	清華

Chiu-chou	九州
Chiu-ho	九河
ch'iu-ch'i-shih	求其是
Ch'iu Ch'ing-ch'üan	邱清泉
Ch'iu-shu	訄書
cho-yao ta-kuei	捉妖打鬼
Chou	周
Chou	紂
Chou Ch'i-ming (Tso-jen)	周豈明
Chou-hua	周化
Chou Keng-sheng	周鯁生
Chou Ku-ch'eng	周谷城
Chou-li	周禮
Chou Mei-sun	周枚蓀
Chou Tso-jen	周作人
"Chou tung-feng yü Yin i-min"	周東封與殷遺民
Chu Chia-hua	朱家驊
Chu Ch'ien-chih	朱謙之
Chu Chih-ch'ing	朱志清
Chu Hsi	朱熹
Chu Hsi-tsu	朱希祖
Chu Hsia	諸夏
chu-i	主義
Chu I-hsin	朱一新
Chu Po-lu	朱柏廬
chu-shih	著史
Chu-tzu-hsüeh lüeh-shuo	諸子學略說
"Chu-tzu wen-chi chih yen-pien"	諸子文籍之演變
Ch'u An-p'ing	儲安平
ch'u-kuan	出官
Ch'u-tz'u	楚辭
Ch'ü Ch'iu-pai	瞿秋白
Ch'ü fu	曲阜
Ch'ü Hsüan-ying	瞿宣穎
chü jen	舉人
ch'ü-wei	趣味
ch'ü wei ts'ung chen	黜偽崇真
chuan-t'i yen-chiu	專題研究
ch'üan-chi	全集
ch'üan k'ao-pu-chu	全靠不住
ch'üan-p'an hsi-hua	全盤西化

ch'üan-pao	全豹
ch'üan-shen-t'ang	全神堂
Chuang-tzu	莊子
chuang-yüan	狀元
chüeh ku-tung	掘古董
chüeh-pao	掘寶
Chün-chi-ch'u	軍機處
chung	忠
chung-chiao	中焦
Chung hsiao-hsüeh wen-yen yün-tung	中小學文言運動
chung-hsüeh-t'ang	中學堂
Chung-hua wen-hua chiao-yü chi-chin-hui	中華文化教育基金會
"Chung-kuo hsüeh-shu ssu-hsiang chieh chih chi-pen miu-wu"	中國學術思想界之基本謬誤
"Chung-kuo-kou ho Chung-kuo-jen"	中國狗和中國人
"Chung-kuo li-tai ta-shih"	中國歷代大事
Chung-kuo-min-tsu ko-ming shih-kao	中國民族革命史稿
chung-tsu	種族
Chung-yang jih-pao	中央日報
Chung-yang yen-chiu yüan	中央研究院
Chung-yang yen-chiu yüan Li-shih yü-yen yen-chiu-so chi-k'an	中央研究院歷史語言研究所集刊
Chung Ying wen-hua chi-chin-hui	中英文化基金會
Dai Toa minzokushi	大東亞民族史
Erh-ya	爾雅
fan-t'ung	飯桶
Fan Wen-lan	范文瀾
Fang Chuang-yu	方壯猷
fang-hsin	放心
Fang Tung-shu	方東樹
Fei Hsiao-t'ung	費孝通
Fei-lien	飛廉
fei-wu	廢物
Feng Yu-lan	馮友蘭
Feng Yü-hsiang	馮玉祥

Glossary

Fu Hsiao-lu	傅曉麓
Fu Hui-tsu	傅回祖
Fu I-chien	傅以漸
Fu I-ling	傅衣凌
Fu-ku-chai shih-i	負固齋試義
Fu Li-ch'üan	傅笠泉
Fu Meng-po	傅孟博
Fu Ssu-nien	傅斯年
Fu Ssu-yen	傅斯嚴
Fu Ta-p'ao	傅大砲
Fu Tseng-hsiang	傅增湘
H. H. Kung (K'ung Hsiang-hsi)	孔祥熙
Hai Jui	海瑞
hai wai yu chieh	海外有截
Han	漢
Han	韓
Han-cho	寒浞
Han Fu-chü	韓復榘
Han-lin	翰林
Han-shu	漢書
Han Yü	韓愈
Hang Li-wu	杭立武
hao-jan-chih-ch'i	浩然之氣
Ho Ch'ang-ch'ün	賀昌群
Ho I-shih	何燏時
Ho Jih-chang	何日章
Ho Ping-sung	何炳松
Ho Ssu-yüan	何思源
Ho Ting-sheng	何定生
Hou-Han-shu	後漢書
Hou-i	后羿
Hou Yen-shuang	侯延塽
Hou-kang	後崗
"Hsi-lun"	戲論
Hsi-nan lien-ta	西南聯大
Hsi-nan min-tsu hsüeh-hui	西南民族學會
hsi-shu	西書
Hsi-tsung shih-lu	熹宗實錄
hsi-t'ung che-hsüeh	系統哲學
hsi-t'ung-te	系統的
Hsi-yu-chi	西遊記

hsia	俠
Hsia	夏
hsia-chiao	下焦
Hsia Nai	夏鼐
Hsia Tseng-yu	夏曾佑
hsiang-jen-ou	相人偶
hsiang-shang te sheng-huo	向上的生活
Hsiang Ta	向達
Hsiang Yü	項羽
hsiao	孝
hsiao erh hao	小而好
hsiao-hsüeh-t'ang	小學堂
Hsiao I-shan	蕭一山
Hsiao-t'un	小屯
hsieh-hsing-wen	蟹形文
Hsieh Kuo-chen	謝國楨
hsieh-ting	寫定
"Hsien-t'an li-shih chiao-k'o shu"	閒談歷史教科書
hsin	小
hsin	心
Hsin-ch'ao	新潮
Hsin-ch'ao she	新潮社
hsin che-hsüeh	新哲學
hsin ch'i po-jo	心氣薄弱
hsin-shu	心術
Hsin-ch'ing-nien	新青年
Hsin fang-yen	新方言
Hsin Han-hsüeh	新漢學
Hsin Ju-chia	新儒家
hsin-kung-ming	新功名
hsin-min	新民
Hsin-sheng-ming p'ai	新生命派
Hsin-sheng-pao	新生報
hsin-shih	新詩
Hsin-shih-hsüeh	新史學
hsin wen-yen	新文言
hsing	性
Hsing-chung-hui	興中會
Hsing ming ku-hsün	性命古訓
Hsing ming ku-hsün pien-cheng	性命古訓辨證
hsiu-shen	修身

Hsiung Shih-li	熊十力
Hsü Chih-heng	許之珩
Hsü Chung-shu	徐中舒
Hsü Fu-kuan	徐復觀
Hsü Hsü-sheng (Hsü Ping-ch'ang)	徐旭生（徐秉昶）
Hsü Ping-ch'ang (Hsü Hsü-sheng)	徐秉昶（徐旭生）
Hsü Te-heng	許德珩
hsüan	玄
Hsüan-ho k'ao-ku t'u	宣和考古圖
Hsüeh-heng	學衡
Hsüeh Hsiang-sui	薛祥綏
hsüeh-pa	學霸
Hsüeh-pu	學部
hsüeh-shu k'an-wu	學術刊物
hsüeh-wen	學問
hsün	訓
hsün-cheng	訓政
Hsün-tzu	荀子
Hu	胡
Hu Fu-lin (Hu Hou-hsüan)	胡福林（胡厚宣）
Hu Han-min	胡漢民
Hu Jen-yüan	胡仁源
Hu Shih	胡適
Hu Shih ssu-hsiang p'i-p'an	胡適思想批判
Hu Shih wen-ts'un	胡適文存
Hua-hsia	華夏
Huai	淮
Huang Chang-chien	黃彰健
Huang Fei-hu	黃飛虎
Huang-fu Mi	皇甫謐
Huang Hsing	黃興
Huang-huo	黃禍
Huang K'an	黃侃
Huang-lung hsien	黃龍見
Huang-ti	黃帝
Hui Tung	惠棟
Huang Yen-p'ei	黃炎培
Hung Pang	洪榜
I	夷
i	義

I-ching t'ung-chu	易經通註
I Hsia tung hsi shuo	夷夏東西說
I-ku Hsüan-t'ung	疑古玄同
i-li	義例
i-li-chih-hsing	義理之性
I Mi-chih	伊密之
i-t'uan mao-tun	一團矛盾
I Yin	伊尹
Jao Tsung-i	饒宗頤
Jao Yü-t'ai	饒毓泰
jen	仁
jen	人
Jen Cho-hsüan (Yeh Ch'ing)	任卓宣（葉青）
jen-hsing	人性
Jen Hung-chün	任鴻雋
jen i	仁義
jen-jen	仁人
jen-lei ch'ing-kan	人類情感
Jen-te-wen-hsüeh	人的文學
jen-wei	人為
jen-wen te li-ming	人文的黎明
Juan Yüan	阮元
Jung	戎
Jung Chao-tsu	容肇祖
Jung Keng	容庚
K'ang Pai-ch'ing	康白情
K'ang Yu-wei	康有為
Kao Ch'ü-hsün	高去尋
kao-teng-hsüeh-t'ang	高等學堂
ken-yüan	根源
ko-hsin	革心
Ko I-ch'ing	葛毅卿
ko-ming-ch'ao-liu	革命潮流
ko-wu	格物
k'o-hsüeh-te	科學的
k'o-hsüeh te cheng-li kuo-ku	科學的整理國故
Ku Ch'eng-wu (Ku Chieh-kang)	顧誠吾（顧頡剛）
Ku Chieh-kang (Ku Ch'eng-wu)	顧頡剛（顧誠吾）
Ku chün k'ao	顧君考
Ku-chin wei-shu k'ao	古今偽書考

Ku-liang chuan	穀梁傳
Ku-shih chieh	古史解
Ku-shih hsü-pien	古史續辨
Ku-shih k'ao	古史考
Ku-shih pien	古史辨
ku-wu	古物
Ku Ying-t'ai	谷應泰
kuan	官
Kuan Chung	管仲
kuan-hsi	關係
Kuan-hsien	冠縣
Kuan Lin-cheng	關麟徵
Kuan-t'ang chi-lin	觀堂集林
Kuan-tzu	管子
kuei	鬼
Kuei Ch'ung-chi	桂崇基
Kume Kunitake	久米邦武
K'un-ch'ü	崑曲
kung-ch'eng	工程
Kung-fei	碩妃
K'ung Hsiang-hsi (H. H. Kung)	孔祥熙
K'ung Keng	孔庚
K'ung-sang	空桑
Kung-yang chuan	公羊傳
kuo	國
kuo-ch'ih	國恥
kuo-chiu	國舅
Kuo-fang ts'an-i hui	國防參議會
Kuo-fu wei-yüan	國府委員
kuo-hsüeh	國學
Kuo-hsüeh chi-k'an	國學季刊
Kuo-hsüeh-kuan	國學館
kuo-hsüeh-yüan	國學院
kuo-hua	國畫
kuo-i	國醫
kuo-ku	國故
kuo-ku shih-tai	國故時代
Kuo Kuo-chi	郭國基
Kuo-li pien-i kuan	國立編譯館
Kuo Mo-jo	郭沫若
kuo-nan	國難

Kuo Pao-chün	郭寶鈞
Kuo-min	國民
kuo-min-hsing	國民性
kuo-min hsün-lien	國民訓練
Kuo-min ta-hui	國民大會
kuo-shu	國術
Kuo-ts'ui	國粹
Kuo-yü	國語
Lao Kan	勞榦
Lao-tzu	老子
Lei Chen	雷震
Lei Hai-tsung	雷海宗
Li	李
Li Ao	李翱
Li Chi	李濟
Li-chuang	李莊
Li Fang-kuei	李方桂
Li Ho-lin	李何林
Li Hsiao-feng	李小峰
li-hsüeh	理學
li-hsüeh chiu-kuo	理學救國
Li Kuang-t'ao	李光濤
li-lun	理論
li-pi-yu-che	理必有者
Li Sheng-to	李盛鐸
Li-shih po-wu kuan	歷史博物館
Li Shih-tseng	李石曾
Li-shih yen-chiu-fa	歷史研究法
Li-shih yü-yen yen-chiu-so	歷史語言研究所
"Li-shih yü-yen yen-chiu-so kung-tso chih-ch'ü"	歷史語言研究所工作旨趣
"Li-shih yü-yen yen-chiu-so pao-kao-shu ti-i-ch'i"	歷史語言研究所報告書第一期
Li Ta	李達
Li Ta-chao	李大釗
Li Tsung-huang	李宗黃
Li Tsung-t'ung	李宗侗
Liang-ch'eng-chen	兩城鎮
Liang Ch'i-ch'ao	梁啟超
Liang Fang-chung	梁方仲
Liang Kuang-ming	梁光明
Liang Shu-ming	梁漱溟

Liang Ssu-ch'eng	梁思成
Liang Ssu-yung	梁思永
Liang Yü-sheng	梁玉繩
Liao-ch'eng	聊城
Liao P'ing	廖平
Lin-tzu	臨淄
Lin Hui-yin	林徽音
Lin Shu	林紓
ling	令
Ling T'ing-k'an	凌廷堪
Liu Chih	劉峙
Liu Chih-chi	劉知幾
Liu-ching yü ju-chia ti-li shang chih kuan-hsi	六經與儒家地理上之關係
Liu Fu	劉復
Liu Hsin	劉歆
Liu Hsiang	劉向
Liu Hsing-en	柳興恩
Liu I-cheng	柳詒徵
Liu Pang	劉邦
Liu-pien	六變
Liu Shih-p'ei	劉師培
Liu Yao (Yin Ta)	劉曜（尹達）
Lo Chen-yü	羅振玉
Lo Chia-lun	羅家倫
Lo Erh-kang	羅爾綱
Lo Wen-kan	羅文榦
Lu	魯
Lu-hsi	魯西
Lu Hsün	魯迅
Lun-yü	論語
Lung-shan shu-yüan	龍山書院
Lü Hsien	呂咸
Lü Ssu-mien	呂思勉
Lü Ta-lin	呂大臨
luan-tang	亂黨
Lungshan	龍山
Ma Hsü-lun	馬敘倫
Ma Yin-ch'u	馬寅初
Ma Yü-tsao	馬裕藻
mai-pan	買辦
Man	蠻

"Man-Mo-Zo wa Shina no ryodo ni arazu ron" 滿蒙藏は支那の領土に非る論"
Mao I-heng 毛以亨
Mao Tse-tung 毛澤東
Mao Tun (Shen Yen-ping) 茅盾（沈雁冰）
Mao Tzu-shui 毛子水
Maruzen 丸善
Mei I-ch'i 梅貽琦
Meng-tzu hsin-te chiang 孟子心得獎
Meng-tzu tzu-i shu-cheng 孟子字義疏證
Meng Wen-t'ung 蒙文通
Miao 苗
Miao Feng-lin 繆鳳林
Miao Man 苗蠻
Miao-ti-kou 廟底溝
min-chu 民主
min-pen 民本
Min-tsu yü ku-tai Chung-kuo shih 民族與古代中國史
ming 命
ming-chiao 名教
ming li-i, chih lien-ch'ih 明禮義、知廉恥
Ming-shih chi-shih-pen-mo 明史紀事本末
Ming-shih-lu 明實錄
Mo-tzu 墨子
Mu Ou-ch'u 穆藕初
Nan-hsi 南溪
Nan-k'ai 南開
nei-pen-lun 內本論
nei-wei-i erh wai-ch'ien-chiu 內違異而外牽就
ni-ku 擬古
"Ni-ku ssu-fan" 尼姑思凡
Nieh Yün-t'ai 聶雲台
Nu-li 努力
o 惡
ou-hsiang 偶像
Ou-hua 歐化
Ou-hua yü-yen 歐化語言
Ou-yang Hsiu 歐陽修
pa-ku-wen 八股文
pa-kung 拔貢
pa-tao 霸道

Pai-hua pen-kuo-shih	白話本國史
Pai-ti	白狄
pan-chia hsien-sheng	搬家先生
P'an-keng	盤庚
pang	幫
Pao Chien-ch'ing	鮑鑑清
pao-hsüeh te nu-ts'ai	飽學的奴才
Pei	邶
Pei-p'ing yen-chiu-yüan	北平研究院
Peita	北大
Peiyang	北洋
pen-neng	本能
"Pen-wei-wen-hua chien-she hsüan-yen"	本位文化建設宣言
p'i-p'an	批判
pien-cheng-fa	辯證法
"Pien-chi fan-li"	編輯凡例
P'ing	平
P'ing-Han	平漢
P'ing-ling	平陵
po	亳
po-hai	渤海
Po-hu-t'ung	白虎通
Pu-jen tsa-chih	不忍雜誌
pu-pien	補編
pu-tou-t'ou	不逗頭
pu-t'ung	不通
San-Chin	三晉
san-kang	三綱
San-tai	三代
shan	善
Shan-hai ching	山海經
shang-chiao	上焦
Shang-shu	尚書
Shao Hao	少昊
Shao-nien Chung-kuo hsüeh-hui	少年中國學會
she-hui	社會
she-hui nei chih-hsü	社會內秩序
she-hui shang chih-hsü	社會上秩序
she-mo shih hsüeh-wen	什麼是學問

Shen Chien-shih	沈兼士
shen-hua fen-hua shuo	神話分化說
Shen Yen-ping (Mao Tun)	沈雁冰（茅盾）
sheng	生
sheng-chan	聖戰
sheng chih wei hsing	生之謂性
sheng-jen-kuan	聖人觀
sheng-yüan	生員
Shih-chi	史記
Shih-chi chih-i	史記志疑
Shih-chieh jih-pao	世界日報
Shih-ching	詩經
shih-hsüeh	史學
shih-hsüeh chi shih-liao-hsüeh	史學即史料學
shih-kuan	史觀
shih-liao p'ai	史料派
Shih-liao ts'ung-k'an ch'u-pien	史料叢刊初編
shih-liu tzu hsin-ch'uan	十六字心傳
Shih p'i-p'an shu	十批判書
Shih-t'ung	史通
Shih-yü-so tang-an	史語所檔案
shu	書
shu-min ch'ang-yu	庶民倡優
shu-sheng	書生
shu-sheng ho i pao-kuo	書生何以報國
Shui-hu chuan	水滸傳
Shun	舜
shuo-hsing chu-i	獸性主義
Shuo-wen	說文
Ssu-ma Ch'ien	司馬遷
ssu-ming shuo	俟命說
su-ch'eng	速成
Su Ping-ch'i	蘇秉綺
sui-kan-lu	隨感錄
Sun Fu-yüan	孫伏園
Sun Hsing-che	孫行者
Sun Ta-ch'en	孫達宸
Sun Tz'u-chou	孫次舟
Sun Wen (Sun Yat-sen)	孫文（孫逸仙）
Sun-wu-k'ung	孫悟空

Sun Yat-sen (Sun Wen)	孫逸仙（孫文）
Sung Chia-shu (Charlie Soong)	宋嘉樹
Sung Chiang	宋江
Sung Ching-shih	宋景詩
Sung Tzu-wen (T. V. Sung)	宋子文
Sung Yüan hsi-ch'ü-shih	宋元戲曲史
T. V. Soong (Sung Tzu-wen)	宋子文
ta-ko-ming	大革命
Ta-kung pao	大公報
ta-ming	大名
"Ta-sheng ch'i-hsin-lun yüan-ch'i"	大乘起信論緣起
Ta Tai chu-i	大傣主義
Ta-tao Wang Wu	大刀王五
"Ta-tung hsiao-tung shuo"	大東小東説
Ta-tung-ya min-tsu-shih	大東亞民族史
ta-tzu-pao	大字報
ta-wen-t'i	大問題
Tai Chen	戴震
Tai Chi-t'ao	戴季陶
T'ai-shang kan-ying-p'ien	太上感應篇
T'aita	台大
T'an P'ing-shan	譚平山
T'an Ssu-t'ung	譚嗣同
tang-hua chiao-yü	黨化教育
T'ang	湯
T'ang Lan	唐蘭
T'ang liu-shih ming-chia chi	唐六十名家集
T'ang Ts'ai-ch'ang	唐才常
T'ang Yung-t'ung	湯用彤
Tao	道
tao-t'ung	道統
T'ao-chai chi-chin lu	陶齋吉金錄
T'ao Hsi-sheng	陶希聖
T'ao Meng-ho	陶孟和
T'ao Pai-ch'uan	陶百川
T'ao Yüan-ming	陶淵明
Teng Kuang-ming	鄧廣銘
Ti	狄
ti	帝
ti-hsia shih-liao	地下史料

Ti K'u	帝嚳
Ti-wang shih-chi	帝王世紀
tiao-min fa-tsui	弔民伐罪
t'iao-li-te	條理的
t'ien	天
T'ien-Han chih-hou	天漢之后
t'ien jen ch'ang tuan	天人長短
T'ien-t'an hsien-fa ts'ao-an	天壇憲法草案
t'ien-ti-chih-hsing jen-wei-kuei	天地之性人為貴
T'ien-wen	天問
T'ien-yen-lun	天演論
Ting	丁
Ting Wen-chiang (V. K. Ting)	丁文江
tsai-hsiang	宰相
Ts'ai Yüan-p'ei	蔡元培
tsao she-hui	造社會
Ts'ao Ju-lin	曹汝霖
tsei-chung	賊種
"Tsen-yang hsieh pai-hua-wen"	怎樣寫白話文
Ts'en Chung-mien	岑仲勉
Tseng Kuo-fan	曾國藩
Ts'eng-lei tsao-ch'eng shuo	層累造成說
Tso-chuan	左傳
Tsou	鄒
Tsou Heng	鄒衡
Tsu-chih-pu	組織部
Tzu-yu Chung-kuo	自由中國
ts'un erh pu pu	存而不補
tsung-fa	宗法
tsung-lun	總論
Tu-ching yün-tung	讀經運動
Tu-li p'ing-lun	獨立評論
Tuan Fang	端方
tu-shu-jen	讀書人
Tuan Hsi-p'eng	段錫朋
Tuan Yü-ts'ai	段玉裁
tuan-p'ing	短評
Tun-huang	敦煌
Tung Chung-shu	董仲舒
Tung I	東夷
"Tung-I chuan"	東夷傳

Tungnan	東南
Tung-pei shih-kang	東北史綱
Tung Tso-pin	董作賓
T'ung-cheng	桐城
t'ung-chung	通種
t'ung-shih	通識
tzu	字
tzu-jan	自然
tzu-pen-chia	資本家
V. K. Ting (Ting Wen-chiang)	丁文江
wai-hsüeh	外學
wai-kuo-jen te yen-kuang	外國人的眼光
wai-wu chu-i	外物主義
"Wan-o chih yüan"	萬惡之源
Wang Cheng-t'ing	王正廷
Wang Ching-hsi	汪敬熙
Wang Ching-hsüan	王敬軒
Wang Ching-wei	汪精衛
Wang Ch'ung	王充
Wang Hsien-t'ang	王獻唐
Wang Hsing-kung	王星拱
Wang I	王逸
Wang Kuo-wei	王國維
Wang Lun	王倫
Wang Mang	王莽
Wang Shih-chieh	王世杰
Wang Su-yün	王素雲
wang-tao	王道
Wang Yang-ming	王陽明
Wang Yü-ch'üan	王毓銓
Wei	衛
Wei	魏
wei-ching	偽經
wei-shu	偽書
wei-tsao	偽造
wen-hua chi-lei	文化積累
Wen-hui pao	文匯報
wen-i-tsai-tao	文以載道
wen-jen	文人
wen-ming-shih	文明史
wen-t'i-tan	問題單
Wen T'ien-hsiang	文天祥

Weng Wen-hao	翁文灝
"Wo pu-yao le"	我不要了
wu	物
wu-chih	物質
Wu Chih-hui (Wu Ching-heng)	吳稚暉（吳敬恆）
Wu Chin-ting	吳金鼎
Wu Ching-ch'ao	吳景超
Wu Ching-heng (Wu Chih-hui)	吳敬恆（吳稚暉）
Wu Han	吳晗
wu-hsing	五行
wu-hsüeh	物學
Wu K'ang	吳康
wu-k'o pien-po	無可辯駁
Wu Kuang	吳廣
wu-liao hsüeh-che	無聊學者
Wu Mei	吳梅
Wu Mi	吳宓
wu-teng chüeh	五等爵
Wu T'i	伍俶
Wu T'ing-hsieh	吳廷燮
Wu Wei-p'ing	吳衛平
ya-hsün	雅馴
Yang Chen-sheng	楊振聲
Yang Chung-chien	楊鍾健
Yang Hsiang-k'uei	楊向奎
Yang Hsing-fo (Yang Ch'üan)	楊杏佛（楊銓）
Yang Hsiung	揚雄
yang-jen	洋人
Yang K'uan	楊寬
Yang Lien-sheng	楊聯陞
yang-pa-ku	洋八股
Yang-shao	仰韶
Yao	堯
Yao Chi-heng	姚際恆
Yao Shih-ao (Yao Ts'ung-wu)	姚士鰲（姚從吾）
Yao Ts'ung-wu (Yao Shih-ao)	姚從吾（姚士鰲）
yeh	也
Yeh Ch'ing (Jen Cho-hsüan)	葉青（任卓宣）
Yeh Ch'u-ts'ang	葉楚傖
yeh-man chu-i	野蠻主義

Glossary

Yeh Shao-chün	葉紹鈞
Yen	燕
Yen Fu	嚴復
Yen Hsi-shan	閻錫山
Yen-shih	偃師
yen-chiu	研究
Yin	殷
Yin Chou chih chi	殷周之際
Yin Chou chih-tu lun	殷周制度論
Yin Hai-kuang	殷海光
Yin-hsü	殷墟
"Yin pen-chi"	殷本紀
yin sha	淫殺
Yin Ta (Liu Yao)	尹達（劉燿）
yin yang	陰陽
Ying Hua	英華
yu-hsin-ju-fen	憂心如焚
yu-hsüeh	遊學
yu-i-shih	有意識
yu tsu-chih te she-hui	有組織的社會
Yung-chia	永嘉
yung-chiu-le	用舊了
Yü	禹
"Yü Hsia liang-hsi shuo"	虞夏兩系說
yü-k'o	預科
Yü-kung	禹貢
Yü P'ing-po	俞平伯
Yü Ta-fu	郁達夫
Yü Ta-ts'ai	俞大綵
Yü Ta-wei (David Yule)	俞大維
yu-wu yu-tse	有物有則
Yü-yen li-shih chou-k'an	語言歷史週刊
Yüan	元
Yüan	院
"Yüan chung hsiao"	原忠孝
Yüan Shih-k'ai	袁世凱
Yüan Tao	原道
Yüan-ch'ü-hsüan	元曲選
Yüeh-fu shih-chi	樂府詩集
yüeh-lü chu-i	約律主義

Bibliography

Allito, Guy. *The Last Confucian: Liang Shu-ming and the Chinese Dilemma of Modernity.* Berkeley, 1979.
An-hui su-hua pao 安徽俗話報. 1904; rpt., Peking, 1983, 2 vols.
Asen, Johannes, ed. *Gesamtverzeichnis des Lehrkörpers der Universität Berlin. Bd. 1, 1810–1945.* Leipzig, 1955.
Bannister, Robert C. *Sociology and Scientism.* Chapel Hill, 1987.
Beasley, W. G., and E. G. Pulleyblank, eds. *Historians of China and Japan.* London, 1971.
Berlin, Isaiah. "Nationalism." In *Against the Current.* New York, 1979.
Bonner, Joey. *Wang Kuo-wei: An Intellectual Biography.* Cambridge, Mass., 1986.
Boorman, Howard L., ed. *Biographical Dictionary of Republican China.* New York, 1968, 4 vols.
Bourdieu, Pierre. *Homo Academicus.* Translated by Peter Collier. Stanford, 1984.
Brandt, Conrad, ed. *A Documentary History of Chinese Communism.* Cambridge, Mass., 1952.
Burke, Peter. *The French Historical Revolution.* Stanford, 1989.
Chan Wing-tsit 陳榮捷. *Religious Trends in Modern China.* New York, 1953.
Chang Chih-yüan 張致遠. "Lan-k'o (Ranke) te sheng-p'ing yü chu-tso" 蘭克的生平與著作. *Tzu-yu Chung-kuo* 自由中國, 7:12 (1952), 382–387.
Chang Chün-mai 張君勱. *Pi-chiao Chung Jih Yang-ming hsüeh* 比較中日陽明學. Taipei, 1955.
Chang Chung-tung 張忠棟. "Hu Shih yü Yin Hai-kuang" 胡適與殷海光. *Kuo-li T'ai-wan ta-hsüeh wen shih che hsüeh-pao* 國立台灣大學文史哲學報, 37 (1989), 123–172.
Chang Hao 張灝. *Chinese Intellectuals in Crisis: Search for Order and Meaning, 1890–1911.* Berkeley, 1987.
"Hsing-hsiang yü shih-chih – tsai-lun Wu-ssu ssu-hsiang" 形象與實質──再論五四思想. In *Tzu-yu mın-chu te ssu-hsiang yü wen-hua* 自由民主的思想與文化. Taipei, 1990, 23–57.
Liang Ch'i-ch'ao and Intellectual Transition in China, 1890–1907. Cambridge, Mass., 1971.
"New Confucianism and the Intellectual Crisis of Contemporary China." In Charlotte Furthe, ed., *The Limits of Change: Essays on Conservative Alternatives in Republican China.* Cambridge, Mass., 1976, 276–302.

Chang Hsüeh-ch'eng 章學誠. *Wen-shih t'ung-i* 文史通義. In *Chang Hsüeh-ch'eng i-shu* 章學誠遺書. 1920; rpt., Peking, 1985, 1–49.
Chang Kwang-chih 張光直. *The Archaeology of Ancient China*. 3rd ed. New Haven, 1977.
The Archaeology of Ancient China. 4th ed. New Haven, 1986.
The Early Chinese Civilization: Anthropological Perspective. Cambridge, Mass., 1976.
"The Origins of Chinese Civilization: A Review." *Journal of the American Oriental Society*, 98 (1978), 85–91.
"Sandai Archaeology and the Formation of States." In David Keightley, ed., *The Origins of Chinese Civilization*. Berkeley, 1983, 495–521.
Shang Civilization. New Haven, 1980.
"Ts'ung Hsia Shang Chou san-tai k'ao-ku lun san-tai kuan-hsi yü Chung-kuo ku-tai kuo-chia te hsing-ch'eng" 從夏商周三代考古論三代關係與中國古代國家的形成. In *Ch'ü Wan-li ch'i-chih jung-ch'ing lun-wen chi* 屈萬里七秩榮慶論文集. Taipei, 1978, 287–306.
"Yin Shang wen-ming ch'i-yüan yen-chiu shang te i-ko kuan-chien wen-t'i" 殷商文明起源研究上的一個關鍵問題. In Tu Cheng-sheng 杜正勝, ed. *Chung-kuo shang-ku-shih lun-wen hsüan-chi* 中國上古史論文選集. Taipei, 1979, 2 vols., 1:263–287.
Chang Li-yang 張利庠. "Lüeh lun Fu Ssu-nien hsien-sheng te hsüeh-shu kung-hsien" 略論傅斯年先生的學術貢獻. *Chin-yang hsüeh-k'an* 晉陽學刊, 5 (1990), 41–45.
Chang Ping-lin 章炳麟. *Chien-lun* 檢論. In *Chang T'ai-yen ch'üan-chi* 章太炎全集. Shanghai, 1984, 6 vols., vol. 3.
Chang Yin-lin 張蔭麟. *Chung-kuo shih-kang* 中國史綱. 1941; Taipei, 1963.
Chang Yü-fa 張玉法. *Chung-kuo hsien-tai-shih* 中國現代史. Taipei, 1977, 2 vols.
Chao Chi-pin 趙紀彬. "Tu 'Hsing-ming ku-hsün pien-cheng'" 讀性命古訓辨証. In *Chao Chi-pin wen-chi* 趙紀彬文集. Honan, 1985, 2 vols., 1:7–14.
Chao Hsiao-i 趙效沂 and Hung Yen-ch'iu 洪炎秋. "Kuan-yü Li Wan-chü yü Fu Ssu-nien" 關於李萬居與傅斯年. *Chuan-chi wen-hsüeh* 傳記文學, 21:2 (1972), 40.
Chao K'o 趙科. "Mao Tse-tung tu-shu i-wen" 毛澤東讀書軼聞. *Li pao* 立報, 14 (1981), 71, 73.
Chao Yüan-jen 趙元任. "T'ai-shan yü-liao hsü-lun" 台山語料序論. In *Fu so-chang chi-nien t'e-k'an* 傅所長紀念特刊. Taipei, 1951, 61–66.
Ch'en Ch'i-t'ien 陳啟天. "Fa-chia te fu-hsing" 法家的復興. In Ts'ai Shang-ssu 蔡尚思, ed., *Chung-kuo hsien-tai ssu-hsiang-shih tzu-liao chien-pien* 中國現代思想史資料簡編. Chekiang, 1982–1983, 5 vols., 3:835–844.
Ch'en Chih-ch'ao 陳智超, ed. *Ch'en Yüan lai wang shu-hsin-chi* 陳垣來往書信集. Shanghai, 1990.
Ch'en Chih-mai 陳之邁. "Kuan-yü Fu Meng-chen (Fu Ssu-nien) hsien-sheng te chi-chien-shih" 關於傅孟真先生的幾件事. *Chuan-chi wen-hsüeh*, 28:3 (1976), 49–51.
Ch'en Han-sheng 陳翰笙. *Ch'en Han-sheng hui-i-lu* 陳翰笙回憶錄. Peking, 1988.
Ch'en, Jerome. "The Chinese Communist Movement to 1927." In John K.

Fairbank and Denis Twitchett, eds., *The Cambridge History of China*. Cambridge, 1983, 12.1:505–526.

Ch'en P'an 陳槃. "Chi Fu Meng-chen shih tsai Chung-shan ta-hsüeh" 記傅孟真師在中山大學. *Chuan-chi wen-hsüeh*, 5:6 (1964), 54.

"Hou yü she-hou" 侯與射侯. *Chung-yang yen-chiu yüan Li-shih yü-yen yen-chiu-so chi-k'an* 中央研究院歷史語言研究所集刊, 22:1 (1950), 121–128.

"Huai ku en-shih Fu Meng-chen hsien-sheng yu-shu" 懷故恩師孟真先生有述. *Hsin-shih-tai* 新時代, 3:3 (1963), 13–14.

"Huai ku en-shih Fu Meng-chen hsien-sheng yu-shu chih erh" 懷故恩師傅孟真先生有述之二. *Chuan-chi wen-hsüeh*, 11:4 (1967), 39–40.

Tso-shih-ch'un-ch'iu i-li pien 左氏春秋義例辨. Shanghai, 1947.

Ch'en Po-ta 陳伯達. *Chung-kuo te ssu-ta-chia-tsu* 中國的四大家族. Hong Kong, 1947.

Ch'en P'o 陳波. "Ch'ing-nien Mao Tse-tung yü Pei-ching ta-hsüeh" 青年毛澤東與北京大學. *Pei-ching ta-hsüeh hsüeh-pao* 北京大學學報, 6 (1984), 90–94.

Ch'en Shu-yü 陳漱渝. "Fu Ssu-nien ch'i-jen ch'i-shih" 傅斯年其人其事. *T'uan-chieh-pao* 團結報 (July 29, August 1, 1990).

Ch'en Teng-yüan 陳登原. *Kuo-shih chiu-wen* 國史舊聞. Peking, 1958, 2 vols.

Ch'en Tu-hsiu 陳獨秀. "Chin-jih chih chiao-yü fan-cheng" 今日之教育方針. In *Ch'en Tu-hsiu chu-tso hsüan* 陳獨秀著作選. Shanghai, 1993, 140–146.

"Hsien fa yü k'ung-chiao" 憲法與孔教. In *Ch'en Tu-hsiu chu-tso hsüan*, 224–229.

"Ta Ch'ien Hsüan-t'ung" 答錢玄同. In *Ch'en Tu-hsiu chu-tso hsüan*, 376.

"Wu-jen tsui-hou chih chüeh-wu" 吾人最後之覺悟. In *Ch'en Tu-hsiu chu-tso hsüan*, 175–179.

"Yüan shih-k'ai fu-huo" 袁世凱復活. In *Ch'en Tu-hsiu chu-tso hsüan*, 238–240.

Ch'en Tuan-chih 陳端志. *Wu-ssu yün-tung chih shih te p'ing-chia* 五四運動之史的評價. Shanghai, 1935; rpt., Taipei, 1986.

Ch'en Wei-p'ing 陳衛平. "Lun Po-ko-sen (H. Bergson) che-hsüeh tsai Chung-kuo chin-tai te ying-hsiang" 論柏格森哲學在中國近代的影響. *Chung-kuo che-hsüeh-shih yen-chiu* 中國哲學史研究, no. 2 (1988), 84–93.

Ch'en Yin-k'o 陳寅恪. *Chin-ming-kuan ts'ung-kao ch'u-pien* 金明館叢稿初編. Shanghai, 1980.

"Ch'ung-k'o *Yüan Hsi-yü jen Hua-hua k'ao* hsü" 重刻元西域人華化考序. In *Ch'en Yin-k'o hsien-sheng lun-wen-chi* 陳寅恪先生論文集. Taipei, 1977, 2 vols., 1:683–684.

"Fu Ch'ing-chu" 傅青主. A poem included in *Han-liu-t'ang chi* 寒柳堂集. Shanghai, 1980, 29.

"Lun Han Yü" 論韓愈. In *Ch'en Yin-k'o hsien-sheng lun-wen-chi*, 2:589–600.

"Ta-cheng-ch'i-hsin-lun wei Chih-i hsü te chen shih-liao" 大乘起信論偽智顗序的真史料. In *Ch'en Yin-k'o hsien-sheng lun-wen-chi*, 2:1343–1347.

Ch'en Yü-hsien 陳毓賢. "Hung yeh i ku-yu" 洪業憶故友. *Ming pao yüeh-k'an* 明報月刊, no. 12 (1987), 103–107.

Ch'en Yüan-hui 陳元暉. "Chung-kuo te Ma-ho (E. Mach) chu-i che" 中國的馬赫主義者. In *Ch'en Yüan-hui wen-chi* 陳元暉文集. Foochow, 1993, 3 vols., 2:79–95.

Cheng Chen-to 鄭振鐸. "Ch'ieh man-t'an so-wei kuo-hsüeh" 且慢談所謂國學. *Hsiao shuo yüeh-pao* 小說月報, 20:1 (1929), 8–13.

Cheng Ho-sheng 鄭鶴聲. "Fu Ssu-nien teng pien-chu *Tung-pei shih-kang* ch'u-kao" 傅斯年等編著東北史綱初稿. *T'u-shu p'ing-lun* 圖書評論, 1:11 (1933), 7–18.

Cheng Shih-hsü 鄭師許. "Cheng Shih-hsü hsien-sheng te i-chien" 鄭師許先生的意見. In *Tu-ching wen-t'i* 讀經問題. Originally a special issue of *Chiao-yü tsa-chih* 教育雜誌 (May 1935); rpt., Hong Kong, 1966, 31–4.

Ch'eng Ai-chin 程愛勤 and Li Hui-ling 李慧玲. "T'ao-Sung-yün-tung te chu-chiang" 討宋運動的主將. In *Fu Ssu-nien* 傅斯年. Shantung, 1991, 187–192.

Ch'eng Ts'ang-p'o 程滄波. "Chi Fu Meng-chen" 記傅孟真. In *Ts'ang-p'o wen-hsüan* 滄波文選. Taipei, 1964, 235–243. Also in *Fu ku hsiao-chang ai-wan-lu* 傅故校長哀輓錄. Taipei, 1951, 47–49.

"Tsai-chi Fu Meng-chen hsien-sheng" 再記傅孟真先生. *Hsin-wen t'ien-ti* 新聞天地, 156 (1951), 49–51. Also in *Fu ku hsiao-chang ai-wan-lu*, 49–51.

Ch'eng Tuan-li 程端禮. *Ch'eng-shih-chia-shu tu-shu fen-nien jih-ch'eng* 程氏家塾讀書分年日程. In Yang Chia-luo 楊家駱, ed., *Tu-shu fen-nien jih-ch'eng* 讀書分年日程, *Hsüeh-kuei lei-pien* 學規類編. Taipei, 1962, 1–132.

Chi-nien Ch'en Yin-k'o chiao-shou kuo-chi hsüeh-shu t'ao-lun-hui lun-wen-chi 紀念陳寅恪教授國際學術討論會論文集. Kwangtung, 1989.

Ch'i Ssu-ho 齊思和. "Chin pai-nien lai Chung-kuo shih-hsüeh te fa-chan" 近百年來中國史學的發展. *Yen-ching she-hui k'o-hseüh* 燕京社會科學, 2 (1949), 1–35.

Chiang Hsin-li 江心力. "Fu Ssu-nien te kuo-min hsing-ko lun" 傅斯年的國民性格論. *Liao-ch'eng shih-fan hsüeh-yüan hsüeh-pao* 聊城師範學院學報, no. 1 (1991), 64–76.

Ch'ien Chi-po 錢基博. *Hsien-tai Chung-kuo wen-hsüeh-shih* 現代中國文學史. Shanghai, 1933; rpt., Taipei, 1976.

Ch'ien Hsüan-t'ung 錢玄同. "Chung-kuo chin-hou chih wen-tzu wen-t'i" 中國今後之文字問題. *Hsin-ch'ing-nien* 新青年, 4:4 (1918), 350–356.

Ch'ien Li-ch'ün 錢理群. *Fan-jen te pei-ai: Chou Tso-jen chuan* 凡人的悲哀：周作人傳. Taipei, 1991.

Ch'ien Mu 錢穆. "Chan-hou chien-tu te wen-t'i" 戰後建都的問題. In *Cheng hsüeh ssu-yen* 政學私言. Chungking, 1945, 137–152.

"Chou ch'u ti-li k'ao" 周初地理考. *Yen-ching hsüeh-pao* 燕京學報, 10 (1931), 1955–2008.

Chung-kuo chin san-pai-nien hsüeh-shu-shih 中國近三百年學術史. 4th ed., Taipei, 1968, 2 vols.

Hsien-tai Chung-kuo hsüeh-shu lun-heng 現代中國學術論衡. Taipei, 1984.

Pa-shih i shuang-ch'in, Shih-yu tsa-i 八十憶雙親，師友雜憶. Taipei, 1983.

"Po Hu Shih chih 'Shuo Ju'" 駁胡適之說儒. In *Chung-kuo hsüeh-shu ssu-hsiang-shih lun-ts'ung* 中國學術思想史論叢. Taipei, 1976–1980, 8 vols., 2: 373–382.

"Yin-lun" 引論. *Kuo-shih ta-kang* 國史大綱. Taipei, 1975, 2 vols., 1:1–32.

Chien Po-tsan 翦伯贊. *Li-shih-che-hsüeh chiao-ch'eng* 歷史哲學教程. 1938; 2nd ed., Changchun, 1949.

Chin Chao-tzu 金兆梓. "Chung-kuo jen-chung chi wen-hua chih yu-lai" 中國人種及文化之由來. *Tung-fang tsa-chih* 東方雜誌, 26:24 (1929), 73–82.

Chin Ching-fang 金景芳. "Chin Yü-fu chuan-lüeh" 金毓黻傳略. *Shih-hsüeh-shih yen-chiu* 史學史研究, no. 3 (1986), 71–74.
"Shang ch'i-yüan yü wo-kuo pei-fang shuo" 商起源於我國北方說. *Chung-hua wen-shih lun-ts'ung* 中華文史論叢, 7 (1978), 65–70.
Chin Yao 金耀. "I Fu Ssu-nien hsien-sheng" 憶傅斯年先生. In *Fu ku hsiao-chang ai-wan-lu*. Taipei, 1951, 59.
Chin Yü-fu 金毓黻. *Chung-kuo shih-hsüeh-shih* 中國史學史. Shanghai, 1944; rpt., Taipei, 1960.
Ch'in Shou-ch'ang 秦綬昌, ed. *Cheng-chih hsieh-shang hui-i shih-mo chi* 政治協商會議始末記. Changsha, 1946.
Ching-chi tzu-liao she 經濟資料社, ed. *T. V. Soong hao-men tzu-pen nei-mu* T. V. 宋豪門資本內幕. Hong Kong, 1948.
Ching Yen 靜弇. "Wei 'kuan yü Fu Ssu-nien' pu-i" 為'關於傅斯年'補遺. *Wen-hui-pao* 文匯報 (November 10, 1946).
Ch'ing-shih-kao chiao-chu pien-tsuan hsiao-tsu 清史稿校注編纂小組, ed. *Ch'ing-shih-kao chiao-chu* 清史稿校注. Taipei, 1986.
Ch'ing-shih lieh-chuan 清史列傳. Shanghai, 1928.
Ch'iu Yung-ming 邱永明. "Ho Ping-sung *Li-shih chiao-hsüeh-fa* shu-lun" 何炳松歷史教學法述論. In Liu Yin-sheng 劉寅生, ed., *Ho Ping-sung chi-nien wen-chi* 何炳松紀念文集. Shanghai, 1990, 199–213.
Chou Ch'ao-min 周朝民. "Ho Ping-sung shih-hsüeh li-lun ch'u-t'an" 何炳松史學理論初探. In Liu Yin-sheng, ed., *Ho Ping-sung chi-nien wen-chi*. Shanghai, 1990, 83–98.
Chou Chih-p'ing 周質平. "Hu Shih yü Feng Yu-lan" 胡適與馮友蘭. *Chih-shih-fen-tzu* 知識份子, no. 3 (1991), 78–88.
Chou Fa-kao 周法高. "Ti-hsia tzu-liao yü shu-pen tzu-liao te ts'an-hu yen-chiu" 地下資料與書本資料的參互研究. *Lien-ho hsüeh-pao* 聯合學報, no. 1 (1970), 1–13.
Chou I-liang 周一良. "Hsi-yang Han-hsüeh yü Hu Shih" 西洋漢學與胡適. In *Hu Shih ssu-hsiang p'i-p'an* 胡適思想批判. Peking, 1955, 7 vols., 7:198–213.
Chou P'ei-yüan 周培源, "Liu-shih-nien lai te Chung-kuo k'o-hsüeh" 六十年來的中國科學. In Chung-kuo she-hui k'o-hsüeh-yüan Chin-tai-shih yen-chiu-so 中國社會科學院近代史研究所編, ed., *Chi-nien Wu-ssu yün-tung liu-shih chou-nien hsüeh-shu t'ao-lun-hui lun-wen-hsüan* 紀念五四運動六十周年學術討論會論文選. Peking, 1980, 3 vols., 1:44–63.
Chou T'ien-chien 周天健. "Fu Ssu-nien" 傅斯年. In *Chung-hua-min-kuo ming-jen-chuan* 中華民國名人傳. Taipei, 1989, 6:340–363.
"Kao-ming-jou-k'o te jen-ko tien-hsing: Fu Meng-chen hsien-sheng shih-shih ssu-shih chou-nien chih-kan" 高明柔克的人格典型：傅孟真先生逝世四十週年誌感. *Lien-ho pao* 聯合報 (December 10, 1990).
Chou Tzu-tung 周子東 et al. *San-shih nien-tui Chung-kuo she-hui hsing-chih lun-chan* 三十年代中國社會性質論戰. Shanghai, 1987.
Chou Yen-sun 周衍孫. "Shen Chien-shih yü Chung-kuo shih-hsüeh" 沈兼士與中國史學. *Min-chu p'ing-lun* 民主評論, 5:14 (1954), 29–30.
Chow Tse-tsung 周策縱. *The May Fourth Movement: Intellectual Revolution in China*. Cambridge, Mass., 1960.

Chu Chia-hua 朱家驊. "Tao wang-yu Fu Meng-chen hsien-sheng" 悼亡友傅孟真先生. In *Fu ku hsiao-chang ai-wan-lu*. Taipei, 1951, 39–40.
Chu Yu-hsien 朱有瓛, ed. *Chung-kuo chin-tai hsüeh-chih shih-liao* 中國近代學制史料. Shanghai, 1986, part 1, 2 vols.
Ch'ü Ch'iu-pai 瞿秋白. "Ou-hua wen-i" 歐化文藝. In *Ch'ü Ch'iu-pai wen-chi* 瞿秋白文集, "wen-hsüeh-pien" 文學編. Peking, 1985, 6 vols., 1:491–497.
"P'u-lo (Proletariat) ta-chung wen-i te hsien-shih wen-t'i" 普羅大眾文藝的現實問題. In *Ch'ü Ch'iu-pai wen-chi*, "wen-hsüeh-pien," 1:461–483.
"Tzu-yu-jen te wen-hua yün-tung" 自由人的文化運動. In *Ch'ü Ch'iu-pai wen-chi*, "wen-hsüeh-pien," 1:498–503.
Ch'ü Wan-li 屈萬里. "Ching tao Fu Meng-chen hsien-sheng" 敬悼傅孟真先生. *Tzu-yu Chung-kuo*, 4:1 (1951), 20–22.
Ch'üan T'ang shih 全唐詩. Peking, 1960, 12 vols.
Chuang Lien 莊練. "Lao-hu Fu Ssu-nien" 老虎傅斯年. *Chung-yang jih-pao* 中央日報 (January 10, 1988).
Chung Kung-hsün 鍾貢勛. "Meng-chen hsien-sheng tsai Chung-shan ta-hsüeh shih-ch'i te i-tien pu-ch'ung" 孟真先生在中山大學時期的一點補充. *Chuan-chi wen-hsüeh*, 28:3 (1976), 51.
Chung-kuo hsien-tai che-hsüeh-shih yen-chiu hui 中國現代哲學史研究會, ed. *Chung-kuo hsien-tai che-hsüeh yü wen-hua ssu-ch'ao* 中國現代哲學與文化思潮. Peking, 1989.
"Chung-kuo-kuo-min-tang ti-i-tz'u ch'üan-kuo tai-piao ta-hui hsüan-yen" 中國國民黨第一次全國代表大會宣言. In *Chung-kuo-kuo-min-tang ti-i-tz'u ch'üan-kuo tai-piao ta-hui shih-liao chuan-chi* 中國國民黨第一次全國代表大會史料專輯. Taipei, 1984, 113–124.
Chung-kuo li-shih wen-hua ming-ch'eng – Liao-Ch'eng 中國歷史文化名城——聊城. Shangtung, 1995.
Chung-kuo she-hui-k'o-hsüeh-lien-meng ch'eng-li wu-shih-wu chou-nien chi-nien chuan-chi 中國社會科學聯盟成立五十五週年紀念專輯. Shanghai, 1986.
Chung-kuo tang-tai she-hui k'o-hsüeh-chia 中國當代社會科學家. Peking, 1982–1990 to date, 11 vols.
Chung-kuo te ch'u-fa 中國的出發. *Hsien-jen-chang* 仙人掌, 1:1 (1977). A special issue commemorating Fu Ssu-nien. Taipei, 1977.
Chung-yang jih-pao 中央日報. Nanking, July 1, 1947.
Chung-yang yen-chiu yüan shih ch'u-kao 中央研究院史初稿. Taipei, 1988.
Coble, Parks M. *The Shanghai Capitalists and the Nationalist Government, 1927–1937*. Cambridge, Mass., 1980.
Creel, Herrlee G. *The Origin of Statecraft in China*, vol. 1, *The Western Chou Empire*. Chicago, 1970.
Dirlik, Arif. "Mirror to Revolution: Early Marxist Images of Chinese History." *Journal of Asian Studies*, 33:2 (February 1974), 193–223.
Revolution and History: Origin of Marxist Historiography in China, 1919–1937. Berkeley, 1978.
Duiker, William. *Cai Yuanpei: Education of Modern China*. Pennsylvania State University Studies, no. 41. University Park, Pa., 1977.

Eastman, Lloyd. *The Abortive Revolution: China under Nationalist Rule, 1927–1937.* Cambridge, Mass., 1974.
Eber, Irene. "Hu Shih and Chinese History: The Problem of *cheng-li kuo-ku.*" *Monumenta Serica,* 27 (1968), 169–207.
Edwards, Paul, ed. *The Encyclopedia of Philosophy.* New York, 1967, 8 vols.
Elman, Benjamin. *From Philosophy to Philology.* Cambridge, Mass., 1984.
Erh-shih-erh shih tsuan-lüeh 二十二史纂略. 1803.
Erikson, Erik. *Young Man Luther.* New York, 1962.
Esherick, Joseph. *The Origins of the Boxer Uprising.* Berkeley, 1987.
Fang Hao 方豪. "Ying Lien-chih hsien-sheng nien-p'u chi ch'i ssu-hsiang" 英斂之先生年譜及其思想. *Kuo-li T'ai-wan ta-hsüeh li-shih-hsüeh-hsi hsüeh-pao* 國立臺灣大學歷史學系學報, 1 (1974), 59–96.
Fang Hsin-liang 房鑫亮. "Ho Ping-sung p'ing-chuan" 何炳松評傳. In Liu Yin-sheng, *Ho Ping-sung chi-nien wen-chi.* Shanghai, 1990, 390–420.
Fan K'ang-fu 樊抗父. "Tsui-chin erh-shih-nien chien Chung-kuo chiu-hsüeh chih chin-pu" 最近二十年間中國舊學之進步. *Tung-fang tsa-chih,* 19:3 (1922), 33–38.
Feigon, Lee. *Chen Duxiu: Founder of the Chinese Communist Party.* Princeton, 1983.
Feng Ch'i 馮契, ed. *Chung-kuo chin-tai che-hsüeh-shih* 中國近代哲學史. Shanghai, 1989, 2 vols.
Feng Yu-lan 馮友蘭. *A History of Chinese Philosophy.* Translated by Derk Bodde. Princeton, 1952, 2 vols.
San-sung-t'ang hsüeh-shu lun-wen-chi 三松堂學術論文集. Peking, 1984.
San-sung-t'ang tzu-hsü 三松堂自敘. In *San-sung-t'ang ch'üan-chi* 三松堂全集, Honan, 1985, vol. 1.
Foreign Relations of the United States, 1945. Vol. 7. Washington, D.C., 1969.
Foreign Relations of the United States, 1948. Vol. 7. Washington, D.C., 1973.
Fu Ch'ung-lan 傅崇蘭. *Chung-kuo yün-ho ch'eng-shih fa-chan shih* 中國運河城市發展史. Szechwan, 1985.
Fu hsiao-chang tsui-hou lun-chu 傅校長最後論著. Taipei, 1950.
Fu I-ling 傅衣凌. "Wo shih tsen-yang yen-chiu Ming Ch'ing tzu-pen-chu-i meng-ya te" 我是怎樣研究明清資本主義萌芽的. In *Fu I-ling chih-shih wu-shih nien wen-pien* 傅衣凌治史五十年文編. Fukien, 1989, 45–50.
Fu Le-ch'eng 傅樂成. *Fu Meng-chen hsien-sheng nien-p'u* 傅孟真先生年譜. In *FSNC* 傅斯年先生全集, 7:2595–2716.
"Fu Meng-chen hsien-sheng te hsien-shih" 傅孟真先生的先世. *Chuan-chi wen-hsüeh,* 28:1 (1976), 3–23. Included in Fu Le-ch'eng, *Shih-tai te chui-i lun-wen-chi* 時代的追憶論文集. Taipei, 1984, 111–128.
"Fu Meng-chen hsien-sheng te min-tsu ssu-hsiang" 傅孟真先生的民族思想. *Chuan-chi wen-hsüeh,* 2:5 (1963), 17–20; 2:6 (1963), 26–31. Included in Fu Le-ch'eng, *Shih-tai te chui-i lun-wen-chi,* 141–167.
"Fu Meng-chen hsien-sheng yü Wu-ssu yün-tung" 傅孟真先生與五四運動. *Lien-ho-pao* (April 23, 24, 1979). Included in Fu Le-ch'eng, *Shih-tai te chui-i lun-wen-chi,* 129–140.
"Hsien-po Meng-chen hsien-sheng te jih-ch'ang sheng-huo" 先伯孟真先生的日常生活. In *Fu ku hsiao-chang ai-wang-lu.* Taipei, 1951, 13–15.

"Hui-i hsien-po Meng-chen hsien-sheng te jih-ch'ang sheng-huo" 回憶先伯孟真先生的日常生活. *Chung-kuo-shih-pao* 中國時報 (January 17, 1977). Included in Fu Le-ch'eng, *Shih-tai te chui-i lun-wen-chi*, 197–205.

"Wo chuan-hsieh Fu Ssu-nien chuan te kou-hsiang" 我撰寫傅斯年傳的構想. *Ta-hua-wan-pao* 大華晚報 (March 24, 1967). Included in *Shih-tai te chui-i lun-wen-chi*, 209–216.

Fu so-chang chi-nien t'e-k'an 傅所長紀念特刊. Taipei, 1951.

Fu Ssu-nien 傅斯年. "Ch'ing-nien te liang-chien shih-yeh" 青年的兩件事業. *Ch'en-pao* 晨報 (July 3, 5, 1920).

"Chou tung-feng yü Yin i-min" 周東封與殷遺民. *FSNC*, 3:894–903.

"Chung-hsi shih-hsüeh kuan-tien chih pien-ch'ien" 中西史學觀點之變遷. *FSNP* II-945.

"Chung-kuo chin san-pai-nien lai tui wai-lai wen-hua chih fan-ying" 中國近三百年對外來文化之反應. In *FSNP*, I-708.

"Chung-kuo shang-ku-shih yü k'ao-ku-hsüeh" 中國上古史與考古學. *FSNP*, I-807.

"Fa-k'an-tz'u" 發刊詞. *Chung-shan ta-hsüeh yü-yen li-shih-hsüeh yen-chiu-so chou-k'an* 中山大學語言歷史學研究所週刊, 1 (1927), 3.

Fu Meng-chen hsien-sheng chi 傅孟真先生集. Taipei, 1952, 5 vols.

Fu Ssu-nien ch'üan-chi 傅斯年全集. (*FSNC*). Taipei, 1980.

Fu Ssu-nien hsüan-chi 傅斯年選集. Taipei, 1967, 10 vols.

Fu Ssu-nien hsüeh-shu lun-wen-chi 傅斯年學術論文集. Hong Kong, 1969.

"Hsien Ch'in wen-chi te yen-hua" 先秦文籍的演化. In *FSNP*, I-433.

"Hsing ming ku-hsün pien-cheng" 性命古訓辨證. *FSNC*, 2:492–736.

"I Hsia Tung hsi shuo" 夷夏東西説. *FSNC*, 3:823–893.

"Liu Ying chi-hsing" 留英紀行. *Ch'en-pao* (August 6, 7, 1920).

"Lun che-hsüeh men li-shu wen-k'o chih liu-pi" 論哲學門隸屬文科之流弊. *Pei-ching ta-hsüeh jih-k'an* 北京大學日刊 (August 10, 1918).

"Lun hao-men tzu-pen chih pi-hsü ch'an-ch'u" 論豪門資本之必須剷除. *Kuan-ch'a* 觀察, 2:1 (1947), 6–9.

(Meng-chen) 孟真. "Mei-kan yü jen-sheng" 美感與人生. *Ch'en-pao* (July 7, 8, 9, 10, 1920).

"O yu t'u-chung shui-kan-lu" 歐遊途中隨感錄. It is mixed up with the administrative archives of the IHP without any serial number.

"She-hui-ko-ming: E-kuo (Russia)-shih te ko-ming" 社會革命：俄國式的革命. *Hsin-ch'ao* 新潮, 1:1 (1919), 128–129.

"Shih-tai te shu-kuang yü wei-chi" 時代的曙光與危機. In Wang Fan-sen and Tu Cheng-sheng, eds., *Fu Ssu-nien wen-wu chih-liao hsüan-chi* 傅斯年文物資料選輯. Taipei, 1995, 34.

"Sung Tzu-wen te shih-pai" 宋子文的失敗. *Shih-chi p'ing-lun* 世紀評論, 1:8 (1947), 5–7.

Ta-tung hsiao-tung shuo 大東小東説, *FSNC*, 3:745–758.

"T'an liang-chien *Nu-li chou-pao* shang te wu-shih" 談兩件努力週報上的物事. *Ku-shih pien* 古史辨. Peking and Shanghai, 1926–1941, 7 vols., 2:288–301.

Tung-pei shih-kang 東北史綱. Peking, 1932. This book was summarized and

Bibliography

translated into English by Li Chi 李濟, *Manchuria in History: A Summary* (Peking, 1932).
(Meng-chen) 孟真. "Yao liu-hsüeh Ying-kuo te jen tsui-hsien yao chih-tao te shih" 要留學英國的人最先要知道的事. *Ch'en-pao* (August 12, 13, 14, 15, 1920).
"Yü Kung Chiu-chou shih-ming" 禹貢九州釋名. In FSNP, II-637.
Fu Ssu-nien 傅斯年, Li Chi, Tung Tso-pin 董作賓, Liang Ssu-yung 梁思永, Wu Chin-ting 吳金鼎, Kuo Pao-chün 郭寶鈞, and Liu Yü-hsia 劉嶼霞. *Ch'eng-tzu-yai* 城子崖. Nanking, 1934.
"Fu Ssu-nien hsien-sheng erh-san shih" 傅斯年先生二、三事. In *Fu Ku hsiao-chang ai-wan-lu*. Taipei, 1951, 6–7.
Fu Ssu-nien Papers. (FSNP). Taipei, Institute of History and Philology, Academia Sinica.
Fu Tseng-hsiang 傅增湘. *Ts'ang-yüan ch'ün-shu ching-yen lu* 藏園群書經眼錄. Peking, 1982, 5 vols.
Fujie, Kira 藤枝晃. "Yano Sensei to Showa rokujunen" 矢野先生と昭和六十年. *Toyoshi kenkyu* 東洋史研究, 28:4 (1970), 30–32.
Furth, Charlotte. *Ting Wen-chiang: Science and China's New Culture*. Cambridge, Mass., 1970.
Gay, Peter. *The Enlightenment: An Interpretation*. Vol. 1, New York, 1966; vol. 2, New York, 1969.
Freud for Historians. New York, 1985.
Gilbert, Felix. *History: Politics or Culture?* Princeton, 1990.
"Leopold von Ranke and the American Philosophical Society." *Proceedings of the American Philosophical Society*, no. 3 (September 1986), 362–366.
Gooch, George P. *History and Historians in the Nineteenth Century*. Boston, 1965.
Graham, A. C. "The Background of the Mencian Theory of Human Nature." In *Ts'inhua hsüeh-pao* 清華學報, 6:1–2 (1967), 215–273.
Grieder, Jerome. *Hu Shih and the Chinese Renaissance*. Cambridge, Mass., 1970.
Intellectuals and the State in the Modern China. New York, 1971.
Han ming-ch'en chuan 漢名臣傳. Rpt., Taipei, 1970.
Higham, John. *History*. Baltimore, 1989.
Hightower, James. *The Poetry of T'ao Ch'ien*. Oxford, 1970.
Historische Zeitschrift (Munich), 1 (1859).
Ho Lin 賀麟. *Tang-tai Chung-kuo che-hsüeh* 當代中國哲學. Rpt., Taipei, 1974.
Ho Ping-sung 何炳松. "Chung-hua min-tsu ch'i-yüan chih hsin-shen-hua" 中華民族起源之新神話. *Tung-fang tsa-chih*, 26:2 (1929), 75–90.
"Lun so-wei kuo-hsüeh" 論所謂國學. *Hsiao-shuo yüeh-pao*, 20:1 (1929), 1–7.
Ho Ting-sheng 何定生. "Sun-shih t'ai ta le" 損失太大了. *Fu ku hsiao-chang ai-wan-lu*. Taipei, 1951, 76.
Ho Yu-sen 何佑森. "Juan Yüan te ching-hsüeh chi ch'i fang-fa" 阮元的經學及其方法. *Ku-kung wen-hsien* 故宮文獻, 2:1 (1970), 19–34.
Hobsbawn, E. J. *Nations and Nationalism since 1780*. Cambridge, 1990.
Hsi I 希夷. "Kuan-yü Chung-kuo wen-ming ch'i-yüan to-yüan te hsin-chia-kou" 關於中國文明起源多元的新架構. *Li-shih yüeh-k'an* 歷史月刊, 10 (1988), 151–154.

Hsia, C. T. *A History of Modern Chinese Fiction, 1917–1957*. New Haven, 1961.
Hsia Nai 夏鼐. *Hsin Chung-kuo te k'ao-ku shou-huo* 新中國的考古收穫. Peking, 1961.
"Liang Ssu-yung chuan-lüeh" 梁思永傳略. In *Chung-kuo hsien-tai she-hui k'o-hsüeh-chia chuan-lüeh* 中國現代社會科學家傳略. Shansi, 1985, 7:376–379.
"Wu-ssu yün-tung ho Chung-kuo chin-tai k'ao-ku-hsüeh te hsing-ch'i" 五四運動和中國近代考古學的興起. *K'ao-ku* 考古, no. 3 (1979), 193–196.
Hsia-shih lun-ts'ung 夏史論叢. Shantung, 1985.
Hsia Tseng-yu 夏曾佑. *Chung-kuo ku-tai-shih* 中國古代史. Peking, 1955.
Hsiao Ch'ao-jan 蕭超然. *Pei-ching ta-hsüeh hsiao-shih (1898–1949)* 北京大學校史. Peking, 1988.
Hsiao Kung-ch'üan 蕭公權. *Chung-kuo cheng-chih ssu-hsiang-shih* 中國政治思想史. Taipei, 1954, 6 vols.
Wen-hsüeh chien-wang lu 問學諫往錄. Taipei, 1972.
Hsin-ch'ao 新潮 (Peking), 1:1–3:2 (January 1919–March 1922).
Hsin-ch'ing-nien 新青年. Shanghai, Peking, and Canton, 1915–1925.
Hsin-sheng-pao 新生報. Taipei, December 22, 1950.
Hsiung Shang-hou 熊尚厚. "Fu Ssu-nien" 傅斯年. In *Min-kuo jen-wu chuan* 民國人物傳. Peking, 1987, vol. 6.
Hsiung Shih-li 熊十力. *Tu-ching shih-yao* 讀經示要. Taipei, 1973.
Hsü Chi-lin 許紀霖. "Chung-kuo tzu-yu-chu-i chih-shih fen-tzu te ts'an-cheng (1945–1949)" 中國自由主義知識份子的參政. *Erh-shih-i shih-chi* 二十一世紀, 6 (1991), 37–46.
Hsü Chih-heng 許之珩. "Tu Kuo-tsui hsüeh-pao kan-yen" 讀國粹學報感言. *Kuo-tsui hsüeh-pao* 國粹學報, 6 (1905), 1–6.
Hsü Chung-shu 徐中舒. "Chin-wen ku-tz'u shih-li" 金文嘏辭釋例. *Chung-yang yen-chiu yüan Li-shih yü-yen yen-chiu-so chi-k'an*, 6:1 (1936), 1–44.
"Tsai-shu Nei-ko-ta-k'u tang-an chih yu-lai chi ch'i cheng-li" 再述內閣大庫檔案之由來及其整理. *Chung-yang yen-chiu yüan Li-shih yü-yen yen-chiu-so chi-k'an*, 3:4 (1933), 538–571.
"Ts'ung ku-shu chung t'ui-ts'e chih Yin Chou min-tsu" 從古書中推測之殷周民族. *Ch'ing-hua kuo-hsüeh lun-ts'ung* 清華國學論叢, 1:1 (1927), 109–113.
"Yin Chou chih chi shih-chi chih chien-t'ao" 殷周之際史蹟之檢討. *Chung-yang yen-chiu yüan Li-shih yü-yen yen-chiu-so chi-k'an*, 7:2 (1936), 137–164.
"Yin-jen fu-hsiang chi hsiang chih nan-ch'ien" 殷人服象及象之南遷. *Chung-yang yen-chiu yüan Li-shih yü-yen yen-chiu-so chi-k'an*, 2:1 (1930), 60–76.
Hsü Fu-kuan 徐復觀. *Chung-kuo jen-hsing lun shih* 中國人性論史. Taichung, 1963.
Chung-kuo ssu-hsiang-shih lun-chi 中國思想史論集. Taichung, 1968.
"K'ao-chü yü i-li chih cheng chih ch'a-ch'ü" 考據與義理之爭之插曲. *Hsüeh-shu yü cheng-chih chih chien* 學術與政治之間. Taichung, 1963, 2 vols., 2:241–263.
"San-shih-nien lai chung-kuo te wen-hua ssu-hsiang wen-t'i" 三十年來中國的文化思想問題. *Hsüeh-shu yü cheng-chih chih chien*, 2:140–152.
"Shih shei chi-k'uei le Chung-kuo she-hui fan-kung te li-liang" 是誰擊潰了中國社會反共的力量. In *Hsüeh-shu yü cheng-chih chih chien*, 2:1–14.
Hsü Hsiao-t'ien 許嘯天, ed. *Kuo-ku-hsüeh t'ao-lun-chi* 國故學討論集. Shanghai, 1927, 3 vols.

Hsü Hsü-sheng 徐旭生 (Hsü Ping-ch'ang 徐炳昶). *Chung-kuo ku-shih te ch'uan-shuo shih-tai* 中國古史的傳說時代. Peking, 1960.

Hsü Kang 徐剛. "Fu Ssu-nien te chiao-yü ssu-hsiang chi ch'i chiao-yü hsüeh-shu shih-yeh" 傅斯年的教育思想及其教育學術事業. M.A. thesis, Cheng-chih University, Taiwan, 1981.

Hsü Kuan-san 許冠三. *Hsin-shih-hsüeh chiu-shih-nien* 新史學九十年. Hong Kong, 1986, 1988, 2 vols.

Hsü Te-heng 許德珩. "Hui-i kuo-min tsa-chih" 回憶國民雜誌. In *Wu-ssu shih-ch'i te she-t'uan* 五四時期的社團. Peking, 1979, vol. 2.

"Wu-ssu yün-tung liu-shih chou-nien" 五四運動六十週年. *Wen-shih-tzu-liao hsüan-chi* 文史資料選集, 61 (1979), 4–39.

Hsü Yüan 徐淵. "Fa-hsi-ssu-ti (Fascism) yü San-min-chu-i" 法西斯蒂與三民主義. In Ts'ai Shang-ssu, ed. *Chung-kuo hsien-tai ssu-hsiang-shih tzu-liao chien-pien*. Chekiang, 1982–1983, 5 vols., 3:690–696.

Hsüan-p'u lun-hsüeh chi 玄圃論學集. Peking, 1990.

Hu Ch'ang-chih 胡昌智. *Li-shih chih-shih yü she-hui pien-ch'ien* 歷史知識與社會變遷. Taipei, 1988.

Hu Feng-hsiang 胡逢祥. "Ho Ping-sung yü Lu-pin-sun (J. H. Robinson) te hsin-shih-hsüeh" 何炳松與魯濱遜的新史學. *Shih-hsüeh-shih yen-chiu*, no. 3 (1987), 31–37.

Hu Hou-hsüan 胡厚宣. "Tung-pei shih-kang ti-i-chüan tso-che shih Fu Ssu-nien" 東北史綱第一卷作者是傅斯年. *Shih-hsüeh-shih yen-chiu*, 3 (1991), 48–49.

"Yin fei nu-li she-hui lun" 殷非奴隸社會論. In *Chia-ku-hsüeh Shang-shih lun-ts'ung ch'u-pien* 甲骨學商史論叢初編. Chengtu, 1944, 4 vols. 1:1–14.

Hu Shih 胡適. Address given at the Royal Institute of International Affairs. *Journal of the Royal Institute of International Affairs*, 6:6 (1926), 265–283.

"Cheng-li kuo-ku yü ta-kuei" 整理國故與打鬼. In *Hu Shih wen-ts'un* 胡適文存. Taipei, 1968, 4 vols, 3:123–132.

"Chih-hsüeh te fang-fa yü ts'ai-liao" 治學的方法與材料. In *Hu Shih wen-ts'un*, 3:109–122.

"Ch'ing-tai hsüeh-che te chih-hsüeh fang-fa" 清代學者的治學方法. In *Hu Shih wen-ts'un*, 1:383–412.

"Fu Meng-chen hsien-sheng te ssu-hsiang" 傅孟真先生的思想. In *Hu Shih chiang-yen-chi* 胡適講演集. Taipei, 1978, 3 vols., 2:336–350.

"Hsin-ssu-ch'ao te i-i" 新思潮的意義. In *Hu Shih wen-ts'un*, 1:727–736.

"Hsin-wen-hua yün-tung yü Kuo-min-tang" 新文化運動與國民黨. *Hsin-yüeh* 新月, 2:6–7 (1929), 1–15.

Hu Shih chia-shu shou-chi 胡適家書手跡. Anhwei, 1989.

Hu Shih lai wang shu-hsin hsüan 胡適來往書信選. Hong Kong, 1983, 3 vols.

Hu Shih te jih-chi 胡適的日記. Taipei, 1989, 18 vols.

"The Indianization of China: A Case Study in Cultural Borrowing." In *Independence, Convergence, and Borrowing in Institutions, Thought, and Art*. Cambridge, Mass., 1937, 219–247.

Jen-ch'üan lun-chi 人權論集. Shanghai, 1930.

"Kuan-yü Fu Meng-chen hsien-sheng sheng-p'ing te pao-kao" 關於傅孟真先生生平的報告. A pamphlet published by the Institute of History and Philology, Academia Sinica. Taipei, 1965.

"Kuo-hsüeh chi-k'an fa-k'an hsüan-yen" 國學季刊發刊宣言. *Kuo-hsüeh-chi-k'an* 國學季刊, 1:1 (1923), 1–26.

"The Scientific Spirit and Method in Chinese Philosophy." In C. A. Moore, ed., *The Chinese Mind*. Honolulu, 1967, 104–131.

"Shuo Ju" 説儒. *Chung-yang yen-chiu yüan Li-shih yü-yen yen-chiu-so chi-k'an*, 4:3 (1934), 233–290.

Tai Tung-yüan te che-hsüeh 戴東原的哲學. Taipei, 1975.

"Wo-men tsou na t'iao lu" 我們走哪條路. *Hsin-yüeh*, 2:10 (1939), 11–12.

"Wu-ssu yün-tung shih ch'ing-nien ai-kuo yün-tung" 五四運動是青年愛國運動. In *Hu Shih chiang-yen-chi* 胡適講演集. Taipei, 1970. 3:548–569.

Hu Shih lai wang shu-hsin hsüan 胡適來往書信選. Hong Kong, 1983, 3 vols.

Hu Sung-p'ing 胡頌平. *Hu Shih nien-p'u ch'ang-pien ch'u-kao* 胡適年譜長編初稿. Taipei, 1984, 10 vols.

Hu Ying-fen 胡映芬. *Fu Ssu-nien yü Chung-kuo hsin-shih-hsüeh* 傅斯年與中國新史學. M.A. thesis, Taiwan University, 1976.

Huang Chang-chien 黃彰健. *Ching-hsüeh Li-hsüeh wen-ts'un* 經學理學文存. Taipei, 1976.

Ming-shih-lu chiao-k'an-chi 明實錄校勘記. Taipei, 1968, 29 vols.

Huang Chi-lu 黃季陸. "I Fu Meng-chen hsien-sheng" 憶傅孟真先生. *Chuan-chi wen-hsüeh*, 1:7 (1962), 17–19.

Huang Chin-hsing 黃進興. *Li-shih chih-shih yü li-shih li-lun* 歷史知識與歷史理論. Taipei, 1992.

Huang Fu-ch'ing 黃福慶. *Chin-tai Chung-kuo kao-teng chiao-yü yen-chiu – Kuo-li Chung-shan ta-hsüeh (1924–1937)* 近代中國高等教育研究——國立中山大學 (1924–1937). Taipei, 1988.

Huang Yen-p'ei 黃炎培. "Yenan Kuei-lai" 延安歸來. In *Kuo-min ts'an-cheng hui tzu-liao* 國民參政會資料. Szechuan, 1984, 463–506.

Humboldt, Wilhelm von. *On Language*. Translated by Peter Heath. Cambridge, 1988.

Hummel, Arthur. *The Autobiography of a Chinese Historian*. Leyden, 1931.

——— ed. *Eminent Chinese of the Ch'ing Period*. Rpt., Taipei, 1972.

——— "What Chinese Historians Are Doing in Their Own History." *American Historical Review*, 34:4 (1929), 715–724.

I-erh-chiu yü-tung shih 一二九運動史. Peking, 1980.

I-erh-i ts'an-an shih-lu 一二一慘案實錄. Kunming, n.d., n.p.

I-erh-i yün-tung 一二一運動. Kunming, 1988.

I-erh-i yün-tung shih-liao hsüan-pien 一二一運動史料選編. Kunming, 1980, 2 vols.

I-ho-t'uan yün-tung-shih lun-wen-hsüan 義和團運動史論文選. Szechwan, 1987.

I Tsung-k'uei 易宗夔. *Hsin shih-shuo* 新世説. 1918; rpt., Shanghai, 1982.

Iggers, Georg. "The Crisis of the Rankean Paradigm in the Nineteenth Century." In Georg Iggers and Konrad von Moltke, eds., *The Theory and Practice of*

History: Leopold von Ranke. Translated by Wilma A. Iggers and Konard von Moltke. Indianapolis and New York, 1973, 170–179.

The German Conception of History. Middletown, Conn., 1969.

Iggers, Georg, and James Powell, eds. *Leopold von Ranke and the Shaping of the Historical Discipline.* Syracuse, 1990.

Isreal, John. *Student Nationalism in China, 1927–1937.* Stanford, 1966.

James, William. *Pragmatism.* Cambridge, Mass., 1979.

Jing Su 景甦 and Luo Lun 羅侖. *Landlord and Labor in Late Imperial China: Case Studies from Shantung.* Translated by Endymion Wilkinson. Cambridge, Mass., 1978.

Juan Yüan 阮元. *Hsing ming ku-hsün* 性命古訓. In *Yen-ching-shih chi* 揅經室集. Taipei, 1964, 3 vols., 1:191–214.

"Lun-yü lun jen lun" 論語論仁論. In *Yen-ching-shih chi,* 1:157–173.

Kan Chih-keng 干志耿, Li Tien-fu 李殿福, and Ch'en Lian-k'ai 陳連開. "Shang hsien ch'i-yüan yü Yu Yen shuo" 商先起源於幽燕說. *Li-shih yen-chiu,* no. 5 (1985), 21–34.

K'ang Chung-p'ing 康仲平. "Lun Chung-kuo kuan-liao tzu-pen-chu-i" 論中國官僚資本主義. *Ch'ün-chung* 群眾, 38 (1948), 14–16; 39 (1948), 14–15.

K'ang Yu-wei 康有為, ed. *Pu-jen tsa-chih hui-pien* 不忍雜誌彙編. Shanghai, 1914; rpt., Taipei, 1968, 2 vols.

Ta-t'ung shu 大同書. Peking, 1959.

Kao Chün 高軍, ed. *Chung-kuo she-hui hsing-chih lun-chan* 中國社會性質論戰. Peking, 1984, 2 vols.

"Ti-i-tz'u kuo-nei ko-ming chan-cheng hou kuan-yü Chung-kuo she-hui hsing-chih wen-t'i te lun-chan" 第一次國內革命戰爭後關於中國社會性質問題的論戰. *Shih-hsüeh yüeh-k'an* 史學月刊, no. 2 (1982), 54–59.

Keightley, David, ed. *The Origins of Chinese Civilization.* Berkeley, 1983.

Keng Yün-chih 耿雲志. *Hu Shih nien-p'u* 胡適年譜. Hong Kong, 1986.

Kohn, Hans. *The Idea of Nationalism.* New York, 1945.

Nationalism: Its Meaning and History. Princeton, 1955.

Kolakowski, Laszek. *The Alienation of Reason: A History of Positivist Thought.* Translated by Norbert Guterman. New York, 1968.

Krieger, Leonard. *Ranke: The Meaning of History.* Chicago, 1977.

Ku Ch'ao 顧潮. *Ku Chieh-kang hsien-sheng nien-p'u* 顧頡剛先生年譜. Peking, 1993.

"Ku Chieh-kang yü Fu Ssu-nien tsai ch'ing-chuang shih-tai te chiao-wang" 顧頡剛與傅斯年在青壯時代的交往. *Wen-shih-che* 文史哲, 2 (1993), 11–17.

Ku Chieh-kang 顧頡剛 "Chan-kuo Ch'in Han chien jen te chao-wei yü pien-wei" 戰國秦漢間人的造偽與辨偽. In *Ku-shih pien* 古史辨. Peking and Shanghai, 1926 1941, 7 vols., 7:1–64.

"Hui-i Hsin-ch'ao she" 回憶新潮社. In *Wu-ssu shih-ch'i te she t'uan.* Peking, 1979, 4 vols.

ed. *Ku-shih pien.* Peking and Shanghai, 1926–1941, 7 vols.

Tang-tai Chung-kuo shih-hsüeh 當代中國史學. Nanking, 1947.

Ku Ying-t'ai 谷應泰. *Ming-shih chi-shih pen-mo* 明史紀事本末. Taipei, 1968.

241

Kuan Pei-liang 關貝亮. "Fu Ssu-nien hsiao-chang erh-san-shih" 傅斯年校長二三事. *Chuan-chi wen-hsüeh*, 48:2 (1986), 69–70.

Kung Yü-chih 龔育之, P'ang Hsien-chih 逄先知, and Shih Chung-ch'üan 石仲泉. *Mao Tse-tung te tu-shu sheng-huo* 毛澤東的讀書生活. Peking, 1986.

Kuo Chan-p'o 郭湛波. *Chin-tai Chung-kuo ssu-hsiang-shih* 近代中國思想史. N.p., n.d.

Kuo Jung-kuang 郭榮光. *K'ung Hsiang-hsi hsien-sheng nien-p'u* 孔祥熙先生年譜. Taipei, 1980.

Kuo-ku 國故 (Peking), nos. 1–4 (1919).

Kuo-li Chung-shan ta-hsüeh jih-pao 國立中山大學日報 (Kwangchou), (June 21, 1927).

Kuo-li Pei-yang ta-hsüeh chi-wang 國立北洋大學記往. Taipei, 1979.

Kuo Mo-jo 郭沫若. "Cheng-li kuo-ku te p'ing-chia" 整理國故的評價. In *Kuo Mo-jo ku-tien wen-hsüeh lun-chi* 郭沫若古典文學論集. Shanghai, 1985, 25–28.

Chung-kuo ku-tai she-hui yen-chiu 中國古代社會研究. Shanghai, 1930.

Kuo Mo-jo shu-chien 郭沫若書簡. Kwantung, 1981.

"Po 'Shuo Ju'" 駁說儒. In *Ch'ing-t'ung shih-tai* 青銅時代. Peking, 1954, 127–156.

Shao-nien shih-tai 少年時代. Shanghai, 1948.

Shih p'i-p'an shu 十批判書. Peking, 1954.

Kuo T'ing-i 郭廷以. *Chin-tai Chung-kuo shih-kang* 近代中國史綱. Hong Kong, 1986, 2 vols.

Kwok, D. W. Y. *Scientism in Chinese Thought, 1900–1950*. New Haven, 1965.

Lao Kan 勞榦. *Chü-yen Han-chien* 居延漢簡. Taipei, 1957, 1960, 2 vols.

"Fu Meng-chen hsien-sheng yü chin erh-shih-nien lai Chung-kuo li-shih-hsüeh te fa-chan" 傅孟真先生與近二十年來中國歷史學的發展. *Ta-lu tsa-chih* 大陸雜誌, 2:1 (1951), 7–9. Also in *Fu ku hsiao-chang ai-wan-lu*. Taipei, 1951, 69–72.

Lao Kan hsüeh-shu lun-wen chi 勞榦學術論文集. Taipei, 1976, 2 vols.

Lao She 老舍 (Shu Ch'ing-ch'un 舒慶春). "K'ang-chan i-lai wen-i fa-chan te ch'ing-hsing" 抗戰以來文藝發展的情形. *Lao She wen-chi* 老舍文集. Peking, 1990, 15 vols., 15:494–514.

Lattimore, Owen. *Inner Asian Frontiers of China*. New York, 1940.

Laue, Theodore H. von. *Leopold Ranke: The Formative Years*. Princeton, 1950.

Lee, Leo Ou-fan 李歐梵. "Literary Trends I: The Quest for Modernity, 1895–1927." In John K. Fairbank and Denis Twitchett, eds., *The Cambridge History of China*. Cambridge, 1983, 12.1:452–504.

"Literary Trends: The Road to Revolution (1927–1949)." In John K. Fairbank and Albert Feuerwerker, eds. *The Cambridge History of China*. Cambridge, 1986, 13.2:421–491.

The Romantic Generation of Modern Chinese Writers. Cambridge, Mass., 1973.

Legge, James, trans. *Chinese Classics*. Hong Kong, 1861.

Lei Hai-tsung 雷海宗. "Periodization: Chinese History and World History." *Chinese Social and Political Science Review*, 20:4 (1937), 461–491.

Levenson, Joseph. *Confucian China and Its Modern Fate: A Trilogy*. Berkeley, 1968.

Liang Ch'i-ch'ao and the Mind of Modern China. Cambridge, Mass., 1959.

Li Chi 李濟. *Anyang: A Chronicle of the Discovery, Excavation, and Reconstruction of the Ancient Capital of the Shang Dynasty*. Seattle, 1977.

Bibliography

"Anyang fa-chüeh yü Chung-kuo ku-shih wen-t'i" 安陽發掘與中國古史問題. *Li Chi k'ao-ku hsüeh lun-wen-chi* 李濟考古學論文集. Taipei, 1977, 2 vols., 2:825–866.

"Anyang tsui-chin fa-chüeh pao-kao chi liu-tz'u kung-tso chih tsung ku-chi" 安陽最近發掘報告及六次工作之總估計. *Li Chi k'ao-ku hsüeh lun-wen-chi*, 1:129–154.

The Beginning of the Chinese Civilization. Seattle, 1957.

"Chih-te ch'ing-nien men hsiao-fa te Fu Meng-chen hsien-sheng" 值得青年們效法的傅孟真先生. *Tzu-yu Chung-kuo*, 4:1 (1951), 19. Also in *Fu ku hsiao-chang ai-wan-lu*. Taipei, 1951, 60–61.

"Chung-kuo ku ch'i-wu-hsüeh te hsin chi-ch'u" 中國古器物學的新基礎. In *Li Chi k'ao-ku-hsüeh lun-wen chi*, 2:867–883.

"Chung-kuo tsui-chin fa-hsien chih hsin shih-liao" 中國最近發現之新史料. *Chung-shan ta hsüeh yü-yen li-shih hsüeh yen-chiu-so cho-k'an* 中山大學語言歷史研究所週刊, 5 (1928): 57–58.

"Hua-pei Hsin-shih-ch'i-shih-tai wen-hua te lei-pieh, fen-pu yü pien-nien" 華北新石器時代文化的類別、分佈與編年. In *Li Chi k'ao-ku-hsüeh lun-wen chi*, 2:925–950.

"Importance of the Anyang Discoveries in Prefacing Known Chinese History with a New Chapter." In *Li Chi k'ao-ku-hsüeh lun-wen chi*, 2:961–972.

Kan chiu lu 感舊錄. Taipei, 1967.

Li-chi chu-shu 禮記注疏. *Shih-san-ching chu-shu* 十三經注疏. 1815.

Li Ch'üan 李泉. "Fu-hai shuo san-ch'ien ti-tzu" 浮海說三千弟子. In *Fu Ssu-nien*. Shantung, 1991, 98–206

Li Ch'üan and Hsü Ming-wen 徐明文. "T'ai Kang chih-ming jen-shih i Fu Ssu-nien" 台港知名人士憶傅斯年. In *Fu-Ssu-nien*. Shangtung, 1991, 272–342.

Li Han-t'ing 李漢亭. "Tsai tung hsi fang te chia-feng chung ssu-k'ao – Fu Ssu-nien hsi-hsüeh-wei-yung te Wu-ssu wen-hsüeh kuan" 在東西方的夾縫中思考——傅斯年西學為用的五四文學觀. *Tang-tai* 當代, 25 (1988), 114–129.

Li Hsiao-feng 李小峰. "Hsin-ch'ao she te shih-mo" 新潮社的始末. *Wen-shih tzu-liao hsüan-chi*, 61 (1979), 82–128.

Li Hsiao-ting 李孝定. *Shih che ju ssu* 逝者如斯. Taipei, 1996.

Li Hsüeh-ch'in 李學勤. *Chung-kuo ch'ing-t'ung-ch'i te ao-mi* 中國青銅器的奧秘. Shanghai, 1987.

Li Huan 李桓, ed. *Kuo-ch'ao ch'i-hsien lei-cheng ch'u-pien* 國朝耆獻類徵初編. 1884–1890; rpt., Taipei, 1966.

Li Jui 李銳. "Hsiang-chiang p'ing-lun yü Wen-hua shu-she" 湘江評論與文化書社. In Chang Ching-lu 張靜廬, ed., *Chung-kuo hsien-tai ch'u-pan shih-liao* 中國現代出版史料. Peking, 1954–1959, 5 vols., 1:31–44.

Li Ling 李零. "Ch'u-t'u fa-hsien yü ku-shu nien-tai te tsai jen-shih" 出土發現與古書年代的再認識. *Chiu-chou hsüeh-k'an* 九州學刊, 3:1 (1988), 105–136.

Li Shang-ying 李尚英. "Yang Hsiang-kuei hsien-sheng hsüeh-shu yen-chiu chi chu-tso pien-nien" 楊向奎先生學術研究及著作編年. *Ch'ing-shih lun-ts'ung* 清史論叢 (1994), 1–13.

Li Shih-hsüeh 李奭學. "Hsiao-po-na (Bernard Shaw) tien ch'i Chung-kuo wen-t'an chan-huo" 蕭伯納點起中國文壇戰火. *Tang-tai*, 37 (1989), 36–55.

Li Ta-chao 李大釗. *Li Ta chao hsüan-chi* 李大釗選集. Peking, 1959.

Li Tse-hou 李澤厚. *Chung-kuo chin-tai ssu-hsiang shih-lun* 中國近代思想史論. Peking, 1979.
Chung-kuo hsien-tai ssu-hsiang shih-lun 中國現代思想史論. Peking, 1987.
Li Tsung-t'ung 李宗侗. "Ku-shih wen-t'i te wei-i chieh-chüeh fang-fa" 古史問題的唯一解決方法. In Ku Chieh-kang, ed., *Ku-shih pien*. Peking and Shanghai, 1926–1941, 7 vols., 1: 268–70.
Li Yün-han 李雲漢. *Ts'ung jung-kung tao ch'ing-tang* 從容共到清黨. Taipei, 1966, 2 vols.
Liang Ch'i-ch'ao 梁啟超. *Chung-kuo li-shih yen-chiu fa* 中國歷史研究法. In *Liang Ch'i-ch'ao shih-hsüeh lun-chu san chung* 梁啟超史學論著三種. Hong Kong, 1984.
Hsin-min shuo 新民說. Taipei, 1978.
Intellectual Trends in the Ch'ing Period. Translated by Immanuel Hsü. Cambridge, Mass., 1959.
Liang Shan 梁山. *Chung-shan ta-hsüeh hsiao-shih* 中山大學校史. Shanghai, 1983.
Liang Shu-ming 梁漱溟. *Chao-hua* 朝話. Shanghai, 1941.
"Ching i ch'ing-chiao Hu Shih-chih hsien-sheng" 敬以請教胡適之先生. In *Hu Shih lun-hsüeh chin-chu* 胡適論學近著. Shanghai, 1935, appendix 附錄, 454–464.
Liang Ssu-yung 梁思永. "Hou-kang fa-chüeh hsiao chi" 後崗發掘小記. In *Liang Ssu-yung k'ao-ku lun-wen-chi* 梁思永考古論文集. Peking, 1959, 99–106.
"Hsiao-t'un, Lungshan yü Yang-shao" 小屯、龍山與仰韶. In *Liang Ssu-yung k'ao-ku lun-wen-chi*, 91–98.
Liao-ch'eng shih-fan ta-hsüeh li-shih-hsi 聊城師範大學歷史系, Liao-ch'eng ti-ch'ü cheng-hsieh kung-wei 聊城地區政協工委, and Shan-tung-sheng cheng-hsieh wen-shih-wei 山東省政協文史委, eds. *Fu-Ssu-nien* 傅斯年. Shangtung, 1991.
Lin Chi-ch'eng 林基成. "Fo-lo-i-te (S. Freud) hsüeh-shuo tsai Chung-kuo te ch'uan-po, 1914–1925" 佛洛伊德學說在中國的傳播 (1914-1925). *Erh-shih-i shih-chi*, no. 4 (1991), 20–31.
Lin Kan-ch'üan 林甘泉. *Chung-kuo ku-tai-shih fen-ch'i t'ao-lun wu-shih nien* 中國古代史分期討論五十年. Shanghai, 1982.
Lin Shou-chin 林壽晉. "Lun Yang-shao-wen-hua hsi-lai shuo" 論仰韶文化西來說. *Chung-kuo wen-hua yen-chiu hsüeh-pao* 中國文化研究學報, 10:2 (1979), 273–277.
Lin Yü-sheng 林毓生. *The Crisis of Chinese Consciousness*. Madison, Wis., 1979.
"Pu-i k'ao-cheng wei chung-hsin te jen-wen yen-chiu" 不以考證為中心的人文研究. In *Ssu-hsiang yü jen-wu* 思想與人物. Taipei, 1983, 263–275.
Linden, Allen. "Ts'ai Yüan-p'ei yü Chung-kuo-kuo-ming-tang (1926–1940)" 蔡元培與中國國民黨. Ts'ai Yüan-p'ei yen-chiu-hui 蔡元培研究會, ed., *Lun Ts'ai Yüan-p'ei* 論蔡元培. Peking, 1989, 281–303.
Ling Yün 凌雲. "P'eng Chao-hsien cheng-hai fu-ch'en hua tang-nien (1)" 彭昭賢政海浮沉話當年(一). *I-wen-chih* 藝文誌, 80 (1972), 20–26.
Link, Perry. "Traditional-Style Popular Urban Fiction in the Tens and Twenties." In Merle Goldman, ed., *Modern Chinese Literature in the May Fourth Era*. Cambridge, Mass., 1977, 327–349.

Liu Ch'i-yü 劉起釪. *Ku Chieh-kang hsien-sheng hsüeh-shu* 顧頡剛先生學述. Peking, 1986.
Liu Ching-pai 劉靜白. *Ho Ping-sung shih-hsüeh te p'i-p'an* 何炳松史學的批判. Shanghai, 1933.
Liu I-cheng 柳詒徵. *Chung-kuo wen-hua shih* 中國文化史. Taipei, 1954.
Kuo-shih yao-i 國史要義. Taipei, 1957.
"Lun wen-hua shih-yeh chih cheng-chih" 論文化事業之爭執. *Shih-hsüeh tsa-chih* 史學雜誌, 2:1 (1930), 1-7.
Liu Ta-p'eng 劉大鵬. *Tui-hsiang-chai jih-chi* 退想齋日記. Shangshi, 1990.
Lo Chen-yü 羅振玉. *Shih-liao-ts'ung-k'an ch'u-pien* 史料叢刊初編. Peking, 1924.
Lo Chia-lun 羅家倫. *Lo Chia-lun hsien-sheng wen-ts'un* 羅家倫先生文存. Taipei, 1988, 7 vols.
"Yüan-ch'i lin-li te Fu Meng-chen" 元氣淋漓的傅孟真. *Chuan-chi wen-hsüeh*, 16:1 (1970), 93-96. Also in *Fu ku hsiao-chang ai-wan-lu*. Taipei, 1951, 41-46.
Lo Erh-kang 羅爾綱. "Liang-ko jen-sheng" 兩個人生. In Sheng-huo Tu-shu Hsing-chih San-lien shu-tien 生活讀書新知三聯書店, ed. *Hu Shih ssu-hsiang p'i-p'an*. Peking, 1955, 7 vols., 2:183-188.
Losee, John. *A Historical Introduction to the Philosophy of Science*. Oxford, 1980.
Lu Hsün 魯迅. "Chiao-shou tsa-yung" 教授雜詠. In *Lu Hsün ch'üan-chi* 魯迅全集. Peking, 1981, 16 vols., 7:435-436.
Liang-ti-shu 兩地書. In *Lu Hsün ch'üan-chi*, vol. 11.
Lü Ssu-mien 呂思勉. *Hsien Ch'in shih* 先秦史. Rpt., Taipei, 1967.
Pai-hua pen-kuo-shih 白話本國史. Shanghai, 1920.
"Ts'ai Chieh-min (Yüan-p'ei)" 蔡孑民（元培）. In *Hao-lu wen-hsüeh chi* 蒿廬問學記. Peking, 1996, 440-445.
Ma Liang-k'uan 馬亮寬. "Ch'ing k'an ti-t'ou-che, jen i t'i ch'i t'ou" 請看剃頭者，人亦剃其頭. In *Fu Ssu-nien*. Shantung, 1991, 169-176.
"P'ang-huang p'ai-huai nien ku-t'u" 徬徨徘徊念故土. In *Fu Ssu-nien*. Shantung, 1991, 193-197.
Ma Liang-k'uan and Wang Ch'iang 馬亮寬, 王強. *Ho Ssu-yüan: Huan-hai fu-ch'en i shu-sheng* 何思源：宦海浮沈一書生. Tientsin, 1996.
Ma Shu 馬驌. *I shih* 繹史. Taipei, 1968, 4 vols.
Mach, Ernst. *Analysis of the Sensations*. Translated by C. M. Williams. Chicago, 1897.
Mao I-heng 毛以亨. "Kuan-yü Fu Ssu-nien te i-feng-hsin" 關於傅斯年的一封信. *T'ien-wen-t'ai* 天文臺 (January, 2, 4, 1951).
Mao Tse-tung 毛澤東. "Tiu-tiao huan-hsiang, chun-pei tou-cheng" 丟掉幻想，準備鬥爭. *Mao Tse-tung hsüan-chi* 毛澤東選集. Peking, 1966, 1487-1494.
Mao Tun 茅盾 (Shen Yen-ping 沈雁冰). *Wo tsou-kuo te tao-lu* 我走過的道路. Hong Kong, 1981.
"Wu-ssu yün-tung te chien-t'ao – Ma-k'o-ssu-chu-i (Marxism) wen-i yen-chiu hui pao-kao" 五四運動的檢討——馬克思主義文藝研究會報告. In *Wen-hsüeh tao-pao* 文學導報, 1:2 (1931), 14.
Yu-chih che 有志者. Shanghai, 1938.
Mao Tzu-shui 毛子水. *Shih yu chi* 師友記. Taipei, 1967.

Mcdougall, William. *The Group Mind*. Cambridge, 1920.
Meinecke, Friedrich. *Cosmopolitanism and the Nation State*. Translated by Felix Gilbert. Princeton, 1963.
Meisner, Maurice. *Li Ta-chao and the Origins of Chinese Marxism*. Cambridge, Mass., 1967.
Meng Wen-t'ung 蒙文通. *Ku-shih chen-wei* 古史甄微. Shanghai, 1933.
Merz, John T. *A History of European Thought in the Nineteenth Century*. London, 1904–1912; rpt., New York, 1965.
Miao Feng-lin 繆鳳林. "Chung-kuo-min-tsu-hsi-lai pien" 中國民族西來辨. *Hsüeh-heng* 學衡, 36 (1924): *shu-hsüeh* 述學, 1–34.
—— "P'ing Fu Ssu-nien chün *Tung-pei shih-kang* chüan-shou" 評傅斯年君東北史綱卷首. *Wen-i ts'ung k'an* 文藝叢刊, 2:2 (1934), 131–163. I have not been able to obtain a published copy of this article. I quote from a pamphlet among Fu Ssu-nien's belongings that was apparently sent to him by someone.
Min-tsu te tou-shih 民族的鬥士. Taipei, 1979.
Ming-Ch'ing tang-an yü li-shih yen-chiu 明清檔案與歷史研究. Peking, 1988, 2 vols.
Moller, Alan Gordon. "Bellicose Nationalist of Republican China: An Intellectual Biography of Fu Ssu-nien." Ph.D. diss., University of Melbourne, 1979.
Mou Jun-sun 牟潤孫. "Chi so-chien chih erh-shih-wu-nien lai shih-hsüeh chu-tso" 記所見之二十五年來史學著作. *Ssu-hsiang yü shih-tai* 思想與時代, 116 (1964), 9–13; 117 (1964), 18–21; 118 (1964), 26–28.
—— "Hsüeh chien Han Sung te Yü Chi-yü (Yü Chia-hsi) hsien-sheng" 學兼漢宋的余季豫先生. In *Hai i tsa-chu* 海遺雜著. Hong Kong, 1990, 129–138.
Mou Tsung-san 牟宗三 et al. "Wei Chung-kuo wen-hua ching-kao shih-chieh jen-shih hsüan-yen" 為中國文化敬告世界人士宣言. *Min-chu p'ing-lun*, 民主評論 9:1 (1958), 2–21.
Na Lien-chün 那廉君. "Chui-i Fu Meng-chen hsien-sheng te chi-chien-shih" 追憶傅孟真先生的幾件事. *Chuan-chi wen-hsüeh*, 14:6 (1968), 56–59.
—— "Fu Meng-chen hsien-sheng i-shih" 傅孟真先生軼事. *Chuan-chi wen-hsüeh*, 15:6 (1969), 61–64.
—— "Fu Meng-chen hsien-sheng liu-shih-chin-ssu ming-tan" 傅孟真先生六十晉四冥誕. *Ta-lu tsa-chih*, 18:5 (1959), 32.
—— "T'a tsou-te t'ai-k'uai – chi Meng-chen hsien-sheng sheng-ch'ien erh-san-shih" 他走的太快—記孟真先生生前二三事. *Hsien-jen-chang*, 1:1 (1977), 31–36.
T'ai-ta hua tang-nien 台大話當年. Taipei, 1991.
Naito, Shunpo 內藤雋輔. "Yano shen sei no omoide" 矢野先生のお思いて. *Toyoshi kenkyu*, 28:4 (1970), 22–25.
Naquin, Susan. *Shantung Rebellion*. New Haven, 1981.
Novick, Peter. *That Noble Dream*. Cambridge, 1988.
Numata, Jiro. "Shigeno Yasutsugu and the Modern Tokyo Tradition of Historical Writing." In W. G. Beasley and E. G. Pulleyblank, eds., *Historians of China and Japan*. London, 1971, 264–287.
Pa-wei-hui t'ung-hsün 罷委會通訊 (Kunming). (December 5, 7, 8, 1945).

P'ang Chen-hao 逄振鎬. *Tung-I ku-kuo shih-lun* 東夷古國史論. Chengtu, 1989.
Pao Han-sheng 包瀚生. "Li-shih cheng-ming Meng-ku shih Chung-kuo ling-t'u" 歷史證明蒙古是中國領土. *Tung-fang tsa-chih*, 31:5 (1934), 53–56.
"Li-shih cheng-ming Tung-san-sheng shih Chung-kuo te ling-t'u" 歷史證明東三省是中國的領土. *Tung-fang tsa-chih*, 30:19 (1933), 78–80.
Pei-ching ta-hsüeh jih-k'an (Peking), nos. 1–2885 (December 1917–September 1932).
Pelliot, Paul. "The Royal Tombs of An-yang." In *Independence, Convergence, and Borrowing in Institutions, Thought, and Art*. Cambridge, Mass., 1937, 265–272.
P'eng K'ang 彭康. "Hsin-wen-hua yün-tung yü jen-chüan yün-tung" 新文化運動與人權運動. In Ts'ai Shang-ssu, ed., *Chung-kuo hsien-tai ssu-hsiang-shih tzu-liao chien-pien*. Chekiang, 1982–1983, 5 vols., 3:101–117.
P'eng Ming 彭明. *Wu-ssu yün-tung shih* 五四運動史. Peking, 1984.
P'eng Ming-min 彭明敏. *Tzu-yu te tzu-wei* 自由的滋味. Taipei, 1995.
Pickowicz, Paul. "Qu Qiubai's Critique of the May Fourth Generation: Early Chinese Marxist Literary Criticism." In Merle Goldman, ed., *Modern Chinese Literature in the May Fourth Era*. Cambridge, Mass., 351–384.
Said, Edward. *Orientalism*. New York, 1978.
Scheler, Max. *Ressentiment*. Translated by William Holdheim. New York, 1961.
Schneider, Laurence. *Ku Chieh-kang and China's New History*. Berkeley, 1971.
Schwarcz, Vera. *The Chinese Enlightenment: Intellectuals and Legacy of the May Fourth Movement of 1919*. Berkeley, 1986.
Schwartz, Benjamin. "A Marxist Controversy in China." *Far Eastern Quarterly*, no. 2 (Febuary 1954), 143–153.
In Search of Wealth and Power: Yen Fu and the West. New York, 1969.
ed. *Reflections of the May Fourth Movement: A Symposium*. Cambridge, Mass., 1972.
"Theme in Intellectual History: May Fourth and After." In John Fairbank and Denis Twitchett, eds., *The Cambridge History of China*. Cambridge, 1983, 12.1:406–451.
Shan Shih-k'uei 單士魁. *Ch'ing-tai tang-an ts'ung-t'an* 清代檔案叢談. Peking, 1987.
Shang Yen-liu 商衍鎏. *Ch'ing-tai k'o-chü k'ao-shih shu-lun* 清代科舉考試述論. Peking, 1958.
Shen Chien-shih 沈兼士. "Ku-kung-po-wu-yüan wen-hsien-kuan cheng-li tang-an pao-kao" 故宮博物院文獻館整理檔案報告. In *Shen Chien-shih hsüeh-shu lun-wen-chi* 沈兼士學術論文集. Peking, 1986, 345–359.
Shen Sung-ch'iao 沈松僑. *Hsüeh-heng-p'ai yü Wu-ssu shih-ch'i te fan Hsin-wen-hua yün-tung* 學衡派與五四時期的反新文化運動. Taipei, 1984.
Shen Yin-mo 沈尹默. "Wo ho Pei-ta" 我和北大. In *Wu-ssu yün-tung hui-i-lu* 五四運動回憶錄. Peking, 1979, 3 vols., 3:157–170.
Sheng-huo Tu-shu Hsing-chih San-lien shu-tien 生活讀書新知三聯書店編, ed. *Hu Shih ssu-hsiang p'i-p'an* 胡適思想批判. Peking, 1955, 7 vols.
Shih Chang-ju 石璋如. *K'ao-ku nien-piao* 考古年表. Taipei, 1952.
"Yin-hsü fa-chüeh tui-yü Chung-kuo ku-tai wen-hua te kung-hsien" 殷墟發掘對於中國古代文化的貢獻. *Hsüeh-shu chi-k'an* 學術季刊, 2:4 (1953), 8–23.

Shih-chieh jih-pao 世界日報. Peking, February 15, 1947.
Shih Ch'üan-sheng 史全生, ed. *Chung-hua-min-kuo wen-hua-shih* 中華民國文化史. Chilin, 1990, 3 vols.
Shih Yüan-kao 石原皋. *Hsien-hua Hu Shih* 閒話胡適. Anhwei, 1985.
Shih-yü-so tang-an 史語所檔案. Taipei, Institute of History and Philology, Academia Sinica.
Shiratori Kukichi 白鳥庫吉. "Kyokuto shijo ni okeru Manshu no rekishi chiri" 極東史上に於ける滿洲の歷史地理. In *Shiratori Kukichi sensu* 白鳥庫吉全集. Tokyo, 1971, 10 vols., 9:399–408.
"Manshu no kako oyobbi shorai" 滿洲の過去與將來. In *Shiratori Kukichi sensu*, 8:17–23.
Shu Hsin-ch'eng 舒新城. *Chin-tai Chung-kuo chiao-yü-shih tzu-liao* 近代中國教育史資料. Peking, 1961, 3 vols.
Shu Wu 舒蕪. "Ts'ai Yüan-p'ei te liang-tz'u shuo-mei" 蔡元培的兩次説媒. *Chung-kuo shih-pao* (February 5, 1992).
Snow, Edgar. *Red Star over China*. New York, 1978.
Ssu-ma Ch'ien 司馬遷. *Shih-chi* 史記. Peking, 1982, 10 vols.
Stern, Fritz, ed. *The Varieties of History*. Cleveland, 1957.
Su Ping-ch'i 蘇秉琦. "Chien-kuo i-lai Chung-kuo k'ao-ku-hsüeh te fa-chan" 建國以來中國考古學的發展. In *Su Ping-ch'i k'ao-ku-hsüeh lun-shu hsüan-chi* 蘇秉琦考古論述選集. Peking, 1984, 299–305.
Su T'ung-ping 蘇同炳. "Shih-yü-so fa-chan-shin" 史語所發展史. Taipei, unfinished and unpublished manuscript.
Su Yün-feng 蘇雲峰. "Min-ch'u chih nung-ts'un she-hui" 民初之農村社會. In *Chung-hua-min-kuo ch'u-ch'i li-shih yen-t'ao-hui lun-wen-chi* 中華民國初期歷史研討會論文集. Taipei, 1984, 2 vols., 2:637–655.
Sun Ch'ang-wei 孫常煒. "Ts'ai Yüan-p'ei hsien-sheng yü Chung-yang yen-chiu yüan" 蔡元培先生與中央研究院. *Chuan-chi wen-hsüeh*, 12:2 (1968), 55–62.
Sun, E-tu Zen. "The Growth of the Academic Community, 1912–1949." In John K. Fairbank and Albert Feuerwerker, eds. *The Cambridge History of China*. Cambridge, 1986. 13. 2:361–421.
Sun T'ung-hsün 孫同勛. "T'an Fu Ssu-nien hsien-sheng te shih-hsüeh" 談傅斯年先生的史學. *Li-shih yüeh-k'an*, 12 (1989), 8–11.
Sung Ching-shih tang-an shih-liao 宋景詩檔案史料. Peking, 1959.
Sung Hsin-ch'ao 宋新潮. "Chin nien lai Shang-tsu ch'i-yüan yen-chiu kai-shu" 近年來商族起源研究概述. *Chung-kuo-shih yen-chiu* 中國史研究, 6 (1990), 14–18.
T'ai-ta Fu ku hsiao-chang Ssu-nien hsien-sheng chi-nien lun-wen-chi 台大傅故校長斯年先生紀念論文集. Taipei, 1952.
T'ai-ta Ssu-liu shih-chien tzu-liao sou-chi hsiao-tzu 台大四六事件資料蒐集小組, ed. *T'ai-ta Ssu-liu shih-chien k'ao-ch'a – Ssu-liu shih-chien tzu-liao sou-chi hsiao-tzu tsung-chieh pao-kao* 台大四六事件考察——四六事件資料蒐集小組總結報告. Taipei, 1997.
T'an Hsün-ts'ung 譚訓聰. *Ch'ing T'an Fu-sheng hsien-sheng Ssu-t'ung nien-p'u* 清譚復生先生嗣同年譜. Taipei, 1980.
T'ang Chün-i 唐君毅. "Chung-kuo chin-tai hsüeh-shu wen-hua ching-shen chih

fan-hsing" 中國近代學術文化精神之反省. *Ming-chu p'ing-lun*, 1:24 (1950), 3–10.

Shuo Chung-hua-min-tsu chih hua kuo p'iao-ling 說中華民族之花果飄零. Taipei, 1974.

T'ang Pao-lin 唐寶林 et al. *Ch'en Tu-hsiu nien-p'u* 陳獨秀年譜. Shanghai, 1988.

T'ang Te-kang 唐德剛. *Hu Shih k'ou-shu tzu-chuan* 胡適口述自傳. Taipei, 1981.

Hu Shih tsa-i 胡適雜憶. Taipei, 1980.

T'ang Ts'ai-ch'ang 唐才常. "T'ung-chung shuo" 通種說. *T'ang Ts'ai-ch'ang chi* 唐才常集. Peking, 1980, 100–104.

T'ao Fei-ya 陶飛亞. "Shantung shih-shen yü fan chiao-hui tou-cheng" 山東士紳與反教會鬥爭. In *I-ho-t'uan yün-tung yü chin-tai Chung-kuo she-hui* 義和團運動與近代中國社會. Szechwan, 1987, 278–286.

T'ao Hsi-sheng 陶希聖. *Ch'ao-liu yü tien-ti* 潮流與點滴. Taipei, 1964.

"Fu Meng-chen hsien-sheng" 傅孟真先生. In *Fu ku hsiao-chang ai-wan-lu*. Taipei, 1951, 51–52.

T'ao Ying-hui 陶英惠. "Ts'ai Yüan-p'ei yü Pei-ching ta-hsüeh (1917–1923)" 蔡元培與北京大學 (1917–1923). *Chung-yang yen-chiu yüan Chin-tai-shih yen-chiu-so chi-k'an* 中央研究院近代史研究所集刊, 5 (1976), 263–312.

Teng Kuang-ming 鄧廣銘. "Chi i-wei Shantung te lao chiao-yü-chia – Wang Chu-ch'en hsien-sheng" 記一位山東的老教育家——王祝辰先生. In FSNP, I-1282.

"Hui-i wo te lao-shih Fu Ssu-nien hsien-sheng" 回憶我的老師傅斯年先生. In *Fu Ssu-nien*. Shantung, 1991, 2–8.

Teng, S. Y. "Chinese Historiography in the Last Fifty Years." *Far Eastern Quarterly*, no. 2 (February 1949), 131–156.

Thompson, James, and Bernard Hohn. *A History of Historical Writing*. New York, 1942.

Ting Shan 丁山. "Yu san-tai tu-i lun ch'i min-tsu wen-hua" 由三代都邑論其民族文化. *Chung-yang yen-chiu yüan Li-shih yü-yen yen-chiu-so chi-k'an*, 5:1 (1935), 87–130.

Ting Wen-chiang 丁文江. *Liang Jen-kung nien-p'u ch'ang-pien ch'u-kao* 梁任公年譜長編初稿. Taipei, 1958.

Ts'ai Shang-ssu 蔡尚思, ed. *Chung-kuo chin-tai hsüeh-shu ssu-hsiang shih lun* 中國近代學術思想史論. Kwangtung, 1986.

Ts'ai Yüan-p'ei 蔡元培. "Chiu-jen Pei-ching ta-hsüeh hsiao-chang chih yeh-shuo" 就任北京大學校長之演說. In Shen Shan-hung 沈善洪, ed., *Ts'ai Yüan-p'ei hsüan-chi* 蔡元培選集. Hangchow, 1993, 2 vols., 1:490–492.

"Wei shuo-ming pan-hsüeh fan-chen ta Lin Ch'in-nan chün han" 為說明辦學方針答林琴南君函. In Sun Te-chung 孫德中, ed., *Ts'ai Yüan-p'ei hsien-sheng i-wen lei-ch'ao* 蔡元培先生遺文類鈔. Taipei, 1961, 32–36.

Ts'ai Yüan-p'ei yen-chiu hui 蔡元培研究會, ed. *Lun Ts'ai Yüan p'ei* 論蔡元培. Peking, 1989.

Ts'ao Chü-jen 曹聚仁. "Kuo-ku-hsüeh chih i-i yü chia-chih" 國故學之意義與價值. In Hsü Hsiao-t'ien, ed., *Kuo-ku-hsüeh t'ao-lun-chi*. Shanghai, 1927, 3 vols., 1:50–93.

Wo yü wo te shih-chieh 我與我的世界. Peking, 1983.

Tseng Fan-k'ang 曾繁康. "Chung-kuo hsien-tai shih-hsüeh-chieh te chien-t'ao" 中國現代史學界的檢討. *Tse-shan pan-yüeh-k'an* 責善半月刊, 1:5 (1940), 13–15.

Tseng Shih-jung 曾士榮. "Chan-hou T'ai-wan chih wen-hua ch'ung-pien yü tsu-ch'ün kuan-hsi" 戰後台灣之文化重編與族群關係. M.A. thesis, National Taiwan University, 1994, 134–136.

Tso Shun-sheng 左舜生. *Chin san-shih-nien chien-wen tsa-chi* 近三十年見聞雜記. Hong Kong, 1954.

Tsui-chin chih wu-shih-nien 最近之五十年. *Shen Pao* 申報, anniversary volume. Shanghai, 1922.

Tu Cheng-sheng 杜正勝. "Chung-kuo ku-tai she-hui-shih ch'ung-chien te hsing-ssu" 中國古代社會史重建的省思. *Ta-lu tsa-chih*, 82:1 (1991), 15–30.

"Kuan-yü hsien-Chou li-shih te hsin-jen-shih" 關於先周歷史的新認識. *Kuo-li T'ai-wan ta-hsüeh li-shih-hsüeh-hsi hsüeh-pao* 國立台灣大學歷史系學報. 16 (1991), 1–45.

Tu Wei-yün 杜維運. *Ch'ing-tai te shih-hsüeh yü shih-chia* 清代的史學與史家. Taipei, 1984.

Tung Tso-pin 董作賓. "Li-shih yü-yen yen-chiu-so tsai hsüeh-shu shang te kung-hsien" 歷史語言研究所在學術上的貢獻. *Ta-lu tsa-chih*, 2:1 (1951), 1–6. Also in *Fu ku hsiao-chang ai-wan-lu*. Taipei, 1951, 64–69.

"Min-kuo shih-ch'i-nien shih yüeh shih-chüeh Anyang Hsiao-t'un pao-kao shu" 民國十七年十月試掘安陽小屯報告書. *Anyang fa-chüeh pao-kao* 安陽發掘報告, 1 (1929), 3–36.

"Ta kuei ssu pan k'ao-shih" 大龜四版考釋. *Anyang fa-chüeh pao-kao*, 3 (1931), 423–441.

"Wu-teng-chüeh tsai Yin Shang" 五等爵在殷商. *Chung-yang yen-chiu yüan Li-shih yü-yen yen-chiu-so chi-k'an*, 6:3 (1936), 413–430.

Yin-hsü wen-tzu chia-pien 殷墟文字甲編. Shanghai, 1948.

Uehara Tadamichi 上原淳道. "Fu Shinen no kodaishi kenkyu ni tsuite" 傅斯年の古代史研究について. *Ko-dai-gaku* 古代學, 1:2 (1952), 119–125.

Wang Fan-sen 王汎森. *Chang T'ai-yen te ssu-hsiang* 章太炎的思想. Taipei, 1985.

Ku-shih-pien yün-tung te hsing-ch'i 古史辨運動的興起. Taipei, 1987.

"Liu Shih-p'ei yü Ch'ing-mo te wu-cheng-fu chu-i yün-tung" 劉師培與清末的無政府主義運動. *Ta-lu tsa-chih* 90:6 (1995), 1–9.

Wang Fan-sen and Tu Cheng-sheng, eds. *Fu Ssu-nien wen-wu tzu-liao hsüan-chi* 傅斯年文物資料選集. Taipei, 1995.

Wang Hsin-ming 王新命 et al., "Chung-kuo pen-wei-wen-hua chien-she hsüan-yen" 中國本位文化建設宣言. *Tung-fang tsa-chih*, 32:4 (1935), 81–83.

Hsin-wen-ch'üan li ssu-shih-nien 新聞圈裡四十年. Taipei, 1957.

Wang Hsün 王勛. *Tung-i wen-hua yü Huai-i wen-hua yen-chiu* 東夷文化與淮夷文化研究. Peking, 1994.

Wang Kuo-wei 王國維. *Ku-shih hsin-cheng* 古史新證. Peking, 1935.

"Lun chin-nien chih hsüeh-shu chieh" 論近年之學術界. In *Wang Ching-an wen-chi* 王靜庵文集. Taipei, 1978, 171–176.

"Shuo tzu Hsieh chih Ch'eng T'ang pa ch'ien" 說自契至成湯八遷. In *Kuan-t'ang chi-lin* 觀堂集林. Peking, 1959, 497–498.

"Wan-hsi-sha" 浣溪沙. *Wang Kuan-t'ang hsien-sheng ch'üan-chi* 王觀堂先生全集. Taipei, 1968, 16 vols., 4:1517.

"Yin Chou chih-tu lun" 殷周制度論. In *Kuan-t'ang chi-lin*, 451–480.

"Yin pu-tz'u chung so chien hsien-kung hsien-wang k'ao" 殷卜辭中所見先公先王考, and "Hsü k'ao" 續考. In *Kuan-t'ang chi-lin*, 409–437, 437–450.

Wang Shih-chieh 王世杰. "Fu hsien-sheng tsai cheng-chih shang te erh-san shih" 傅先生在政治上的二三事. *Chuan-chi wen-hsüeh*, 28:1 (1976), 14–15.

Wang Shu-shih 汪漱石. "Kuan-yü Fu Meng-chen hsien-sheng chih Li Tzung-jen shu" 關於傅孟真先生致李宗仁書. *Chuan-chi wen-hsüeh*, 3:3 (1963), 16.

Wang Yü ch'üan 王毓銓. *Early Chinese Coinage*. New York, 1951.

Wang Yün 王雲. "Fu Ssu-nien yü Pei-ching ta-hsüeh" 傅斯年與北京大學. In *Fu Ssu-nien*. Shantung, 1991, 92–101.

Wang Yün-wu 王雲五. "Shih-nien lai te Chung-kuo ch'u-pan shih-yeh" 十年來的中國出版事業. In Chang Ching-lu, ed. *Chung-kuo hsien-tai ch'u-pan shih-liao*. Peking, 1954–1959, 5 vols., 2:335–352.

Wang Yung-chen 王永貞. "Wu-ssu shih-ch'i te Fu Ssu-nien" 五四時期的傅斯年. *Min-kuo tang-an* 民國檔案, no. 3 (1989), 74–77.

Wellmuth, John. *The Nature and Origins of Scientism*. Milwaukee, 1944.

Wells, H. G. *The Outline of History*. New York, 1971.

Wu Ching-heng 吳敬恆. "I-ke hsin hsin-yang te yü-chou-kuan chi jen-sheng-kuan" 一個新信仰的宇宙觀及人生觀. In *Wu Ching-heng hsüan-chi* 吳敬恆選集. Taipei, 1967, 10 vols., *che-hsüeh* 哲學 volume, 11–128.

"K'o-hsüeh-chou-pao pien-chi-hua" 科學週報編輯話. *Wu Ching-heng hsüan-chi, k'o-hsüeh* 科學 volume, 34–116.

"Ssu-shih-nien ch'ien te hsiao ku-shih" 四十年前的小故事. In Ts'ai Chien-kuo 蔡建國, ed., *Ts'ai Yüan-p'ei hsien-sheng chi-nien-chi* 蔡元培先生紀念集, Peking, 1984, 89–92.

"Ssu-shih-sui jih-chi hsüan-lu" 四十歲日記選錄. In *Wu Ching-heng hsüan-chi, hsü-pa* 序跋, *yu-chi* 遊記, *tsa-wen* 雜文 volume, 218–221.

Wu Chung-k'uang 吳忠匡. "Wu shih Ch'ien Chi-po hsien-sheng chuan-lüeh" 吾師錢基博先生傳略. *Chung-kuo-wen-hua* 中國文化, 4 (1991), 190–198.

Wu Han 吳晗. "Wo k'o-fu le ch'ao-chieh-chi kuan-tien" 我克服了超階級觀點. *Wu Han wen-chi* 吳晗文集. Peking, 1988, 4 vols., 4:101–110.

Wu Hsiang-hsiang 吳相湘. "Fu Ssu-nien" 傅斯年. *Chuan-chi wen-hsüeh*, 23:3 (1973), 104–105.

"Fu Ssu-nien hsüeh-hsing ping-mao" 傅斯年學行並茂. In *Min-kuo pai-jen chuan* 民國百人傳. Taipei, 1971, 4 vols., 1:215–236.

Wu Hsüeh-chao 吳學昭. *Wu Mi yü Ch'en Yin-k'o* 吳宓與陳寅恪. Peking, 1992.

Wu-ssu shih-ch'i ch'i-k'un chieh-shao 五四時期期刊介紹. Peking, 1958, 4 vols.

Wu-ssu shih-ch'i te she-t'uan. Peking, 1979, 4 vols.

Wu T'i 伍俶. "I Meng-chen" 憶孟真. *Tzu-yu Chung-kuo*, 4:1 (1951), 18. Also in *Fu ku hsiao-chang ai-wan-lu*. Taipei, 1951, 62–64.

Wu Yüan-chao 吳元釗. "Li Ta yü Chung-kuo she-hui hsing-chih she-hui-shih wen-t'i lun-chan" 李達與中國社會性質社會史問題論戰. *Shih-hsüeh-shih yen-chiu*, no. 4 (1988), 27–33.

Yang Hsi-mei 楊希枚. "Hsi-yang chin-tai te tung-fang-hsüeh chi yu-kuan Chung-kuo ku-shih te yen-chiu" 西洋近代的東方學及有關中國古史的研究. *Ta-lu tsa-chih*, 24:4 (1962), 1–6.

Yang Hsiang-k'uei 楊向奎. "P'ing Fu Meng-chen te I Hsia tung hsi shuo" 評傅孟真的夷夏東西說. In *Hsia-shih lun-ts'ung*. Shantung, 1985, 151–158.

Ta-i-t'ung yü Ju-chia ssu-hsiang 大一統與儒家思想. Chilin, 1989.

Yang Hsiang-k'uei and Chang Cheng-lang 楊向奎, 張政烺. "Tao-nien Yin Ta t'ung-chih" 悼念尹達同志. *Li-shih yen-chiu* 歷史研究, no. 5 (1983), 73–77.

Yang K'uan 楊寬. "Chung-kuo shang-ku-shih tao-lun" 中國上古史導論. In *Ku-shih pien*. Peking and Shanghai, 1926–1941, 7 vols., 7:148–156.

Yang Lien-sheng 楊聯陞. Review of *Fu Meng-chen hsien-sheng chi*. *Harvard Journal of Asiatic Studies*, 16:3–4 (1953), 487–490.

Yang Pu-wei 楊步偉. *Tsa-chi Chao-chia* 雜記趙家. Taipei, 1972.

Yano Jinichi 矢野仁一. "Man-Mo-Zo wa Shina no ryodo ni arazu ron" 滿蒙藏は支那の領土に非は論. *Gaiko jiho* 外交時報, 35:412 (1931), 56–71.

"Rokujunen no omoide" 六十年の思い出. *Tohogaku* 東方學, 28 (1964), 131–147.

"Yeh Ch'ing hsien-sheng te i-chien" 葉青先生的意見. In *Tu-ching wen-ti*. Shanghai, 1935, 120–131.

Yeh Kuei-sheng 葉桂生 and Liu Mao-lin 劉茂林. "Lü Chen-yü te chih-shih tao-lu" 呂振羽的治史道路. *Wen-hsien* 文獻, no. 2 (1980), 7–44.

Yeh Shu 葉曙. "Ch'u-ch'i T'ai-ta te jen ho shih" 初期台大的人和事. *Chuan-chi wen-hsüeh*, 48:6 (1986), 71–75.

"Wo so jen-shih te pa-wei T'ai-ta hsiao-chang" 我所認識的八位台大校長. *Chuan-chi wen-hsüeh*, 49:1 (1986), 46–70.

Yeh Wen-hsin. *The Alienated Academy: Culture and Politics in Republican China, 1919–1937*. Cambridge, Mass. 1990.

Yeh Yüan-lung 葉元龍. "Ch'ung-ta hsiao-chang Yeh Yüan-lung ch'ing-li Ma Yin-ch'u shih-chien" 重大校長葉元龍親歷馬寅初事件. *Chuan-chi wen-hsüeh*, no. 3 (1992), 67–70.

Yen Fu 嚴復. "I-yü chui-yü" 譯餘贅語. In *Ch'ün-hsüeh i-yen* 群學肄言. Shanghai, n.d., 2:1–3.

"Lun chih-hsüeh chih-shih yi fen erh t'u" 論治學治事宜分二途. In Chiang Chen-chin, 蔣貞金, ed., *Yen Chi-tao wen-ch'ao* 嚴幾道文鈔. Taipei, 1971, 163–168.

"Lun shih-pien chih chi" 論世變之亟. In Chiang Chen-chin, ed., *Yen Chi-tao wen-ch'ao*, 15–24.

Yen Keng-wang 嚴耕望. "Wo tui Fu Meng-chen hsien-sheng te kan-nien" 我對傅孟真先生的感念. *Hsien-jen-chang*, 1 (1977), 25–29.

Yin Hai-kuang 殷海光. "Wo i Meng-chen hsien-sheng" 我憶孟真先生. *Tzu-yu Chung-kuo*, 4:2 (1951), 78–80.

Yin Ta 尹達, ed. *Chung-kuo shih-hsüeh fa-chan shih* 中國史學發展史. Honan, 1985.

Hsin-shih-ch'i shih-tai 新石器時代. Peking, 1955.

Yin Ta shih-hsüeh lun-chu hsüan-chi 尹達史學論著選集. Peking, 1989.

Ying Ch'ien-li 英千里. "Hui-i yu-nien shih-tai te Fu hsiao-chang" 回憶幼年時代的傅校長. In *Fu ku hsiao-chang ai-wan-lu*. Taipei, 1951, 8.

Ying Lien-chih hsien-sheng jih-chi i-kao 英斂之先生日記遺稿. Taipei, n.d.
Young, Ernest. *The Presidency of Yüan Shih-k'ai*. Ann Arbor, 1977.
Yü Chan-pang 余湛邦. "Mao Tse-tung chu-hsi tsai Ch'ung-ch'ing t'an-p'an ch'i-chien" 毛澤東主席在重慶談判期間. *Ch'ung-ch'ing wen-shih tzu-liao* 重慶文史資料, 24 (1985), 152–174.
Yü Chia-hsi 余嘉錫. *Ku-shu t'ung-li* 古書通例. Shanghai, 1985.
Yü Heng 于衡. "I shen hsün chiao te Fu Ssu-nien" 以身殉教的傅斯年. *Chuan-chi wen-hsüeh*, 22:5 (1973), 57–62.
Yü-p'i li-tai t'ung-chien chi-lan 御批歷代通鑑輯覽. 1874.
Yü Ta-ts'ai 俞大綵. "I Meng-chen" 憶孟真. *Hsien-jen-chang*, 1 (1977). Included in *FSNC*, 2577–2591.
Yü Tan-ch'u 俞旦初. "Erh-shih shih-chi ch'u-nien Chung-kuo te hsin-shih-hsüeh ssu-ch'ao ch'u-k'ao" 二十世紀初年中國的新史學思潮初考. *Shih-hsüeh-shih yen-chiu*, no. 3 (1982), 54–74.
Yü Ying-shih 余英時. "The Changing Conceptions of National History in Twentieth Century China." In Erik Lönnroth, Karl Molin, and Bagmar Björk, eds., *Conceptions of National History*, Proceedings of Nobel Symposium 78 (New York, 1994), 155–174.
"Ch'ien Mu yü Hsin-ju-chia" 錢穆與新儒家. In *Yu-chi feng ch'ui shui shang lin* 猶記風吹水上鱗. Taipei, 1992, 31–98.
"Chung-kuo chih-shih fen-tzu te pien-yüan-hua" 中國知識份子的邊緣化. *Erh-shih-i shih-chi*, 6 (1991), 15–25.
"Chung-kuo chin-tai ssu-hsiang te chi-chin yü pao-shou" 中國近代思想的激進與保守. In *Yu-chi feng ch'ui shui shang lin*, 199–242.
Chung-kuo ssu-hsiang ch'uan-t'ung te hsien-tai ch'üan-shih 中國思想傳統的現代詮釋. Taipei, 1987.
Li-shih yü ssu-hsiang 歷史與思想. Taipei, 1976.
Lun Tai Chen yü Chang Hsüeh-ch'eng 論戴震與章學誠. Hong Kong, 1976.
"T'an Kuo Mo-jo te ku-shih yen-chiu" 談郭沫若的古史研究. *Ming-pao yüeh-k'an*, no. 10 (1992), 28–35.
"Wu-ssu – i ke wei wan-ch'eng te wen-hua yün-tung" 五四———一個未完成的文化運動. In *Wen-hua-p'ing-lun yü Chung-kuo ch'ing-huai* 文化評論與中國情懷. Taipei, 1988, 65–72.
"Wu-ssu yü Chung-kuo ch'uan-t'ung" 五四與中國傳統. In *Shih-hsüeh yü ch'uan-t'ung* 史學與傳統. Taipei, 1976.
Yüeh Yü-hsi 岳玉璽. "Fu Ssu-nien sheng-p'ing p'ing lüeh" 傅斯年生平評略. *Liao-ch'eng shih-fan hsüeh-yüan hsüeh-pao*, no. 3 (1989), 65–81.
"Kuo-min ts'an-cheng hui ch'i-chien te liang-chien-shih" 國民參政會期間的兩件事. In *Fu Ssu-nien*. Shantung, 1991, 164–165.

Index

Academia Sinica: founded, 69; and KMT as funding source, 92
academic world: as autonomous sphere of learning, 3–5. *See also* objectivity
academic freedom: and debate on social role of scholarship, 93–7; Fu supports at T'aita, 188–9
Ancient China and Ethnicity (Fu Ssu-nien), 152
Anyang excavation, 82, 83, 85–7, 118, 124
archaeology, 83–4, 85; and deethicization of ancient Chinese history, 131; and Fu's leadership, 7–8; and IHP research projects, 91; supports Fu's theories, 110–11, 121, 122. *See also* Anyang excavation; Ch'eng-tzu-yai excavation

Bacon, Francis, 78
Bagehot, Walter, 59
behaviorism, 191
Bergson, Henri, 129
Berlin University, 58–9
Bernheim, Ernst: influence on Fu, 63
Black Pottery culture, 19; distinguished from Painted Pottery culture, 111
Book of Great Harmony (K'ang Yu-wei), 24
book readers (tu-shu-jen): Fu's condemnation of, 76–7
Borodin, Michael, 161
Boxer Rebellion, 12
Buckle, T., 60
Bulletin of the Institute of History and Philology, 63, 73

Ch'an Buddhism, 137
Chang Cheng-lang, 132
Chang Hsüeh-liang: and kidnapping of Chiang Kai-shek, 163
Chang Hsün, 21
Chang Kwang-chih, 100, 121
Chang Ping-lin: as champion of true learning, 4; and conservatives at Peita, 24–5; and decline of Confucianism, 2, 26; influence on Fu, 128; and oracle bones, 86; and reliability of non-Confucian texts, 102
Chang T'ai-lei: and Communist attempt on Fu's life, 71; and Kwangchow Riot, 161
Chang Yen-ch'ing, 179
Chao Yüan-jen: and IHP, 69; 81
Ch'en Li, 138
Ch'en P'an: and deethicization of ancient Chinese history, 131–2
Ch'en Pu-lei, 169
Ch'en Shou-i, 71
Ch'en Tu-hsiu: influence on Fu, 23, 33; and New Culture Movement, 21; at Peita, 5; and savagism, 130; and single origin theory, 99; and vernacular versus literary style, 49
Ch'en Yin-k'o, 81; and Fu at Berlin University, 63–4; 67; and IHP, 69
Cheng Lieh: and wartime corruption, 169
Cheng-li kuo-ku yün-tung, 126
Ch'eng-tzu-yai excavation: and black pottery, 111; supports Fu's theories, 110

255

Chiang Kai-shek, 160–1, 162, 163, 176, 202–3, 207; appoints Hu Shih president of Peita, 174; and funding for Academia Sinica, 92; and political intervention in Anyang excavation, 85–6; and wartime corruption, 168, 169
Chiang T'ing-fu: and Debate over Democracy or Absolutism, 161
Ch'ien Hsüan-t'ung, 124; influence on Fu at Peita, 25; and vernacular versus literary style, 49
Ch'ien Mu: defends traditional historiography, 93
Chien Po-tsan, 143
China Foundation: and funding for Academia Sinica, 92
chin-shih-hsüeh: and archaeology, 84
Chinese civilization: plural origins theory, 99, 101–14; western origins theory, 87, 100
Chinese medicine: Fu's criticism of, 72
Ch'ing. See Ming and Ch'ing Cabinet Archives
Ch'ing evidential research, 127; contribution to decline of Confucianism, 26; and Western methods, 41–2
Ch'ing New Text School, 104
Chiu-chou, 116
Chou culture, 87, 100, 109, 124
Chou, Duke of, 103, 112, 113
Chou Tso-jen: and "Humane Literature," 37; influence on Fu, 24, 33; and New Tide Society, 27
Chu Chia-hua, 92, 155, 168
Chu Hsi, 137–8, 194
Chu Hsi-tsu: and Fu's criticism of *History of Ming*, 75
Chung-kuo li-tai ta-shih: and single origin theory, 99
Chung-yang yen-chiu yüan Li-shih yü-yen yen-chiu-so chi-k'an. See *Bulletin of the Institute of History and Philology*
Chung Ying wen-hua chi-chin-hui: and funding for Academia Sinica, 93
Chungshan University: Fu's tenure, 65, 70–1
Citizen: competition with *New Tide*, 29, 31, 32; and protests at Peita, 30

citizenship training: and creating society, 46; advocated by Fu, 155
civil service examinations: abolished, 3; as buttress of traditional system, 2; as cause of China's lack of society, 43
class: in leftist historical thought, 95; and May Fourth ideas, 201. *See also* common people
Columbia University, Teachers College, 72
common people: in Fu's thought, 34; and leftist critique of May Fourth ideas, 201
Communist Party (CCP): 9, 32, 162, 204; and Fu as emissary from People's Political Council, 170–1; Fu rejects, 161–2; and Kunming Student Movement, 177
Comte, Auguste: influence on Fu, 44
Confucian Classics: studied by Fu, 16–17
Confucian texts. *See* non-Confucian texts
Confucianism: as buttress of traditional system, 2; decline as precursor to May Fourth Movement, 26; and human nature according to Fu, 132–4; reinterpretation of, 127
Council of National Defense: and Fu's wartime service, 166
cultural nativism, 153–6

Debate of Problem and Cause, 47
Debate on the Nature of Chinese Society, 140–8
Debate over Democracy or Absolutism: Fu's nonparticipation, 161
Debate over Science and the Philosophy of Life: and positivism, 128
December Ninth Student Movement: Fu's contribution to, 73
"Declaration for Cultural Construction on a Chinese Basis," 140, 153, 155
deethicization: of ancient Chinese history, 131–9
"Disputation and Vindication of the Ancient Glosses on Nature and Destiny," 126, 132

"East-West Theory of I and Hsia" (Fu Ssu-nien), 8, 111–12
eight-legged essay, 12

Index

Erikson, Erik, 50
ethicization, 113; as weakness of Confucian Classics, 103. *See also* deethicization
ethnology: IHP research projects, 91
Eucken, Rudolf, 129
Evidential Analysis of the Meaning of Terms in the Mencius (Tai Chen), 128
Evolution and Ethics (Thomas H. Huxley), 1–2

Fei Hsiao-t'ung: criticized by Fu, 173
Feng Yu-lan, 122
Five Elements, 112, 116
Franke, Herman: influence on Fu, 64
Fu Hui-tsu, 11
Fu I-chien, 14–15
Fu Li-ch'üan: influence on Fu Ssu-nien, 13–14
Fu Ssu-nien: as academic hegemon, 81, 92; advocates positivism, 60; advocates scientific method applied to humanities, 79, 80; anti-Japanese stand, 73; attacked by CCP, 186; attacks wartime corruption, 167–70, 180–3, 203; attitude toward politics, 9–10; at Berlin University, 58–9; "bundle of contradictions" as characteristic of, 47, 48–54; and Chinese language and mentality, 37–40; and Chou colonization, 118–19; and conversion to New Culture philosophy at Peita, 25–7; and *New Tide*, 27–30; and criticism of Chinese educational system, 72; as cultural critic, 34–9; death of, 195; and deethicization of ancient Chinese history, 131–9; on democracy, 197; on dualism in Han thought, 137–9; on economic equality, 189–90; on genetic or evolutionary creation of ancient texts, 114–17, 119, 122; on human nature, 34–6, 190–1; and KMT, 159–60; and Kunming Student Movement, 174–7; at London University, 56–8; on Manchurian history, 149–52; and May Fourth demonstrations, 30–2; on need to create society, 42–8, 198; on objectivity in historical studies, 141, 146–7, 194; opposes "national learning," 155–6; and plural origins theory, 101–14, 199; and preservation of Ming and Ch'ing Cabinet Archives, 89–90; as president of T'aita, 186–9; on primary and nontextual sources, 73–7; and pro-Japanese faculty, 177–9; reevaluates Confucius and Mencius, 191–3; rejects Confucian Classics, 40–1; and research methods, 77–9; and role in modern Chinese intellectual world, 5–10; as student at Peita, 19–27; as student leader, 30–1; upbringing, 15–19; and U.S. visit, 183–4; and westernization, 158, 194, 197; as young proselyte, 33–4

Han Empire: and cultural dominance of eastern China, 112
Han people: and single origin theory, 99–100
Han Yü, 137
historical materialism, 144
Ho Jih-chang: and Anyang excavation, 85, 86
Ho Ping-sung, 96
Hou Yen-shuang, 18
Hsi-tsung shih-lu, 90
Hsia Dynasty, 124; and east-west confrontation, 112, 113
Hsia Nai, 121
Hsia Tseng-yu, 100, 107
Hsiao Chen-ying, 73
Hsiao-t'un: and Shang bronzes, 86
Hsin-ch'ao she, 24
Hsing ming ku-hsün pien-cheng, 79, 126
Hsiung Shih-li: and role of mind, 94
Hsü Chung-shu: and plural origins theory, 108–10
Hsü Fu-kuan, 7
Hsü Hsü-sheng: and plural origins theory, 99, 101, 104, 105; and influence of Fu's theories, 121
hsüeh-wen. *See* Western learning
Hsün-tzu: and Fu's reinterpretation of Confucian philosophy, 127; praised by Fu, 134, 135–6, 137
Hu Fu-lin: and leftist historians, 147
Hu Han-min, 160

257

Hu Shih, 7, 64, 72, 138–9, 148; as advocate of gradual change, 47; and blueprint for historical studies, 73, 74; and Ch'ing evidential research, 42; and cultural nativism, 157–8; and Debate over Democracy or Absolutism, 161; and importance of new data, 94; and influence on Fu, 23, 24, 33; and need for academic excellence, 68; and Movement for Rearranging the National Heritage, 153; and New Tide Society, 27; opposes introspective moral philosophy, 128–9; "On the Origin of the 'Ju' and Their Relation with Lao-Tzu and Confucius," 122; *Outline of the History of Chinese Philosophy*, 117; and plural origins theory, 105; and reevaluation of Confucius and Mencius, 192–3; and reinterpretation of Chinese tradition, 127; and Shang culture, 83, 86; and single origin theory, 99; and vernacular versus literary style, 49
Huang K'an: as conservative influence on Fu at Peita, 25
human nature: and Fu's reevaluation of Confucianism, 132–4

I: and east-west confrontation, 112; Fu's contribution to study of, 122; in Fu's theory of Chinese history, 101
I-Hsia tung hsi shuo (Fu Ssu-nien), 8, 111–12
Institute of History and Philology (IHP), 68–97; influence of, 198; phonetics studied at, 79; postwar publications, 179; research projects, 90–1; wartime moves, 166, 186
intellectuals: as agents of change, 3

Japan: and defeat of Chinese in Sino-Japanese War, 1; and KMT, 160. *See also* Mukden Incident
Jen Cho-hsüan, 162
Juan Yüan, 133, 138; and anti-introspective moral philosophy, 127–8, 129
Jung Chao-tsu, 82
Jung Keng: and Fu's efforts to punish pro-Japanese faculty, 178

K'ang Yu-wei, 1, 2, 20, 23, 26; and Westernization, 158
Kao Ch'ü-hsün, 121
King Wu, 103
Korea, 151
Ku Chieh-kang, 40, 55, 124, 205–6; and authenticity of ancient texts, 114, 116; on Chinese antiquity, 101, 103; and Chinese historiography, 8; and *Ku-shih pien*, 104, 105; and KMT, 66; and need for academic society, 68, 69; on nonwritten sources, 74; on Shang culture, 83, 86–7; and single origin theory, 99
Ku-shih pien (Ku Chieh-kang), 104
Kuan-t'ang chi-lin (Wang Kuo-wei): influence on Fu, 108
Kung, H. H.: attacked by Fu for corruption, 167–70, 180, 181, 203
Kunming Student Movement, 174–7
kuo-hsüeh: opposed by Fu, 153–4, 155
Kuo Kuo-chi, 195
Kuo-min. *See Citizen*
Kuomintang (KMT): and conflicts with intellectuals, 175, 181–2; Fu joins, 71; and funding for Academia Sinica, 92; Fu's support and criticism of, 160–3, 202–3
Kuo Mo-jo, 65, 70, 142, 147
Kuo Pao-chün: and scholars' desire to serve country, 165
Kuo-yü, 124
Kwangchow Riot: and Fu's hatred of CCP, 161

Lattimore, Owen: and influence of Fu's theories, 121
learning: autonomy and objectivity of, 93–4
leftist historians: and criticism of Fu's research style, 95
Li Ao, 137
liberalism: and socialism, 190
Li Chi, 81, 121; and Anyang excavation, 84, 85, 86; and archaeology as support for traditional texts, 154; and IHP, 69; on need for nontextual sources, 74; and scholars' desire to serve country, 165

Li Kuang-t'ao: and Ming and Ch'ng Cabinet Archives, 90
Li Shih-tseng, 4, 5, 69–70
Li Ta-chao, 24, 27, 42, 47
Li Tsung-t'ung, 83
Liang Ch'i-ch'ao, 1, 2, 3, 80; and history of civilization approach, 142
Liang Kuang-ming, 82
Liang Shu-ming, 127; and debate on nature of Chinese history, 148
Liao-ch'eng: effect of decline on Fu's upbringing, 11–13
Liao P'ing: and non-Confucian texts, 102–3
linguistics, 79, 91
Liu I-cheng, 93, 95, 123
Liu Fu: influence on Fu at Peita, 24
Lo Chen-yü: and archaeology, 83, 84
Lo Chia-lun, 24, 49
Lo Erh-kang, "Two Kinds of Lives," 95–6
London University, 56, 57
Lu Hsün, 33, 49, 65, 70–1
Lü Ssu-mien: and western origins theory, 99–100
Lü Ta-lin: and archaeology, 84
Lungshan culture: and black pottery, 111
Lungshan Expansion theory, 121
Lytton Commission, 149, 150, 151

Ma Yü-tsao, 25
Mach, Ernst, 60–2, 128
Manchuria: Fu's history of, 149–52
Mao I-heng, 57
Mao Tse-tung, 6, 29, 49, 170–1
Marco Polo Bridge Incident, 164
Marxism, 145; and May Fourth intellectuals, 67
May Fourth generation: challenged by Chinese society, 9; and conflict between patriotism and academic objectivity, 200
May Fourth Movement, 5, 201–2; and creation of society, 44; impact on politics, 32
May Fourth youth: and KMT, 162
Mcdougall, William, *The Group Mind*, 56–7
men of letters: Fu's attack on, 34
Mencius, 102, 127, 134, 135, 136; Fu's reevaluation of, 191–3, 204
Meng-tzu tzu-i shu-cheng (Tai Chen), 128

Meng Wen-t'ung: and non-Confucian texts, 102, 103; and plural origins theory, 101
Miao, 107–8; and single origin theory, 99
Miao Feng-lin, 93, 123; criticism of *An Outline History of Northeastern China*, 149, 150–1, 152
Miao Man: and plural origins theory, 105
Miao-ti-kou excavation, 121
Ming and Ch'ing Cabinet Archives, 88–90
Ming Shih-lu, 90
Moller, Alan, 5–6
Movement for Rearranging the National Heritage, 26; and deethicization of ancient Chinese history, 131
Movement of Doubting Chinese Antiquity, 8, 83, 86
Mukden Incident, 9, 73, 160, 164; as impetus for politicization of historiography, 140, 149, 150, 152

national medicine, 153; and Fu's rejection of, 157
Nationalist Party (KMT): attracted former New Tide members, 32; purge, 69. *See also* Kuomintang
National Past Society: competition with New Tide, 28
Nationalist government: and Confucianism, 152–3; Fu's support of, 65, 202–3
Neo-Confucianism, 128, 134, 137, 138
New Citizen, and Comte's social organism theory, 44
New Culture Movement: and anti-introspective moral philosophy, 128; ideological splits in, 8; and KMT, 162
New Tide: audience, 28–9; and criticism of Chinese traditions, 27–8; decline after Fu leaves, 32; founded, 24; and psychology, 53–4
New Youth: and *New Tide*, 27
Nietzsche, Friedrich, 130
non-Confucian texts: reliability of, 102
Northern Expedition, 69

objectivity: and professionalization of academic culture, 69, 79–80; versus politics in academic research, 165–7, 171–4, 183, 202

"On Government and the Championing of Morality" (Fu Ssu-nien), 155
oracle bones, 83–4, 111
An Outline History of Northeastern China (Fu Ssu-nien), 149–52, 202

Pao Chien-ch'ing: and Fu's efforts to punish pro-Japanese faculty, 179
Pearson, Karl: influence on Fu, 59–60
Peita (Peking University): 4–5, 22–3
Pelliot, Paul: and Anyang excavation, 87
Pen-wei-wen-hua chien-she hsüan-yen, 140
People's Political Council, 9, 164, 167
Philology and History Weekly of Chungshan University, 66
positivism, 60–2, 190–1
primary sources: value of emphasized by Fu, 73–7, 198
psychology, 53–4
Pu-jen tsa-chih: read by Fu at Peita, 23–4

Rankean school of historiography (Leopold von Ranke), 144; influence on Fu, 62–3, 90, 198
Rites of Chou, 103, 124
Robinson, James Harvey, 96
Russian Revolution: and Fu's thinking on social construction, 42; influence on Li Ta-chao and New Tide Society, 24, 46

Said, Edward, 156
savagism: as alternative to traditional introspective moral philosophy, 130
Shan-hai ching: as non-Confucian text, 102
Shang Dynasty, 87, 101, 109, 112, 113, 124; and Black Pottery culture at Ch'eng-tzu-yai excavation, 111; culture as revealed by Anyang excavation, 83, 86; and debate on nature of Chinese history, 145
she-hui nei chih-hsü. *See* social order
she-hui shang chih-hsü. *See* social order
Shen Chien-shih: influence on Fu, 25
shih-liu tzu hsin-ch'uan, 100–1
Shirokogorff, Sergei Mikhailovich, 82
Sino-English Boxer Indemnity Foundation: and funding for Academia Sinica, 93

Sino-Japanese War (1894–1895): impact on Fu's generation, 1, 203
Six Classics, 133; as Confucian forgeries according to K'ang Yu-wei, 26
Sixteen-Character Transmission: and traditional Chinese history, 100–1
social responsibility, 45
social order: as distinguished from order within society, 44
socialism: and liberalism, 190
society: Fu on need to create, 42–8
Soong, T. V., 167, and postwar corruption, 180–1, 203
Southwest Associated University: organization proposed by Fu, 166–7
Southwest Ethnic Research Association, 173
Ssu-ma Ch'ien: and western origins theory, 100
Stalinists: and debate on nature of Chinese history, 145
"Studies on the Ancient Meanings of 'Nature' and 'Destiny'" (Fu Ssu-nien), 79
Su Ping-ch'i: and Shang dynasty, 86
Sun Yat-sen, 1

Tai Chen, 128, 138
T'aita (Taiwan University), 204
T'an Ssu-t'ung, 2
tang-hua chiao-yü: and Academia Sinica, 69
T'ang Yung-t'ung, 172
T'ao Hsi-sheng: and cultural nativism, 157
Temple of Heaven Draft Constitution: and Confucianism as state religion, 20
Three Dynasties: and Fu's theories, 8, 100–1, 198
Ting Wen-chiang, 60, 72, 92
Trevelyan, G. M., 77
Trotskyites: and debate on nature of Chinese history, 145
Ts'ai Yüan-p'ei, 2, 4–5, 20; and Anyang excavation, 85; as architect of New Culture Movement, 21–2; and funding for Academia Sinica, 69–70, 92; impact on Peita, 22–3
Ts'ao Ju-lin, 31
Tso's Commentaries, 124
Tsou Heng, 122

Tuan Fang: and archaeology, 84
Tu-li p'ing-lun, 71
T'ung-ch'eng school: conservative literary school, 25
Tung-I: and plural origins theory, 105
Tung-pei shih-kang, 149–52
Tung Tso-pin: and Anyang excavation, 83, 84; and leftist historians, 147
tu-shu-jen. *See* book readers

Veritable Record of the Hsi-tsung Reign, 90
vernacular language and literature, 201; advocated by Fu, 36–9
von Humboldt, Wilhelm, 133

Wang Ching-wei, 4, 160
Wang Hsien-t'ang: and influence of Fu's theories, 121
Wang Hsing-kung: and positivism, 60
Wang Kuo-wei, 51, 83, 108, 109, 113
Wang Lun Rebellion, 12
Wang Mang: and fabrication of ancient texts, 117
Wang Shih-chieh, 169
Warring States Period, 104; and ethicalization of history, 113
Watson, John, 130, 191
Wells, H. G., 57
Wen-t'i yü chu-i lun-chan. *See* Debate of Problem and Cause
Weng Wen-hao: and conflict with Soong, 182; and scholars' desire to serve country, 165
wen-jen: Fu's attack on, 34. *See also* men of letters

Western learning: as true learning, 55
Western origins theory, 106–7
Wu Chih-hui, 5, 49, 92; critique of Movement for Rearranging the National Heritage, 153–4; and funding for Academia Sinica, 70; and political intervention in Anyang excavation, 85; and scholarly community as transformative force for society, 4
Wu Ching-ch'ao: criticized by Fu, 173
Wu Han: and leftist history, 95
wu-hsing, 112, 116
Wu K'ang: and psychology, 54
Wu T'ing-hsieh: rejected by Fu, 81

Yang Hsiang-k'uei, 121
Yang Hsing-fo: and funding for Academia Sinica, 70, 92
Yang-shao painted pottery, 111
Yen Fu: advocates true learning, 4; and European political and economic philosophy, 1–2
Yin, 124; and Chou, 108–9
"Yin Chou chih-tu lun," 108
Yin Hai-kuang, 195
Yin Ta: and scholars' desire to serve country, 165
Ying Hua, 18
Youth (Ch'ing-nien): and beginning of New Culture Movement, 21
Yü P'ing-po, 56, 155
Yü Ta-fu, 65
Yü Ta-ts'ai: marriage to Fu, 72–3
Yüan Shih-k'ai: as supporter of traditional culture, 20–1